EMPIRE

WILLIAM S. PALEY
AND THE MAKING OF CBS

Lewis J. Paper

ST. MARTIN'S PRESS / New York

To Lindsay and Brett

EMPIRE: WILLIAM S. PALEY AND THE MAKING OF CBS. Copyright © 1987 by Lewis J. Paper. All rights reserved.
Printed in the United States of America. No part of this book may be used or reproduced in any manner whatsoever
without written permission except in the case of brief quotations embodied in critical articles or reviews. For
information, address St. Martin's Press, 175 Fifth Avenue, New York, N.Y. 10010.

Design by Trish Parcell Watts

Library of Congress Cataloging in Publication Data

Paper, Lewis J.
   Empire : William S. Paley and the making of CBS.

   1. Paley, William S. (William Samuel), 1901–
2. Broadcasters—United States—Biography.
3. CBS Inc.—Biography.   4. Broadcasting—United States—
History.   I. Title.
HE8689.8.P34P36 1987   384.54′092′4   [B]   87-4368
ISBN 0-312-00591-1

First Edition
10 9 8 7 6 5 4 3 2 1

C O N T E N T S

Choices

I t was not just another celebration. CBS was about to commemorate its fiftieth anniversary, and for board chairman William S. Paley, it was indeed a special occasion. In September 1928, he had assumed the presidency of United Independent Broadcasters—a fledgling radio network with sixteen affiliate stations and mounting debts. Paley was two days shy of his twenty-seventh birthday and without experience in broadcasting. Nonetheless, through shrewd business deals, charm, and a little luck, he reversed UIB's predicament, renamed the network the Columbia Broadcasting System, and established the course that would make CBS, Inc., a billion-dollar empire by 1978.

CBS meant more than financial success to Bill Paley. It represented the best in broadcasting—the premier network in news and entertainment. After all, he was the one who had brought Edward R. Murrow, Walter Cronkite, Bing Crosby, Lucille Ball, Jackie Gleason, and all those other top journalists and performers into America's homes. It was no small achievement, and Paley had ample reason to look forward to the prime-time television special that CBS had scheduled to mark its fiftieth anniversary.

Norman Lear had a different reason for looking forward to that special, and he wanted to share it with Paley in a meeting they were to have shortly before the program aired. Lear was the creator and original producer of "All in the Family," one of CBS's most revolutionary (and profitable) television programs. Ironically, Paley had initially opposed any broadcast of "All in the Family." To him, Archie Bunker was too coarse, too vulgar, and too bigoted to be a part of the CBS schedule. It was not the kind of show he wanted for his network. But others at CBS, most especially network president Bob Wood, were enthusiastic and had pushed it relentlessly. Paley believed in backing his subordinates (as long as they performed), and he had finally agreed to allow the program to be used as a replacement series in January 1971. The rest, of course, was history, and no one was more pleased than Paley. He loved success.

Lear and Paley had more in common than an interest in "All in the

Family." Like Paley, Lear presented a well-manicured appearance (although Lear, more fit and trim than Paley, preferred designer suits to the dark business suits that Paley favored). Lear also possessed the same kind of charm and magnetism that had made Paley so attractive to so many people over the years. Still, Lear approached his meeting with the CBS chairman with some trepidation. Paley was twenty years his senior and, more than that, a giant in the broadcasting industry. "That's part of the mystique," Lear observed. "His accomplishments are there in the anteroom before you go in to see him. You're expecting to see strength and charm. And it's a self-fulfilling prophecy." For all these reasons, Lear could never get himself to call the CBS chairman "Bill." It was always "Mr. Paley."

Whatever the salutations, Lear had a request when he met with Paley shortly before the fiftieth anniversary special. They were in Paley's office at CBS headquarters on Fifty-second Street in Manhattan, a building known to industry insiders as "Black Rock." Almost all of the offices in the tall building were modern, sleek, almost sterile. Paley's office was a notable exception. The walls had a rich paneling. Paintings by Picasso, Matisse, and other masters were conspicuous. And yet, at the same time, there was a certain informality to the office. The old CBS radio microphone, the cigar-store Indian, and the French gaming table that served as Paley's desk—these and other items conveyed a sense of warmth and, not incidentally, intimated the breadth and depth of Paley's interests.

After an exchange of pleasantries, Lear came to the point. It was time, he said, for the establishment of new standards. Television had been dominated by a concern for ratings and higher profits. The emphasis seemed to be on winning—at whatever cost. Quality seemed to be a forgotten commodity. And it was not just on television. To Lear, it had become the dominant ethic of American life. So Lear had a suggestion for Paley. The chairman of the board of CBS should use the fiftieth anniversary prime-time special to make a dramatic announcement that CBS would no longer concern itself with ratings, that there would be a return to first principles—a dedication to quality, not higher profits. It would rock the industry and reaffirm Paley's place as a pioneer.

Lear had even gone to the trouble of preparing a draft of the statement Paley could make, but the CBS chairman would not bite. "He's very good at the net," Lear recalled. "I just couldn't get through. He never said no, but he never said yes." The dramatic announcement was never made.

For Lear, it was a lost opportunity. For Paley, it was just another choice among thousands he had to make in his long stewardship of CBS. Paley of course understood what Lear wanted. He had heard the argument many times before. Like Lear, he appreciated the importance of quality—indeed, it was something he always emphasized in conversation with performers, producers, and CBS program executives. But Paley also liked the notion of being number one in the ratings, and he would often say that a program that entertains sixty million people—and does it with style—can't be all bad. Others might see an inconsistency between quality and high ratings, but Paley believed that CBS could have it all.

He feels the same way about his personal life. His zest for life is extraordinary, and he has had both the means and the desire to satisfy it. As one colleague observed, "Bill has lived a life that few people could comprehend. He is a man of tremendous wealth who knows how to enjoy it." He has always felt free to cater to whatever whim suited his fancy—from homes in the Caribbean to good food to travel in Europe to tailor-made suits. But more than that, Paley has enjoyed these pleasures with a remarkable, almost unbridled, enthusiasm. In fact, one of his associates observed that writing a biography would be no easy matter because of the difficulties in capturing Paley's love of life. "One of the things that could get lost among the chronology," said this associate, "would be the laughter, of which there has been a lot."

In pursuing goals for himself and CBS, Paley could not, and did not, please everyone. There are many—including professional colleagues, independent observers, and even family members—who sometimes questioned the wisdom of his choices. But Bill Paley is a man without regret. And largely for good reason. He is the single most important person in the history of broadcasting. And while there have been mistakes a long the way, he has been, on balance, a force for good in that ever-expanding medium of communications.

His stature, however, extends beyond individual achievements. He has established an image that seems larger than life. And that image goes a long way in understanding the CBS board's decision to ask Bill Paley, age eighty-four, to step out of retirement in September 1986 to help repair the divisions and turmoil that had plagued the company for almost two years. To be sure, Paley's resurrection was made possible through his alliance with Laurence A. Tisch, the Loews Corporation board chairman who owned 24.9 percent of CBS's outstanding stock. Together the two men owned a third of the company, a formidable position under almost any circumstance. But Paley plainly represented something more than stock ownership. His presence in the CBS governing structure could help provide assurances to employees and observers alike that the setbacks were temporary and that soon all would be well. He provided a link to the past, a rallying point to return to those early days when, in the haze of memory, quality and stability reigned supreme.

And so the story of Bill Paley's life involves far more than a recounting of one man's life. It also shows how one man's choices shaped an industry that now dominates American life.

They did not yet see, and thousands of young men . . . , now crowding to the barriers of their careers, could not see that if a single man plant himself on his convictions and then abide, the huge world will come round to him.

—*Ralph Waldo Emerson*

EMPIRE

CHAPTER ONE

Chicago

Ey the late nineteenth century, Chicago was on the move. Because of its favorable location at the southern tip of Lake Michigan, it was only natural that the city should attract people with an entrepreneurial spirit. And attract them it did. Stockyards were established by 1848, and soon whole industries had been spawned to accommodate the industrial growth. It was here, for example, that Gustavus Swift and Philip Armour built their competitive meat-packing plants; George Pullman and others built railway cars and developed huge railway facilities; and Marshall Field erected large department stores. The city had its cultural and intellectual life, but business was the order of the day. Chicago was, said the writer Henry B. Fuller, "the only great city in the world to which all its citizens have come for the avowed purpose of making money. There you have its genesis, its growth, its object; and there are but few of us who are not attending to that object very strictly."

Chicago also offered opportunities for those who needed a break from the hectic pace of business development. Theater was limited, but there was an abundance of saloons, gambling houses, and brothels. Most of them were located in an area known as the Levee, and, until progressive reform became the order of the day in the early twentieth century, they promoted their wares and services freely. Indeed, one of the more popular brothels, the Everleigh Club, became immortalized when Ada and Minnie Everleigh, the sisters who owned the club, distributed brochures adorned with photographs of the club's facilities and "staff."

The city's population, like most of urban America at the time, was largely white and Protestant. But Chicago also had a growing population of Jewish immigrants from Eastern Europe, and among them were Isaac and Zelda Paley and their seven children. Isaac had been a man of some wealth and position in his native town of Brovary in Russia. Although Jews had begun to experience increasing persecution with the ascension of Alexander III as czar in 1881, Isaac was able to use his connections to protect his family. But he no doubt saw what was coming, and around

1884 he traveled to the United States with his son Samuel to investigate the possibilities. He liked what he found, and in 1888 he returned with his entire family.

A tall man with a Vandyke beard, Isaac Paley saw the United States as a place where he could freely enjoy the wealth he had earned from his lumber business in Russia. His investments did not equal his hopes, however, and his children were soon forced to undertake work to maintain their father in the style to which he aspired.

Samuel Paley was then just a thirteen-year-old boy, but he was up to the challenge. In his family, the father's needs and wishes assumed top priority. So Sam quit school and began working, first selling newspapers, then toiling in a piano factory, and finally accepting a position as an apprentice in a cigar factory. That clicked. Sam discovered he had a natural affinity for recognizing quality tobacco and knowing how to blend it into an appealing cigar. But Sam Paley was more, much more, than a backroom cigar-maker. He was a shrewd businessman, a person who knew then, as he would for most of his life, how to take advantage of a good opportunity. So while he kept his job at the cigar factory, he opened his own cigar store across town, placing a man in the window who would roll the cigars and attract attention from the passing crowd. Before long Sam's own cigar business had expanded to the point where he could no longer keep two jobs. He left the factory and concentrated on his own business. By the time he turned twenty-one in 1896, Sam Paley was a very wealthy man.

Sam's money, however, did not enable him to reach beyond the confines of the Jewish community. Like most American cities at the turn of century, Chicago had only limited tolerance for Jewish immigrants, especially those from Eastern Europe. Unlike their German brethren, Eastern European Jews seemed less refined and almost always spoke English with heavy accents—traits that made their assimilation that much more difficult. But Sam Paley was not one to be inhibited by such matters. He was young, full of energy, and, above all, financially successful. And then he fell in love. Her name was Goldie Drell, a young girl of medium height with brown hair, attractive features, and a sweet disposition. Like Sam, she was the offspring of Jewish immigrants from Eastern Europe and spoke English with a heavy accent. Their relationship ripened quickly, and they got married in 1898 when she was only sixteen.

It would be a long and happy marriage. But it was not an equal partnership. Like many orthodox Jewish families, the Paley household was dominated by the husband. Conditioned by his own upbringing, Sam had come to expect a certain deference as the man of the house, and Goldie saw no reason to disappoint those expectations. The scope of Sam's control over the family made a striking impression on many visitors, including Dorothy Hart, Bill Paley's first wife. "Bill's father was someone who had to be taken care of," she recalled many years later. "Everything was done his way. You ate dinner when he wanted to eat. You did things at his pleasure. And his wife catered to him." The lesson was not lost upon Sam Paley's only son, and decades later his wives would similarly observe that Bill Paley also liked to have things—even minor matters like a table setting—done *his* way.

In the meantime, Sam Paley was prepared to follow opportunity wherever it took him, and in the early 1900s it took him to Detroit. By then, he and Goldie had had their first child, a boy whom they named William Samuel Paley. He was born on September 28, 1901, and from all appearances he seemed to be bright and healthy. But childhood was not to be all tranquillity for young Willie, as his father was soon calling him. In 1905 Goldie gave birth to another child, Bill's sister Blanche.

As time would reveal, Blanche did not possess Bill's charm, his drive, or his entrepreneurial skills, perhaps in part, if not largely, because she was not expected to succeed in business. In later years Sam took considerable pains to educate his son—but not his daughter—about every aspect of the cigar business. But Blanche did not lack for attention. Goldie, who dominated the children's early years, doted on Blanche, showering her with praise and affection. Bill, in contrast, felt left out, removed, and even unwanted. Years later his wife Dorothy would remember the resentment that Bill felt toward Blanche. "He always recalled the excessive attention Blanche received from their mother," said Dorothy, "and in particular the devotion which Goldie gave to Blanche during a childhood illness." And Paley himself, looking back on a long and successful life, would still feel the hurt of those early years. "The worst of it was my impression," he ruminated, "that [my mother] did not find me attractive. . . . I am not sure now if she really felt that way about me or was just trying to make me try harder. But the effect on me was a feeling of inferiority. I felt sorry for myself. I believed I was born unattractive." Not surprisingly, he speculated that his driving ambition reflected an attempt to overcome an antagonism he sensed in his mother.

There was never any open rift between mother and son, or between brother and sister. Goldie Paley was not one to be so blatant about her feelings, and the children seemed to follow her lead. So, as the years passed, the words among them would almost always be warm and proper, but observers also seemed to notice a certain reserve between Bill Paley and the women in his immediate family.

The same was not true of the son's relationship with the father. "Sam Paley was a small, jovial guy who liked to laugh," said Bill Paley's friend

Henry Gerstley, "and he had a good relationship with Bill." The seeds of the relationship were sown in the early years when Sam would regale the family at dinner with stories about his business. Young Willie listened intently and with awe. The cigar business sounded fascinating, and Bill Paley decided then and there that his future lay with his father. "I admired him enormously," Paley recalled many years later, "and thought of doing great things to help him."

The relationship blossomed as Bill grew older and Sam recognized that his son had the intelligence and common sense to work in his business. Willie began to spend many hours in his father's offices and factories, learning about every aspect of the cigar business. Sam would take his son almost everywhere he went—to business negotiations across town, to Puerto Rico or Amsterdam to buy tobacco, and to distant cities to investigate possible sites for new factories.

Through this close contact, Bill Paley began to sense his father's extraordinary skills at negotiation—how his father, for example, would feign indifference to attract better offers. (Years later the son would employ that same technique to great advantage as the head of a billion-dollar broadcasting empire.) But something more than mutual respect emerged from the Paleys' collaboration in the cigar business. It was love. Their mutual admiration merged into an affection that seemed to grow with time. And nothing—not even the formality of a CBS Board of Directors meeting— could suppress those deep feelings. When Sam Paley entered the meetings, almost always late and out of breath, his son, then the board chairman, would move to greet his father with a warm embrace and a kiss. And those who spent time with the CBS chairman outside board meetings found that sooner or later the conversation would drift into a description of Sam Paley's character and exploits.

Not every move made by the elder Paley was a success, however. Things did not go well in Detroit in the early 1900s. One of Sam's major customers went bankrupt, and Sam lost the bulk of his fortune. So he took his family back to Chicago—a town he knew, a place where he felt comfortable, and, most importantly, the home where he had first made his fortune. He bought a house on Marshfield Avenue just west of the Loop, an area heavily populated by other Jewish immigrants from Eastern Europe. And then Sam Paley went about rebuilding his cigar business.

Despite uncertainty about his mother's feelings, Willie did well in school and soon found that girls did indeed find him attractive. Like the young Paley, Chicago was also starting to blossom. Skyscrapers eighteen and twenty stories tall were being built, railways were expanding their reach from bustling depots, and automobiles were starting to clog the downtown streets (to the point where the South Park Board banned all automobiles from Michigan Avenue that emitted "offensive odors" and traveled at a speed greater than eight miles per hour).

However distasteful to traditionalists, automobiles were a sign of success, and Sam Paley decided he wanted one for himself—even though he had no idea how to drive. The first experiment behind the wheel did not turn out well. While Goldie and Willie waited at the house, Sam took Blanche for a ride around the corner. After a while, Sam and Blanche returned—without the car. As he was negotiating a corner, Sam placed his foot on the accelerator instead of the brake, and the car crashed headlong into a brick building. Still, Sam would not forego the status of owning an automobile. He had another car delivered to the house within two weeks, but he himself would never drive again. Sam did not like to be in situations where he was not in control—a trait his son would later emulate.

Being Jewish was another circumstance over which Sam had no control, but it was not, as in the case of automobiles, one from which he tried to run away. Sam never forgot the persecution his parents left behind in Russia, and he appreciated—especially after Hitler—the importance of a Jewish homeland in Palestine. Not surprisingly, in later years he became an ardent supporter of and contributor to the Zionist cause.

Sam's interest in Zionism did not reflect a commitment to organized religion. He was too practical to follow rituals and traditions. But he had no objection if Goldie wanted to take the children to her father's house on Friday nights to celebrate the Sabbath. Morris Drell was an orthodox Jew who cherished the teachings and rituals of Judaism. The grandfather's enthusiasm was not shared by Willie. He found the Friday evening services boring. They were conducted primarily in Hebrew, which Willie did not understand. And, more than that, he found little meaning in the ancient history and religious ritual that surrounded the Sabbath ceremony. "When I was fourteen years old," Paley later recalled, "I started asking questions and couldn't get decent answers. I said, My God, that's a lot of bull." Like his father, Willie was more concerned with the realities he could observe and experience than with the seemingly abstract lessons of a time gone by.

Fortunately for Bill Paley, his parents did not pressure him to adopt a different view. His parents had joined a Reform temple in Chicago that reduced the amount of Hebrew in services and generally tried to adapt Judaism to American ways. Willie did receive a "confirmation" at the Reform temple, which required him to recite the Ten Commandments in Hebrew. But he found the whole process to be rather meaningless. He had memorized his confirmation statement and had virtually no idea what he was saying. His only goal was to be free of these formal obligations as an adult.

Not surprisingly, Bill Paley made few visits to temple after those early days in Chicago. But he could not escape his Jewish heritage. Anti-Semitism was rampant in the first half of the twentieth century, and Paley found evidence of it almost everywhere. Even as the president and later board chairman of CBS, he learned that there were apartments he could not rent, restaurants he could not patronize, and resorts he could not visit—all because he was Jewish.

For Dorothy Hart, his first wife, it was an eye-opening experience. "I talked with him about places I'd like to go on vacation," she remembered years later, "and he would say how we couldn't go here or there because they don't accept Jews. He was pretty matter of fact about it, but I found it shocking." One of the places he disliked visiting was Palm Beach—even after his parents had retired to the Florida coastal community. Sam learned very quickly that many of the private clubs were anti-Semitic, a rejection that led him to organize a local club that would cater to Jews. But Paley was not prepared to endure the discomfort of anti-Semitism. "I'll be damned," he once told a friend, "if I'll take my wife and children on a vacation where I'll have to worry about that kind of thing."

Even the most careful planning, however, could not completely insulate Paley from blind bigotry. The time in Bermuda in the 1930s was particularly traumatic. Dorothy and Bill had rented a cottage, and were on the beach playing with their dog, Angus, when a man came walking toward them, yelling at Paley, "You goddamn Jew, you goddamn Jew." Paley was stunned and stood there openmouthed. Dorothy, always feisty and full of fight, began yelling at the man to get off their beach, while Angus barked and ran circles around the intruder. Later, Dorothy recalled, Paley was "philosophical" about the experience, saying that there was simply no way to understand why some people behaved the way they did.

Even so, it had to hurt. In many respects, Paley was and is a shy person, a man concerned about other people's reactions, a man who very much wants to be accepted, and, more than that, respected. Some incidents, like the one in Bermuda, were so beyond the pale of reason that they could be dismissed as aberrant human behavior. But it could not have been as easy to dismiss other insults. For example, Paley very much wanted to be admitted to the prestigious F Street and Metropolitan Clubs in Washington, D.C., but neither would have him at first. (David Sarnoff, Paley's chief rival at RCA and another Russian Jew, took great pride in being able to use his connections to wrangle an invitation from the same Metropolitan Club that initially rejected Paley.)

The specter of anti-Semitism was particularly glaring in the dark years of blacklisting and Senator Joe McCarthy in the 1940s and 1950s. The heads of all three television networks were Jewish, and that only helped to fuel anti-Semitic feelings in many quarters. So being Jewish was not a major advantage for anyone interested in a career at CBS (or the other networks), and few of CBS's top executives during that time were Jewish. (When Louis G. Cowan became president of the CBS Television Network in 1958, Paley told him that the appointment could not have been made if Cowan's name had been Cohen—which is what Cowan's name had been before he changed it.)

For business purposes, then, there was little advantage and much cost in advertising a Jewish heritage. But like his father, Paley did not try to escape his own background. He remained a generous contributor to Jewish causes, including Israel, and funded the construction of a modern art center in Jerusalem in the 1970s in honor of his mother. And even as his circle of friends shifted to "high society" in the gentile world (his Long Island home, for instance, was located in the "Gold Coast" region populated by the WASP rich), Paley had no qualms about his Jewish origins. There was the time in the 1960s, for example, when Paley and CBS Vice President Michael Burke (who was not Jewish) traveled on the company plane for a business meeting in Chicago. As they got into the limousine, Paley began to reminisce about his childhood in Chicago and then asked whether Burke would like to see the neighborhood where he had grown up. The CBS vice president was not about to say no, so Paley asked the driver if he knew where Marshfield Avenue was. The driver, unaware of the conversation that had been going on in the back seat, said of course he knew where Marshfield Avenue was, but he was sure the CBS chairman did not want to go there. "Why not?" asked Paley. "Because," said the driver, "it's an old run-down Jewish neighborhood." At that, Paley broke into uncontrolled laughter—a man, recalled Burke, who seemed very comfortable with his background.

However comfortable he felt, Paley never forgot the discrimination he faced as a Jew—the friends who had turned on him, the places that had rejected him. As he entered the twilight years of his life, his conversation turned more and more frequently to such incidents. Some colleagues (especially those who are *not* Jewish), considerably younger than Paley and strangers to the world of anti-Semitism, viewed his recollections as a sign of an inferiority complex—or even senility. It was, somehow, a sign of weakness.

In large part, however, the opposite is true. The confrontations with anti-Semitism left Bill Paley unruffled. His disappointments and frustrations were real, but they had little impact on his resolve to be the best at whatever he did—even if it meant doing business with gentiles. But when Paley's father picked up and took the family to Philadelphia in 1919, he had no idea that that business would involve broadcasting. For Paley, the attractive opportunities lay in the field of cigar-making.

CHAPTER TWO

Philadelphia

When his business continued to grow in Chicago, Sam Paley moved his family to a nicer neighborhood. Willie attended public schools and almost always finished at or near the top of his class. He also displayed a sense of mischief and playfulness that probably went over better with other students than with teachers. Paley himself had only one real fear: the wrath of his father. There was the time, for example, when Paley was a teenager and was given the family car to go out on a date. His father instructed him to be home by eleven o'clock. The instruction was completely forgotten in the pleasure of the moment, and Paley found an unhappy man when he confronted his father at one o'clock in the morning. "You remember when I asked you to be home at eleven, a friend of mine was present?" demanded the senior Paley. The friend had scoffed at the idea that Paley's son would abide by the instruction, but Sam Paley had great confidence in Willie. "I took a very strong stand," Sam explained, "and you let me down, son, you let me down."

Paley was crushed, and he was not about to endure experiences like that too often. But not long afterward he was caught speeding while having his arm around a girl companion. The police officer threatened the young driver with a fate worse than jail—a call to his father. Paley rushed back to the apartment house where his family was then living and begged the desk clerk to take the call and pretend to be Sam Paley. The accommodating clerk did as he was asked, and Paley escaped unscathed.

Sam Paley nonetheless seemed to understand his son's potential to be distracted, and in 1917 Willie was sent to Western Military Academy in Alton, Illinois, to complete his high school education. There he wore his cadet's uniform, participated in daily drills, and engaged in mock battles. The Spartan environment did not hurt his academic performance. He earned two years of high school credits in one and was admitted to the University of Chicago in 1918 at the age of seventeen.

Paley devoted his first semester to the singular goal of getting good grades, and he was not disappointed. The dean wrote Sam after that first semester that his son was one of the best students the university had ever had. But then love and pleasure took over. By this time Paley was almost six feet, slim, handsome, and possessed an infectious smile. His self-effacing manner and charm only made him that much more attractive to women. His first love affair was with an older woman who lived far from the university on the north side of the city. No matter. As in later years, there were few obstacles that could discourage Paley in the pursuit of pleasure. Every evening he took the elevated train to the north side, spent several hours with his new friend, and then left in the early morning hours for the return trip. It was a grueling schedule and, in the end, something had to suffer. By the end of the second semester Paley ranked at the bottom of his class.

None of this was to have any bearing on his future. By the spring of 1919 his father had decided to relocate his factories. Chicago had long been a focus of social reform and, more significantly from Sam Paley's perspective, a center for the championing of labor rights. It was, after all, the site of the famous Haymarket riot in 1886 and the Pullman strike in 1894, events that had generated violence and polarized public opinion. Coinciding with these incidents were the efforts of Florence Kelley, Jane Addams, and others to have the government play a more active role in protecting the rights of workers and their families.

Because of its history and stature as an industrial base, Chicago had been a favorite target of the burgeoning labor movement. In 1919 Samuel Gompers, the venerable leader of the American Federation of Labor, authorized a strike against Sam Paley's cigar factories. It was not the first strike he had endured, but Sam vowed it would be the last. He took Willie on a trip East to explore the alternatives. The first stop was New York City (where Bill Paley, captivated by tales of sin, waited in hotel lobbies—without success—to be accosted by seductive women). Sam, spending his time more productively, was not convinced New York was the best location for his business and traveled on to Philadelphia.

Although smaller than New York, Philadelphia had much to offer. Located on the Delaware River, with access to major sea routes, it had a growing economy and enjoyed an expanding work force (in large part due to the immigration of blacks from the South and Caucasians from Eastern Europe). Of equal significance for Sam Paley, unions had established only limited strength in Philadelphia. Indeed, local employers had been so successful in thwarting the labor movement that Philadelphia was generally known as a "graveyard of unionism." For the senior Paley it was an unbeatable combination, and he soon obtained a lease on a site for a factory.

These plans were soon disrupted by the death of Isaac Paley. Sam rushed back to Chicago to attend to the details of his father's funeral and to be with his family. Willie was left behind to take care of the new factory. It was an assignment his father could make with confidence. Willie had already spent his summers in Chicago working in the cigar factories, and he had been introduced to all aspect of the business. He had swept floors, purchased the bonding stamps that had to be placed on the cigar boxes, and worked in the "kitchen" where the tobaccos were mixed. His keen intelligence, coupled with a deep desire to please his father, had made him very knowledgeable very quickly. So he felt fully capable of minding the business while his father took care of family matters in Chicago.

Sam had promised to return within a week or so. But the weeks dragged on and it was almost a month before he was able to return to Philadelphia. In the meantime, his son had to confront his first major crisis. Despite Sam Paley's hopes to the contrary, the industry was hit with a strike. Then, as in later years, Bill Paley was prepared to follow his own instincts as to what was fair, and he thought the strike was very unfair to the Paley cigar business. He explained to the union leaders that the Paley business had not yet initiated operations, so there could be no quarrel with its labor practices. And to dispel any notion that they might be unfair, Paley struck bargains concerning wages and working conditions that represented improvements over the packages offered by the other cigar manufacturers (bargains that Paley justified on the belief that the Paley cigar would be a higher quality and more expensive than those produced elsewhere in Philadelphia).

Paley's success with the striking union did not go over well with the other manufacturers. An industry group marched over to the Paley office to demand an explanation and to urge unity in the face of labor's threat. They no doubt expected to deal with an experienced businessman and must have been shocked to see a teenager sitting behind the president's desk. They made their arguments, but Willie knew where his interests lay—and he knew what his father expected of him. He held his ground and later recalled the encounter as a turning point in his life. His self-confidence had been rewarded by his father, who congratulated Bill upon his return. In later years, Paley would often feel uncertainty as to where his best interests lay, but once that decision was made, he rarely lacked the self-confidence to do whatever was necessary to protect those interests.

By the summer of 1919 Sam had moved his family into a big Victorian home on Chadwick Street. Although the lot was not large, it was beautifully landscaped with a pool in the back. The family loved the home, and years later Bill Paley would always speak glowingly of that house on Chadwick Street. His father was equally pleased with business developments. The Congress Cigar Company began expanding almost as soon as it commenced operations in that summer of 1919. And he looked forward to the day when his son had completed his college education and could join him on a full-time basis.

In the meantime, Bill had transferred to the Wharton School at the University of Pennsylvania in Philadelphia. The school offered a variety of business courses, but Paley had lost whatever interest he had left in academic life. His future lay in the Congress Cigar Company, and he would not need good grades to secure a decent job. With this certainty about post-graduate employment, he felt free to take full advantage of the college's social life. He continued his membership in Zeta Beta Tau, the Jewish fraternity he had first joined at the University of Chicago. ("We didn't have to worry about anti-Semitism," said Paley's college friend Nathan Hamburger, "because we had almost no social contact with gentiles.") Paley had no difficulty making friends on campus. "He was a very modest, very charming fellow," said Hamburger, "and he became very popular." The fraternity house on Spruce Street was the focus of his life, with its camaraderie and its rituals and its parties. By his senior year Bill Paley was ZBT's president.

However much he enjoyed the fraternity, Paley's social life was not confined to campus. Although Prohibition had already been established, Philadelphia offered many opportunities for extra-curricular activities— especially if money was no object. There was some wisdom in exercising caution—bootleg whiskey was often made with industrial alcohol, and the city coroner estimated at one point in the 1920s that its consumption was causing about ten deaths every day. Whatever the risks, it was a time for self-indulgence. That very much suited Bill Paley, and in later years he would look back upon those days with much delight. He would use the Essex automobile his father had given him to escort his friends and their dates to parties, restaurants, and nightclubs. The only limitation on this fun occurred on Saturday nights, when Paley would drive his parents to any place of their choosing (since Sam Paley still refused to drive a car).

After graduation in the spring of 1922, Paley, as expected, began working full-time at the Congress Cigar Company. At first he had no title and was asked only to assume a variety of responsibilities in order to get even better acquainted with the business. One of his more memorable experiences from this period involved his attempt to blend some tobacco into a rough cigar—Paley started smoking it and, after a few puffs, fainted dead away, the victim of a bad mix.

Other ventures proved more successful. Shortly after he began working full-time, his father explained that Bill would be placed in charge of the building of a new factory-office building for the Congress Cigar Company. By that time the company had expanded its markets throughout the East

Coast, with six factories producing some 500,000 cigars every day. Sam felt the business warranted a newer, more modern building. His son accepted the task with his usual enthusiasm. He reviewed the needs of the business, examined various architectural plans, and visited numerous sites. Eventually he concluded that the factory should be air-conditioned in order to prevent the tobacco from drying out. When the new plant was constructed at the corner of Third and Spruce, it became one of the first factories to have air-conditioning.

President Calvin Coolidge had said that the "business of America is business," and Sam Paley had no reason to quarrel with that. Between 1922 and 1927 his profits doubled and the company's factories reached a production level of 1.5 million cigars every day. He had perfected the technique of mass production while still maintaining his product's quality. And more than that, by the mid-1920s he had ceased producing a variety of cigars and instead focused his energies on a single brand, La Palina (an obvious play on the family name). A woman with golden locks graced the wrapper, and rumors later circulated that it was an image of Paley's mother (though he himself was never sure).

As the years passed, Bill began to assume more responsibilities. By 1927 he had been made a vice president with a salary of $20,000—no small amount in those years. Sam had also begun to trust his son to take trips by himself to Puerto Rico to buy tobacco. Bill was up to the task. He had developed a talent for selecting the right blends, and, under Sam's tutelage, had learned the art of making good purchases. On one occasion, for example, he found that the tobacco farmers on the island had produced a large crop, which threatened to drive prices down and force some farmers out of business. As the largest buyer, the Congress Cigar Company played a pivotal role in the farmers' fate. Instead of exploiting his momentary advantage, Paley offered the farmers a higher price than the market warranted. He reasoned that the farmers' long-term survival was in the company's best interests and that any immediate benefit in lower prices would be offset in later years by difficulties in acquiring needed qualities and quantities of tobacco. When told of his son's decision and the reasons behind it, Sam very much approved. It was exactly the kind of foresight that had made him so successful.

Sam Paley's financial success did not guarantee his acceptance into the mainstream of Philadelphia society. Ethnic and class distinctions still remained powerful influences in the community, and roots of intolerance ran deep in the City of Brotherly Love. The Main Line Protestants were suspicious of Jews, blacks, and other ethnic groups that could not trace their lineage back to colonial days. Even classified ads for domestic servants stated that they should be white and Protestant. This kind of atmosphere helped to foster divisions among the Jewish community. As in Chicago, Philadelphia's German Jews, like the Gimbels and the Scullenbergs, had arrived earlier, had prospered, and had made considerable strides in their efforts to be assimilated into Philadelphia society. Eastern European Jews, with their heavy accents and unsophisticated ways, were viewed as a threat to social acceptance. Financial success was often deemed to be an irrelevant factor, and many German Jews considered the Paleys "vulgar" people who had changed their name from Palinski (since Paley sounded too American for an Eastern European Jew). Still, Sam Paley remained undaunted, and he used his wealth and his connections to secure a membership in the Philmont Country Club that catered to German Jews. There he played bridge and established relationships with Ellis Gimbel and other stalwarts of the German Jewish community. (Indeed, Gimbel had to cover most of his losses at bridge, because Sam, despite his enormous wealth, was opposed to any extravagance in gambling and refused to play for more than a tenth of a cent a point.)

Sam's son was equally adept in forming friendships with members of the German Jewish community, and two of his closest friends in those days immediately after college were Ben Gimbel and Henry Gerstley. Paley had rented a one-room apartment at the Warwick hotel, and he and his friends pursued the pleasures that he had first tasted as a college student. He maintained memberships in clubs whose only goals were to play cards and plan parties. He frequented speakeasies, saloons, and gambling houses. He danced and dated show girls (and once, after taking a girl to a hotel room, had his lovemaking constantly interrupted by his friend Ben Gimbel, who purposely rented the room next door and pounded on the walls). It was, all in all, a carefree time when Paley could leave his business concerns at the office and give no thought to the future. Perhaps the only disruption to all this enjoyment was the time when Boo Boo Hoff sent two thugs to see Paley about $5,000 in debts which he had accumulated at Hoff's well-known casino. Paley quickly eliminated the debts with a loan from his Uncle Jay (since Paley did not want to compound the problem by incurring his father's displeasure)— but none of this dissuaded Paley from continuing his patronage of gambling houses.

Paley's social life was not confined to Philadelphia. Every spring his family would travel to Europe. He and his father would spend days inspecting tobacco lots and preparing bids for tobacco auctions in Amsterdam. The Palina wrapper was Java tobacco from the Dutch colony, and it was considered a principal factor in the cigar's success. So no effort was spared in trying to buy the necessary amount of high quality Java. Paley was impressed with his father's thoroughness in the process, and years later most CBS executives found that Bill Paley could, when the spirit moved him, devote similar care to his business, asking pointed questions so that important details did not escape his attention.

Both before and after the establishment of CBS, Paley saw European travel as one of the rewards of hard work. After the tobacco auctions in Amsterdam, Sam and Goldie would travel to Vichy in France. Sam was a hypochondriac, and he was convinced that Vichy's spring waters could ease his ailments and prevent their recurrence. Bill went directly to Paris, where his parents would ultimately join him.

Paris in the 1920s was host to the American expatriates, a place where literary giants like Ernest Hemingway, F. Scott Fitzgerald, and Gertrude Stein lived a life of seeming glamour and romance. For Paley, who had no literary inclinations, Paris was simply an extension of the carefree life he pursued in Philadelphia. He would stay at the fashionable Ritz hotel, dine at elegant restaurants, and frequent the nightclubs and bistros that would soon make Montmartre famous. As in later years, there was almost no limit to his interest in sensual and material comfort. One highpoint was reached in the spring of 1928 when he purchased an Hispano Suiza from Hibbard and Darrin, one of the world's most exclusive automakers, for $16,000—which was more than most Americans' annual salaries. The car was large, beautiful, unique, and, for Paley, irresistible. His father was prone to chastize his young son for the purchase, but Goldie convinced Sam that it was an indulgence of youth and should be tolerated.

Paley was not entirely casual in his approach to pleasure. He had come to appreciate how hard his father worked to make his business a success. Day in, day out. There seemed to be no end to it. His father had always talked of retiring to California and buying an orange grove as soon as he had $25,000 in the bank, but, when the magic day arrived, Sam could not leave his business. Paley vowed that he would not be so tied to his work and that he would enjoy the fruits of his labor while he was still young. "I thought quite a bit about it," he later recalled, "and recognized that my father and men like him got caught up in the web of business and constantly postponed retirement and the pleasures of leisure. In order not to get caught that way myself, I made an oath to myself and a solemn vow that I would retire, no matter what, at age thirty-five." But when the time came, Paley found, like his father, that it was not so easy to leave your business—especially if it happened to be in the exciting new world of broadcasting.

CHAPTER THREE

New York

On September 30, 1966, CBS Chairman William S. Paley gave a short speech in New York at a testimonial dinner for David Sarnoff, the guiding presence behind the National Broadcasting Company which, in CBS circles, was known as "the other network." Sarnoff and Paley had been competitors, both professionally and, to some extent, personally, for almost forty years. The rivalry had always been intense and almost always costly. But Paley put aside those differences to pay tribute to his archrival. "There are many here who can speak with more authority than I of David Sarnoff's qualities of leadership, endurance, and inexhaustible energy," said Paley. "But no one can speak with greater authority of his strength and perseverance as a competitor. He never relaxed in his efforts and I've got the scars to prove it."

Many forces and events had brought Sarnoff and Paley into conflict over the previous four decades. But there was a bond between them that ran deeper than any fleeting controversy. For, in one of history's ironic twists, David Sarnoff had been instrumental in creating Bill Paley's opportunity to enter the world of broadcasting in 1928.

Unlike Paley's, Sarnoff's rise to power was a true rags-to-riches story. Born in the village of Uzlian in southern Russia in 1891, his early years were not ones of joy and laughter. From the time he was a small boy, Sarnoff knew little except hard work and fear. His family was orthodox, and he spent most of his daylight hours studying the Talmud and learning about Jewish traditions and laws. The study was interrupted on occasion by Cossacks and vigilantes rampaging through the Jewish settlements, and years later he could still recall vividly the experience of clinging to his mother's skirts while Cossacks rode into a political demonstration, whipping the crowd and trampling men, women, and children under their horses' hooves.

Sarnoff was rescued from a life of desolation by his father, who almost literally starved himself in order to save enough money to bring the family to America. After landing at Montreal, the family traveled by train and then boat to New York City, reaching its harbor in July of 1900. Little David did not speak a word of English, a liability that soon caused him considerable embarrassment at school. But none of that affected his ambition or willingness to work hard. "I knew that I would have to work twice as hard as most other boys . . . to get my education, as it were, on the run," he once remarked. "I didn't think it was unfair and I wasn't bitter. I accepted the handicap calmly, as facts of life, to be faced and overcome."

And overcome them he did. He developed his own newspaper route in the neighborhood known as Hell's Kitchen on New York's West Side; worked as a messenger boy for the Commercial Cable Company (where he learned Morse Code); and then, in his most fateful move, became a messenger for the Marconi Wireless Telegraph Company in September 1906. The company, founded through the efforts of Marchese Guglielmo Marconi, proved to be the forerunner of RCA, the parent company of NBC. Sarnoff worked his way up the corporate ladder, impressing almost everyone with his diligence and intelligence. His first public acclaim came in reporting the *Titanic* tragedy in 1912. Although there is some conflict in contemporaneous accounts concerning the precise nature of Sarnoff's role, there is no dispute that the twenty-one year old station operator did obtain important information about the disaster and its aftermath. Sarnoff was manning the wireless radio for Marconi in the Wanamaker department store in Manhattan when he heard faint messages from another ship confirming that the *Titanic* had struck an iceberg and was sinking fast. Sarnoff immediately relayed the communication to the press. Other messages followed, and Sarnoff was soon surrounded by crowds of people eager for further details.

Other stations were also reporting vital information, but Sarnoff's view of himself was not restricted by historical fact. In succeeding years he would recount the incident to interviewers, each time exaggerating his role more and more until, by 1930, he became *the* central figure in first reporting the *Titanic*'s fate, staying glued to his station for seventy-two consecutive hours while hordes of people gathered around him. However fanciful the recollection, the episode did have a very real impact on Sarnoff's career. His new status as a public figure brought him to the attention of executives in the Marconi company, and they saw that David Sarnoff was very talented and very dedicated. He would tackle problems with enthusiasm, especially those concerning technological advancements in the development of radio.

Sarnoff's interest in these technological matters seemed to be compensation for his lack of formal education. Engineering was a matter of science, a field that could be mastered only by the educated elite. But the interest in these scientific matters was not academic. Sarnoff wanted his ideas to have practical application. In 1916 he wrote a memorandum to the president of American Marconi proposing the use of radio as a "music box" that would bring concerts, lectures, and entertainment into the American home and become something of a "household utility." Edward McNally, the company president, considered Sarnoff's proposal to be "harebrained," but Sarnoff persevered, and in 1921 he presented the idea to Owen D. Young, board chairman of the Radio Corporation of America, which had been formed only two years earlier. Young responded favorably to the proposal—not because he saw radio as a significant medium of entertainment and news but because he thought Sarnoff's proposal, if implemented, would help RCA sell the radio sets it was manufacturing.

Coincidentally, radio had just made its first mark in the distribution of information. Westinghouse Broadcasting Company's station in Pittsburgh, KDKA, had broadcast the presidential election returns in 1920, and soon thereafter the four hundred or so radio stations sprinkled throughout the country began to take those first tentative steps toward becoming a genuine medium of mass communication. The progress, however, was slow. One major obstacle concerned payment for the concerts, lectures, and other programs that a radio station aired. No one, not even David Sarnoff, contemplated that advertisers would foot the bill. He suggested instead that a national broadcast service be established and that it be funded by a surtax on the sale of radio equipment. Although his proposal did not win wide support, most people involved with the fledgling industry agreed with the sentiments behind it. Secretary of Commerce Herbert Hoover, whose department then regulated radio, commented that "[i]t is inconceivable that we should allow so great a possibility for service to be drowned in advertising chatter."

AT&T broke ranks when it introduced "toll broadcasting" in 1922 over its New York station, WEAF. In what it described as an "experiment," AT&T stated that it would make air time available to anyone who wanted to buy it. Company officials likened it to a person placing a coin in a telephone booth to make a call. The experiment posed some difficult problems of decorum, such as whether advertisements for toothpaste were too "personal" to be mentioned in public. But AT&T's sensitivity to these problems did not enhance its position within the industry—at least not initially. Periodicals and public figures condemned the practice, some calling for legislation to prohibit it. But economics prevailed.

Industry leaders began to recognize that AT&T's experiment offered the best solution. Soon Hoover and other observers were speaking out against only "direct" advertising, whatever that meant. Other stations began to sell air time but warned advertisers that certain standards had to be followed and that the price of products could not be mentioned under any circumstance.

In the meantime, AT&T had become embroiled in a controversy with RCA, General Electric Company, and Westinghouse Broadcasting—the giants in the burgeoning radio field—over various agreements that had been signed in the early 1920s concerning AT&T's right to become involved in broadcasting. Although WEAF had proven extremely profitable, AT&T was still smarting under the criticism it had attracted. Sarnoff, then an RCA vice president, saw AT&T's posture as a guide to settlement. He proposed that a national broadcast organization be formed, that it buy WEAF from AT&T, that the organization then affiliate with other radio stations around the country to form a network, and that this new radio network then lease telephone lines from AT&T to transmit programming to the affiliated stations.

The parties debated and refined this proposal throughout 1926. In July of that year an agreement was reached to create the National Broadcasting Company. Ownership of the company was distributed among RCA (50 percent), General Electric (30 percent), and Westinghouse (20 percent). AT&T would sell WEAF to NBC and then lease lines to NBC for an annual fee of $1 million. Everyone seemed satisfied, and in September of 1926 RCA purchased full-page advertisements in newspapers around the country announcing the creation of NBC. In the face of charges by Congress and others that it was creating a "radio trust," RCA stated in the announcements that it "is not in any sense seeking a monopoly of the air."

Some readers of the announcement may have believed RCA's disclaimer. Arthur Judson, for one, did not. He was a forty-five-year-old entrepreneur who managed orchestras and performing artists. (He had earlier earned a living as a violinist, but decided to lock up his violin when "I discovered that I was neither a Kreisler nor a Heifetz.") Judson saw great potential—for himself—in radio. He went to see Sarnoff, then generally acknowledged as the moving force behind NBC, and proposed that NBC book some of Judson's clients on programs that would be sponsored by advertisers. Sarnoff said he would consider the proposal, but Judson soon realized that NBC was planning to move forward on the idea without Judson or his clients.

Judson was not about to walk away from radio and its enormous potential. He formed Judson Radio Program Corporation with the hope that he could peddle his clients to other radio stations. He recognized, however, that life would be much simpler if he could sell his programs to a chain of radio stations instead of having to approach individual ones throughout the country. The problem, of course, was that NBC had the only chain of radio stations. So Judson marched back to Sarnoff's office and adopted a more aggressive approach. He told Sarnoff that he had formed Judson Radio Program Corporation and that he was prepared to sell to other stations unless NBC agreed to do business with him.

David Sarnoff had many attractive qualities, but modesty was not one of them. He had come from nowhere to establish himself as an acknowledged authority in an important new industry before he was thirty-five. He saw himself as a leader beyond challenge. ("In a big ship sailing an uncharted sea," he once said, "one fellow needs to be on the bridge. I happen to be that fellow.") He was not the kind of man to be intimidated by Arthur Judson or any other promoter. So when Judson asked Sarnoff what he was going to do about his proposal, Sarnoff had a one-word answer: "Nothing." Judson, letting his anger overrule his better judgment, responded by saying he would organize his own chain of radio stations and challenge NBC's monopoly. Sarnoff threw his head back in laughter. "You can't do it," he said. "I have just signed a contract to take one million dollars' worth of long lines from the telephone company. In any event, you couldn't get any wires even if you had a broadcasting station. It can't be done."

Had Sarnoff been a little more humble and accommodating, he might have preserved NBC's position as the only radio network (at least for a while longer). But his cavalier dismissal of Arthur Judson set in motion the events that would lead to the formation of the Columbia Broadcasting System.

As a practical matter, Sarnoff knew what he was talking about. The obstacles to establishing a second radio network were considerable. But it was too late for Arthur Judson to turn back. He recruited some associates and formed United Independent Broadcasters. He then tried to lease telephone lines, but AT&T was not very responsive. They sent an executive and an engineer to see him; the executive patiently explained the difficulties of providing the lines while the engineer motioned in the background that it was indeed possible. As they were speaking, Judson received a telegram from a colleague in Washington stating that he had been able to use his contacts and $11,000 to "persuade" AT&T to cooperate.

That was not the end of Judson's problems. He had been able to enlist sixteen stations as affiliates of UIB. He had promised to pay each of them $500 per week for ten hours of UIB's programming. Unfortunately, Judson had neither the programs nor the money to give to affiliates. (When Betty Fleischmann Holmes, a potential financial contributor, asked Judson what he was doing with UIB, he replied, "[L]osing our shirts.") But he persisted and was finally able to secure an agreement with the Columbia Phonograph Company that entitled the record company to become UIB's broadcast operations arm, which was renamed Columbia Phonograph Broadcasting Company. In exchange, the record company gave UIB $163,000 (which, according to Judson, "was probably arrived at by the amount of money we needed").

UIB finally began to distribute its programs on September 18, 1927, but even that accomplishment was not enough to put the company in the black. Each week UIB was losing about $20,000. A financial angel was sorely needed and, by coincidence, it came through one of UIB's affiliates.

Because of its location in Philadelphia—one of the country's largest radio markets—WCAU was recognized as an important affiliate for UIB. The station was owned by Ike Levy and his younger brother Leon. The two men were not at all alike. "Leon was suave and gentile," said one friend who knew both men, "and Ike was not." A hardnosed lawyer who recognized the need to establish a practice with someone who was not Jewish, Ike had formed a partnership with Daniel Murphy, a skilled trial lawyer. Ike was also a person who believed in taking risks, and he and Murphy had purchased WCAU for $25,000 in 1922. When Murphy later tired of the business, Ike approached his younger brother. Leon was a dentist, but he recognized the potential of radio and agreed to become a partner if Ike would revamp the entire program schedule (to which Ike replied, "You've filled your last tooth, kid").

As an affiliate of UIB, the Levys were only too happy to help the fledgling network, and they interested Jerome Louchheim, a client of Ike's who also happened to be a millionaire. Louchheim purchased a controlling interest in UIB, and for weeks afterward he and Ike would make periodic trips to New York (after having an early morning breakfast of frog legs at Louchheim's house). But Louchheim broke his hip and felt that the venture was too draining. A younger man was needed to take over (since Judson also felt that management was not his forte). Ike discussed it with his brother, but Leon did not want to leave Philadelphia to manage an operation that was constantly on the verge of bankruptcy.

It was then that Louchheim approached Sam Paley. Sam was younger than Louchheim and, more importantly, he had a product he could advertise over UIB's stations. Sam, however, had little interest in what seemed to be a losing proposition. His son had a different reaction. When Sam conveyed the substance of his conversation with Louchheim, Bill became interested immediately. To begin with, his future at the Congress Cigar Company did not seem as secure as it once had. Sam had taken part of the company public in 1926, and in 1927 he sold the controlling interest to the Porto Rican-American Tobacco Company for almost $30 million. Sam and his brother Jay, who also worked at Congress, were given contracts to continue working there, but Bill had not been given any contract.

True, his father could keep him on the payroll for as long as Sam was there, but who knew when the senior Paley might finally decide to pursue that long-deferred dream of retirement?

All of these financial details, however, were of minor significance. One factor overrode all others: Bill Paley did not like the cigar business and yearned for a job with more excitement. "He never liked the cigar business," said Henry Gerstley. "The one thing he liked was to meet people of prominence and importance, and you couldn't meet many people like that in the cigar business." Nathan Hamburger agreed with this assessment. "Bill didn't like the tobacco business," he remembered. "It wasn't glamorous enough for him. He didn't like looking at tobacco and he didn't like smelling tobacco. The only part he liked was the advertising end."

Paley's principal involvement in advertising had been with WCAU, which was still owned by the Levys. There was a certain irony in the connection. Leon Levy had begun dating Blanche, and at first Bill was not at all pleased with his sister's choice in men (and on one occasion he locked her in her room when Levy showed up at his parents' house for a date). But Blanche persisted, eventually marrying Levy in September 1927, and, through increased contact, Bill too came to have a high regard for his new brother-in-law. The relationship with Leon and his brother deepened when they sold a share in WCAU to the Paley family. So it was only natural for Bill to turn to the Levys when he decided to experiment with a radio advertisement for Congress cigars. Paley made the purchase of air time while his father and Uncle Jay were away on business, and Jay had cancelled it upon his return, calling it a frivolous expenditure. But afterwards people kept asking Sam Paley what happened to "La Palina Hour," and Jay was forced to admit that Bill's judgment had been sound. So they asked Bill to develop a regular program, which became identified as "La Palina Smoker." It featured an orchestra, a female singer, and a comedian as a master of ceremonies. Cigar sales shot up immediately, and everyone at the company seemed satisfied that radio was a powerful instrument.

"La Palina Smoker" was carried over UIB's network, and Bill was required to make frequent trips to UIB's offices in New York. He met Arthur Judson, he reviewed their operation, and he felt the excitement of this new enterprise, however shaky it might be from a financial standpoint. So when his father mentioned Louchheim's desire to sell his interest in UIB, Bill knew that it was the kind of opportunity he had to exploit. "I went to my father," Paley remembered decades later, "and said that I'd been giving an awful lot of thought to broadcasting, and what did he think . . . if I bought Mr. Louchheim's position."

Sam's reaction was critical to his son. He had received $1 million from the sale of stock in Congress Cigar Company, and he proposed to use part of that money to purchase Louchheim's interest. While the money might be in an account with his name, Bill Paley knew that no part of those stock proceeds could be used without his father's permission. And beyond the issue of money was his father's hopes and expectations. Sam had been grooming him to take over the cigar business, plans that would be frustrated if Bill went to manage UIB in New York.

Paley did not know how his father would react. Sam was, as Paley later recalled, "a broad-minded person." But business judgments could not be clouded with sentimentality or abstract principles. Real dollars were at stake, and Paley feared that his father might prefer the security of a known enterprise like cigar-making to the risk of a fanciful venture called broadcasting.

Other forces, however, were pushing Sam to accept his son's proposal. Coincidentally, Ike Levy had visited with Sam and had suggested that he buy UIB for his son. Ike had great faith in radio's future, and more than that, UIB's financial ills had just been alleviated—at least for the moment—with a new $750,000 advertising contract from a Warner Brothers subsidiary.

After thinking it over, Sam told his son that he approved of the UIB purchase, that Bill should use $400,000 of his stock funds to buy Louchheim's interest, and that the family would contribute another $100,000. Paley was delighted and surprised, but most of all surprised. He had convinced himself that Sam would never release him from the cigar business, and he could not resist asking his father why he had yielded. Sam replied that it was all a matter of good business sense. "Well," he told Bill, "if you succeed, it'll be a bigger business, and more interesting business, and a more broadening business than what you're in now; and if you don't succeed," his father added, "you will have had a lot of experience which might be very useful in the cigar company and to me, and so, on balance, I think you ought to try it."

Paley had no doubt about his ability to enjoy the new venture—or to succeed at it. He rushed over to see Louchheim and, after some hard negotiating, reached an agreement on September 19, 1928 to buy almost all of Louchheim's controlling interest. In exchange for $503,000, Louchheim gave Paley 50.3 percent of UIB's stock. On September 26 Bill Paley was elected UIB's president and the next day he was in New York to assume his new position. He was one day shy of his twenty-seventh birthday.

Paley was no doubt excited when he arrived at UIB's office on an upper floor in the tower of the Paramount Building in midtown Manhattan. But his reception was something less than he had hoped for. A stocky office boy refused to admit the boyish-looking president, demanding to see credentials and to know the purpose of his visit.

After finally gaining admittance, Paley tackled UIB's problems with great energy. UIB then had about sixteen employees, and they were, for the most part, taken by the presence of their new leader. He seemed very affable, very accessible, and, perhaps most importantly, willing to listen. Ann Honeycutt, a UIB staff member, was among those who witnessed Paley's ascension to power at UIB. "Everyone of course was nervous about the new boss," she remembered, "but he moved freely from office to office, speaking with us, asking questions about any suggestions we had. And," she continued, "you could always count on him to bum a cigarette whenever he came into your office."

However impressed he may have been with the existing staff, Paley knew that additions would have to be made. His father had advised him before leaving Philadelphia to hire smart people and to have the good sense to listen to them. Paley had great respect for his father and certainly did not want his father to lose money in the venture. Paley recognized that one of his first needs was to have an assistant whose first loyalty was to him, so he asked his good Philadelphia friend, Larry Lowman, to join him at once. He then retained the services of Edward L. Bernays, the most respected name in public relations. A diminutive man with a small black moustache, Bernays had won acclaim for his imagination in promoting all kinds of businesses, especially theater and other entertainment ventures. Paley had read Bernays's book, *Crystallizing Public Opinion,* and was excited by the prospect of having access to a public relations adviser. As he later explained, "I thought, my God, to be important enough to have a public relations man. Somebody who could tell you what to do and what not to do." It was not simply a question of prestige, however. Paley knew that UIB's success would depend on its credibility with affiliate stations, advertisers, and the public, and Bernays would, Paley hoped, create the kind of image that UIB desperately needed.

Like the UIB staff, Bernays was impressed with Paley. "He was affable, cool, suave, polite, soft-spoken, and well groomed," Bernays later recalled. Bernays did not have the same respect for the UIB operation. It seemed totally disorganized; even the smallest matters seemed to get fouled up. There was, for example, no receptionist on hand after five o'clock, a void that meant late-evening calls about news items or schedules—of which there were many—often went unnoticed.

Bernays gave advice freely, and Paley seemed to accept almost all of his suggestions. Paley would listen intently, ask some questions, retreat to his office, and then telephone Bernays in a day or two with his approval. To Bernays, the whole process seemed a little mystifying. "I never knew how he made his decisions," he later commented, "and it puzzled me because I didn't think there was anyone else at his office to consult. And I used to think, well, maybe he's communing with Nature."

Paley was not one to seek divine inspiration, but he did like to absorb information and dwell on it before reaching any conclusions. And one conclusion soon became obvious enough: UIB needed more affiliate stations. If it was going to attract advertisers and charge remunerative rates, UIB needed a wider audience. Paley studied the matter and decided that the network's affiliation contract was the major obstacle to expansion. Louchhcim had amended the original contract drawn up by Judson. Under the amended contract, UIB was still paying the affiliates $500 per week for commercially sponsored time; but UIB had also demanded that the affiliates pay it for their use of any unsponsored, or "sustaining," programming supplied by the network. The UIB sustaining programs were not particularly good, and the affiliate stations were not cash-rich. The result: very few stations bought UIB's sustaining programs.

Paley decided to amend the affiliation contract one more time. Instead of the present ten-hour weekly commitment, he promised to provide the affiliates with twenty hours of commercially sponsored programs. There was, however, one catch—the first five hours would be free to the network. In return, the network would provide sustaining programming at no cost to the affiliates. The final amendment was one Paley regarded as critical. The affiliates could not associate with any other network (meaning NBC) and, in addition, they had to identify the programs with their network— which Paley had by then renamed the Columbia Broadcasting System.

Initially, Paley proposed to offer the new affiliation contract to stations in the South, since the network had none in that region. Telegrams were sent out, and twelve stations sent representatives to the meeting at the Ambassador Hotel in New York. Paley was magnificent in his presentation. Smooth, deliberative, smiling (even Ike Levy, who later had a falling out with Paley, admitted that he was a terrific salesman who "was very good at making you want things you really didn't want"). The results were spectacular. A very excited and happy Bill Paley watched as all twelve representatives came up after the presentation to sign the new affiliation agreement. Overtures in other parts of the country were equally successful, and on January 8, 1929, CBS President Bill Paley went on the air to announce that his network now had the largest number of affiliates, with forty-nine stations in forty-two cities.

Technically, Paley's claim was accurate. But that was only because NBC was divided into two separate networks, the "Red" and the "Blue," and neither of those *individual* networks had more affiliates (although considered together, NBC had far more). But Paley already knew that success depended on image, and he was not about to sacrifice a successful image for the sake of a more complete truth.

Although he devoted long hours and considerable energy to his new company, Paley did not forsake his social life. It was too important to him to be neglected. For years he had read *Vogue, Harper's Bazaar,* and other magazines that whetted his appetite for the excitement of New York's nightlife. Initially, he rented an apartment at the Elysee, a small, elegant hotel on Fifty-fourth Street between Madison and Park Avenues. By the end of the decade he had moved into a triplex apartment at 480 Madison Avenue. No expense was spared to outfit it with every convenience. The interior was done by Lee Simonsin, a well-known theater designer, at a reported cost of $10,000 per room—an astronomical sum in those Depression years. Every room had a radio, and Paley could use a remote control from his bed to change stations; a piano (which Paley had once attempted to play in his younger years) was almost completely hidden behind a wall, with only the keyboard visible; and the closets were large enough to hold three hundred suits, a hundred shirts, and a hundred ties to match.

Paley did not try to manage all this himself. When he left for Philadelphia, his mother had told him not to do what he could get someone else to do for him. So he hired an English butler who also substituted as a valet when needed. With a quick telephone call to his apartment, Paley could plan sumptuous dinner parties to entertain his friends and companions. Although he remained somewhat shy, especially among those he did not know well, his manner was engaging and ingratiating. Friends and companions found that he displayed what seemed to be a genuine interest in whatever topic concerned his guest. There would almost always be questions, compliments, and a ready smile. If anyone suggested a new game or activity, he would be one of the first to express enthusiasm for the idea. It was all so natural and endearing. Few could resist Bill Paley's charm when he decided to turn it on.

There were occasions when Paley's social activities created problems, and one of the first arose after a housewarming at his Madison Avenue triplex where some of the guests included journalists. Although Prohibition was in effect, Paley wasn't worried about serving liquor. After all, speakeasies, saloons, and private clubs were found in abundance in Manhattan and seemed to attract little media attention. Late that evening, however, Bernays received a telephone call from a reporter at the *Chicago Tribune,* asking for confirmation that liquor had been served at the apartment of the new CBS president. Bernays used all of his considerable charm to persuade the reporter that the story should not be used because it would brand the young Paley as a bootlegger and unfairly taint a promising career.

For Bill Paley it was an instructive experience. As a broadcaster, his activities—both in and out of the office—would attract public attention; if he was to keep his social life private, measures would have to be taken. From then on, few outsiders would be given access to that private world, and seasoned reporters would say that Bill Paley was something of an enigma because he gave few interviews and jealously guarded his privacy.

There were other measures Paley had to take to accommodate his socializing. He soon realized he had difficulty getting up in the morning. So he hired another man whose only job was to come to the apartment and make sure he got up, even if it meant pulling him out of bed. The CBS president did not always appreciate these early morning visits, and his hired hand was fired many times, only to be told (after Paley had had a shower and massage) to be back the next morning.

All in all, it was an exciting time both professionally and socially. It was the kind of life that Paley had dreamed of in Philadelphia, the kind of life he felt suited to pursue and enjoy. And as CBS advanced in audience ratings and corporate profits, the dream only seemed to get better.

CHAPTER FOUR

Success

On the morning of October 17, 1934, CBS's thirty-three-year old president, with his brown hair slicked back and dressed in a dark, double-breasted suit, took a seat at the table before the seven members of the Federal Communications Commission. Congress had created the FCC the previous June and had charged it with the responsibility of regulating interstate communications facilities, including broadcasting. Congress had also asked the FCC to report back on a proposal that would require a certain percentage of all radio stations to be dedicated to educational and other noncommercial uses. The proposal reflected the view of some, like Senator Henry D. Hatfield of West Virginia, that radio's reliance on commercial advertisements had produced "pollution of the air." Not surprisingly, commercial broadcasters—including the Columbia Broadcasting System—took a different view. The FCC had scheduled hearings to consider these divergent viewpoints, and Bill Paley had been among those asked to make a presentation.

Paley's comments on the issue would be given considerable weight. In the short time since he had assumed the presidency of United Independent Broadcasters in 1928, Paley had become a leading figure in broadcast circles. No one, least of all RCA, thought that Paley—so young and so inexperienced—could develop UIB into a major force that would challenge NBC's dominance. But Paley had surprised them all. In 1928 CBS showed a net loss of $179,000. One year later the company made a net profit of $474,000. By 1931 the net profit had skyrocketed to $2.35 million, and in 1934 the company was on its way to a profit of $2.27 million. This performance seemed even more remarkable when viewed against the backdrop of the Depression when most business firms were more concerned with survival than with astronomical profits.

Of course, there were many factors behind CBS's success, and many of them had little or nothing to do with Bill Paley's talents. Still, much of the credit was his. His amendment of the affiliate contract and his active courtship of stations across the country had increased the number of CBS affiliates to one hundred by 1934. He had also refined and expanded the network's programs, and by 1934 CBS was providing sixteen hours of programming every day. Approximately one-third of these had commercial sponsors, and the rest were sustaining programs that CBS made available to its affiliates free of charge. One could argue about the quality of these programs, but no one in 1934 needed to ask—as President Franklin D. Roosevelt once had at a press conference—what the initials CBS stood for.

CBS's development had required considerable effort, and Bill Paley had given it everything he had. He worked twelve, fourteen, even sixteen hours a day, talking with affiliates, charming performers, and cajoling advertisers. But however stretched his schedule might be in New York, he was almost always prepared to take the train to Washington to speak with government officials. Congress had been considering broadcast legislation from the time that UIB had been formed, and Paley was frequently asked to testify before congressional committees or meet with members of Congress. He also spent considerable time talking with officials at the FCC as well as the Federal Radio Commission, the regulatory agency that had preceded the FCC (and whose powers had been transferred to the FCC in the Communications Act of 1934). The FCC (and the FRC before it) had authority to issue three-year licenses that entitled the holder—like CBS for example—the exclusive use of a radio frequency for the duration of the license (which was usually renewed). A broadcaster could not operate without a license, and it made obvious sense for Paley to spend time cultivating relationships with the commissioners and their staffs.

At first, Paley enjoyed these forays into the nation's capital. The political process fascinated him, and it was exciting to be involved in decisions that would shape a new industry for decades to come. But then Paley tired of these trips. To begin with, he never felt completely comfortable as a spokesman for CBS or the broadcast industry. In private meetings with subordinates he could be direct, quick, and incisive. But with strangers he was more self-deprecating, almost shy, and that part of his personality collided with the open and exposed role required of a public spokesman. He did not adjust to the public role, and his speeches often lacked the precision and charm that were so evident in private conversation.

There was also the social side of it. Washington was little more than a sleepy Southern town with tree-lined boulevards and government buildings. There were few restaurants, no casinos, and no nightclubs. The evening social life consisted almost entirely of private dinners. Paley found it all too tranquil for his more sophisticated tastes. Joe Ream, a young Yale-trained lawyer, had been hired to organize a law department at CBS, and he used to accompany Paley to Washington. "We almost never went to dinner parties or cocktail parties," Ream recalled. "Paley never seemed to like that kind of socializing. I think one of his chief pleasures on those trips was to sneak out around ten P.M. and go to a hamburger stand near the Carlton Hotel, where we usually stayed."

Paley would have gladly asked someone else to assume the responsibility as CBS's spokesman in Washington. But he recognized that it was a vitally important role, and there was no one—at least not yet—who had the stature and talent to take his place. So he continued to shoulder the burden. And he was not going to let his personal discomfort undercut the message he had for the FCC on that fall day in 1934.

There was, Paley told the commissioners, no advantage and much cost in any proposal to reserve a substantial portion of the radio spectrum for educational and other noncommercial purposes. Radio had prospered under the "dictates of good business practice" and would grow only if "conducted on sound business principles. . . ." In Paley's mind, it was a matter of simple logic. Radio programs cost money, and since the government was not going to pay for them, another source had to be found, and that source was the advertiser.

There was nothing nefarious about this reliance on advertisers, Paley explained. After all, newspapers and other bastions of free speech also relied on advertisers for their financial survival. He of course recognized that the dependence on advertisers limited the broadcaster's discretion in deciding what programs to air, but that was all to the good. The need for advertisers forced broadcasters to develop an audience for their programs. Paley frowned on the idea that the broadcaster should unilaterally decide—without regard to listener interest—what programs to air. "We cannot," he told the commissioners, "calmly broadcast programs we think people ought to listen to, if they know what is good for them, and then go on happily unconcerned as to whether they listen or not." No, he continued, responsible broadcasting required that all programs—even educational and and cultural programs—"must appeal either to the emotions or the self-interest of the hearer, and not merely to his intellect. . . . Experience has taught that one of the quickest ways to bore the American audience is to deal with art for art's sake, or to deify culture and education because they are worthy gods."

Paley said that his ideas had been applied with great success in developing CBS's program schedule. True, only 30 percent of its programming had commercial sponsors. But CBS tried to develop sustaining programs that would attract a wide audience and eventually secure commercial sponsorship. As an example, Paley cited the Columbia School of the Air, an educational program series that included dramatic episodes on history, geography, and science. CBS's criterion of success in these programs, Paley said, was to develop "a presentation so dramatic that the listener could distinguish it from pure entertainment only with difficulty." (This approach was exemplified in CBS's "Mercury of the Air Theatre" in 1938 by Orson Welles's simulated news bulletins of an invasion from outer space, causing thousands of people, believing the invasion to be real, to flee New York City for the safer environs of the country.)

Paley did not personally draft all of his FCC statement, but it reflected his personal views on broadcasting—views that would remain largely unchanged over the next fifty years. In his private life he would cultivate exquisite tastes in art, in food, in clothing, and even in programming. But he would rarely impose his personal preferences on the CBS program schedule. Almost always the question was not what *he* would like, but whether the program could attract a large enough audience to justify the time and expense that were usually required to produce it. And always— whether stated or not—a key, if not overriding, factor was a program's potential to generate large profits. Because in the end, as Paley explained to the FCC, broadcasting is a business, and "[i]t must render a service so important that someone . . . must be willing to pay for it."

Paley's views commanded wide support both inside and outside the broadcast industry, but they were not universally accepted—especially as radio (and later television) assumed more and more influence in American life. Many critics argued that broadcasters—whose FCC licenses were a government-guaranteed monopoly over the airwaves—had a responsibility to broadcast informational programs even if they could not generate commercial sponsorship, and the Communications Act of 1934 itself stated that broadcast licensees had a duty to serve the "public interest, convenience and necessity." Paley recognized this duty, and there were occasions—particularly in the early days of radio, when time was always available and production costs were minimal—when he would air a program that had considerable informational value and little or no commercial value. But he never forgot that CBS was—first and last—a business that had to make money, and the more the better.

These views constituted the heart of Bill Paley's philosophy in broadcasting. But philosophy alone did not carry Paley and his network to the point where it could—and eventually did by the 1936–37 season—overtake NBC in the ratings. Shrewd bargains, substantial investments, and good timing had laid the necessary foundation.

One of the first needs had always remained the acquisition of stations and affiliates. Paley wanted a flagship station that would be owned by CBS and provide the setting for the origination of network programs. Two stations—WOR in Newark, New Jersey, and New York City's WABC (which was not part of any network)—were the prime candidates, and in December 1928 Paley purchased WABC for $390,000, primarily because the asking price was lower and because the acquisition included a programming studio in Steinway Hall on West Fifty-seventh Street. The deal required Paley to purchase $200,000 more of CBS stock and for the other stockholders to increase their investments as well.

Despite the infusion of additional capital from the Paley family and other CBS shareholders, there was still not enough money on hand to insure adequate funds to develop programs and attract affiliates. A new, larger source of revenue was required, and it soon appeared in the person of Adolph Zukor, the Hollywood movie mogul.

In 1929, Zukor was fifty-six years old—exactly twice Paley's age. Like Paley's father, Zukor was an Eastern European Jew who had emigrated to the United States in the 1880s. Unlike Paley's father, however, Zukor had not been able to rely on his family's wealth—he had only the forty dollars that his mother had sewn into his waistcoat before placing him on the boat going to America. But Zukor was ambitious and tough. He soon made his way to Chicago and opened a furrier business. Chicago's growing entrepreneurial class provided a natural market for luxury items, and Zukor's business did well—so well that he decided to open an office in New York and then to diversify. The diversification included the purchase of a penny arcade with another enterprising Eastern European Jew named Sam Goldfish (who later changed his name to Goldwyn). By 1912 Zukor's involvement in the entertainment business had led him to buy the U.S. rights to the silent French film, *Les Amours de la Reine Elisabeth,* starring the incomparable Sarah Bernhardt. The great popularity of the movie led Zukor to abandon his furs in New York for movie lots in a dusty suburb of Los Angeles called Hollywood. Not one addicted to humility, Zukor called his new company Paramount Pictures.

Zukor was fascinated by the developments in broadcasting—not because he was attracted to radio but because he thought it inevitable that sound would soon be wed to pictures and that television was just around the proverbial corner. For that reason, he tried to buy an interest in UIB (which had its offices in the Paramount Building) in 1927, but Arthur Judson resisted when Zukor insisted on renaming the company Paramount Broadcasting. Zukor's interest in UIB had never flagged and he was willing to make another approach when UIB's ownership changed hands in 1928.

For his part, Bill Paley was a willing listener. UIB—now renamed the Columbia Broadcasting System—definitely could benefit from an association with an established movie company. It had stature, financial resources, and programming facilities. It was a natural fit. But Paley was not about to rush into Zukor's arms just for prestige and promises alone. CBS had already started to expand operations and generate revenues. Radio sets were being purchased at an explosive rate. It seemed more and more likely that radio would become—as David Sarnoff had envisioned—a household utility.

All of this gave Bill Paley great faith in CBS's future. So when William Fox of Twentieth Century-Fox offered to buy half of CBS at the same price Paley had paid for his shares less than a year earlier, the young network executive picked up his hat and walked out of the meeting feeling very insulted. And when Adolph Zukor's representative inquired about the price for half ownership of CBS, Paley calmly replied it was $5 million—ten times the amount he and his family had invested for their controlling interest. Zukor's representatives tried to negotiate, finally offering $4.5 million, but Paley held firm. The price was $5 million—and it was not subject to negotiation.

Adolph Zukor was a man used to getting his way, and he found Paley's intransigence difficult to understand. A meeting was arranged, and Paley was ushered in to see the legendary movie mogul. The two men could not have been more different in appearance. Zukor was about five feet tall, with short graying hair and perpetually squinting eyes. In contrast, Paley was tall, boyish-looking, and dressed in fashionable clothes—a dark suit with a high starched collar, which he wore in part to make himself seem older. Although happy to meet the famous movie producer, Paley had no interest in lowering his price. Zukor persisted. Paramount's bid of $4.5 million was a fair counteroffer, he said; didn't Paley understand that counteroffers were an accepted form of negotiation? Paley, soft-spoken and polite, stood his ground. Zukor did not like being turned down, but he respected a tough negotiator—and he wanted badly to get into broadcasting. Shortly after the meeting ended, Zukor's representative informed Paley that Paramount would accept his offer and buy half of CBS for $5 million.

The agreement meant that CBS was now worth ten times more than when Paley had purchased his half interest less than a year earlier. There were, however, important particulars still to be negotiated. The first concerned operating control of the company. With Paramount owning exactly half the CBS stock and the other shareholders (including Paley and his family) owning the other half, no one had majority control; either side could create a stalemate in the decision-making process. To avoid that dilemma, the agreement called for Paley to continue managing the company's day-to-day operations.

A second problem concerned the method by which Paramount would pay for the CBS stock. Paley wanted cash. Zukor wanted to pay with an exchange of Paramount stock, which in those pre-Depression days was selling for $65 a share. Paley could not reach an agreement with Zukor's representative, so another meeting was arranged with Zukor himself. Zukor told Paley that acquisition of Paramount stock was a better deal than the young network executive had sought. Although $65 a share now, said Zukor, the stock was bound to reach $150 a share within a year; the market was going up, and there seemed to be no limit to stock prices.

This time it was Paley who made the counteroffer. He told Zukor that he would take the Paramount stock with the following condition: if CBS made $2 million in profits within the next two years, Paley and the other CBS stockholders could require Paramount to buy its stock back at $85 a share. Zukor, feeling he had the better part of the deal, quickly accepted Paley's offer. The CBS stockholders were given 58,823 shares of Paramount stock worth a total of $3.8 million and the right to have Paramount repurchase its stock two years later for $5 million—if, and only if, CBS made $2 million in profit during that time.

The final papers were signed on June 13, 1929, and Paley had every reason to feel good. He had come a long way in a very short time.

Like Paley, Zukor had great faith in *his* business. But like most people, Zukor did not anticipate the stock market crash of October 1929 and the economic depression that ensued. By the time the two-year period had elapsed, in March 1932, Paramount's stock was selling for $9 a share. Since CBS had netted more than $2 million in those two years, Zukor was obligated to pay Paley and the other stockholders $85 a share for the Paramount stock they held. Not relishing the thought of paying the $5 million in cash, Zukor asked Paley for an extension. After all, he argued, no one in early 1929 could have predicted the economic collapse that had affected almost every business (broadcasting being a notable exception).

Paley was sympathetic; no doubt he recalled his earlier experience with the Puerto Rican tobacco farmers. It was not always prudent—or fair—to exploit every short-term economic advantage. Paley discussed the issue with other CBS stockholders, including his family and the Levys. Ike Levy took a hard stand, saying that a deal was a deal and that Paramount should be forced to buy the stock back now—no extensions. Levy pressed his viewpoint, and Paley finally acceded—especially after Zukor's representatives tried to overpower him in negotiations, patronizing him as a "young man" who did not fully understand standard business practices.

At the same time, Paley knew that Paramount did not *have* $5 million in cash. So he made Zukor another proposal: he and the CBS stockholders would buy back the CBS stock in Paramount's possession. The price: $4 million. That way, Paley and his group would have Zukor's $5 million and *all* the CBS stock.

Paramount did not have to sell the CBS stock back to Paley and his associates, and Paramount representatives complained that Paley's offer of $4 million was low in light of CBS's past earnings and potential earning power in the future. But Paley again held firm, knowing that no one else would offer to buy the CBS stock (because under the agreement the CBS stockholders had a right to match any offers from other sources) and knowing that Paramount needed the cash to pay off CBS.

Paramount finally yielded. As a result, Paley and the other CBS stockholders once again had all the CBS stock (now at its greatly appreciated value) as well as their money. Paley converted part of the returned CBS stock into cash and walked away from the closing with a check for more than $2 million for himself and the other stockholders. Bill Paley, age thirty-one, had become a wealthy man in his own right.

The successful conclusion of the Paramount deal coincided with positive developments in affiliate relations. Paley had been able to use the amended affiliation contract to attract affiliate stations in the South, the East, and the Midwest, but CBS had little penetration in the West. The imbalance became critical in early 1929 when CBS—in a rush to expand its operations—assumed some AT&T radio line leases on the West Coast. The only way to defray the added expense was to acquire some additional affiliates in that region—and fast.

The most attractive prospect was Don Lee, who owned a string of stations in Los Angeles, San Francisco, and other West Coast cities. Paley was not about to wait for formal introductions. He telephoned Lee in Los Angeles, explained the situation, and inquired whether Lee might be interested in affiliating his stations with the new CBS network. Lee's response was vague but encouraging. The prospect of a CBS affiliation could be intriguing, but Lee said it was too important to discuss on the telephone. Paley would have to come to Los Angeles if he wanted to pursue the issue.

That was no simple invitation in 1929. There were no commercial airline flights to California. The trip required a week on a train just to get there. But CBS needed a stronger presence on the West Coast, Don Lee had numerous stations in the area, and Paley wanted those stations affiliated with his network.

When Paley got off the train in Los Angeles in the early summer of 1929, Lee's chauffeur was waiting to take him to a sumptuous suite in the Ambassador Hotel. Paley expected to complete the negotiations within a couple of days and return to New York and CBS's ever-present problems. Don Lee had different expectations. He told Paley to pack a bag for a few days at sea on his magnificent yacht, *The Invader*. Paley resisted, saying that he had to return to New York as soon as possible. But Lee was adamant, and Paley yielded. Once on the boat, however, Lee explained that no business could be discussed until they returned to Los Angeles. Paley yielded again and, always capable of self-indulgence, enjoyed himself enormously with the other guests.

When they returned to Los Angeles, Paley raised the issue of Lee's affiliation with CBS, but Lee was not about to be rushed. "I'll discuss business only if you'll agree to come back on the boat for another three or four days," he told the young CBS president. "You still look tired." Exasperated, Paley protested that he really had to get back to New York. But Lee knew better. Unless Paley returned to the boat, there was nothing to discuss. Paley picked up the cue that there *would* be something to discuss if he took one more cruise. So he agreed to another sail, and raised the possibility of affiliation as soon as they had returned to Los Angeles. Lee, having gotten to know Paley from the many days of social interaction in close quarters, was now prepared to do business. He called in his secretary and told her to transcribe the terms of his affiliation with CBS— which Paley was to unilaterally dictate then and there.

Paley resisted. He had already been dealing with Fox, Zukor, and others in the entertainment field. Although he did not want to negotiate the price of Paramount's purchase of CBS stock, he *did* want to negotiate the terms of Lee's affiliation with CBS. But again Lee persisted—knowing, by then, as Paley also knew, that he would respond to Lee's confidence by giving him better terms than he would have to if they bargained with each other. But Lee's stations were important to CBS, and on July 16, 1929, the parties executed the contract that Paley had dictated.

In dealing with Lee and Zukor, Paley had recognized the importance of superior physical plant in building a radio network. After all, NBC's technical facilities—backed by the vast resources of RCA—were of the highest quality, and Paley initially felt his own network had to match, or at least approach, NBC's technical quality if CBS were to compete successfully. But Paley soon had second thoughts about the significance of technical superiority. Obviously, the sound had to be clear for the listener at home, but audiences were not attuned to fine differences in technical quality. The most important factor for them was the programming. Paley compared it to movie theaters: the most resplendent theater in Manhattan would not draw crowds if the movie being shown was mediocre. Conversely, a more modest theater *would* draw crowds if the movie being shown was one that people wanted to see.

From that point forward Paley believed that virtually all decisions— whether in corporate affairs, affiliate relations, or technological developments—had to be gauged against their contribution to better programming. This new insight also cast a new light on another factor—the advertiser.

In inaugurating its radio network, NBC had said that its primary purpose was to develop better programming for the American people. To that end, commercials would be allowed—but only as a means to enable the network to afford the best programs. And if by chance NBC made profits, they would be reinvested in the network's facilities and programming (a commitment that NBC gamely tried to honor until the 1930s). In the beginning, then, NBC was able to boast that it truly was dedicated to public service.

NBC could afford to make this boast because it was wholly owned by RCA and did not have to account to stockholders whose only interest was NBC. And, since it viewed NBC largely as a vehicle to sell the radio sets it manufactured, RCA saw little risk—and considerable benefit—in promoting NBC as a public service corporation that had little interest in retaining profits.

CBS did not have the cushion of a wealthy parent corporation, but, in the heat of competition, Paley too had to emphasize the public service goals of his network. So in early testimony before Congress (drafted by Bernays), Paley had stated that he would welcome new regulatory legislation because "[t]here is perhaps today no other force touching the people of America more broadly and vitally than does this new form of communication, education, and entertainment." And in conformance with NBC's posture, Paley told the Senate Interstate Commerce Committee in 1930 that CBS would not allow "direct" advertising—which had now been defined as advertising in which the sponsor publicized the price of its service or products.

Paley began to rethink some of these commitments as he began to appreciate more fully the importance of the advertiser (who usually *did* want to promote the price of its products and services). The advertiser was the one who made *all* programs financially feasible by sponsoring some programs and by paying the network enough money for those programs to support the other, sustaining shows that had no specific sponsor. Advertisers made it clear from the outset that their names and products had to be prominently displayed on any program they sponsored (and rarely would a single advertiser in those days agree to share sponsorship with another advertiser—each wanting complete control over any program it sponsored).

In this context, it made sense to Paley to cater to the advertiser's needs and desires—even if it meant mentioning the price of a product on the air. His experience with George Washington Hill offered an apt and dramatic example of this new attitude.

Hill was much older than Paley, much more eccentric, and, most importantly, president of the American Tobacco Company, which made—and advertised—Lucky Strike cigarettes. Paley had little hope of obtaining the Lucky Strike account (which was then handled by NBC), but an American Tobacco subsidiary corporation did produce the popular Cremo cigars, and Paley thought CBS might have a chance of securing that account.

In early 1931 Paley made an appointment to meet with Hill in his New York office. He went to the meeting in his usual conservative suit and high starched collar. He walked into Hill's office, only to find the American Tobacco president—a heavyset man with bushy eyebrows—sitting at his desk dressed in a black bow tie, a jacket with suede elbow patches, and a cowboy hat. Paley explained his purpose. When he finished, Hill handed him a pad and a pencil. Perplexed, Paley asked Hill what he had on his mind. Hill said curtly that he bought ideas and that Paley should return when he had some program proposals that could be used to advertise Cremo cigars.

Encouraged by Hill's invitation, Paley returned to CBS headquarters and developed several program proposals that he and his staff thought were sure to appeal to Hill. But in a subsequent meeting with Paley, Hill rejected all of them. They did have merit, Hill said, but they were not quite right. He urged Paley to return again when he had developed some other ideas. There was still hope, so Paley and his staff formulated some additional program concepts, again confident that Hill would find at least one of them satisfactory. But Hill had the same reaction as before. He again complimented Paley on his creativity, but none of the proposals was suited for Cremo cigars. As before, however, Hill invited Paley to return when he had some more ideas.

Paley was frustrated and saw little prospect of selling any program concept to Hill. But then instinct took over, and Paley sensed Hill's real objection to Paley's proposals—Hill could not claim credit for any of them. So Paley developed a new strategy. He arranged a meeting with Hill on the pretext of discussing something other than CBS's programming ideas. After the discussion was concluded, the American Tobacco president asked Paley if CBS had come up with any new program ideas. Paley demurred, saying that he had despaired of ever satisfying Hill. And then he set the bait, adding that his staff had suggested an idea that Paley had rejected as inappropriate.

His curiosity piqued, Hill told Paley not to be discouraged—and, by the way, what was the idea that Paley had rejected? Oh, it's nothing, really, said Paley. CBS would get the popular Arthur Pryor Band to play martial music, the kind that would make men—purchasers of Cremo cigars—

"puff their chests out" and feel proud to be Americans. Paley could see the excitement creeping across Hill's face. "Paley, wait a minute, wait a minute," exclaimed Hill. He summoned his staff and described the idea— now *his* idea. At first the staff didn't like the concept, and Paley's hopes sank. But Hill was now enthralled with the proposal, and he explained it again and again, each time speaking in a louder voice and marching around the office to give the staff the full flavor of his wonderful idea. The staff finally acceded, and CBS had the Cremo account.

That was not the end of Paley's effort to accommodate Hill. He also advised Hill that the Cremo advertisements could include a reference to the cigar's five-cent cost (in addition to the claim that it was a "no spit" cigar, since it was manufactured by machine and therefore not wrapped with the aid of human saliva). In discussing the Cremo account a year later, Paley told a trade journalist that the art of radio advertising was developing rapidly and that CBS's "specific contribution toward this end is the permitting of price mention."

Paley and his network were now on a roll, and nothing—not even public protest—could compromise Paley's interest in pleasing CBS advertisers. In the mid-1930s, CBS was criticized for allowing laxative commercials over its network. If toothpaste usage was too personal to be considered, laxatives were beyond the realm of rational discussion. Always the diplomat in public, Paley announced that CBS would discontinue laxative commercials as soon as the "present commitments" expired. Paley was applauded for his sense of public responsibility. He did not mention, however, that the "present commitments" included options for renewal that could extend the laxative ads for years to come. But Paley had deflated the public controversy. The commercials continued, and the issue was soon forgotten.

Paley used similar ingenuity in trying to find programs that would please audiences and attract commercial sponsors. Indeed, broadcast historian Erik Barnouw concluded that the "outburst of creative activity that came to radio in the second half of the 1930s was largely a CBS story. The first stirrings were at CBS, and while these eventually awakened much of the industry, the most brilliant moments were at CBS—in drama, in news, and almost every other kind of programming."

This creative accomplishment did not reflect Paley's abstract interest in innovation. In fact, he avoided innovation where possible. He wanted performers and programs that were known quantities likely to draw audiences and secure commercial sponsors. In the beginning, staff members in CBS's programming department (such as it was) were frustrated by their president's lack of interest in new ideas; his only interest seemed to be in the acquisition of popular programs from NBC or the solicitation of performers who were sure to attract large audiences. (Paley's approach changed little over the ensuing decades; CBS program executive Mike Dann, who spearheaded the development of the network's television programs in the late 1950s and 1960s, observed that "Paley was not innovative. He was not a gambler. He was interested only in building a better mousetrap. He knew what was a proven hit—and that's what he wanted for his network.")

Paley's focus on established performers and programs—at least in the early days of CBS—was understandable. The network had just been organized, it faced stiff competition from another network with access to vast resources, and it needed popular programs to establish quick rapport with audiences and advertisers. These needs were satisfied initially by bands and orchestras. It was relatively simple to broadcast music, and Arthur Judson had imbued CBS with the notion that musical fare would draw wide audiences. So Paley pursued the popular ensembles of the day—the New York Philharmonic, the Paul Whiteman Band, the Arthur Pryor Band, the Dorsey Brothers, and Guy Lombardo.

This focus on musical talent did make Paley sensitive to new performers who might become popular with mass audiences. One day in 1929 CBS program executive Ralph Wonder urged Paley to delay lunch and listen to four black teenagers from Cincinnati; after listening for an hour, Paley agreed with Wonder that the Mills Brothers should be signed for CBS. Similar auditions eventually led CBS to hire Kate Smith, Morton Downey, and, in later years, Frank Sinatra. But Paley's proudest moment in the popular music field was the signing of Bing Crosby.

Paley was on a cruise ship to France in June 1931 when he heard a melodious voice on a record being played repeatedly by a fellow passenger. Intrigued, he asked the singer's name and then cabled his office: "Sign up singer named Bing Crosby." When he returned to New York several weeks later, he discovered that his instructions had not been followed. The CBS staff had located Crosby, a singer with the Paul Whiteman Band, in California, but, after some investigation, had decided not to sign him. He had a fear of the microphone, he sometimes imbibed too much liquor, and, as a result, he was unreliable, often missing scheduled appearances.

Paley was furious. He explained to his staff that he wanted to acquire Crosby's voice, not his reliability. Howard Barlow, director of CBS's own symphony and Paley's general adviser on music, counseled against signing Crosby, saying that his voice lacked the proper qualities. But Paley knew better. The word went out again to sign Crosby. Within a short time Crosby appeared in CBS's New York offices, accompanied by an able lawyer demanding $1,500 a week for his client on sustaining programs and

$3,000 a week if a sponsor was found. Paley considered Crosby's demands to be outrageous, but he was very talented and, more importantly, NBC had also entered the bidding for his services. Then, as in later years, Paley was willing to spend large sums to secure good programming (in marked, and often decisive, contrast to David Sarnoff, who did not appreciate the importance of programming as much as Paley and was willing to see a performer walk away from NBC if the financial demands exceeded Sarnoff's preconceived limits). Despite Crosby's excessive demands, Paley met them and afterward happily took Crosby on a tour of CBS's offices, introducing him to the staff as CBS's next star attraction.

At first Paley had to have doubts about the wisdom of the contract. As the CBS staff had predicted, Crosby was unreliable (and even missed his first scheduled appearance on CBS). But Crosby quickly became popular, being mobbed by crowds after personal appearances. Within a short time George Washington Hill dropped the Arthur Pryor Band and substituted the ex-big band singer for his Cremo cigar program. From there Crosby's fame and stature only increased, and for decades afterward Paley would repeatedly cite his "discovery" of Bing Crosby as one of the more magical moments in his long career at CBS.

Despite Crosby's growing popularity in the early thirties, CBS could not crack NBC's dominance of the "ratings war." The competition had begun in 1930 when the first Crossley rating—based on telephone calls asking people to recall the programs they had recently listened to— reported that NBC had completely swamped the fledgling CBS. The ratings showed that many NBC programs had ratings of 25 percent or better, that only two CBS programs had ratings better than 12 percent, and that no other CBS program had done better than 3.3 percent. The revelation shocked Paley, and he asked the accounting firm of Price Waterhouse to do a separate survey for CBS—one that showed that CBS was doing far better than the primitive Crossley survey had indicated.

His confidence restored, Paley went on the offensive, knowing that ratings were now a major, if not *the* major, barometer of a program's popularity—and, at a minimum, information that would guide advertiser decisions. Ratings were scrutinized closely, and a program's fate was often determined by how well it had done or would do in the ratings (which became more and more sophisticated over time). And when CBS still failed to break NBC's lead, only one course was left: to acquire NBC's programs. And so in 1936 Paley pursued some of NBC's stars, and in the 1936–37 season CBS, for the first time, was able to take the lead in the ratings (now called the Hooperatings, which were based on telephone surveys asking people to identify the programs they were listening to *at that moment*). CBS's new ratings leadership was not based on innovation; it reflected instead Bill Paley's success in wooing three major stars away from NBC—Major Bowes, Eddie Cantor, and Al Jolson.

CBS's success also reflected Paley's recognition that vaudeville, sketches, and comedy had started to replace musical performance as the audience's first choice in programming. By the mid-thirties, Jack Benny, who continually played off his stinginess, was king of radio. (Robber to Benny: "Your money or your life." Long pause. Robber to Benny: "Well?" Benny: "Wait a minute. I'm thinking.") Benny's popularity on NBC was so great that CBS didn't even try to sell time in its competing slot between 7:00 and 7:15 P.M. on Sunday nights.

Paley was especially sensitive to Benny's success because Benny had started out on CBS, only to be lured to NBC by the prospect of larger audiences. Other comedians like George Burns and Gracie Allen also moved over to NBC after breaking in on CBS, and Paley no doubt felt that "raiding" the other network's stars was fair game in the ratings war. But he could still take pride in the comedians he had brought to the attention of the American public—in addition to Benny and Burns and Allen, a list that included Will Rogers, Fred Allen, and the team of Stoopnagle and Budd.

In bringing these and other performers to radio, Paley tried to serve two separate goals: quality and popularity. It was not always possible to have both at the same time, but Paley bowed to quality alone when the air time would otherwise go unused. And since commercially sponsored time occupied only about one-third of CBS's program schedule, there was ample opportunity to explore new concepts. An apt example was the "Columbia Workshop," which aired opposite NBC's Jack Benny program on Sunday nights. Inaugurated in 1936, the program consisted of dramatic presentations that, as Paley had explained to the FCC two years earlier, used technical devices to create an aura of realism. In March 1937 the series won wide critical acclaim when it broadcast "The Fall of the City," an adaptation of the poem of the same name by the Pulitzer Prize-winning poet Archibald MacLeish that addressed the tensions of the civil war then raging in Spain.

Paley was delighted with the program's success, and he gladly accepted the accolades that programs like this generated. But these successes did not belong to Paley alone. Increasingly, he benefitted greatly from the efforts of a growing and dedicated staff.

When he had first assumed the presidency of UIB, there was some skepticism among the existing staff about the ability of their new boss. Word spread that he was a spoiled rich boy who had received the position as a gift from his father. This early (and unfounded) skepticism was soon replaced by admiration and even enthusiasm. Paley was smart, a good listener, and unpretentious. He always seemed to have a smile and a kind word for everyone. Jap Gude, an early CBS staff member (and later agent for Edward R. Murrow), remembered Paley as informal and accessible, "the kind of guy you could meet and talk to in the men's room."

As CBS began to grow in the 1930s, Paley spent less and less time with the entire staff. Part of the reason was simple physical separation. By 1929 Paley had moved CBS into six floors of a new, large office building at 485 Madison Avenue, near the intersection of Fifty-second Street; program studios occupied two floors, and the remaining space was divided among the staff, with the executive offices located on the twentieth floor. All of the executive offices were of modern design, except for Paley's. Monarch Studios, the commercial decorator hired to orchestrate the move, had recommended that the rich paneling in the president's office at the Paramount Building be moved into the president's new office at the Madison Avenue building, and Paley had agreed. Paley's new office became the site of meetings to discuss major problems on every front. In contrast with his first days at UIB, Paley now took few tours of staff offices to chat with employees. In his ever-growing organization, his staff contact was largely limited to those who attended meetings in his office. Joe Ream, who headed the CBS legal department, was among those who recognized the difference. "Paley was not very accessible to the staff," Ream remembered. "In many ways he was cold and aloof and remote. He never jollied around with the troops."

Two staff members, however, had almost constant contact with the network president: Edward Klauber and Paul Kesten. Klauber was the older and more senior employee of the two. Born in Louisville in 1887, he was a complicated man who inspired respect and disdain as well as love and hate in those who knew him best. Childhood had not been a happy time for him. His father had died when he was young, and he and his mother, brother, and sister were forced to move in with another family member, a move he always resented. His unhappiness was compounded by the fact that Klauber was Jewish and frequently experienced the humiliation of anti-Semitism.

After he joined CBS in 1930 Klauber impressed Paley as a tireless worker, spending days, nights, and weekends at the office. But Klauber told his wife that, at bottom, he was really a lazy person. "He used to say," she recalled, " 'I was destined to be a ne'er-do-well, and I almost succeeded.' " He recounted, for example, that he once thought of becoming an electrician but abandoned the idea when he learned that the position required years of study.

His drift into CBS was full of coincidences. His uncle was a drama critic for *The New York Times* and got him a job there as a copyeditor. Klauber loved words. He spent much of his spare time doing crossword puzzles and reveled in his new job, refining a reporter's rough copy into fluid sentences. Within a short time he was promoted to city editor and, under different circumstances, could have anticipated even greater success at the *Times.* But his personality made that impossible.

To his subordinates at the *Times,* Ed Klauber was a hateful man. He was taciturn, quick to criticize, and slow to compliment. If a reporter mentioned that he was about to go on vacation, Klauber would issue an assignment to disrupt those plans. It was an intolerable situation, and a *Times* executive mentioned it to Edward Bernays, CBS's outside public relations counsel. Klauber was clearly a talented man, and Bernays became convinced that his personality might be better suited to a smaller organization like Bernays's. But it was not to be, and Bernays soon decided that Klauber needed another work environment.

In one of their many meetings, Bernays raised the issue with Paley. Klauber was smart and tough-minded, and perhaps he could help CBS develop the discipline the company badly needed. Paley met with Klauber and was not impressed. At forty-three, Klauber seemed like an old man. And in contrast to Paley's pleasant, gregarious demeanor, Klauber, so heavy-set and so quiet, seemed out of place. Bernays persisted, though. Klauber could be very useful to CBS, and there would be little harm in giving him a try. Paley was receptive to this argument. "I was looking around for an assistant . . . ," he later said, "somebody who could help me with the myriad of things that were coming across my desk, and I had to have an extra pair of hands." So Klauber was hired in early 1930 as assistant to the president of CBS and soon became vice president and then executive vice president, taking on the administrative tasks (except the trips to Washington) that Paley found distasteful.

Klauber would not have won any popularity contests among the CBS staff. Most viewed him as a cantankerous "old" man without feeling. As at the *Times,* it seemed that he could execute decisions without regard for people's feelings. "I don't like to say men are evil," said CBS's outside counsel Ralph Colin, "but Ed Klauber was evil. He adored his wife and he adored CBS and that's all he cared about. He would call in staff and humiliate one member in front of the others." Although he recognized Klauber's talents, Colin felt that Klauber had to go and told Paley as much. But Paley deflected that suggestion. Paley acknowledged that Klauber was "very rigid"; and he knew that Klauber could be indifferent to people's feelings—even those of his former benefactor, Edward Bernays, whose contract with CBS was cancelled shortly after Klauber was hired. (Klauber casually explained to Bernays at lunch one day that he was handling public relations for the network now and there was no need for two public relations counsels.) But Paley needed that kind of toughness in an administrator.

There was the personal side of it as well. From his first days at the company, Klauber could see that the young CBS president was being pulled in too many directions. Klauber decided that he would ease the burdens, deflect the pressures, and give Paley the time to focus on what mattered most to him—programming. For Klauber it was a charge, a mission, that overrode everything else. "Ed had a very paternalistic feeling toward Paley," Klauber's wife later said. And Paley, for one, welcomed it. Others might find Klauber's personality objectionable, but Paley always appreciated Klauber's dedication to CBS generally and to him personally. And years later, when Klauber was forced to resign because of ill health, Paley would take time from a hectic schedule to visit Klauber in his apartment to explain the pension benefits that would give Klauber the financial security which, in Paley's eyes at least, was richly deserved.

Ironically, Klauber's growing importance at CBS in the early 1930s collided with the success of Paley's other chief lieutenant, Paul Kesten, who was also hired in 1930. A thin man with a receding hairline and bulging eyes, Kesten was thirty years old at the time and had worked his way up the corporate ladder to become a copyeditor for an advertising agency in New York. Klauber had seen Kesten's work, was greatly impressed, and hired him shortly after he joined CBS.

Kesten and Paley hit it off immediately. They were contemporaries and had much in common. Like Paley, Kesten recognized the importance of personal appearances and was a fastidious dresser (although Kesten went to greater lengths than Paley, such as polishing the soles of his shoes so that he could put his feet up on his desk without feeling self-conscious). Kesten was also very good in developing promotional copy for CBS. He could make the most mundane concepts seem intriguing, and Paley was repeatedly amazed at Kesten's creativity. He "had one of the most brilliant advertising and merchandising minds I've ever come across," Paley later observed. "He was a genius at making the public aware of radio—not just CBS, but radio."

Kesten knew, however, that marketing ideas were not enough. The network needed to learn more about the public's views. What did they like about the existing program schedule? What did they not like? And what would insure their loyalty to CBS? Kesten needed answers to these and many other questions, and he was always in search of better survey techniques to assess public opinions. So when a young psychology Ph.D. candidate from Ohio State wrote CBS in the spring of 1935 about some market research he was conducting, Kesten wrote back himself, inquiring about the student's findings and raising other problems CBS was confronting. An exchange of correspondence followed, and in September 1935, Frank Stanton, a twenty-seven-year-old Ph.D. graduate with no experience in broadcasting, joined CBS, was made head of the research department, and then spent the rest of his career with the company, including twenty-eight years as president and chief operating officer. ("I got on the elevator when it was moving," Stanton later recalled, "and it was wonderful.")

Kesten's relationship with Stanton, like his relations with other CBS employees, was open, friendly, and stimulating. Kesten rarely had the heart to criticize an employee directly. He believed in positive reinforcement and would encourage better performance by asking questions and suggesting new ideas. There was little need for him to worry about Stanton, however. He was extremely intelligent, a methodical thinker, and a tireless worker. And, as Kesten had hoped, Stanton had the imagination and ambition to develop better audience survey techniques. He developed the new system with Professsor Paul Lazarsfeld of Columbia University. People were randomly selected from the streets of New York or Los Angeles (wherever the studio was), placed in specially designed seats, given a pre-distribution airing of a program, and asked to press certain buttons attached to their chairs to record their reactions to every aspect of the program as it progressed. The system, affectionately called "Little Annie" in CBS circles, defied some established principles of market surveying but proved to be extremely effective in predicting a program's popularity.

Kesten no doubt felt that Stanton's achievements reflected the rewards of his positive management style—a style that stood in sharp contrast to Klauber's. Not surprisingly, the two men had many acrimonious battles over the best approach to particular problems. While Kesten's view might prevail on a specific issue, Klauber had a higher position in the company and therefore the final say (subject of course to Paley's approval).

Despite their disagreements over management style, Klauber and Kesten were of one mind when it came to Bill Paley. They both had great respect for his talents and accomplishments, and they both dedicated themselves to making CBS the premier network. Their admiration for Paley and their commitment to CBS gave them the incentive to cooperate when necessary.

For his part, Paley remained congenial in dealing with both men, recognizing the different contributions each made to the network (although Paley preferred Kesten's company to Klauber's). In meetings with them and other CBS executives, however, Paley did not rely on the charm he used so effectively with the network's performers and advertisers. He listened intently and asked pointed questions that cut to the heart of the issue. He seemed to have a knack for quickly spotting the weakness in an argument and often raised his concerns before the speaker had even finished his presentation. Rarely did he issue directives or commands to resolve those concerns. Instead, he made suggestions or raised questions that left no doubt as to how he felt but left the final decision to subordinates.

In time, Paley's approach to decision-making would create uncertainty and breed resentment among some CBS executives. But in the 1930s the results were impressive. CBS had come from nowhere to establish a leadership position in the broadcast industry, and in June 1935, *Fortune* magazine paid tribute to CBS's achievements and the leadership of its young president. The article called CBS's success "spectacular" and credited it all to Paley: "It wasn't his idea, but he built it, he controls it, he is it. In six packed years he has become the idol of stockholders, the hero of subordinates and employees." The company's directors were equally impressed, telling *Fortune* that "never in all their lives . . . have they been associated with anybody as clever at business. Not only is he a master advertiser and feeler of the public pulse, but these gentlemen say that he is the greatest organizer, the best executive, the quickest thinker, the coolest negotiator they have ever seen."

According to *Fortune,* Paley's most outstanding characteristic "is enthusiasm—for radio, for his friends, for his hobbies, for anything he does. Yet," the article continued, "his executives have seen him as cold as a fish, as calculating as a Metternich. . . . He is known as a devil for detail. He listens with amazing patience to everybody, takes advice, . . . and seems not to care who got the right answer, whether William Paley or someone else." The article said that Paley's achievements as an executive reflected his ability to be "fast and tense in his thinking" and to work "quietly" without the necessity of browbeating his subordinates.

For anyone concerned about public image, the article was all one could ask for. But however fulsome the praise, Paley could not escape the undercurrent of anti-Semitism. In what the author no doubt regarded as the highest compliment, the *Fortune* article concluded that Bill Paley "has the grace of an educated Jew. . . ."

CHAPTER FIVE

Dorothy

It was the winter of 1986, and Dorothy Hirshon sat in the main living room of Willow Pond, her wooded estate in Glen Cove, Long Island. The room seemed to reflect Dorothy's personality and interests. With floor-to-ceiling bookshelves lining the walls, heavy wood beams traversing the ceiling, and large comfortable chairs, the room conveyed a sense of warmth and stimulation, the environment of a person who cared about learning—and who also enjoyed the good life that money made possible.

Although now seventy-eight, Dorothy seemed much younger than her years. With a full head of silvery hair, a slim figure, and dressed smartly in well-cut slacks and a trendy top, she conveyed a sense of elegance, of someone who appreciated the elements of high fashion. On this Saturday morning in 1986, she sat in one of her overstuffed chairs, very relaxed, and, interrupted only by the demands of her nine dogs and five cats, spoke of Bill Paley and their fifteen-year marriage. While the smoke of an everpresent Benson & Hedges cigarette curled upward, she talked in a throaty voice about the man and their time together with apparent detachment, as though she had been nothing more than a dispassionate observer of events.

Before they met, Paley had been enjoying the bachelor's life in New York. He worked hard, but he played hard, too. There seemed to be no end to the women he could meet and the places he could go. And he wanted to take advantage of it all. He spent almost as much time planning his social life as he did addressing CBS's problems. One night it could be the Central Park Casino, frequented by public figures, including New York's flamboyant mayor, Jimmy Walker; another night it could be ballroom dancing at the private Mayfair Club Dance in the Crystal Room of the old Ritz Carlton; and other times it could be El Morocco on Fifty-fourth Street, *the* place for people interested in late-night dancing and in being seen. In all of this, Paley displayed a zest that set him apart from everyone else. (Marietta Tree, a longtime friend, who first saw Paley at El Morocco some years later, vividly remembered watching "this man,

surrounded by beautiful women, with a marvelous smile and laughing and having an absolutely wonderful time—which seemed so unusual because people did not have *that* much fun at El Morocco.")

Bill Paley, so young, so attractive, and so charming, had little trouble finding female escorts. Even so, he did not like to take chances and, as in business, wanted to keep his options open. On occasion he would ask Ralph Colin, then a fellow bachelor and CBS's outside counsel, to keep a second date on call if the need should arise (a role that Colin later likened to being a "wet nurse").

Paley's social life was not confined to New York. Through CBS's connections with Paramount Pictures and Don Lee, Paley began to make numerous trips to California and Los Angeles in particular. Although most of the movie studios were run by Jews, Los Angeles was a very "restricted" town in some respects, and there were many clubs, restaurants, and other establishments that limited their patrons to those with the "right" background. Still, there was much to enjoy, and Paley found himself intoxicated with the beauty and glamour of Hollywood. Most movie moguls felt that television was imminent and that CBS might soon become a partner (or antagonist) in the entertainment business, a view that was reinforced by Sarnoff's participation with Joseph Kennedy in forming what ultimately became RKO. In either case, it made good sense to maintain good relations with Paley. He was wined and dined at parties with stars like Loretta Young, Jean Harlow, and Norma Shearer, and studio heads like Louis B. Mayer, Sam Goldwyn, and Harry Cohn. No pleasure seemed beyond his reach, and Bill Paley considered marriage to be an option for other men but not for him. And then he met Dorothy Hart.

It happened in the summer of 1931 at Alley Pond, a fashionable home on Long Island's North Shore, where Paley often attended parties with the rich and famous. Dorothy was captivating. She was, by all accounts, beautiful. But there was much more to her than beauty. She had a vibrancy that matched Paley's. The daughter of a Los Angeles insurance executive, Dorothy had socialized with society all her life and had spent many nights attracting attention at Cocoanut Grove, Los Angeles' answer to El Morocco. (Irene Selznick, who spent many nights as a young woman observing the scene at Cocoanut Grove, remembered being especially taken by the beauty and charm of two belles—Jane Peters, later known as Carole Lombard, and Dorothy Hart.)

Dorothy was on a fast track, and by the age of nineteen she married Jack Hearst, son of the legendary William Randolph Hearst. It was an exciting time for Dorothy. Every material comfort was within her grasp, and she had the varied lifestyle of the Hearsts besides—with their interests in journalism, politics, art, and social pleasures. Dorothy was especially taken by William Randolph Hearst himself, whom she called "W.R." He was polite and approachable, but it was not easy to get close to him. But Dorothy, with her warmth and her questions, broke through the facade, and "W.R." developed a special affection for her, spending hours talking with her about all kinds of subjects and even taking her on some of his trips to buy art (which he did with great frequency and at extravagant prices). Dorothy continued to be fascinated with "W.R." There was so much to learn and enjoy with him, and she treasured the time they spent together.

After a while Dorothy went with Jack to Atlanta, where he could complete his college education. Then they transferred to New York, where Jack was put in charge of some Hearst magazines. New York suited Dorothy well. The Hearst name opened many doors, including invitations to high society parties on Long Island.

Although still married to Jack Hearst, Dorothy had an immediate attraction to Bill Paley. He was handsome, debonair, smart, and accomplished. The affair soon began in earnest, and in the space of months Dorothy was divorced from Jack. She and Bill went to Kingman, Arizona, in May 1932 for a small, private ceremony (Paley having learned the costs of living life in a fishbowl), and then to Honolulu for several weeks for a honeymoon. Upon their return to New York that summer, they rented a house in Sands Point, Long Island, and then in the fall moved into a rented apartment on Beekman Place, a quaint street on Manhattan's Upper East Side (a favorite residential neighborhood for upscale German Jews). At first they liked Beekman Place so much that they bought another house on the street, tore it down, and had it completely rebuilt with a modern design. But Paley found the modern touch too sterile, and they eventually moved to another apartment on East Seventy-fourth Street.

To all appearances, Bill and Dorothy seemed made for each other. She had a grace and style that complemented his image as president of CBS (and she used her flair to help CBS, redecorating a stark studio into a comfortable room that would help put interview guests at ease). Within a short time photographs of Dorothy began appearing regularly in *Vogue, Harper's Bazaar,* and other fashion magazines. She was selected as one of the country's best-dressed women, and people frequently identified the Paleys as one of New York's more glamorous couples.

Despite their affinity for style and material comfort, Dorothy and Bill were very different people. Paley was a man with few convictions, except in broadcasting (and even there he was still learning). Dorothy, in contrast, had definite opinions about many subjects, a reflection of her wide-ranging interests and her willingness to spend time educating herself. (If an important guest was coming to dinner, she would spend hours boning up on topics that were likely to come up in conversation.) And Dorothy had no hesitancy in sharing her opinions with guests or urging them upon her new husband.

Politics, for example, was a matter of considerable importance to Dorothy. She was a liberal Democrat committed to President Franklin D. Roosevelt (and would later expend efforts working for the election of Adlai Stevenson, John F. Kennedy, and Robert F. Kennedy). To Dorothy, the government had an obligation to help the less advantaged, especially in those Depression times, and she applauded Roosevelt's efforts to provide relief to millions of Americans.

Paley's politics were based more on personal relations than on deeply held views. His early fascination with the political process was diminishing rapidly, and he had no philosophy or perspective that motivated him to make a commitment to any party or platform. To the extent he gave the matter any thought, his political affiliations were influenced by people he liked and respected. For example, he was taken by Dorothy, he valued her opinions, and FDR seemed to be a magnetic and effective leader. So he was receptive to her support for the Democratic president. (In later years friendships with Dwight Eisenhower and other Republican stalwarts would lead Paley to switch party affiliations and support Republican presidents.)

Psychology was another interest of Dorothy's that she tried to to push on her husband. Freud's theories were still relatively new, and Dorothy was intrigued by their implications. She read whatever she could find, talked to knowledgeable people, and developed definite opinions. When friends had family members with mental or emotional problems, they would ask Dorothy for her thoughts and recommendations. Dorothy herself underwent psychoanalysis for an hour every day (unless she was out of town). She convinced Bill to join her in the quest for self-understanding, and he too began to undergo psychoanalysis.

Like most people, Bill Paley had foibles and weaknesses that probably could have been helped by greater self-understanding. For one thing, he had inherited his father's hypochondria (a legacy that Paley himself freely acknowledged, although he would claim that his father's concern for health was more extreme than his own). Paley had an almost childlike fear of illness and death and would display concern with almost any ache or ailment. (He also seemed to develop back pain that required secluded rest and sometimes traction whenever a crisis erupted at CBS.) Friends also noticed that he took an unusual interest in the course of their illnesses, asking questions that reflected an in-depth knowledge of medical matters. Whatever its causes, the hypochondria was not cured by the hours of psychoanalysis. Nor did they have an impact on his obsession with food. From the beginning Dorothy noticed that her husband had a voracious appetite and an enjoyment of culinary delights that surpassed anything she had previously known. It wasn't merely the great quantities of food that he consumed (which seemed especially impressive, since he never seemed to gain weight); it was also the zeal with which he approached a meal or snack. He almost seemed to inhale the food, and those who dined with Paley over the years—both professional colleagues and social companions—were usually overwhelmed by the performance. "I never saw anyone eat with such gusto," one CBS executive remembered. "He devoured food like a longshoreman."

On occasion this enthusiasm for food could prove embarrassing. In the company of people he knew and felt comfortable with, Paley had a habit of reaching across everyone's plate to sample whatever they were having. One time Paley was present at an elegant dinner hosted by Jock and Betsey Whitney, who were then his brother- and sister-in-law. In front of Betsey Whitney was a plate of what appeared to be sugar-coated candies. After finishing his dinner, Paley reached across Betsey's plate and, before anyone could say anything, popped one of the candies into his mouth. A look of anguish came over his face, and he spit the candy out, asking, "What is this? What is this?" Mrs. Whitney laughed and said, "Oh, it's a dog yummy. It's for the dog."

Paley's interest in food was an open secret at CBS, and most executives knew he was much more receptive to their suggestions in the presence of a good meal. But it had to be good. CBS executive Mike Dann learned the importance of quality when he discussed programming issues with Paley in the 1960s. In anticipation of an important luncheon meeting, Dann had ordered delicatessen food—a favorite of Paley's—from the Stage Delicatessen, generally regarded as one of New York's best. But the food was delivered in the morning, and by lunchtime it was cold and unappealing. The meeting did not go well, and Dann decided to do things differently the next time. The food was ordered shortly before lunch, the hot pastrami sandwiches were wrapped in foil to preserve their warmth, the pickles were delivered in their brine, and the condiments remained sealed in containers until the last minute. At the appointed hour, Paley's butler wheeled in the lunch from the private kitchen attached to his office. Smells of pastrami, pickles, and celery tonic filled the room, and Paley's head picked up immediately. "At that point," Dann recalled, "I knew I had him. And it was one of the best meetings I ever had."

Paley attributed his interest in food to his mother's good cooking, and he did show a preference for fare found in Jewish homes and restaurants. But his enthusiasm for food seemed to exceed any Jewish mother's greatest hopes. In one sense it seemed to provide an escape from the burdens and responsibilities of his hectic life. Whatever the explanation, food was and remained one of Paley's favorite activities, and he could and often did spend hours each day eating food, thinking about food, and talking about food.

He did not have the same obsession with his children. From the beginning, he told Dorothy he wanted a family, and soon after their marriage Dorothy became pregnant. But then she had a miscarriage, and the doctors warned her about the dangers of future pregnancies. Bill was still intent upon having children, so they adopted a son, Jeffrey, in 1939, and then a daughter, Hilary, in 1940. At first Paley was absorbed in the new babies, delighting in their activities and physical progress. But the interest started to wane as the children got older. "He loved them when they couldn't talk back," Dorothy observed, "but as they got older and developed, I became more interested in them and he became less so." Visitors to the Paley home similarly noticed that Bill paid little attention to the children.

He did, however, pay considerable attention to his expanding social life, and Dorothy joined him in that pursuit. Paley was by now a millionaire many times over, a wealthy man who could afford any material comfort and who wanted very much to be accepted by New York's social aristocracy. He knew who they were and he cultivated their friendships. Dorothy remembered Bill's tension the evening they first went to the home of John D. Rockefeller II. Although normally relaxed and carefree before social engagements, Paley was plainly concerned that they not be late and create the wrong impression on the Rockefellers.

This courtship of the social elite also helped explain the Paleys' frequent visits to Long Island's North Shore. Called the "Gold Coast" by some, the North Shore was the playground of New York's very rich—and, in most cases, families that were not Jewish. It was certainly scenic, with vast expanses of tall trees and dramatic vistas of Long Island Sound, where pleasure yachts dotted the horizon from spring through fall. It was here that Paley first saw Kiluna Farm, the magnificent eighty-five-acre estate in Manhasset that belonged to Ralph Pulitzer, son of newspaper magnate Joseph Pulitzer. The estate was anything but a farm. It featured a large, rambling, white clapboard house that was hidden from the main roadway by tall trees. The grounds included gardens, guest cottages, stables, a pool, and a tennis court encased in glass to allow for play throughout the year. On one of his trips to Long Island (before his marriage), Paley had occasion to visit Kiluna, and he coveted it at once. It possessed the elegance and comfort that suited his interests and tastes. Then and there he vowed to acquire the house if it ever came on the market.

Several years later he and Dorothy rented Kiluna Farm for the summer. Their love of the place was immediately apparent to the rental agent, who suggested that Paley make an offer to purchase it from Pulitzer. Paley demurred, saying he didn't think he could meet the high price that Pulitzer would surely demand. But Pulitzer's asking price was more reasonable than Paley anticipated, and in 1938 he and Dorothy became the proud and happy owners of Kiluna Farm.

Both of them enjoyed the home, living there in the summer and spending weekends there during the rest of the year. There was also a constant flow of guests with varied backgrounds and interests. Broadway producer Leland Hayward, Orson Welles, Sam and Frances Goldwyn, Tyrone Power, and Jane Steuart were among the more frequent guests. Paley tried to keep his social life separate from his business life, and, with rare exception, the only CBS colleagues to visit Kiluna for weekends were those with whom Paley had established social relationships. These included his Philadelphia friend Larry Lowman and, in later years, Edward R. Murrow and Charles Collingwood.

He was ever the congenial host. "He was obviously interested in his guests," one visitor remarked, "and he had a talent for making them feel comfortable." He playfully flirted with the women and offered everyone activities and conveniences so that they could fully enjoy themselves. Croquet was then the rage among Long Island's estates, and few had as much enthusiasm for the sport as Paley. Tennis and later golf were also favorites, and Paley played them all with his guests. The conversation at meals and around the pool ranged far and wide, but Paley rarely discussed CBS (except to relate a humorous anecdote or a particularly significant event).

Although his social contacts continued to expand each year, Paley still had few close friends. He was pleasant and accommodating to all, was never at a loss for pointed questions about his guests' interests and concerns, and seemed to bask in the presence of their company. But there remained a certain reserve about Bill Paley, a wall that allowed him to maintain the privacy of his innermost feelings. Any number of causes could be cited to explain his reserve: heredity, childhood doubts about his mother's love, his father's stoicism, his family's general reluctance to openly discuss their feelings for one another. Whatever the explanation, Paley felt uncomfortable discussing his feelings and freely acknowledged in later years that he was a difficult person to know well and that he feared the dependence that might come from revealing too much of himself to family or friend.

There were, however, a select few with whom Paley felt close. Averell Harriman was one. The son of the famed railroad magnate, E. H. Harriman, Averell in many ways embodied the kind of lifestyle that Paley tried to emulate. Wealthy beyond imagination and a major force in the corporate world, Harriman embarked on a long and distinguished career in public service during Roosevelt's administrations, ultimately playing a vital role in FDR's negotiations with Winston Churchill and Joseph Stalin (and subsequently becoming governor of New York and, under the Kennedy and Johnson administrations, undersecretary of state and then ambassador-at-large). At the same time, Harriman continued to travel in privileged social circles. A tall handsome man with a jutting jaw, Harriman was the accomplished sportsman he appeared to be. He played polo with the best, enjoyed croquet on Long Island's North Shore (and would bring his own mallet to Kiluna for the weekend), and went hunting with aristocracy in Europe. Paley never did become an equestrian, but Harriman did persuade him to take up shooting on one of their European trips, and Paley later took great pleasure in his growing skills as a huntsman (although he rarely hunted anything other than fowl). Harriman also gave Paley advice on how to live a longer life (put socks on in the morning to prevent cold feet) and urged him to take up art collecting, a hobby that Paley could afford and was willing to pursue, eventually developing a large and admirable assortment of Impressionist and post-Impressionist paintings (and also accepting the Rockefellers' invitation to serve as a trustee for the newly formed Museum of Modern Art in New York).

Despite the time and interests they shared, there remained a certain distance between the two. Harriman was almost ten years older than Paley, and, partly because of this age difference, Paley had mixed feelings toward Harriman, viewing him as both mentor and peer, companion and competitor.

If Paley had an intimate friend during the thirties and forties, it was the movie producer David O. Selznick. The two men were almost identical in age and had similar views of life. Selznick was over six feet tall, with curly hair, horn-rimmed glasses, and a broad smile. He had started his career at Paramount Pictures, married Louis B. Mayer's daughter Irene, and became one of Hollywood's few successful independent producers (the production of *Gone With the Wind* being his most conspicuous achievement). He was an indefatigable worker who, like Paley, pursued his social life with vigor. As his wife Irene later recalled, "From the first, our life together was dominated by parties, gambling, and—most of all— work. For though David believed in fun, more fun, and still more fun, his chief priority always remained the job."

Paley met Selznick on one of his trips to Hollywood, and their friendship grew each year, evolving into a bond that was unusual for each of them. It was a carefree relationship in those days, and the two men would spend hours together talking and joking and partying. But it was entirely social. Both men were eager to avoid the complications from doing business with each other. After Paley's marriage to Dorothy, the two couples spent considerable time with each other at their respective homes on the West and East Coasts. The four of them seemed completely compatible, with Irene developing a friendship with Dorothy that matched Bill and David's.

On the surface, then, there seemed to be considerable strength in Bill and Dorothy's marriage. He enjoyed her company, welcomed her opinions, and even inquired about the visits that her many dogs seemed to be making to the local veterinarian. ("We've made that vet a rich man," he once told a Kiluna guest.) But there were underlying tensions, and some of them were exposed in a dramatic manner.

On March 8, 1940, a woman registered under the assumed name of Mrs. J. Stoddard committed suicide by leaping from the seventeenth floor of the Book-Cadillac hotel in Detroit. Enterprising reporters soon learned that the woman had used oil paint to list the the names of some prominent men on the bathroom mirror, and one of them was William S. Paley. The reporters also discovered and copied a letter dated December 8 that was addressed to Paley:

Dearest Bill,

I just wanted to thank you for you [*sic*] kindness. You know how things were with me. I may have said things in desperation that I didn't mean. I hope you do not hate me. I'm not well. My lungs are in a precarious state, where I have to be so careful.

I still love you, but I guess you were right. I only fought so hard because my heart hurt so. You've been very right about everything. I can only hope to emulate you and try to do something good with my life. I am very tired.

Goodbye darling.

Johanna

The discoveries were flashed across the newswires and created havoc at CBS. Because of his paternalistic feelings toward Paley, Klauber was especially disturbed. Something had to be done—and fast. A trained journalist, he of course wanted more facts. But he was not interested in using them to advance the news stories; he wanted to squelch them.

In time it was learned that Johanna Stoddard was really Geraldine

Kenyon and had left her husband, Dan Bourque, in Pontiac, Michigan, some time before she had met Paley. She had been introduced to him as Johanna Stoddard, an aspiring actress who had apparently sought fame and glory in New York, and had somehow encountered and succumbed to Bill Paley's charms. They had spent only one night together, but Johanna obviously had hopes that the relationship would last longer, and she invested considerable emotional energy to make those hopes a reality.

Dorothy was shocked by the news stories and disturbed by their implications for all concerned. Initially, she felt hurt for herself and for what it said about her relationship with Bill. "I also felt sorry for that woman," she remarked many years later. "She has a short affair with Bill that can't mean anything to either of them and then she tries to pin her suicide on him." As for Paley, he was overcome by the disclosures and had difficulty discussing it with Dorothy. "But let's face it," she said. "Bill was a womanizer. I understood that in him. He always had to be reassured that he was still the most attractive guy around. There was some kind of insecurity in him that made all those conquests necessary."

Despite her emotional turmoil, Dorothy stood by her husband. For his part, Klauber drafted a statement for his boss that was released to the press:

I MET MISS STODDARD ABOUT A YEAR AGO IN A RESTAU-
RANT WITH A GROUP OF PEOPLE. ALTHOUGH I HAD SEEN HER
ONLY THAT ONCE, SHE WROTE LETTERS TO ME SIX MONTHS
LATER ASKING HELP ON THE GROUND THAT SHE HAD TUBER-
CULOSIS. SHE TOLD ME SHE WAS AN ENTERTAINER, BUT SHE
HAD NO TALENT AND, SO FAR AS I COULD FIND OUT, NO
EXPERIENCE THAT WOULD JUSTIFY PUTTING HER ON THE
AIR.

MRS. PALEY AND I BOTH TALKED TO HER SEVERAL TIMES,
TRYING TO STRAIGHTEN HER OUT, BUT SHE BECAME MORE
MENTALLY DISTURBED ALL THE TIME. FINALLY SHE BEGAN
TO WRITE LETTERS TO ME, DECLARING THAT SHE HAD DE-
VELOPED AN EMOTIONAL ATTACHMENT FOR ME.

SHE HAD SPOKEN OF SOME RELATIVES IN MICHIGAN, AND
THROUGH MY LAWYERS WE TRIED TO LOCATE THOSE RELA-
TIVES IN THE HOPE THAT THEY COULD TAKE CARE OF HER
AND INDUCE HER TO COME HOME. NO RELATIVES COULD BE
FOUND, AND MEANWHILE SHE KEPT WRITING AND TELE-
PHONING ME THAT HER HEALTH WAS GETTING WORSE AND

THAT SHE WANTED TO GO OUT TO ARIZONA. SHE REFUSED TO
ACCEPT MEDICAL ATTENTION HERE AND ALL MY EFFORTS TO
CONVINCE HER THAT AN ASSOCIATION WITH HER WAS IMPOS-
SIBLE WERE IN VAIN.

A FEW DAYS AGO I WAS INFORMED THAT SHE WAS GOING
TO MICHIGAN AND THEN TO ARIZONA. THAT WAS THE LAST
I HEARD FROM HER.

Within a short time the press lost interest in the affair. In contrast to later
years, the prevailing ethics frowned on prolonged press inquiries into the
private lives of public figures. But Paley no doubt appreciated Dorothy's
willingness to support him during what had to be a difficult time for her
as well. Loyalty was important to Bill Paley in both his professional and
personal lives, and he would, if consistent with his needs, reciprocate. So
their life went on as before with the dinners at their apartment in New
York and parties at Kiluna. And as before, Paley continued to solicit
Dorothy's opinions on all kinds of subjects, including one of growing
concern to CBS and the country: the network's coverage of news.

CHAPTER SIX

News

I n the summer of 1979, Don Hewitt and his wife, Marilyn, were strolling down the main street of Southampton, one of the more charming towns on the Eastern Shore of Long Island and a summer meeting place for New York's fashionable set. Hewitt certainly qualified on the latter score. He was the creator and producer of "60 Minutes," the CBS news interview program that had consistently placed number one in the television ratings and had been one of the most—if not *the* most—profitable programs in the network's history. Hewitt's income and stature had soared with the program's success, and he and Marilyn had used the increased income to buy a condominium in Southhampton.

As they were walking down the main street that summer afternoon, the Hewitts unexpectedly bumped into William S. Paley, chairman of CBS's board of directors. Although Hewitt had been with CBS News for thirty years, and although he had earlier earned a reputation as one of the more imaginative producers of the "CBS Nightly News," first with Douglas Edwards and then with Walter Cronkite, he did not know Mr. Paley well. He was, as Hewitt later recalled, just an "eminence" whom he had met on a few fleeting occasions. But Hewitt was not shy. He had progressed in his career by being direct and plainspoken. So he stuck his hand out and, on the off chance that Mr. Paley did not recognize him, introduced himself and his wife.

The years had been good to Paley. Although a paunch was starting to protrude over his belt, he still looked remarkably fit for a man of seventy-seven. His hair was now a blondish-white (which led some to speculate that it had been colored) and, in keeping with the style of the times, combed loosely to one side with a small lock dangling elegantly over his forehead. His enthusiasm for friends and fun had remained intact, and he was all smiles when Hewitt said hello. They chatted for a few minutes, Hewitt explaining that he and his wife had a home in Southampton and came there quite frequently. Paley replied that he too had a home in Southampton and that they should plan to get together some time soon.

He pulled out an address book and asked Hewitt for his telephone number. Marilyn interrupted and playfully said, "We normally don't give out our telephone number." Paley, who knew how to disarm almost anyone with charm, smiled broadly and said, "I bet you'll give it to me, though, won't you?"

Thus began a strong friendship. Paley began to spend considerable time with the Hewitts in the Hamptons and New York. On Friday afternoons in the summer they would often meet at the heliport on top of the Pan Am Building in Manhattan for the trip to eastern Long Island. And in winter months they would get together at restaurants or at each other's apartments. Rarely did they discuss business, however. It was exclusively a social relationship. And in those relaxed moments, Paley would reminisce about the past, about how he had started CBS and developed its radio programs. He would mention early CBS stars, like Bing Crosby, but he usually focused on CBS's coverage of news. "Paley is a showman and a newsman. P. T. Barnum and Adolph Ochs rolled into one," said Hewitt. "But he is especially proud of CBS News. And he knew you couldn't mix apples and oranges. So he didn't let his concern for show business get in the way of the need to inform. And because of him CBS News always glittered more brightly."

To some extent, they were the uncritical observations of a close friend. But not entirely. Because CBS News *was* special, and Bill Paley had every reason to feel proud of its history and achievements.

When he first assumed the presidency of United Independent Broadcasters, Paley had no notion that this network, now *his* network, would play any significant role in news coverage. True, radio had already covered some special events, including the tortuous Democratic Convention in 1924 and Calvin Coolidge's inauguration early the following year. But newspapers were plainly the organ of current events information, and newspaper publishers were a power to be reckoned with (as Paley would soon discover). The political climate was another factor that explained radio's reluctance to cover national news. In 1927 Congress adopted the Radio Act, the first comprehensive scheme for government regulation of broadcasting. One of Congress's primary concerns in enacting the law was to prevent the creation of a "radio trust" by RCA and its new radio network, the National Broadcasting Company, which would enable a single company to dominate the distribution of information by the new medium. As one congressman explained during the legislative debate on the act, "[P]ublicity is the most powerful weapon that can be wielded in a republic, and when such a weapon is placed in the hands of one, or a single selfish group is permitted to either tacitly or otherwise acquire ownership and dominate these broadcasting stations throughout the country, then woe be to those who dare to differ with them." In response to this concern, the Radio Act, and later the Communications Act of 1934, seemed to direct federal regulators to license broadcasters who would focus on local rather than national information needs.

In some respects, this legislative command was based more on hope than on reality. As future events would make clear, radio (and later television) networks required a national audience to survive. But NBC was not about to argue with Congress in 1927, and that network consciously refrained from undertaking any major role in the coverage of news. There was too much risk that a national radio news service would only heighten the congressional concerns and lead to legislation that would unduly restrict (if not eliminate) the network's ability to grow. So NBC concentrated on entertainment.

UIB did not pose the same threat of monopoly as NBC (in fact, it's doubtful that many members of Congress even knew UIB existed when the Radio Act was adopted in 1927). But as in most matters, UIB simply followed NBC's lead and did little in the way of news coverage or political commentary. Paley had no reason to challenge the policy when he took over. He had invested in the company and assumed the presidency because he was interested in radio as a medium of entertainment (and profit), not because of any preconceived notions of fulfilling some majestic public service in news. UIB did provide coverage of the presidential election of 1928 (with commentator Ted Husing predicting Herbert Hoover's election before the final tally), a daily fifteen-minute political commentary by Frederick W. Wile, and a five-minute newscast during the day. But it was not until Ed Klauber's arrival in 1930 that Paley focused on the network's potential for news coverage, as well as the manner in which it should be handled.

Klauber had deep feelings about journalism. He would often say that a consumer can tell the difference between two brands of the same food— all he had to do was taste each to decide which was better. A consumer could not make the same kind of distinction between a good newspaper and a bad one. Most consumers simply did not have enough information to know which one was providing more complete and more accurate reports. So the consumer was at the mercy of those who published newspapers, and, in Klauber's mind at least, this dependence imposed a high responsibility on every editor to be diligent and fair in news coverage.

Klauber knew, of course, that many, if not most, newspapers ignored or abused this public trust. But he vowed to insure that his network would honor these high ideals. So he talked with Paley often about the network's obligation to offer balanced news coverage. He felt that radio could provide millions of listeners with immediate access to the news of the day, and that it was an opportunity that should be seized. It was vital, however, that the network be neutral and that no preference be shown for any one viewpoint in the discussion of controversial issues.

Paley was impressed by these arguments and the force with which Klauber made them. His approach was fair and, of equal if not greater importance, would comport with the principles on which the Radio Act of 1927 was based. Indeed, in 1929 the Radio Commission itself had issued a decision stating that the law required "ample play for the free and fair competition of opposing views" and that "the principle applies . . . to all discussions of issues of importance to the public." So Paley agreed to proceed as Klauber proposed—although implementing the guiding principles proved to be far more difficult than he ever imagined.

Father Charles Coughlin provided an early example of the tensions that could be generated by Paley's desire to be fair in the presentation of news and political commentary. Coughlin had been given air time on the CBS network to discuss religious matters from WJR in Detroit, which was located near his church in Royal Oak, Michigan. Coughlin was not content to limit his talks to ecclesiastical matters, however. As the Depression worsened, he began to criticize President Hoover and other national politicians, adding comments that were plainly anti-Semitic—all of which led Klauber to demand that Coughlin allow CBS to preview his scripts before he read them over the air. Coughlin took the issue to his audience, asking them to write CBS President Paley to complain about this "censorship." Paley remembers getting some half a million letters in response to Coughlin's plea, but they had no impact on his policy. By April 1931 Coughlin was no longer getting air time from CBS; instead, CBS instituted a series called "Church of the Air" that featured speakers of different denominations on a rotating basis.

Coughlin was not Paley's only headache in the implementation of CBS's policy on fairness in political commentary. It seemed that almost everyone had opinions that they wanted to express over the air if given the chance. Even in moments of glory the network could not escape the dilemma. In October 1931, for instance, CBS's director of foreign talks finally persuaded George Bernard Shaw to come to a studio in London so that he could convey a message to America over the radio. CBS's elation in securing an appearance by the famed playwright was soon deflated by the substance of Shaw's message praising the communist system in Russia: "Hello all my friends in America! How are all you dear old boobs who have been telling one another for a month that I have gone dotty about Russia? . . . Russia has the laugh on us. She has us fooled, beaten, shamed, shown up, outpointed, and all but knocked out . . ." The public outcry quickly led CBS to arrange for a rebuttal by a vice president of Georgetown University who also happened to be a reverend (a criterion that was felt necessary because Shaw's comments seemed to imply divine favoritism toward the communist system).

Of course, no one anticipated the problems that Shaw's broadcast would create, and, since there was no plan for him to speak again on the network, no one spent any time worrying about what he might say if given another opportunity. But CBS did have other programs in which people *were* given the opportunity to speak out week after week, and those series were cause for concern. "Forum of Liberty," for example, was sponsored by *Liberty* magazine. Each week the head of a major corporation was invited to sit next to *Liberty* publisher Bernard Macfadden and express his views on almost any topic. Few speakers caused the sensation created by George Bernard Shaw, but Klauber and Paley worried that the public might not be getting a balanced presentation of controversial issues. This fear was heightened by the commentary of William J. Cameron, a Ford Motor Company executive who had access to CBS's audience every Sunday evening on time purchased by his company. The primary feature of the program was supposed to be classical music, but Cameron used "intermissions" to talk about current issues, including the shortcomings of unemployment compensation, the National Recovery Act, and other aspects of Roosevelt's New Deal programs. Not surprisingly, Cameron's comments drew fire from a wide range of groups that supported Roosevelt, all demanding time on the network to present their contrasting viewpoints.

To Paley and Klauber, however, it was not simply a matter of insuring balanced presentations on controversial issues. It was, at bottom, a question of control. By allowing commercial sponsors to determine who could speak and what they could say, CBS had lost the power to determine what went out over the network—*their* network. This lack of control was dramatized by the experience of Alexander Woollcott, a respected writer and radio commentator who spoke on the issues of the day every Sunday on "The Town Crier," a CBS program sponsored by Cream of Wheat. On one occasion in 1935 Woollcott decided to devote his commentary to the dangers of Hitler's anti-Semitic and jingoistic policies. The National Biscuit Company, Cream of Wheat's parent company, received a torrent of mail criticizing Woollcott. Nabisco asked Woollcott to use better judgment in the future; he refused, and the sponsor cancelled the series.

This episode must have been particularly painful to Paley, who knew about the dangers of anti-Semitism from firsthand experience. He and Klauber again discussed the problem at length. CBS wanted to satisfy its sponsors. The network couldn't survive without them. But there were limits. And shortly after the Woollcott incident, Paley and Klauber decided that CBS would no longer sell time to anyone for a discussion of controversial issues. From now on CBS itself would be in charge. Always the diplomat, Paley explained the new policy in terms that few could oppose. In a 1937 speech on educational broadcasting, he said it was inherently unreasonable to sell time for someone to use as their personal soapbox. Such a policy, said Paley, would create "the danger that the side with the most money would win the argument and . . . that the special interests would drown out the voice of the public." To combat this danger, Paley said that CBS had adopted a policy that he called "fairness of the air." Under this policy, CBS would strictly control who could discuss controversial issues in order to insure that any such discussion included presentation of conflicting viewpoints. The only exception to this policy would be the sale of time to political candidates during election campaigns, and in that instance, CBS would obviously honor the requirement established by the new Communications Act which mandated that all political candidates be given equal access to the airwaves.

In all of this, Paley continued, CBS itself would remain strictly neutral and would never issue any editorial to support any position or any political candidate. His reasoning on this point reflected the same concerns that had been expressed by Congress in adopting the Radio Act of 1927. "Broadcasting as an instrument of American democracy must forever be wholly, honestly and militantly non-partisan," Paley declared. "This is true not only in politics but in the whole realm of arguable social ideas." Otherwise, he said, there was a risk that a broadcaster's own views would unfairly slant the public's perception of candidates and issues.

In taking this position, Paley knew that he was imposing restrictions on CBS that would have been unthinkable if he were the publisher of a newspaper. But there were differences in the two mediums that justified his more restrictive approach. As Paley explained in his 1937 speech, there was no physical obstacle to anyone publishing a newspaper—it only required money and the will to do it. Broadcasting was different. There were a limited number of frequencies, and the broadcaster's right to exclusive use of a frequency required the protection of a government license. These conditions required broadcasters, in Paley's eyes at least, to guard against misuse of the new medium, especially in the arena of information and opinion. And that obligation, in turn, required a broadcaster to refrain from issuing editorials and to otherwise insure that "all sides are fairly treated."

Paley soon discovered that articulating these new policies was no guarantee that they would be honored—even by his own employees. Hans V. Kaltenborn was CBS's foremost political commentator at the time, and also one of the early and frequent offenders of the network's policy prohibiting editorials.

As a columnist for the *Brooklyn Eagle* in the twenties, Kaltenborn had earned a reputation as a perceptive observer of the political scene. In 1929 CBS hired the thirty-eight-year-old journalist to provide political commentary. Kaltenborn adapted well to the new medium, creating thoughtful pieces that also coincided with the necessary time limitations. Paley, who often had to struggle in crafting speeches, was continually amazed by Kaltenborn's performance, and years later he would remember that "you could give Kaltenborn a subject and say, 'We need seven and a half minutes,' and he would speak exactly seven and a half minutes, in perfect sentences, making a beginning, a middle, and an end, finishing on the dot without ever looking at a watch." Audiences also appreciated Kaltenborn's skills, as well as his energy, and he won acclaim for his firsthand reporting of the Spanish Civil War in 1936 as well as his tireless commentary on the Munich crisis in 1938, when Germany took over Sudetenland, then a part of Czechoslovakia. Kaltenborn, who spoke fluent German, would translate Hitler's statements almost verbatim and then immediately offer an astute analysis of their significance.

Kaltenborn was the pride of the CBS radio network, but in Paley's eyes he did have one major shortcoming. He had freely expressed his opinions as a newspaper columnist, and he saw no reason to proceed any differently on radio. This approach resulted in repeated departures from Paley's policy, but the network president was not the one to confront him with the problem. That job fell to Klauber, who tried to coax Kaltenborn away from the expression of personal opinions. "Now you can do the same thing without seeming to editorialize," Klauber would tell Kaltenborn. "All you've got to do is to say, 'a prominent authority declared,' or 'it is said in informed circles,' or 'there is good reason to believe that . . .' You can always use a qualifying phrase. Why do you have to say 'I think' and 'I believe'?" Kaltenborn would reply that his approach was more honest, and besides, many people listened to him precisely because they were interested in his opinions. Klauber was not impressed, and the discussions would continue, month after month, year after year, until Kaltenborn finally left in 1940 to go to NBC, where he thought he would have more editorial freedom.

CBS did not fare much better with Elmer Davis, Kaltenborn's successor. Like Kaltenborn, Davis was a highly respected print journalist when CBS hired him in 1939 to provide a five-minute commentary at 8:55 P.M., peak listening time on radio. Davis had many insights and firm opinions on the turmoil confronting the country and the world, and he did not keep them to himself. Every couple of weeks Paley himself would have lunch with Davis to review the situation. "Do you believe in our policies or not?" Paley would ask. "We can change them—they're not chiseled in marble—if you think they're wrong." Davis would insist that he fully agreed with CBS policies, but he would then return to the microphone, air his opinions, and after the passage of two weeks have another lunch with Paley to review the issue again. Paley was frustrated by Davis's persistent editorializing, but, as with Kaltenborn, he respected his talents, saying that Davis "could pack more into five minutes . . . than any man who ever lived."

In part, Paley's tolerance of Kaltenborn and then Davis was made possible because of his faith that CBS would, as he had promised, provide an overall balance in discussions of controversial issues. If one viewpoint received air time, Paley wanted conflicting viewpoints aired as well—even if he personally disagreed with them. In Paley's mind, "freedom of the air," as he called it, entitled speakers to the right to express their views "regardless of how the operators of the network or station may themselves feel. . . ." So when presidential candidates Franklin D. Roosevelt and Alfred Landon were given radio time during the 1936 election campaign, Paley felt compelled to give time to Earl Browder, the Communist Party candidate. The decision was strongly condemned in the print media (with the Hearst newspapers carrying a cartoon that showed Paley receiving his orders from Moscow). But none of the criticism caused Paley to regret his decision. The law mandated equal opportunities for all candidates, Browder was a presidential candidate, and Paley thought Browder's view deserved to be broadcast even if he personally disagreed with it. (Decades later Paley would recall that Browder's speech was not that radical and, compared to more contemporary rhetoric, would probably cause people to "think it was being spoken by a right-wing Republican.")

Paley not only had great faith in the policies of balance and equal opportunities; he also had confidence in the CBS staff that enforced those policies. And nothing—not even a desire to accommodate CBS performers—could shake that support. Eddie Cantor learned the hard way. He was one of CBS's star attractions as a comedian. In private, however, Cantor could be demanding, and insulting, and anything but funny. One day he telephoned Helen J. Sioussat, who was then CBS's director of radio talks, and told her he wanted air time to express his views on a current political controversy.

A slight woman with firm opinions of her own, Sioussat was the only female executive at CBS at the time. She had achieved success by withstanding the pressures in an industry dominated by males, and she had no difficulty rejecting Cantor's request, telling him that CBS's presentation on that particular issue was already balanced and that she had no time to give him. Cantor persisted, finally telling Sioussat, "Well, I'll talk to my friend Bill Paley and see what he has to say." Sioussat replied that she would give Cantor time if Paley told her to, but until he did, she was sticking by her decision.

Cantor hung up in a huff, and a few minutes later Sioussat received a telephone call from Paley saying that Cantor had just called him in a rage and asking what Helen had done to offend him. Sioussat recounted the incident quickly, and Paley wasted no time in supporting her decision. "Helen," he said, "you did the right thing. I'll call Cantor back and explain it to him."

Preserving balance was not Paley's only challenge in developing a quality news department for his network. Another formidable obstacle was competitive pressure from the print media. Indeed, if the newspapers had had their way, there would not have been any news department at CBS. And they almost succeeded.

Because of congressional concerns with the "Radio Trust," and because it remained uncertain as to what role it should play in reporting the events of the day, CBS offered only minimal news coverage in the late twenties and early thirties. There was a daily five-minute newscast, and most of the stories were picked up from newspapers. However, the network did provide extended coverage of cabinet meetings, congressional hearings, and other governmental proceedings. Several factors explained this focus on the federal government. CBS's only news bureau outside New York was located in Washington, D.C.; government proceedings did not require much in the way of equipment or expense; and, last but not least, the coverage gave CBS an easy way to fill its vast blocks of unsponsored time.

Still, for those interested in current events, CBS provided ample satisfaction. The amount of time devoted to public affairs was considerable, and the sheer volume heightened the chances that the public would have immediate access to the news of the day. But sometimes the access was entirely accidental. On one occasion, for example, a CBS affiliate was broadcasting a concert from a prison when a raging fire swept through the institution, destroying buildings and taking hundreds of lives; an inmate grabbed the CBS microphone and provided a riveting on-the-spot description of the tragedy.

However satisfactory from the public's perspective, CBS's coverage of current events did not sit well with newspaper publishers (many of whom had purchased radio stations and hoped to keep the medium confined to entertainment). By 1931 the American Newspaper Publishers Association had proposed that radio's use of newswire services (United Press, Associated Press, and International News Service) be strictly regulated and that radio schedules be published only as paid advertisements. Tensions increased considerably after the kidnapping of Charles Lindbergh's baby in 1932. CBS received a tip about the event from a New Jersey newspaper, sent a reporter to the Lindbergh home in New Jersey, and then began airing periodic bulletins on the sordid affair—hours before newspapers could hit the stands with the story. (NBC, anxious to maintain cordial relations with the print media, withheld its reports until the newspapers published their stories.)

The newspapers increased the pressures on the wire services to withhold all services from radio, and the United Press finally yielded, cancelling its contract with CBS just before election day in 1932. As a result of what Paley later called a comedy of errors, UP reinstated its contract on election eve, *after* CBS had been able to retain the services of the Associated Press, which did not know of UP's cancellation and wanted to remain available to any facility that it thought was being used by its chief competitor. The reprieve for CBS was short-lived. By April 1933 all three wire services—fearful of losing contracts with newspapers, their principal clients—adopted policies prohibiting the sale of their services to radio.

Paley and Klauber were angered and frustrated. News had become a major weapon in CBS's competition with NBC, which seemed content to focus on entertainment fare. The junior network had already begun to advertise itself as "Columbia—'The News Network' "—a claim that could hardly be substantiated if the network had no access to the wire services and only one news bureau of its own. And then luck intervened. In the summer of 1933 General Mills advised Paley that it would pay half the tab of a new Columbia News Service if the cost did not exceed $3,000 a week.

The offer was almost too good to be true, and Paley quickly accepted. Arrangements were made to buy the Dow Jones ticker and the Exchange Telegraph news service based in London. Paley and Klauber also decided to add news bureaus in Chicago and Los Angeles and to line up free-lance reporters, or "stringers," in every city with a population of 20,000 or more. The two men then turned their attention to the standards that would govern the CBS news service. Klauber argued, as before, that the reporting should be—both in fact and in appearance—thorough and dispassionate. Paley, by now well tutored in Klauber's principles, agreed, and Klauber was asked to communicate the news policy to the staff. "Columbia is to proceed on the principle that the primary purpose of a news broadcast is to convey information," Klauber wrote in his memorandum to the staff, "and that the time has gone by when excited, fevered, hysterical outbursts of words are an adequate technique. . . . Bear in mind that the audience is primarily interested in what is happening and not in the personal feelings of the announcer. . . ."

The news department was placed under the direction of Paul White, an overweight man with a rumpled appearance. White had gained extensive experience in the news business with UP and knew how to organize a news team. By the fall of 1933 CBS had three daily newscasts—a five-minute one at noon, another five-minute segment at 4:30 P.M., and a fifteen-minute program at 11:00 P.M. Coverage of current affairs expanded, and CBS seemed to be on the leading edge of a new era.

The newspapers remained unconvinced, and they used their leverage to great advantage. Many papers refused to carry any radio program listings, and a number of commercial radio sponsors received visits from newspaper representatives who explained the folly of advertising on radio. And to make sure CBS got the message, the newspaper publishers threatened to take their concerns to Congress, which was then considering a new regulatory law for broadcasters (which ultimately became the Communications Act of 1934).

CBS had more to lose than NBC from this attack, so Paley took the lead in exploring ways to deal with it. There were, however, few alternatives—or so it seemed. The networks were still fledgling organizations, the publishers were a powerful influence in national politics, and, for its part, NBC had no inclination to fight for something that represented only a minor part of its program schedule. Paley appreciated the differences in his competitor's position, but he needed NBC's help in developing a face-saving solution. He met with David Sarnoff, now RCA's president, and NBC president M.H. Aylesworth, and they agreed to jointly seek an accommodation with the newspapers. Paley then arranged for a conference to be held at New York's Biltmore Hotel in December 1933. Those in attendance included representatives from the networks, members of the National Association of Broadcasters (representing local stations), the wire services, and editors of major newspapers. The debate was spirited, the conclusions foregone. By the end of the conference Paley agreed to dissolve the Columbia News Service and NBC agreed to discontinue its limited news-gathering facilities. The networks (along with other radio stations) also agreed to limit the number of newscasts to two, to broadcast them at times when they would not be competing with morning and evening newspapers, and to rely almost exclusively on news summaries prepared by a newly created Press Radio News Bureau (which would be controlled by the newspapers).

The Biltmore agreement was hardly a show of courage by the networks, and Paley himself later agreed that the arrangement was "a big mistake."

But economics took precedence over principle, and Paley was not about
to risk his network's financial health to preserve the independence of the
CBS news department. The newspapers had declared war, and they
seemed to have the resources to prevail in any combat with broadcasters.
Only the public—through its listening habits—could demonstrate otherwise, but, survey techniques being what they were at the time, no one
really knew what the public thought, and Paley could not afford the risk
of rejection. And so the newspapers emerged with a victory, but it was
only temporary.

Paley and other broadcasters soon discovered that the public was indeed enamored of this new medium. Unlike the cold print of the newspapers, radio was alive. Radio had made Franklin Roosevelt a friend and
neighbor; radio had brought Jack Benny and laughter into homes that
knew only despair in those Depression times; radio had become a part of
the family, a source of comfort when people had nowhere else to go. The
more they listened, the more they seemed to want, and Paley gave it to
them. Aside from more entertainment programming, he increased coverage of Washington affairs and expanded the use of news bulletins—the one
crucial exception to the Biltmore agreement (which had recognized
radio's right to advise the public of developments of "transcendent importance"). The networks continually inflated the definitions of those terms,
and by 1934—one year after the Biltmore agreement had been signed—the
exception had swallowed the rule, and almost everything was deemed to
be of "transcendent importance." The public demand for news on radio
made it clear to the wire services—as well as to advertisers—that considerable profits could be made through this new medium and that a boycott
made no business sense. The newspapers, once the primary bastion of
profit for the wire services and advertisers, lost their leverage, and by 1935
the arrangement was dead.

The demise of the Biltmore agreement coincided with another event of
paramount significance for broadcast journalism in 1935: CBS hired Edward R. Murrow as its new director of talks. He was about six feet tall,
slim, and twenty-seven years old. He was also strikingly handsome, with
a lean, angular face, soulful eyes, and dark hair combed straight back. He
dressed in high style, wearing tailored double-breasted suits and shirts
with detachable collars. And he conveyed a sophistication that was remarkable for one so young (and to avoid those kinds of questions, he told
CBS that he was thirty-two rather than twenty-seven).

For all his poise, Ed Murrow was a man beset by conflicting impulses—
and someone whose exterior could camouflage the turmoil that often
brewed inside. He had been born Egbert Roscoe Murrow in Polecat,
North Carolina, in 1908. While he was still a young boy, the family picked

up and left for a place that offered a better economic future, finally settling in a rural part of the state of Washington.

The Murrow family—which included four boys, of whom Egbert was the youngest—was close-knit, and much of the credit belonged to their mother. A Bible-reading Quaker, Ethel Murrow believed in simple virtues. She instructed her sons on the importance of love, honesty, and hard work, and these were the principles she invoked to get the family past tough times. As Murrow once told a friend, "She kept us together. We'd have gone *down* without her." But Ethel Murrow pursued her principles to unreasonable extremes. To her, life was meant to be a struggle. It was not merely a matter of circumstance. Hardship fostered discipline, and for Ethel, discipline was essential to good character. To her children she seemed to be in a constant state of martyrdom. Almost any pleasure was sinful, and she did not bring gaiety and laughter into the Murrow home. A true ascetic, she even refused to attend family weddings and seemed unable to accept almost anything unless it involved sacrifice.

All of this left an indelible imprint on Murrow's psyche. Throughout life he was given to moods of deep despair, so troubling and uncontrollable that he felt obligated to warn Janet Brewster, his future wife, that he would not always be agreeable, and years later Janet Murrow would confirm that "Ed was a sufferer."

Murrow at least had the inner strength to recognize his own weaknesses, and he felt they could be traced back to his upbringing. Speaking of his childhood, he once told a CBS colleague, almost plaintively, "I never learned to play." And years later, when he had achieved fame and glory as *the* American presence in London during World War II, he would write to his parents that "small boys don't really ever grow up. They never escape from their early training, and when the going is tough they return to a few fundamentals, distilled into them between the ages of six and ten. . . ."

Although he did not go to his mother's ascetic extremes—he could indulge himself with the pleasures that money and fame made possible—he never drifted far from her simple view of good and evil in the world. Murrow, too, was prone to see the world in those black-and-white terms, and his greatest moments in broadcast journalism coincided with times when the forces of good and evil could be easily distinguished and when he could assume the mantle of the moral crusader—the days in London when Britain withstood the onslaught of Nazi planes, and later, the television broadcasts in the 1950s, when he had dared to speak out against Senator Joe McCarthy and those who embraced his philosophy of intimidation.

Experience also played a role in shaping Murrow's view of the world.

His family was never financially secure, and, beginning in his teens, he did what he could to contribute. By the summer of his fourteenth year he was working in a logging camp in Washington's forests. It was hard work, but the setting and physical demands were exhilarating. Perhaps the only downside of the experience was his first name, which seemed so out of place among men so rugged. In due course Murrow rectified the problem and changed his name from Egbert to Edward. But the pleasant memories of those summers never left him. Years later, when he was wealthy and wanted a place to escape to from the tensions of broadcasting, Murrow selected a farm in upstate New York that had much in common with the logging camps in which he had worked as a youth.

However relaxing, the outdoors was not where Murrow wanted to spend his professional life. His mother had imbued him with the importance of education, and young Egbert was a good student who felt comfortable in the world of books and ideas. His academic success was enhanced by his friendly manner and considerable skills as a debater. At Washington State College he performed well, and by his senior year he was elected president of his class as well as the student government.

When Murrow graduated in 1930 the country was in the throes of the Depression. It was a time of economic and political uncertainty, and Murrow very much wanted to be among those who pursued solutions. His first vehicle toward this end was the National Student Federation, an organization that represented the student governments of more than one hundred colleges and universities. Murrow had been elected president of the federation before his graduation and had agreed to go to New York to direct its efforts to improve relations with student associations in Europe, which was also suffering from economic depression. Murrow's position gave him an opportunity to travel across the Atlantic to meet with counterparts in European student organizations. It was a stimulating time for him, but the job did not entail a long-term commitment. After a year at the federation, Murrow continued his involvement in international education by accepting a position as assistant to Stephen Duggan, director of the Institute for International Education. One of Murrow's responsibilities was to help Duggan prepare lectures he delivered on CBS's educational program series entitled "School of the Air," and Fred Willis, for one, was impressed with Murrow's work.

That was the turning point for Murrow, because Willis happened to be an assistant to CBS's young president, William S. Paley. In 1935 Paley and Klauber had just decided that CBS would no longer sell time for the discussion of controversial issues and that CBS would instead present balanced debates among speakers of its own choosing. All the idea needed was someone to implement it, and, after interviewing him, Paley and

Klauber decided Murrow was that someone. In Paley's eyes, Murrow seemed to fit the CBS image—which was closely molded after the network's president. The chain-smoking Murrow was articulate, thoughtful, and well-groomed.

Murrow worked directly with Klauber and, in contrast to most of the staff, found the relationship rewarding. "Ed had great respect for Klauber," recalled Janet Murrow, who had married Ed the year before he joined CBS. "Ed would continually remark that Klauber was so clever and knowledgeable in news. Klauber may have been tough, but Ed was tough on himself." The two men functioned well together, and in 1937 Klauber asked Murrow to go to London to be CBS's director of foreign talks. It was an exciting opportunity and one well suited to Murrow's background. So he accepted the offer, and, after a send-off dinner with the Klaubers, the Murrows left for Europe.

Murrow had little contact with Paley after arriving in London. He spent most of his time traveling through Europe lining up lectures and musical performances for "Columbia's American School of the Air"—hardly the kind of responsibility that required communication with the network president. But Hitler changed all that.

As part of his expansionist policy, Hitler had set his sights on the annexation of Austria. The Führer claimed that Austria was really part of Germany and that annexation was the appropriate vehicle to insure Austria's lasting bond with the Fatherland. Others—including the Austrian government—took a different view, but their arguments were futile. Hitler's aggressive policies were now supported by a greatly expanded army, England and France were reluctant to engage Germany in armed combat, and Nazi forces inside Austria had developed wide support among the populace. In an act of desperation, the Austrian government scheduled a plebiscite for early March 1938 to determine whether the Austrian people favored independence or annexation. But Hitler was taking no chances. He gave the German army the order to move into Austria before the plebiscite could be held.

While German tanks rolled into Austria, Murrow was in Warsaw trying to arrange an appearance by a children's choir on "Columbia's American School of the Air." When he returned to his hotel room he found several urgent telephone messages asking him to call Bill Shirer in Vienna. Although a contemporary of Murrow's, Shirer cut a completely different figure—overweight, balding, and dressed in suits that always seemed to need a pressing. But he was an experienced reporter and tenacious in pursuit of news. Murrow had hired him for CBS after arriving in London in 1937. Murrow felt he needed someone to cover Central Europe, and Shirer—who had worked for a wire service in Berlin—seemed to have the right temperament and background. For Shirer, it was not precisely the kind of position for someone with aspirations in journalism. His principal responsibility would be to arrange lectures, concerts, and other performances, and under no circumstances was he to give news reports over the radio. If he or Murrow uncovered items to be included in any news broadcast, the material would be turned over to experienced newsmen with the right kind of voice. The conditions may not have been ideal, but Shirer needed the work and no one else was making him an offer.

Any reservations about the job had to be far from Bill Shirer's mind when Ed Murrow finally returned his urgent calls. Shirer came directly to the point, using metaphors that Murrow was sure to understand. "The opposing team has just crossed the goal line," said Shirer. Murrow: "Are you sure?" Shirer's short response spoke volumes: "I'm paid to be sure." The two men explored their alternatives and decided that Shirer would go to London to report his observations, since the Nazis had shut down RAVAG, the Austrian national broadcasting company. For his part, Murrow would go to Vienna so that he could report on subsequent developments there if the Nazis reopened the broadcast lines.

Back in New York, Klauber, White, and other CBS officials were frantically trying to determine how to present the news of the Austrian crisis. One of the first decisions was to allow Murrow and Shirer to broadcast their reports themselves. There simply was no time to package their information for others to read, and besides, the firsthand accounts would have more drama if related by those who had actually witnessed the events. The next step was to schedule the reports to be aired over the CBS radio network, and on that point Paley himself took charge.

The CBS president was then in bed in his New York apartment with a 102-degree fever and a bad case of the flu. Still, it did not deter him from speaking with Klauber, and the two men were constantly exchanging telephone calls. When told that the Nazis had prohibited CBS's use of the Austrian broadcast facilities, Paley decided to take matters into his own hands. He knew the director general of RAVAG, having met him several times on trips to Salzburg. Paley called the overseas operator and placed a call to the Austrian director. Surprisingly enough, the call was put through. Paley inquired about CBS's use of the Austrian facilities, but it was to no avail. In a voice choking with emotion, the director said only that the Germans were there and that he was no longer in charge. He then broke down and cried. The phone clicked and his voice was gone.

The telephone call had an immediate impact on Paley. The European conflict was no longer a distant reality. It had swallowed up people he knew, and it obviously had broader implications for the peace that Americans enjoyed at home. It was vital that the American people fully appreciate the dimensions of the tragedy. Paley telephoned Klauber and proposed that CBS organize simultaneous reports from CBS contacts in London, Berlin, Vienna, and other European capitals. Klauber called back to say it couldn't be done, but Paley was not about to accept no for an answer. He remained adamant. "I said, Goddamnit, there's no reason in the world I can think of why it can't be done. It has to be done. You go back to them," Paley recalls telling his chief assistant. Within an hour Klauber called back again to say that there were risks, it might not work—but it now seemed possible. And so the first CBS "European News Roundup" (later renamed "World News Roundup") was broadcast over the CBS radio network at 8:00 P.M. on Sunday, March 13, 1938.

The program was introduced from New York by Robert Trout, one of the network's most seasoned political reporters. At his disposal were CBS stringers in Paris, Berlin, and Rome, as well as a United States senator speaking from Washington. But the heart of the "Roundup" consisted of Murrow and Shirer's reports, and their participation involved a certain irony: Shirer, who was based in Vienna, spoke from London, and Murrow, who was based in London, spoke from Vienna (where the Nazis had been cajoled into reopening the broadcast lines). Both men performed exceedingly well, capturing the drama of the situation with their detail and analysis. For Shirer, it was not all that surprising, since his background was in journalism; but Murrow's was not, and that made his performance all the more remarkable. (Elmer Davis later wrote that he was "scandalized" that Murrow could perform so well as a reporter without having worked on a newspaper.)

After the "Roundup," it was obvious that Murrow could no longer be relegated to on off-air position with CBS. He had a voice and a gift for description that seemed tailor-made for radio. It was enjoyable to listen to him, and he could make distant events seem very real to the listener at home. No doubt it reflected, in part at least, his love of learning. He very much wanted people to understand—and care.

Having won wide acclaim, the "Roundup"'s were frequently repeated, reaching another high point in September 1938 during the Munich crisis when British Prime Minister Neville Chamberlain proclaimed that he had signed an agreement with Hitler promising "peace in our lifetime." The commentary from Murrow, Shirer, and others was superb, and no one was happier than Paley. "Columbia's coverage of the European crisis is superior to its competitors," Paley cabled Murrow, "and probably the best job ever done in radio broadcasting." Shirer was beginning to sense the importance that Paley attached to news coverage, an impression that was reinforced when he met the network president the following summer. Paley was full of praise for what Murrow and Shirer had accomplished, and it was clear that foreign news coverage was now and would continue to be a significant part of the CBS program schedule. To be sure, the increased news coverage provided a public service of which Paley could be justly proud; but he also recognized that foreign news was an arena in which his network could compete effectively with NBC.

Paley and Klauber also understood, however, that expanded news coverage required an expansion of the foreign news staff. Murrow was now recognized as the network's principal news reporter in Europe, and he was given the budget and authority to hire additional staff. There were no established company standards, so Murrow focused on personality and background, giving little value to how a person's voice would sound over radio. By the early 1940s his approach had resulted in the recruitment of a number of talented people with exceptional skills in news reporting and analysis: Eric Sevareid, Charles Collingwood, Winston Burdette and Howard K. Smith. To all of them Murrow stressed the need to speak in terms that could be easily understood by a diverse audience. "Imagine yourself at a dinner table back in the United States with a local editor, a banker, and a professor, talking over coffee," Murrow would say. "You try to tell what it was like, while the maid's boyfriend, a truck driver, listens from the kitchen. Talk to be understood by the truck driver while not insulting the professor's intelligence."

Although Murrow was given great scope in choosing his staff and directing its activities, he was not entirely free from network control. As tensions and hostilities mounted in Europe, Paley and Klauber reviewed CBS news policies and their application to the European conflict. Paley and Klauber of course supported the Allies' cause, but they continued to believe that CBS had an obligation to report the news in a dispassionate fashion: people needed access to facts, not the opinions of CBS or its personnel.

The need to reinforce this basic principle with the CBS staff became apparent after September 1, 1939, when Germany invaded Poland and England declared war on Germany. Emotions were running high in the country and in much of the media. Paley did not want those feelings reflected in his network's news reports, and he asked Klauber to issue another memorandum to the staff. Klauber was happy to oblige. After all, Paley's sentiments echoed views that Klauber had been urging on him for years. Klauber's memo of September 5, 1939, explained that there would be "no basic change" in CBS's news policies, that the network "has no editorial opinions about the war" or "what this country or any other country should or should not do," and that CBS should not report selected newspaper editorials "because somebody here had some personal desire to influence public opinion on some given question." It was a high standard of integrity, one that Paley would honor long after Klauber had gone.

News policies were not the only arena in which Paley sought Klauber's assistance as World War II approached. The FCC had declared its own war on the radio networks. But unlike CBS's coverage of the European conflict, the outcome could not be controlled through the issuance of a memorandum.

CHAPTER SEVEN

War

The approach of Paley's eighty-fifth birthday in September 1986 was a cause for celebration in his family, and not just because of his good health. Only weeks before he had come out of retirement to rejoin CBS as acting chairman of the board, a move that pleased Paley enormously. So Paley's family arranged to congregate in New York to make sure that this party was equal to the joy they all felt. In anticipation of the event, his son, Billy, thirty-eight, picked up his father's 1979 autobiography and started leafing through it. "And I came across this part where he promised himself that he would retire at the age of thirty-five," he told a caller, "and that was pretty amazing to me. I just can't imagine he would have ever left CBS." Neither could his father. When the appointed time came in 1936, Paley recalled the commitment he had made to himself, gave it passing consideration, and moved on. Bill Paley could not leave his work. It was not because he needed the money. He already had more than he could ever spend. It was the job. Although he had been with the company for eight years, he still enjoyed being CBS president. The network was still growing, and he continued to find the day-to-day challenges exciting. And more than that, as the head of a radio network Paley had occasion to meet a vast assortment of interesting people—corporate magnates, newsmen, entertainers, and even the president of the United States.

Although the contact was sporadic, Paley took considerable pride in the communications he had with Franklin D. Roosevelt. Most of the contact was through correspondence, and much of that was orchestrated by Harry Butcher, a CBS vice president who supervised government relations from an office in Washington, D.C. Butcher maintained a relationship with Stephen Early, FDR's press secretary, as well as other members of the White House staff, and he used those relationships to obtain letters from the president when the need arose.

One occasion involved the dedication of CBS's new programming studios at Columbia Square in Hollywood in April 1938. As the years had passed, CBS had been able to find more and more commercial sponsors for its programming. One of its more successful ventures included dramatic series whose story lines were continued from one day to the next. Because these series were sponsored by soap manufacturers, they were soon called "soap operas." Many soap operas and other programs could be produced from CBS studios in New York, but CBS had a coast-to-coast network, and the network frequently used its station in Los Angeles, KNX, to produce programs. The KNX facilities were limited, however, and, after discussing the matter with Paul Kesten and other CBS executives, Paley decided that the network should look to the future and construct a large, modern studio in Hollywood that would enable them to take full advantage of the resources in the country's movie capital. One year and $1.75 million later, the new studios—located on Sunset Boulevard—were ready to be opened. A gala all-day celebration was planned to mark the event. Paley and Kesten thought it would be wonderful if the president used a special photoelectric cell to open the curtain that hung across the main stage. Butcher discouraged the idea, however, saying it would be inappropriate and would set an unfortunate precedent for companies that wanted to use his services. Butcher suggested that the company settle for a letter instead, and, after some debate, his suggestion was accepted.

Butcher wrote to Early to make the request and enclosed a draft of a letter the president could send. In addition to congratulating CBS on its new studios, the letter commended the network for its "announced policy of making your facilities available for important discussions of national public topics by representative spokesmen arguing different points of view. The maintenance of such a policy," the letter continued, "is essential in preserving freedom of the air and in preventing abuse of a public franchise which is entrusted to qualified licensees." In due course the letter was sent with the president's signature, and on April 26 Paley responded, telling Roosevelt that he appreciated the congratulations and FDR's support for CBS's policy "governing the broadcasting of discussions on public questions."

The exchange was all for show and all for CBS's benefit. But there were later occasions when the communication was genuine, and few were of more significance to Paley than his meeting with Roosevelt to discuss the extension of the CBS radio network into Latin America. CBS had always recognized the need for international communications, but most of the effort in the early days concentrated on Europe. That began to change in the mid-thirties. There was, to begin with, Roosevelt's "Good Neighbor" policy, which was announced in 1934 and focused public attention on our "neighbors to the South." The turning point for CBS was the outbreak of war in Europe. There was no longer any hope of expanding the CBS network across the Atlantic. Latin America, in contrast, was at peace and seemed to be an inviting and untapped market.

Paley began to sense that a radio network in Latin America—one linked to CBS operations in the United States—could be beneficial to CBS financially and simultaneously serve important national security interests. He discussed the matter with Nelson Rockefeller in the summer of 1940 when both were vacationing in Maine. (Because of the war, Bill and Dorothy had had to forsake their customary August trip to Europe and settled instead for a rented house in Northeast Harbor near the Rockefellers' retreat at Seal Harbor.) Although seven years younger, Rockefeller had much in common with Bill Paley—wealth, an interest in art, and an enjoyment of the good life in New York. For his part, Paley was drawn to the younger man. He was vivacious, fun, and full of energy—the kind of person with whom Paley liked to socialize. So Bill and Dorothy spent a fair amount of time that summer with Nelson and his wife, whom everyone called Todd, and Latin America could not have been far from their minds.

Earlier that summer Paley had received a telephone call from James Forrestal, a sometime golfing partner who also happened to be an assistant to President Roosevelt. Forrestal had asked if Paley might be interested in a presidential appointment as Coordinator of Inter-American Affairs, a new post designed to help shape American policies on Latin America. Paley had had no desire to leave CBS and had declined. But he did have an alternative for Forrestal: Nelson Rockefeller. After all, Rockefeller had business concerns in South America, spoke Spanish, and had an interest in government service. Paley's recommendation was eventually accepted, and Rockefeller's long and distinguished political career was launched.

Although he did not want to coordinate Latin American policy, Paley did hope to expand CBS's radio network into Latin America. "He was very enthused about that Latin American venture," Dorothy recalled, "and he spent a lot of time talking about it and making plans for it." After months of work, Paley was satisfied that the time had come to make an approach to Latin American stations and invite them to become CBS affiliates. "Our plan," Paley said, "was to offer these network affiliates exclusive rights to rebroadcast free of charge our Latin American programs created by a special program department in this country; they in turn would build up programs for retransmission throughout the U.S., thus affording a true exchange rather than a one-sided dumping of cultural achievements and ideas. On the commercial side," Paley continued, "we were prepared to offer the network service to U.S. advertisers interested in the Latin American market and to pay the affiliated stations in American dollars for time purchased from them."

Paley intended to present these plans to the owners of the stations directly. In the meantime, Rockefeller apparently told FDR about the trip, because Paley soon received an unexpected summons to the White House shortly before he was scheduled to leave. He was beginning a lunch in Washington with Jesse Jones, then Secretary of Commerce, when Jones's secretary interrupted with a message that Mr. Paley was expected at the White House to dine with the president. Paley knew nothing about the appointment, but neither he nor Jones was about to ignore the presidential invitation. He was whisked off to the White House in a limousine and soon found himself seated in the Oval Office with President Roosevelt.

While a butler wheeled in a metal tray with sandwiches and drinks, the president, ever gracious and informal, explained that he had heard of Paley's imminent trip to Latin America and wanted to talk with him about its possible utility to the United States. Both Mussolini and Hitler had sensed the potential benefit of allies in South America and had made concerted efforts—including the use of radio broadcasts touting the virtues of fascism—to win public sympathy there. Roosevelt was concerned that this propaganda might be succeeding, and, if so, that it might interfere with American defense policy. He asked Paley to review the level of propaganda and to make recommendations as to how the United States could counteract it. Paley was honored to be given the assignment and quickly accepted.

He was scheduled to leave New York on November 8, 1940, for the seven-week swing through Latin America. He was to be accompanied by Dorothy, Paul White, and Edmund Chester, CBS director of shortwave broadcasts (the technology to be utilized in establishing the network). Before departing, Paley sent a note to Missy LeHand, Roosevelt's personal secretary, enclosing a handwritten letter for the president himself, who had just won re-election to an unprecedented third term. "Dear Mr. President," the letter began, "Few things have meant as much to me, or have given me such full gratification, as the decision of the American people to have you lead us during the next four years. . . . I am confident that you will take us in the right direction, and because I think I know you, even ever so slightly, I am satisfied that you will do so with strength and courage." Paley explained that he was about to leave for South America and that he anticipated "the pleasure of a meeting" with Roosevelt upon his return.

The group went first to Miami and then on to Panama. From there they traveled down the west coast of South America and then returned up the east coast, with a final stop in Cuba. At each port of call Paley met with radio executives, offering the CBS affiliation and trying to arrange for the exchange of programs. Although business discussions dominated the day, he was fully able to enjoy the nightlife as well. And on that score, he regarded Santiago as the "high point in good will, good company and good time." Dorothy agreed with that assessment, although she could not help adding, somewhat ruefully, "I must say, we heard an awful lot of music."

On the whole, the trip lived up to Paley's expectations. He was able to reach agreement with large stations in most of the countries he visited. He was also able to evaluate the extent of fascist penetration, which was considerable. Italians and Germans bought time on stations to play music interspersed with diatribes against the United States. And while Paley felt that the "anti-Yankee" sentiments among the populace were not as widespread as he had anticipated, he also sensed that the fascists' radio broadcasts were effective and could make it more difficult for the United States to strengthen the bonds of friendship with certain Latin American countries, especially Argentina.

In January 1941 Paley submitted a five-page memorandum to Roosevelt summarizing his observations and recommendations. He found that FDR's "Good Neighbor" policy had improved Latin American perceptions of the United States, that the "Nazis are efficiently organized and well financed throughout Latin America," that Latin Americans were nonetheless unconcerned about the Nazi threat, and that Latin Americans tended "to view us as alarmists who are determined to find a fifth columnist under every palm tree." Paley concluded that the greatest danger was not an overt Nazi takeover of any country but "Nazi domination by a deal made with those in power, or through a revolution headed by local stooges representing a legal party. . . ." Consequently, Paley recommended that Roosevelt consider "the desirability of considering a policy under which the Americas will not tolerate the control of any American republic by a foreign nation, irrespective of the methods used to gain and maintain such control."

Paley no doubt emphasized these points when he met with Roosevelt in the Oval Office for ten minutes on the morning of February 26, 1941. Although the meeting was short, Roosevelt gave serious consideration to Paley's findings and recommendations. He sent Paley's memorandum to Sumner Welles, the under secretary of state and one of Roosevelt's principal advisers on foreign policy matters. Welles reported back to the president that Paley's observations were "exceedingly sound." However, Welles opposed adoption of any policy threatening intervention if the United States determined that a Latin American country was under foreign domination. According to Welles, that kind of policy would "afford exactly the opportunity which the Nazi propagandists are seeking to raise

[in] the old charge of Yankee imperialism." Welles proposed instead that the United States rely on inter-American cooperation to counteract any Nazi influence.

Roosevelt did not take any specific action on the issue because other questions dominated his agenda as America moved closer to war. The advent of global war also prevented Paley from implementing his plans for the Latin America network. The shortwave broadcasts to Latin America began in 1942, but shortly afterward the United States government took over the facilities. Nazi activity in South America had escalated, and the government believed that CBS's Latin American facilities would be useful in its counterintelligence effort.

Paley certainly understood and accepted that CBS's commercial plans had to yield to the higher interest of the country. Still, he felt that his memorandum and meetings with the president would make Roosevelt receptive to his requests for assistance on other matters. And the need for such presidential assistance arose almost immediately after Paley had submitted his Latin American report.

The problem was the FCC. In the late 1930s the commission began to receive complaints from stations affiliated with CBS and others affiliated with NBC. In essence, the local radio stations charged that on some occasions the networks were forcing them to carry programs they did not want and at other times refusing to give them programs if they had an affiliation with the other network. CBS was aware of the complaints and tried to prevent them from being presented. Joe Ream, the young lawyer in charge of CBS affiliate relations, would repeatedly tell the affiliates, "We're in a corporate marriage, and you want to cheat on your wife." But it was to no avail. The complaints persisted, and in 1938 the FCC initiated proceedings to investigate network practices. Because the networks were viewed as a "chain," the proceedings were said to concern "chain broadcasting."

Shortly after the proceeding began the FCC acquired a new chairman: James Lawrence Fly, the former general counsel to the Tennessee Valley Authority. Fly was an ardent supporter of Roosevelt's New Deal philosophy, and that support proved to be a point of prime significance. In contrast to his first New Deal programs, Roosevelt no longer pursued relief programs that relied on cooperation with big business. He had tried that and, in the president's eyes at least, big business had stabbed him in the back and undermined the National Recovery Act and other measures. So Roosevelt's "second" New Deal programs were more anti-business and, more specifically, geared to combat monopoly wherever it emerged.

Roosevelt did not have any particular vendetta against NBC or CBS and, in fact, had cordial relations with both Sarnoff and Paley. But Fly did not worry about such fine distinctions. A monopoly was a monopoly, and in Fly's view, NBC and CBS were trying to monopolize control of the nation's radio stations. So he decided to push the FCC's chain broadcast proceedings to a successful conclusion. Extensive hearings were held in 1939, briefs were filed in 1940, and in early 1941 Fly and the FCC staff began to put the finishing touches on an FCC order which would prohibit numerous network practices and require many changes in their structures. On Thursday, May 1, Fly received an unexpected telephone call from Roosevelt himself, saying that he had just received the results of an independent study of radio regulation and that Fly should place any new network regulations on hold until they could study the matter further. Fly did not like the sound of that. He had already invested too much in his commission's decision to see it undone by opposing political forces. He told the president—falsely—that it was too late, that the order had already been approved for public distribution. As a result, some commissioners—especially the two dissenters—found themselves with less than twenty-four hours to review the document and prepare their opinions.

The commission released the order to the public on Saturday, May 3, saying that it had been approved by the FCC the day before. The networks knew that Fly was an adversary and that the chain broadcasting report would not be favorable to their interests. But even they were surprised by its sweep. Among other things, the order said, in effect, that NBC could not operate two radio networks (the Red and the Blue) and would have to sell one, that the networks could not require an affiliate to carry any program, that the networks could not retain an unrestricted option to utilize an affiliate's air time, that the networks could not maintain exclusive relationships with individual stations in a market, and that a network could not own more than one station in a market.

People were frantic at CBS. To them, the FCC's order would prohibit CBS from functioning as a network. Paley was among the most concerned. He had acquired control of the struggling United Independent Broadcasters and built it into a thriving coast-to-coast radio network. The FCC's order, in his eyes, threatened the very viability of CBS, and Paley was not about to stand for it. He had friends, important friends, and he would try to enlist them in his cause.

He had already had some communication with Roosevelt on the matter. By late winter 1941 Paley, as well as others in the broadcast industry, had gathered some indications of what the FCC might do on chain broadcasting. Paley, for one, was not going to wait until the axe fell. He sent a telegram to the president in early March—two weeks after his Latin American meeting with Roosevelt—requesting an appointment to discuss "an urgent radio matter." Major General Edwin M. Watson, FDR's appointments secretary, discussed the matter with press secretary Steve Early, who told Watson to disregard the request, apparently because Roosevelt had already asked for (but not yet received) an independent study of radio issues, including chain broadcasting.

Paley did not let this rejection deter him from further communications with the president. On Monday, May 5, 1941, Paley sent a telegram to Roosevelt advising him of the FCC's "bombshell" and urging the president to "take steps to stay the damaging venture of the Commission." Paley said that the FCC's actions "threaten the freedom of American broadcasting and if enforced will seriously damage radio service in America. I am not an advocate of the status quo," Paley continued, "and sincerely believe that people should have the broadcasting they want and need." But, Paley added, any needed changes "should be accomplished by an orderly process and not by a torpedoing operation by a body of men whose legal authority is sorely in question." This dramatic appeal—and a similar one from David Sarnoff—prompted a reply from Fly and total silence from the White House. Roosevelt was not going to involve himself in a complicated regulatory matter—especially given his other, more pressing burdens.

All was not lost for CBS. The Senate Interstate Commerce Committee scheduled hearings in June to consider the FCC's order. CBS would have an opportunity to make its case and obtain legislative relief. Klauber took the lead in proposing a strategy. The principal problem, he told Paley, was the networks' legal position. Unlike stations, networks were not licensed by the FCC. Therefore, said Klauber, the networks had no legitimate standing to make their voice felt at the FCC. To Klauber, the solution was obvious: propose a new law that would enable the FCC to license networks.

Klauber made his arguments with great vigor, but he did not persuade all those who listened. Joe Ream, for one, thought the notion of having the FCC license networks was "completely cockeyed." "Klauber was a brilliant guy," Ream later observed, "but occasionally he would act too quickly and shoot himself in the foot. And that was one example." Paley, however, had great respect for Klauber's judgment. Klauber had been right so many times before, and his assessment of the problem seemed entirely reasonable. If the networks were licensed, Paley thought, the networks would not be in this mess. So he authorized Klauber to prepare a statement along those lines that he could present at the Senate hearings.

In early June Paley and his lieutenants traveled to the nation's capital and sat in the back of the Senate chamber while Chairman Fly answered senators' questions over the course of several days. Paley was greatly disturbed by what he heard. Fly seemed to have all the answers, and he gave the senators quick assurances that the chain broadcasting order would not undermine the networks' financial viability or the programming available to the American public. But to Paley, Fly's comments reflected a total lack of understanding of how the networks operated. The FCC chairman seemed to think that a network could survive even if it didn't offer considerable financial incentives to advertisers or affiliates. In Fly's world, thought Paley, the networks were public-service corporations that had no cause to worry about profits under any circumstance. Paley knew better, and he tried to convey that knowledge when he had his turn to testify.

Paley gave the Senate committee precise details concerning the formulation and distribution of network programming. There were, said Paley, two kinds of programming: "Commercial programs are normally designed to attract the widest possible audiences. In our sustaining service, on the other hand, we not only keep in mind the broad popular taste but also cater to smaller groups who also have their rights." CBS, the network president observed, went to great lengths to insure quality programming in either event. As one example, he cited children's programming, which reflected input from a child psychologist as well as an advisory committee consisting of educators, parents, and others. None of this would be possible, said Paley, without the advertisers who provided the network with revenue. The advertiser, in turn, wanted assurances on the size of CBS's audience, and CBS could not give those assurances unless it had exclusive contracts with affiliate stations—contracts that gave the network an option to use the station's time when needed.

In Paley's view, the quality and quantity of radio programming would be far more limited without the networks. But he noted that "the commission seems to have been obsessed in its whole thinking by the fact that it is radio stations and not networks that hold the licenses. It seems to feel that under the circumstances the success of the networks must be in some way improper. From this," he continued, "they have gone on to reason that virtually every practice which we in long experience have found to be essential is wrong and must be stopped, regardless of the effects on programs and the public service. That is why . . . I think the time has come when the Congress should recognize the validity of the networks and should license them."

Paley had other proposals to be included in a new radio law. One of the most important concerned discussions of controversial issues. Paley reminded the Senate committee that he had established a policy of "fairness" for CBS six years earlier and that he believed "more emphatically than I did six years ago that such fairness is absolutely essential on the part of a limited medium if it is to fulfill its social obligations in a democracy." CBS, he said, had been scrupulous in following this fairness policy, but he knew that some observers had expressed concern about the power of radio in general to slant the news. "[A]s long as uneasiness does exist," said Paley, "I see no reason why the new law should not embody this requirement so long as there is proper machinery for a competent determination of performance."

This proposal did not mean that Paley wanted to place his faith in a commission whose only guidepost was, as stated under the Communications Act, the "public interest, convenience and necessity." In Paley's mind, that phrase sounded good but left too much discretion to the regulators. The chain broadcasting order was a case in point. "I believe that anyone who has heard the statements in this hearing up to now," he told the committee, "will understand that any businessman . . . would wisely prefer the risks involved in the precision of a well-drawn statute to the vagaries of men who almost seem to make up the law as they go along." Therefore, said the CBS president, Congress should more carefully define the duties and powers of the FCC in regulating radio.

Klauber must have been satisfied with Paley's performance. It embodied all the principles that he had urged on Paley in the weeks leading up to the hearings. But not everyone was persuaded by the CBS president's arguments, and among those was Senator Burton K. Wheeler of Montana, chairman of the Senate Interstate Commerce Committee. He was shocked by Paley's proposal that the FCC be empowered to license the networks. Fly had already made that proposal earlier in the hearings—not to protect the networks but to give the commission greater control over their practices. Wheeler thought that Paley was misguided in believing that an FCC license would really benefit the networks, and he did not pursue the idea (although Wheeler would later tease CBS representatives who complained about FCC regulation, saying, Well, your president wanted to be licensed by the FCC, didn't he?)

In the end, Congress did not take any action to help the networks. The FCC amended the order in October to make it less objectionable to the networks, but the heart of the regulations remained intact. NBC and CBS filed lawsuits in federal court, and eventually the matter was taken to the United States Supreme Court. In a six-to-one decision (with two justices not participating), the Court upheld the FCC's action in a decision issued in May 1943. Ironically, the Court's opinion was written by Felix Frankfurter. While the matter was still pending before the FCC, Justice Frankfurter had discussed the proceedings with Joseph Rauh, one of his former law clerks. Rauh was then an assistant general counsel at the FCC and a major participant in the decision-making process of the commission. He told Frankfurter that the networks were vigorously opposing the adoption of any chain broadcast regulations, that the opposition was not likely to succeed at the FCC, and that the only outcome would be to fuel anti-Semitic sentiment toward the broadcast media (since both Sarnoff and Paley were Jewish). Rauh thought the networks' interests would be better served if they tempered their opposition, and Frankfurter suggested that Rauh speak with Herbert Bayard Swope, retired editor of *The New York World* and someone who had entertained Paley on numerous occasions at his Long Island estate. Rauh spoke with Swope, but the networks did not retreat.

Despite his clear breach of judicial ethics—discussing the merits of a case that might come before the Court—Frankfurter assumed responsibility for explaining why the FCC's action was justified. However troubling to Paley, Frankfurter saw great benefits in the Communications Act's vague public-interest standard. According to Frankfurter, that criterion was "as concrete as the complicated factors for judgment in such a field of delegated authority permit." The language may have been contorted, but its meaning was clear: the FCC had broad powers to regulate radio programming, even if it meant that some networks (like NBC) would have to sell some of their interests or that other networks (like CBS) would have less freedom in making contracts with affiliate stations.

A few months after the Court issued its decision, Paley went to Washington to testify again before the Senate Interstate Commerce Committee. In his view, the Court's decision "marked, for American broadcasting, the end of one world and the beginning of another. . . . No longer can broadcasters gauge their program service by the yardstick of listener survey and audience response. Now they must scan the latest speech by a commissioner for the current pronouncement on what the public should hear." It was, in Paley's eyes, an intolerable situation, and he urged Congress to pass a new radio law that would "leave to broadcasters the widest possible liberty and the most complete freedom from regulation."

Unlike his earlier testimony, Paley did not suggest that Congress pass a law requiring the FCC to license networks. That idea had not been well received at CBS, in the industry, or even in Congress. Paley did not have to worry whether his change of position would offend his executive vice president because Klauber was no longer with the network. Despite tireless and largely productive service for CBS and Paley, Klauber was forced to resign through a convergence of unfortunate factors. His wife became ill with cancer, an experience that drained him physically and emotionally. Klauber himself suffered two heart attacks, with the resulting loss of the stamina that had made him so valuable. All of this made Paley more sensitive to the staff's criticisms of Klauber and raised questions in Paley's mind as to whether Klauber could effectively exercise executive leadership in the event of his absence. That was perhaps the overriding factor, because Bill Paley was about to leave the company to join the war effort.

He had known for a long time that America would probably enter the war. He had visited Murrow in London in 1940, and CBS's new correspondent was convinced that the vast expanse of the Atlantic Ocean would not restrain Hitler's ambitions. Murrow's judgment seemed impeccable. He had access to almost everyone in London, including Prime Minister Winston Churchill and his cabinet. Murrow had also seen the devastation wrought by the Nazi war machine, reporting from rooftops in London while Nazi planes transformed quiet city streets into blazing infernos.

In early December 1941 Paley had sponsored a black-tie dinner for more than one thousand notables at New York City's Waldorf-Astoria to honor the thirty-three-year-old Murrow. The following Sunday was December 7. "When the attack on Pearl Harbor was heard over the air," Paley remembered, "somebody rushed into my room on Long Island and told me about it. I jumped into the car and rushed to the studio immediately, where everything was going a hundred and fifty miles an hour. Everybody was stunned and the newsroom, of course, was the busiest place imaginable in trying to get every scrap of information that it could in order to elaborate on the initial announcement."

America's entry into war further enhanced the importance and stature of CBS's news team. The staff was further expanded, and while no one would ever think of departing from the entrenched policy of network neutrality, news director Paul White issued a memorandum to the staff admonishing them that "public confidence in our news . . . should prove a valuable machine tool in the production of victory" and that there should always be an "assurance that we are doing good and not harm" in reporting the news. Stateside reporters who departed from this standard—like Cecil Brown, who once reported from New York that "a good deal of enthusiasm for this war is evaporating into thin air"—found themselves subject to sharp rebuke.

White tried to impose similar restraints on foreign correspondents, but he sometimes encountered a formidable obstacle—Bill Paley. In the eyes of the network president, the foreign correspondents were in a class by themselves. They were, almost without exception, a highly educated and talented group. And more than that, they were the stars of the news department, if not the entire network. The world was at war, and they provided the American public with a window onto the tragedy. They gave CBS a special aura, and Paley, for one, was determined to stand behind their judgments.

Charles Collingwood was a case in point. He had joined CBS in 1941 with impressive credentials. A native of Three Rivers, Michigan, he had graduated from Cornell University, won a Rhodes scholarship to study at Oxford, and worked for United Press covering the London blitz. Although just twenty-five, Collingwood exuded a certain charisma. He was handsome, with a broad smile and wavy hair, spoke fluent French, and dressed stylishly. Murrow took an immediate liking to him and hired him with the expectation that he would quickly fit the new mold of the CBS foreign correspondent. Collingwood, affectionately called "Duke" by his peers, did not disappoint, and by 1943 his coverage of the war had earned him a Peabody, one of the news profession's most prestigious awards.

None of this meant that Collingwood was above criticism, and one of those to complain was Harry Butcher, the former CBS vice president who had become an important aide to General Dwight D. Eisenhower. On one of his trips back from Europe, Butcher stopped by to see his old boss at 485 Madison Avenue. As they talked, Butcher told Paley that he really had to get rid of that brash young man Collingwood because his reports were creating problems for the military command—discussions of the Free French underground, Jewish protest groups, and the like. Paley was not moved. Collingwood was part of CBS's elite news corps. And absent some clear error or obvious danger, Paley was not going to restrict Collingwood's reporting activities—even if the complaint came from General Eisenhower's aide. So Butcher left the meeting without getting any satisfaction.

Paley's confidence was not based entirely on awards and news reports. In August 1942 he flew to London on a Pan American clipper to view the war from a closer vantage point. It was an eye-opening experience for the forty-year-old network president. War, of course, was horrible in the death and dislocation that it caused. But there was also a sense of excitement about the city, and the times, and Paley found it irresistible.

His frequent escort was Murrow. As head of an American radio network, Paley had some status of his own, but Murrow was one of the most revered people in London, and he helped give Paley access to almost everyone and everything—royalty, government, and military. "He was greatly admired, completely trusted," Paley remembered years later, and "probably the most important American there." The two men went almost everywhere together, even into bomb shelters to escape Nazi bombing raids. But for Paley, the most dangerous part of the trip was probably driving with Murrow in the countryside. Being in a car seemed to be a release for the newsman, and he would drive at high speeds with great abandon, and Paley would invariably think that he would meet his end in a car with Murrow long before he succumbed to a Nazi bomb.

Fortunately, both men survived the car rides and the Nazi bombs. They also learned to enjoy the social life that whirled in London even during wartime. Paley had already developed numerous friendships in London, including one with Randolph Churchill and his wife, the former Pamela Digby. Churchill had taken Paley to the family estate in Chartwell during one of his peacetime visits to England, and the CBS president had listened with growing boredom as Winston Churchill rambled on about his country's failure to prepare for war. All of that had changed, of course, and he now had great respect for the new prime minister's foresight. He also had developed a considerable fondness for Pamela Churchill. She was intelligent, engaging, articulate, and extremely attractive, with fine features and deep blue eyes. She and Paley developed a special relationship that would endure the ensuing decades. Ironically, she would eventually marry two of Paley's closer friends—Leland Hayward and Averell Harriman. But long before then she became entwined with another of Paley's close associates—Ed Murrow. "Pamela was the great love of Ed's life," one of Murrow's friends later remarked. "He could never leave Janet, though, partly because Janet became pregnant toward the end of the war, and Ed had a high sense of responsibility."

War did more for Murrow, however, than introduce him to a new love. It also had a lasting effect on his relationship with Paley. "That period cemented their friendship," said one long-time broadcast journalist. "They spent all that time talking, meeting Churchill, seeing royalty, carousing around. It was a special time and created a special bond."

The 1942 London visit also marked the beginning of another important relationship for Paley: he met General Eisenhower for the first time. Shortly after arriving in London, Paley received an invitation to lunch at Eisenhower's flat in the Dorchester. Eisenhower had just been appointed commander-in-chief of the Allied Expeditionary Force, but the meeting was nothing more than an opportunity for the two men to get acquainted. Paley was impressed, finding Eisenhower to be bright and engaging. They had another meeting before Paley left London, and, again, Paley was favorably impressed. When he arrived back in New York at the end of September, he sent the general a telegram. "The great interest and fascination I found in my trip [were] due in no small measure to your kindness and courtesies," said Paley. "It was also a great pleasure meeting you. I have felt better about our side of things ever since."

In a way, the telegram also implicitly reflected the uneasiness that Paley felt upon his return to New York. After the tension and excitement of London, it was not easy to adjust to the relative calm of 485 Madison Avenue. Paley longed to return to the action, and he was not one to wait for things to happen. "I remember him constantly talking about how he wanted to go over there," Dorothy commented. "He kept saying, 'I've got to enlist, I've got to enlist,' and I kept saying, 'What's the matter with you? Are you crazy?' "

Paley's hopes finally materialized in the summer of 1943 when Robert Sherwood, the playwright and sometime presidential adviser, arranged for Paley to join the Psychological War Branch of the Office of War Information. He was not told what his specific duties would be, except that they would somehow involve propaganda distributed to the enemy. In Paley's eyes, those were only small details that would take care of themselves later. Nor was he concerned that he would actually join as a civilian and wear the uniform of an honorary colonel. Only one thing mattered—that he was in and would soon be a part of the war effort. Within a few weeks he had made all the necessary arrangements to leave CBS. With Klauber gone, Paul Kesten was the logical choice to assume the temporary reins of power and Paley felt very comfortable with that choice.

Having settled the questions of CBS management, Paley immediately undertook the happy task of preparing for his new position—one that would eventually take him overseas. One of his first moves was to have dinner with Louis G. Cowan at the latter's Park Avenue apartment. Lou Cowan, then thirty-three, was a large friendly man who would periodically enter Bill Paley's life over the next two decades. He had been blessed with both talent and money, and in later years it would be said that Lou Cowan was born to a fortune, married a fortune, and made a fortune. Although his parents' marriage had ended in failure, Cowan grew up in Chicago under the watchful eye of a wealthy uncle. From his earliest days in grammar school he was fascinated by radio, and, looking back on his career, he would say, "I was born to be a communicator." After graduating from the University of Chicago in 1931, Cowan struggled through various jobs in the entertainment field. His real niche, however, was the creation and promotion of radio programs. He felt he knew what would work and knew how to market it. By 1940 he had established a national reputation with the broadcast of his latest venture, "Quiz Kids," a panel show that gave listeners a chance to ask bright children questions on any number of topics.

By then he had also married Polly Spiegel, a member of the family that owned the national mail-order house, and life seemed very much under control for Lou Cowan. America's entry into war changed all that. Among other things, a war machine needed a vehicle to absorb, digest, and distribute information over radio. An Office of War Information was created, and one of the first to be enlisted in its cause was Cowan. He knew how to produce and promote radio programs. He could be instrumental in shaping propaganda to be carried to the enemy. At first Cowan was stationed in Washington, D.C.; later he was sent to New York, where OWI had many of its studios.

After Paley was recruited for OWI, Cowan was designated to brief him on the organization's duties and operations. After their dinner Cowan took the CBS chairman down to OWI offices at 224 West Fifty-seventh Street and explained the operations. Paley had no background in engineering and had shown little interest in the technical side of CBS operations. But this was different. This was war, and who knew what he would need to know when he went overseas. "[H]e was greatly interested in the whole machinery there," Cowan remembered. "It was a very long evening, because he was quite meticulous and specific about wanting to see just what was going on. . . ." But Paley did not stop there. Shortly afterward he went to the OWI indoctrination school at the vast Marshall Field estate on Long Island for a week of study and exercise. By the middle of November 1943 he was ready to depart for OWI headquarters in Algiers, full of excitement and wearing a brand new dog tag made by Cartier.

Paley's arrival had already been the subject of much discussion in Algiers. The OWI Psychological War Branch overseas was a joint American–British operation, but he would report to the American co-director, C.D. Jackson. On September 12, 1943, Jackson had received a cable from an OWI officer in Washington who explained that "Bill Paley is interested in working under your direction and has good relationship with BBC. Have talked with him and think he would assist you in operating in radio situation under your direction. . . ." A tall man with blond hair and the right connections (including a degree from Princeton), Jackson had begun his climb up the corporate ladder at Time, Inc., before joining OWI. He knew Paley, and he knew that the CBS president could be invaluable. On September 14 Jackson cabled back to Washington: "Send Paley airborne."

Jackson began to have second thoughts about his cable almost as soon as he sent it. He received word of publicity in the United that suggested the CBS president would have a larger role than the one he envisioned. On October 9, Jackson sent a cable to Robert Sherwood at OWI offices in Washington asking for "advice as to exactly what you expect [Paley] to be doing. Also need confirmation," said Jackson, "[that] he will be part of PWB organization subject to our work assignment rather than free-wheeling radio hotshot, which publicity seems to indicate." On October 16, Sherwood cabled Jackson back that "Paley understands thoroughly that he will be part of and subject to the authority of PWB. Therefore, no need for you to be bothered by publicity." Jackson accepted Sherwood's assurances, but he strongly opposed OWI's proposal that Paley be allowed to bring two former CBS executives with him. "Do not believe,"

Jackson explained in his cable of October 17, "either you or PWB should lay themselves open to inevitable gossip and eventual newspaper comment that CBS is 'taking over' PWB radio here or in Italy." And so Paley was soon given orders to proceed without his assistants.

However clear these arrangements may have been in the minds of the Washington hierarchy, there was still some uncertainty in Algiers as to the precise duties Paley would assume upon his arrival. Simon Michael Bessie was among PWB's senior officers at Algiers, and he later remembered the debate. "We kept asking what Paley would do," Bessie commented, "and no one had a specific answer. Someone jokingly said that there was a shortage of office space and maybe he could help out there." It was not only the vagueness of Paley's assignment that troubled the PWB staff; they remained concerned, despite Sherwood's assurances, that Paley would not accept a subordinate position in PWB operations. After all, he had owned and operated his own radio network, now a sprawling organization, for fifteen years. It was hard for them to believe that he would readily yield to orders issued by others. But he surprised them.

In a way, the OWI assignment provided Paley relief from the daily tensions that went hand-in-hand with the responsibilities assumed by a president of a large corporation. And more than that, Paley was not the kind of person to establish authority through self-centered demands. Despite his fantastic success at CBS, his personality had changed little over the years. He remained the same unassuming person that had taken over United Independent Broadcasters, and he continued to rely on charm as a vehicle for establishing relationships. All of that became apparent after he arrived at PWB offices in Algiers. "He was wonderful to be with," Bessie recalled, "not at all stuffy or pretentious. He just wanted to be one of the boys. He disarmed you with his charm. He said that he had come to be useful and that he would do anything that was asked of him." Edward Barrett, another colleague in the Psychological War Branch, agreed with Bessie's assessment: "He was a warm, engaging guy, a little on the quiet side." But Barrett knew about Paley's inner strength. "I knew Ed Klauber," Barrett recalled, "and he told me that Paley could be a pretty tough guy even though he appeared to be soft." True to Klauber's prediction, Barrett remembered that Paley "would stick to his position whenever he made his mind up."

Paley's toughness never seemed to taint his relations with superiors. Algiers was then Eisenhower's headquarters as well, and Paley spent considerable time at the general's offices. Jackson also got on well with Paley and tried to give him an assignment equal to his talents, eventually asking the CBS president to revamp broadcast operations in Italy, which had surrendered to the Allies in September 1943. Jackson hoped that Paley would be able to develop programming that would expand the stations' audiences and make them receptive to propaganda developed through other PWB operations. To help him accomplish this goal, Paley was given orders to travel to Italy. In advising his representative in Italy of Paley's departure, Jackson said, "Of Paley's competence there can be no question, but I would like to add that he is also one of those rare individuals who doesn't have to throw his weight around to establish himself as a bigshot."

These plans became stalled when Nazi resistance in Rome precluded the Allied forces from fully occupying Italy. But that was not the only change in circumstance that affected Paley. Eisenhower had decided to move his headquarters to London where he could begin preparations for "Overlord," the operation that would begin with the D-Day landings on June 6, 1944. Paley was asked to stay in Algiers as co-director of the psychological war unit there, but he rejected the offer. Eisenhower was leaving, and with him would go the center of activity. Paley preferred a subordinate position near the hub rather than a leadership position on the periphery. And so he traveled to London in January 1944 to become chief of radio broadcasting within the Psychological War Branch of SHAEF, the Supreme Headquarters, Allied Expeditionary Forces.

For Bill Paley, going to London was, in a way, like going home. He knew the city, he knew the people, and he loved its life. He had always had a special attraction to English taste in architecture, furnishings, and clothes, and he felt very comfortable taking up residence in his new role while living at the Claridge's Hotel. To be sure, danger remained ever-present. Germany no longer relied on its air force. Instead it was blitzing London with large unmanned rockets known as the V-1 and later the V-2 (which, unlike the V-1, gave no warning buzz of its arrival). Even so, London remained an exciting place for Paley. He was involved in the most momentous decisions of the day, and it was something that caused him to feel considerable pride.

His principal activities were, as before, to develop programming that would attract listeners among Europe's peoples. There were both "white" stations—which truthfully reported information—and "black" stations— which transmitted false information to mislead the German military and political leadership. As plans for Overlord progressed, he also had responsibility for the broadcasts that would inform Europe of the Allied invasion, which required him to obtain recorded statements from the exiled leaders of the various occupied countries. It also required him to arrange for the broadcast of Eisenhower's personal statement, which had been prerecorded. As the day of reckoning approached, Bob Sherwood, then stationed in London, reviewed Eisenhower's statement and expressed his immediate concern, saying, "My God, he can't say that." The statement directed the European peoples to continue "your passive resistance, but do not needlessly endanger your lives before I give you the signal to rise and strike the enemy." Paley recognized Sherwood's concern at once. Eisenhower seemed to be suggesting that people could "needlessly" endanger their lives as soon as he gave the word. Eisenhower's staff was opposed to the general spending any more time on the matter, but Paley insisted and a new message was prerecorded.

Soon after the initial successes of the Allied invasion, Paley returned to the United States for a short visit, using the time to report to Washington and also to inquire about obtaining additional mobile loudspeaker units, which were being used to urge pockets of German soldiers to surrender. Although the matter was a trivial one relative to the invasion as a whole, he was given an appointment with General George C. Marshall, the Army's chief of staff. Marshall talked openly with Paley about the war's progress, Allied plans to invade southern France, and his assessment of enemy strength. After listening to this unexpectedly broad review of the Army's plans for the European theater, Paley was almost embarrassed by his request. But Marshall treated it seriously, and Paley had his loudspeaker units in place by the time he returned to Europe.

With the focus of war having shifted to the continent, London was now more tranquil. Although his work still required incredibly long hours, Paley also found time to enjoy the social life and his friends, including Bessie, who had been transferred to London and asked Paley to fulfill an Algiers promise of taking him to a good Jewish delicatessen. Afterward, Paley said to Bessie, "I'm going to my tailors. Why don't you come along?" They went to Kilgour, French & Stanbury on Dover Street, where Paley ordered a hand-tailored suit for the then-extravagant price of $75. Bessie could see that Paley knew quality in clothes and accepted his invitation to order one for himself.

However much he enjoyed his life in London, Paley could not stay there. He was soon transferred to Paris along with the rest of his division. As before, his responsibilities centered on developing programs that would attract listeners and enable the Allies to feed information to the local populations. The physical and emotional demands of the job were extraordinary, and he soon found himself almost literally working around the clock. In the midst of his labors he was summoned by General Robert A. McClure, director of the Psychological War Branch, who asked Paley if he would accept an appointment as his deputy to succeed Jackson, who had returned to Washington. Paley agreed to take the position. The post not only expanded his duties but also resulted in him being commissioned a full colonel in the Army.

Paley was accustomed to achievements and rewards in the broadcast business, but few gave him as much satisfaction as his promotion in the Army. It marked success in a new arena, and he derived considerable pleasure from that. Cowan met up with him in Paris and recalled having lunch with him shortly after Paley received his commission as a colonel. Paley related that he was staying at the George V hotel, which was reserved for officers with the rank of colonel and above. All in all, Cowan observed, Paley "was quite pleased that he'd made it."

Paley's principal responsibility as deputy of the Psychological War Branch was to supervise the preparation of a manual that would guide the Allies' control of all information in Germany, including radio, magazines, newspapers, and theater. It was a broad assignment, and he continued to work at a feverish pace, putting in fourteen, sometimes sixteen, hours a day. While his enthusiasm for the task knew no limits, his body did. Eventually, he fell seriously ill and was rushed to the American Hospital in Paris. At first the doctors suspected a heart attack, but after prolonged testing his condition was diagnosed as simple exhaustion. He was instructed to rest in the hospital for a week—without his customary three to four packs of cigarettes a day.

Within a short time Paley felt well enough to resume his hectic schedule. He caught up with his division, which was following in the wake of the Allies' march toward Berlin. By April Paley had been in Germany long enough to recognize that controlling information services posed problems that did not admit to quick or easy solutions. In the short run, however, he believed that the foremost consideration should be the mental state of the German audience. "There is an almost universal lack of sense of responsibility by the German individual for the policy or the actions of the Nazi government," Paley advised his superiors in a memorandum dated April 16, 1945. "There is an equally widespread lack of sense of war-guilt." In addition, Paley noted that there "is a widespread and almost incredible ignorance, and often an abject lack of interest, in world affairs, or, indeed, in anything which does not immediately affect the German personally." To deal with this mentality, Paley proposed that media reports and programs should focus "on such themes as the truth about how the war started" and "how the propaganda ministry deceived the German people." Paley also suggested that "considerable space be devoted to atrocities, but here it should be remembered that 'atrocity propaganda' will be ineffective unless the atrocities are coldly treated within a framework of convincing and authoritative facts."

Paley celebrated V-E day on May 8, 1945, with Richard Crossman, his

British counterpart, in a small hotel in Heidelberg. They had found a bottle of wine and chilled it by placing it under the running water of a faucet. The setting was far from luxurious, but the emotions were magnificent. For Paley, that bottle of wine would remain one of his more pleasurable memories.

After the surrender of Germany, the Psychological War Branch set up headquarters in Hamburg and began to implement the manual that Paley had prepared. It was an enormous operation, with the division involved in the management of all German media. But Paley knew that it was only temporary and that he would soon be returning to New York. In July Eisenhower disbanded SHAEF, a move that narrowed the scope of Paley's responsibilities: instead of working for the Allies, his obligation now ran only to the American armed forces. General Lucius Clay, who had replaced Eisenhower, invited Paley to remain on his staff, a position, he had been advised, that would result in his promotion to general. But stars of that kind no longer held any appeal for him. He had a family and a business in the States, and they now required his attention.

Paley left Germany on August 24, first flying to London and then on to New York. On the whole, his experience with the Army had been a positive one. Bessie would occasionally see Paley afterward, and, said Bessie, "when the conversation turned to that period, he always recalled that time as one of the best in his life." Still, Paley returned to New York with mixed emotions. "I came home with a disconcerting conflict of feelings experienced by many other returning men," he later observed. "The indelible impressions of the horrors of war commingled in my mind with a feeling that life had never been so exciting and immediate and never would be again."

The first priority was his relationship with Dorothy. He had sensed since the middle of the war that their marriage was probably over. The change in his feelings reflected a variety of factors, some more apparent than others. Part of it no doubt involved Dorothy herself. She had never been afraid to voice her opinions—even if Bill disagreed. And while Paley was not the kind to engage in open, heated arguments, friends noticed his growing discomfort whenever Dorothy forcefully urged her opinions on him—especially when they concerned him. "Dorothy is quite intelligent and quite intuitive," said one friend, "and had an answer for every problem. She understood him better than he understood himself—and was willing to let him know this."

One of the things Dorothy knew was that Bill's experiences in London and Paris had contributed to the distance that had grown between them. She knew, for example, that he had not been faithful. "When he got to London," she later remarked, "that was a gold mine. He hit the motherlode there. He had stature, he was a handsome American soldier, and I'm sure he had his pick."

Dorothy was not prepared to end the marriage, however, and, at first, she was not sure that Bill wanted to either. She knew that he had been under incredible physical and emotional strains and that adjustment to civilian life would not be easy. "He had always had a slight tic on his face, but now it was horrible," she remembered. "He had lots of them and was constantly twitching." To Dorothy, he seemed less than sure of himself. "Bill was in terrible shape," she continued. "He didn't know what he wanted to do. He wanted to stay married, he wanted not to be married. He wondered whether he should leave CBS, and then said he couldn't leave CBS. Finally, he just said, 'I've just got to be free, I've got to be free.' "

Still, he could not tell Dorothy that he was sure he wanted a divorce. He needed more time by himself, to consider where he was, what he wanted to do. Life seemed so unsettled. He went to Colorado Springs for a week, then on to California to spend some time with David Selznick, who was having his own marital problems. Selznick never hesitated when it came to enjoying good friends and good times, but pleasure was not Paley's only preoccupation. He knew that it was over between Dorothy and himself. There was no one else. He just wanted his freedom. So he returned to New York, told Dorothy of his decision, and moved into the St. Regis Hotel, located only blocks from CBS offices. Ironically, he spent one of his first nights of "freedom" attending a performance of *Carousel* with Irene Selznick, who had just separated from David.

His marital status was not Paley's only concern. He still owned a broadcast network, and the former Army colonel had already begun to devise strategies for a new war with NBC—one that would keep the broadcast industry in turmoil for years.

CHAPTER EIGHT

Transition

There was a time when Frank Stanton thought he might never be able even to begin his broadcasting career. He had taken his undergraduate degree at Ohio Wesleyan and had then moved on to graduate school at Ohio State in 1930. He wanted to study radio. It was a fascinating new phenomenon. And one of the great mysteries was the impact of radio on listening audiences. People seemed to enjoy what they heard, but no one knew why. The ratings services were primitive, leaving room for speculation on what audiences really thought. So Stanton proposed to undertake a project that would explore methods to measure audience reaction. The only problem was the dean of the graduate business school—he thought any study of radio was pointless. Decades later Stanton recalled the conversation with amusement: "He said, well, radio is just a passing fad. Nothing is going to come of that. Why waste your time on that, young man?" Stanton was forced to pursue his project elsewhere and finally persuaded the dean of the psychology department to accept him. And so Frank Stanton, eager for a business career in broadcasting, wound up with a doctorate in psychology.

That same persistence helped explain Stanton's rapid rise at CBS. He was a tireless worker in the fledgling research department. It was not merely the effort, however. And it was not just the intelligence he applied to any task. Stanton was a perfectionist. He wanted precision in everything—from audience measurement to program design to program balance. That dedication was greatly appreciated by Paul Kesten, his supervisor, and by 1942 Stanton was appointed a vice president. It was a turning point for Stanton, because shortly afterward Bill Paley left for Algiers, leaving Kesten to run the company.

Kesten knew he could not do everything by himself, and he leaned heavily on Stanton and Joe Ream, who by then was also a CBS vice president. The three men stepped into the breach left by Paley and tried to keep the network afloat. They worked in perfect harmony, eating lunch together almost every day, working hard, and enjoying each other's company. "We had the most wonderful time," said Ream, and Stanton agreed, saying, "Oh, it was a ball. . . . [T]hat was a really stimulating period. You had to live by your wits because you were losing people [to the draft] all the time."

They all recognized that changes would be made when Paley returned, but no one, not even Paley, could have anticipated what transpired. To begin with, Paley himself was unsure as to exactly what he wanted to do when he did return. The war had raised many questions in his mind, but one thing he knew for sure: he was not going to handle all the details of management that had crossed his desk before the war. He had never had much patience for those matters, and now he resolved to delegate them almost entirely to someone else. He would reorganize the company's structure and appoint a president to deal with day-to-day management problems. He would make himself chairman of the board and reserve his time for programming matters—the lifeblood of the network and the one area that still held great appeal for him.

There was, of course, no question about who would become the new CBS president. Paul Kesten was a kindred spirit, a man who was talented, dedicated, and, above all, loyal to Bill Paley. It was all set in Paley's mind—until Kesten explained that he couldn't take the job. It was not that he didn't want to. He just couldn't. While Paley had been fighting the enemy in Europe, Kesten had been fighting to preserve his health, and it was a losing battle. Kesten had a severe case of arthritis that had become almost unbearable by the war's end. Joe Ream could not help noticing the deterioration in Kesten's physical appearance. "He had become a pretty emaciated guy," said Ream. "I remember one time during the war we went to Chicago, and he was in real pain. You could see how bad it was. And I said you don't have to do this. But Kesten was insistent. 'I would have done it even if I had to crawl,' he said."

Kesten explained the problem when Paley asked him to become CBS president. There was just no way he could handle the physical demands of the job, he said. The war was one thing, but he could push himself only so far. All was not lost, however, because someone else could fill the job just as well. And Kesten proceeded to tell Paley about Stanton, about his intelligence, his dedication, and his stamina for work. Kesten's remarks were critical, because Paley hardly knew Stanton. They had seen each other only occasionally before the war, and Paley had never considered him for the top management position. But Paley needed someone to take over soon, and he respected Kesten's judgment. And so a meeting was arranged at a Friday afternoon reception that CBS held to welcome back its leader. Paley, dressed smartly in his Army waistcoat, casually asked Stanton whether he would be working on Saturday. For Stanton there was no such thing as a day off, and he said of course. Well, said Paley, why don't we have lunch, and he invited Stanton and his wife out to Kiluna.

Stanton rented a car and drove out to Long Island with his wife, expecting that Kesten and Ream would be there to review their stewardship of CBS in Paley's absence. But no one else from CBS was there. It was just family and friends. Stanton's moment came right after lunch while everyone was sitting around the table. "It was raining cats and dogs," he remembered, "and Bill looked out the window and said, 'Gee, I feel like a walk. Does anybody want to take a walk with me?' " Stanton took that as his cue and said, yes, he also felt like taking a walk. So the two men walked outside and sat under an umbrella by the pool and talked about their futures.

Stanton felt a certain awkwardness. He had never met with Paley alone before and had no idea what the CBS chairman wanted to discuss. Paley explained his own uncertainties and then asked Stanton to become president of the company. Stanton was taken aback. Kesten was the logical choice, and he asked Paley, Why not Paul? Paley related that Kesten felt he could not take the job for health reasons and that Kesten had recommended Frank instead. Stanton asked all the right questions. What exactly would he be doing under this new organizational structure? What would Paley be doing? Stanton did not like uncertainty, but the CBS chairman refused to be pinned down. "Indeed," said Stanton, "I was so uncertain when he made the offer to me that I said, 'Can I have some time to think about it?' And he said, 'Sure.' And we walked back to the house, and as we were going in the back door, one of these split doors, sort of a Dutch door, he reached in and opened the latch and said, 'Well, maybe you'll take care of the announcement on Monday.' And I said, 'Mr. Paley, I thought the agreement was that I could think about it until maybe next week.' 'Oh yes,' he said, and he smiled, and that was that."

On Monday morning Stanton took Kesten into the boardroom and offered to support him if he would take the presidency. For a moment Kesten's eyes sparkled, and Stanton thought he might agree. But Kesten remained adamant. He could not do it, and Stanton should take it. And so Frank Stanton, age thirty-seven, became the new CBS president.

The relationship with Paley evolved slowly, but it soon became apparent that the two men complemented each other. Stanton had the passion for detail that Paley lacked in almost everything except programming. He would review the most minute details of every management matter, and he was meticulous about everything he did, even the memos he wrote. "Stanton had the most orderly mind of anyone I've ever seen," said Richard Jencks, who rose to become CBS general counsel and then executive vice president. "He was also a lawyer's dream. He actually read memos. And his memos were a model of perfection in language and appearance. Every Stanton memo could have been displayed in a glass case in a museum."

None of this came easily to Stanton. He toiled mightly to attain perfection, spending almost every waking hour at the job and inspiring one colleague to remark that Stanton's idea of a day off was to come to the office on a Saturday in a sports coat. In the eyes of many at CBS Stanton appeared to be the exact opposite of Bill Paley—dry, humorless, unexciting, the paradigm of the worker bee. "They really were the the odd couple," said one CBS executive, who became president of CBS News and first became acquainted with both men after the war. But Stanton's devotion to CBS concealed interests that ranged far and wide—from carpentry to art to driving sports cars at breakneck speeds (one of the few traits he shared with Ed Murrow). And in those rare moments when he felt relieved of the burdens of his office, Stanton could be an engaging and entertaining companion, with an intellectual curiosity that far exceeded Paley's. "Stanton is a liberal human person and cerebral," said Dick Salant, another CBS News president who worked closely with both men. "Paley is not. Paley is visceral."

The differences in personality and outlook enabled Stanton to assume responsibility for what had become known as "the Washington beat." He happily began taking trips to the nation's capital to talk with FCC commissioners and members of Congress. Paley had little tolerance for the pettiness and incompetence that seemed so rampant among politicians. Stanton, in contrast, accepted it and was willing to take the time to manipulate it to CBS's advantage. He would literally spend days isolated in a hotel room preparing testimony so that he could master any question a congressman might throw at him.

Although he was prepared to yield the role of CBS spokesman in Washington, Paley was not ready to retreat completely from the public eye. In October 1946 he traveled to Chicago to address the 24th annual convention of the National Association of Broadcasters. It was not simply a ceremonial appearance. Paley was once again concerned that the FCC was being too aggressive in its regulation of broadcasting, and he wanted a forum in which to address the issue. After all, he had taken the lead in fighting the commission's chain broadcasting regulations, and he felt an obligation to continue in that leadership position.

The problem had arisen with the FCC's issuance of its "Blue Book"—a manual that detailed the broadcaster's programming obligations to the public. The document was a response to listener complaints that stations were broadcasting too many commercials and too few informational programs. The commission, dominated by activist Democrats, responded that it would no longer automatically renew station licenses and that it would carefully review a station's past performance to determine whether it had adequately served its community. As support for its action, the commission order had quoted statements by Paley and other industry leaders, but the flattery did little to dampen Paley's anger. He told the NAB members that the Blue Book represented "the most direct threat yet made by government to interfere with programming." Paley rejected the commission's argument—which he had heard many times before—that the stations and networks were devoting too much time to entertainment and too little time to news and other informational programming. "Let's remember," said Paley, "that we exist to serve the people. Is it conceivable, in a democracy governed by the majority will of its people, that broadcasting should not be responsive to that will—the will of the majority? To me it's as unthinkable as that the owners of American baseball should eliminate the sport of millions and substitute cricket matches or chess games! . . . Certainly I see no reason for us to be apologetic for giving the great majority of the American people what they want in the peak listening hours, and in quantities and with a quality found nowhere else in the world." At the same time, Paley conceded some validity to the FCC's criticism. There was, he said, a scarcity of good public-affairs programming, and he asked his audience whether "our real failure has been in not devoting to them the same high quality of showmanship, of good writing, of ingenuity and imagination as we devote to entertainment shows." There was, he continued, a need for "new and sparkling ideas in the presentation of educational, documentary and controversial issues. . . ."

Paley tried to meet this challenge at CBS. He continued to believe the network should devote a substantial amount of air time to controversial issues and that any discussion on those issues should be balanced. To that end he placed his faith in Helen Sioussat, who was still CBS's director of radio talks, and "he kept saying," remembered Sioussat, "that fact always had be to kept separate from opinion." Sioussat was also impressed by Paley's repeated inquiries to determine if she was satisfied with her work. "I would see him both inside and outside the office," she remembered, "and he would always ask, 'Helen, are you pleased with the way things are going? I want to make sure we're doing the best job for the country.' And one time I told him I was not happy," Sioussat continued, "and that I needed more air time. He said not to worry, that he would take care of it. And he did."

The infusion of more air time alone would not suffice to meet the challenges that Paley saw in the coverage of news and public affairs. New directions required new blood. And so Paley decided to change Ed Murrow's role by appointing him vice president for news and public affairs, a newly created position that seemed equal to Murrow's talents and stature. To be sure, Murrow's wartime success had been in front of the microphone and not behind it, but Paley felt that CBS and the country would benefit if Murrow moved from the studio to an office. "I saw in him a top executive," Paley remembered. He "had more than just good technical skill about news. I thought he had deep insight into what was happening in various parts of the world, particularly Europe . . . and that he would give us very good leadership and the kind of depth of knowledge about some of the important issues . . . that maybe very few other people would be able to produce." And more than that, Murrow was a leader, a man who had assembled and guided a pool of foreign correspondents with extraordinary talent. If he could do that under the pressures of armed combat overseas, Murrow could do at least as well under the competitive pressures of peacetime America.

More than business interests were involved, however. Paley had a special relationship with Murrow. Although the friendship had germinated outside the corporate structure, Paley hoped to keep it alive by keeping Murrow close to him inside the corporate hierarchy. At one point Paley had suggested that Murrow buy some land in Manhasset near Kiluna, but Murrow resisted. "Ed felt that he was close enough to Bill at work," Janet Murrow recalled, "and he wanted some space in the relationship, some breathing room to get away from all the problems and tensions." So the Murrows purchased a farm in upstate New York. They would occasionally visit Paley at Kiluna, and he would sometimes come to their country home, where he and Ed would hunt the pheasants Murrow raised for shooting. But the social proximity they knew in London was gone, and their social contacts were largely confined to a business setting.

Whatever the setting, Paley still had a high regard for Murrow and the correspondents who had served with him in the war. They remained a special group, being among the few CBS employees who could still address the CBS chairman as "Bill." It was not simply a matter of social relations, although Paley had developed friendships with several of the correspondents during the war. The news group in general, and the foreign correspondents in particular, had catapulted CBS over NBC to become the number one radio network in news and information. More and more, people had turned to radio to learn about the war's progress, and CBS was always there with better and better coverage. Eric Sevareid, one of the more accomplished members of Murrow's group, understood the significance of this turning point. Looking back years later, Sevareid observed that the news staff "gave CBS, as a network, its first leg up. . . . I think one reason Bill still has a soft spot in his heart for news and the news people was that. This gave him a great breakthrough."

David Schoenbrun learned to appreciate his special status as a CBS foreign correspondent when he returned to the United States in 1947 to cover proceedings at the United Nations in New York. Like many of Murrow's recruits, Schoenbrun's early career had been in education; he had accepted a teaching position in the New York City school system as a French teacher. By the time war had broken out, however, he was a reporter with the Overseas News Agency. Ironically, he eventually left that job to accept a position with the Psychological War Branch, the same office that recruited Paley, and like Paley, he wound up working for Eisenhower, first in Algiers and then on the Continent as the Allied forces moved toward Berlin. It was during his service in Algiers that Schoenbrun first met Murrow, and he was immediately impressed. "Murrow walked in, tall, elegantly groomed and darkly handsome," Schoenbrun remembered. "Eisenhower greeted him warmly and then introduced us. I had all I could do to restrain myself from gushing. Murrow was a special hero. His voice from London under the blitz had brought the war home to Americans and won much-needed sympathy for the brave British." Thus began a sporadic contact that eventually led Murrow to hire Schoenbrun as CBS's Paris correspondent. For Schoenbrun, nothing could have been better. He spoke French fluently, he loved the French people, and he felt knowledgeable about their affairs. Now all of this enthusiasm could be put to work for CBS, the premier radio news service.

Schoenbrun was still riding high when he came back to cover the 1947 U.N. proceedings, and he was surprised and delighted when he found a message in his hotel room for him to call Bill Paley. Although he had served with the Psychological War Branch in Algiers, Schoenbrun had never met the CBS chairman. He traveled over to the CBS offices at 485 Madison Avenue with some trepidation, but Paley quickly put him at ease, smiling and saying how much he respected the news department and how critical it was to CBS's future. "You know," he told Schoenbrun, "having these stations is like having a license to print money. And the news department justifies it. It's the most important part of CBS." There was something else, however. Paley went on to tell Schoenbrun that he loved Paris, that Schoenbrun was now the Paris correspondent, and that he hoped Schoenbrun would be nice to him whenever he was in town. Whatever you want, said Schoenbrun, you're the boss. But Paley didn't want to look at it that way. No, said Paley, it can't be just an employer-employee relationship. It's got to be something more than that.

Schoenbrun left Paley's office feeling very happy. This is a wonderful company, he thought. The chairman invites a lowly correspondent in, someone he's never met, to tell him how important he is and to say that they have to have a relationship that goes beyond the normal working situation. But later Schoenbrun began to have doubts about what that special relationship entailed. On one of Paley's visits to Paris, Schoenbrun arranged a party at his apartment so that the CBS chairman could mingle with the elite of French society—government leaders, writers, performers, the kind of people that Bill Paley, man of the world, bon vivant, would want to meet. Paley was indeed impressed, and midway through the party he walked up to Schoenbrun and quietly asked, How much are we paying you so that you can throw a party like this? Not enough, said an irritated Schoenbrun, and he walked away thinking that maybe things were not quite what they seemed in New York.

Howard K. Smith had a similar experience—although the ending was happier. Like Collingwood, Smith was a Rhodes Scholar. And like Collingwood, he had left Oxford University to join the United Press as a reporter when war broke out in Europe. After working for *The New York Times* briefly in Berlin, he had escaped to Switzerland, arriving on December 7, 1941, where he was told by a Swiss guard that Japan had just bombed Pearl Harbor (to which Smith replied, "Where's Pearl Harbor?"). Articulate and intelligent, Smith attracted Murrow's attention and soon joined his coterie of correspondents, reporting from London and the Continent.

When Murrow left London in 1946 to accept his vice presidency, Smith was appointed to replace him as CBS's chief foreign correspondent. But unlike Murrow, Smith did not have a special relationship with the network chairman and did not know how to deal with Paley's social demands. At first they didn't seem too intrusive. Paley had resumed his periodic trips to Europe and asked for Smith's assistance on travel arrangements whenever he went to London. But on one occasion things did not go smoothly, and Paley expressed annoyance that Smith had failed to make proper arrangements for his limousine, baggage, and hotel. Smith did not take the criticism well—he was a reporter, not a valet. "So I wrote Paley a note," Smith remembered, "telling him how annoyed *I* was, that he had people in New York to do things like that, that my job was to be a journalist, and that I had enough difficulties trying to do that job." Paley did not stand on ceremony. He wrote Smith a note of apology, and the next time he came to London he made a point of having a leisurely lunch with Smith and his wife.

Not all of CBS's correspondents fared as well. Elmer Davis was one. He had served as director of OWI during the war and, in a technical sense, had been Paley's superior. But that was all behind him, and Davis wanted to return to CBS. The problem was that Paley didn't want him back. True, Davis was a talented commentator, one of the best in the business. But those opinions. Paley did not relish the notion of resuming his arguments with Davis over fairness, balance, and the prohibition against editorializing. He did not have the heart to be candid with Davis, so when Jap Gude, Davis's agent, made inquiries with CBS, he got no response. Finally, Gude got the message and secured a position for Davis at ABC.

Paul White, director of the news department, was another victim of CBS's new look, and his departure marked the beginning of the end for Murrow's tenure as an executive. White had always had a propensity to drink, and the appointment of Murrow did not seem to help matters. It meant that his former subordinate was now his superior. White's drinking began to get out of control, and, of greater embarrassment for him and the network, there were occasions when he appeared on the air while under the influence of liquor. There was great sadness in the newsroom. White had been with CBS almost from the beginning, someone who had been instrumental in shaping the network's news policies. Now someone had to fire him, and that someone was Murrow; it was a task he did not relish. "Ed didn't like the corporate job," his wife recalled, "and the thing he hated most about it was that he had to fire people."

The tensions on Murrow increased considerably when the employee in question was William L. Shirer, the first person he had hired in Europe. Shirer was perhaps the only member of the Murrow group who could claim to have had more experience as a foreign correspondent than their leader. He was also a man of considerable ego, a quality that did not abate when his 1941 book, *Berlin Diary,* made the best-seller lists and transformed him into an instant celebrity. One product of his fame was a contract with the J.B. Williams Company (producers of shaving lotions) to do a fifteen-minute commentary for the network. It was a profitable arrangement for Shirer, and he used the time slot to analyze events of national and international importance.

Shirer's contract extended after the war ended, and one of the topics that dominated his postwar broadcasts was Truman's policy of containment. The president said that it was necessary for the United States to actively support anti-communist forces in Greece and Turkey, a position well supported among the public at large but not by Shirer. He of course opposed communism, but he had doubts about the wisdom and morality of the interventionist role proposed by Truman. Shirer made no secret of his views in his broadcasts, and in early 1947 J.B. Williams advised Shirer's agent that it was cancelling his contract.

Shirer publicly complained that he was being censored, and he expected CBS to stand behind him. After all, the executive with authority over news and public affairs was Ed Murrow, the very symbol of truth and justice. But Murrow had some doubts about Shirer's position. To begin with, he had long felt that Shirer was too arrogant—perhaps an outgrowth of his status as a reporter and writer whose work had commanded attention throughout the United States and Europe. And then there were Shirer's work habits. It seemed to Murrow, as well as to Paley, that Shirer was not doing the necessary legwork, that he was relying entirely on published information for his commentaries, that he was, in a word, lazy. Not at all the right CBS image.

Murrow discussed the matter at length with Paley, agonizing over what they could do, what they should do. Whatever their misgivings, Murrow said, Shirer was a respected journalist who had contributed much to the network. They could not simply desert him. But Paley had other ideas. He did not appreciate Shirer's public comments that he was being censored and that the network was somehow part of the conspiracy. Paley, for one, took note that Shirer's ratings had dropped and that political censorship may have had little or nothing to do with the cancellation of his contract. So Paley was not very receptive when Murrow came to him with a solution, a face-saving statement that Shirer, sensing the inevitable, had almost forced upon his former colleague. Whatever he felt toward Murrow, Paley was not about to succumb to pressure from an employee. "He wanted me to crawl," Paley said of Shirer, "and I wasn't crawling." On March 31, 1947, Shirer gave his last broadcast for CBS, with Murrow and Stanton standing in the control room to cut him off in the event he tried to use the opportunity to criticize CBS and its chairman.

Paley claims that the falling-out with Shirer was just another episode in his management of CBS and that, unlike Murrow, he did not take it personally—although one can search in vain through Paley's 1979 autobiography for any mention of the matter. Whatever Paley's true feelings, Murrow made no secret of his. He never complained, but his anguish was plain to see. Despite his hope to the contrary, Paley soon realized that Murrow was not meant to be an executive. His talents as a newsman could not be transferred to management, and Paley proposed to put Ed back where he belonged. "I suggested his going back on the air at least twice before he finally decided to do so," Paley later recalled. "Each time he said no, he was happy and wanted to stay where he was. I knew in my heart that he wasn't, but that he wanted to prove that he could stick to any assignment or any challenge that had been given to him. It was only the third time I asked him that he said, 'Well, if you order me to go back on the air, I will.' I turned to him and said, 'Okay, Ed, I order you to go back on the air.' I never saw such a wonderful smile on a man's face after I said that."

Coincidentally, Ward Wheelock of Campbell's Soup approached Frank Stanton around this time in 1947 and asked if Murrow might be interested in returning to the air with a fifteen-minute news commentary that Campbell's could sponsor. Stanton suggested that they go ask Ed directly, and Murrow could not have said yes any faster than he did. And so Murrow resumed his role as a newscaster—not as a foreign correspondent but, for the first time, as an observer of the domestic scene.

Although Murrow enjoyed the microphone more than the executive's desk, he was not entirely comfortable with his future in broadcasting. The world was changing rapidly, and one change in particular troubled him greatly: television. Whatever the value of radio in the past, television would completely alter the broadcast landscape, and, in Murrow's eyes at least, it would not be to the good. Murrow conveyed his concerns to Mike Bessie shortly after he had returned to the air. Paley had great respect for Bessie. He was an experienced journalist, a man of good judgment, and, not incidentally, someone with whom Paley felt comfortable. So Paley wanted Bessie on the CBS team. More specifically, he wanted Bessie to run the news department. Paley figured that he had no better salesman than Ed Murrow, and he asked Murrow to have lunch with Bessie and persuade him to accept the offer. Murrow, always a man with his own opinions, did the exact opposite. He told Bessie not to take the job. "Do you have any idea what's going on in broadcasting?" Murrow asked the former OWI officer. Bessie confessed that he didn't. Murrow gave him the one-word answer: "Television." Murrow explained that it would cause profound changes in the broadcast industry. News would be eclipsed by entertainment. And more than that, it would become a "big-money world" where concern for current events would be dwarfed by an obsession with the latest ratings.

Bessie was taken aback by Murrow's lecture. This was not what he had expected when the lunch had been scheduled. But Bessie was not only concerned for himself, and he put it to Murrow: "Does Bill know about this?" Murrow replied that he certainly did. In fact, said Murrow, Paley was then in the process of negotiating a $20 million loan from the Equitable Assurance Society so that CBS would have the resources to move into television.

Bessie took Murrow's words to heart and rejected Paley's offer. He did not advise the CBS chairman about Murrow's concerns, however. Not that it would have mattered. Because television was a necessity if CBS wanted to survive.

Paley had been thinking about television's introduction for many years. The network had been operating two experimental stations since 1931, and Paley himself would marvel as he drove through Manhattan and noticed the increase in television antennas on apartment buildings. In 1939 NBC and then CBS introduced commercial television service, but the quantity and quality of programs were extremely limited. Even this limited service was suspended with the outbreak of war. The FCC reasoned that the country's radio facilities should be devoted to aid the war effort and that the development of new technologies should await the war's end.

Although service was suspended during the war, Paley spent much of his time while in Africa and Europe trying to devise a strategy for CBS in the postwar years. At one point he wrote a letter to Kesten to describe his thinking. He began the letter by saying he was riding in the command car, and afterward Kesten and Stanton, who also reviewed it, would continually refer to the document as the "command car letter." The letter recited Paley's belief that there would have to be a drastic change in the development of programs if CBS was ever to overtake NBC in the entertainment field. Until then, the advertisers had controlled much of the creative process. The advertiser would decide what programs it would sponsor and would then supervise all aspects of their production, from music to performers to settings. The networks, in a very real sense, did little more than to provide the transmission facilities. Paley knew that much of that would have to change with television. The cost of production would escalate manyfold and be prohibitive for most advertisers. To Paley, the solution seemed obvious. Instead of selling an entire program to a single advertiser, the network would produce the program and sell the advertiser a minute or more of air time.

It was not simply a question of finances, however. For CBS, another factor was of equal, if not greater, importance. The "bottom line" of Paley's command car letter, said Stanton, was that CBS will "never be strong vis-à-vis NBC until we own and produce our own programs. As long as the advertiser controls the program, the advertiser is free to move it from one network to another. . . . The way that Bill saw that we could pull ourselves into a stronger position was by having our own schedule and controlling it, and saying to the advertiser, you want to advertise on this particular program, then you come to CBS."

There were of course risks in this approach. It was, to begin with, a sharp break from tradition, and advertisers might not be quick to relinquish control. In the meantime, CBS might be forced to spend millions of dollars on programs without any assurance of finding a sponsor to absorb those costs. These concerns were debated by Kesten and Stanton in Paley's absence, and, by the time Paley returned, Kesten gave him a long letter proposing a completely different approach than the one Paley had in mind. Instead of trying to appeal to the entire population, CBS should produce high-quality programs that would be directed to the intellectual elite of society, programs that would be more stimulating and thought-provoking than anything that would be tolerated by the broad masses. However much he respected Kesten's judgment on other matters, Paley had no hesitation in rejecting the proposal. Radio was, after all, a mass medium, and that, in Paley's eyes, required CBS to cater to the masses and not just the elite. Ego was also involved. Paley wanted to be number one, and he was not about to concede victory to NBC and move into a different arena. He would take NBC on in its own terms—and he was determined to win.

With a strategy in place, Paley moved forward. The key, of course, would be the programming itself. "That word, 'programming,' " Paley would say, "has a sort of cold, mechanical sound. But it gets down to a certain gut instinct about what people will respond to, a kind of mystical connection between the broadcaster and his audience. If he has that instinct and can establish that connection, he can build an audience." Understandably, Paley could not define good programming for his staff. He would have to be satisfied imparting general principles and hoping that his staff could produce programs that would make that "mystical connection" with the audience.

The vice president for programming in 1945 was Douglas Coulter, and one of his better decisions was to hire Ernie Martin to produce programs in Hollywood. Martin, then in his mid-twenties, was a self-described "country boy" from California who knew little about the intricacies of corporate hierarchy or finance, but he had that special feel, that creative spark, to know what would work with mass audiences. And Paley gave him the freedom to apply that creative genius. "I had about one million dollars in budget—and that was a lot of money then—with no strings and no specific directions," Martin recalled. "And that was the great thing about Paley. He left you alone. He had a hands-off policy. No one ever dictated to me what I should produce. If it was good, he would write me a note and say how much he liked it."

Martin used his freedom to develop the mystery series "Suspense," the comedy series "My Friend Irma," another comedy series called "Duffy's Tavern," and many other popular programs, most of which ultimately secured commercial sponsorship. He did not develop these programs in complete isolation from CBS headquarters in New York, however. Every month he would go to the Lockheed Air Terminal in Los Angeles and board a triple-tailed Constellation for the flight to New York, where he would attend meetings of the CBS Program Board. The board consisted of Paley, Martin, Coulter (and later his replacement, Davidson Taylor), Murrow, and the vice president for sales. Paley always led the discussions. "He was," Martin remembered, "calm, inquisitive, deliberate. He listened, he was animated, and he was always interested in the programs. Because he knew that was how CBS would succeed."

Success was not Paley's only criterion, however. He wanted to be proud of CBS's programming, and he was not afraid to turn down programs that might be offensive. One incident in particular stood out in Martin's memory. "I remember one time," said Martin, "we were considering a program in which the lead character was a black cook. And we had a long discussion about the ethics of that—whether it would be a slur against blacks. And we decided not to air the program—although NBC later took it. But that was like Paley," Martin added. "An enormous interest in taste."

When it came to programming matters, Paley also had a great deal of patience, much more so than for other matters. To many of the staff it seemed that there was no limit to his tolerance as long as programming was involved. At one Program Board meeting, for example, someone reported a complaint from an advertising agency that the network had been double-billing the time sold on Martin's mystery program, "Suspense." Paley immediately summoned Isaac Becker, the staff person who directed business affairs for programs. When Becker got to the meeting, Paley quietly asked, "Zack, how much are we making on 'Suspense'? " Becker knew the chairman was a bottom-line man, and he thought he gave the right answer: "Enough." Paley was not satisfied. "No, really, Zack," he persisted, "how much are we making?" Becker continued on the same tack, saying, "Really, we're doing okay." After a few more exchanges Stanton stepped in and said, "Zack, that's not good enough. You're going to have to give us some specific numbers." With those numbers, it turned out that the agency had been charged too much, and Paley ordered that an immediate credit be given. But for Martin, Paley's manner in handling Becker overshadowed the substance of the problem they were discussing. "That was typical of Paley in those days," he said. "Very tolerant."

For his part, Paley very much appreciated Martin's talents and dedication. He had the instinct to know what would work and what wouldn't, a skill that was all the more remarkable given Martin's youth. Paley did not let that prevent him from relying on Martin's judgment. He had been young too, and he remembered all too well the disbelief that one so young could lead a radio network and make a success of it. So one day in late 1947 Paley telephoned Martin and asked him to take the next plane to New York. He had a critical matter to discuss with him.

When Martin arrived at CBS headquarters, Paley explained that Davidson Taylor was changing jobs to take over Murrow's position, that the company would need a new vice president for programming, and that Paley wanted Martin's recommendations. Martin had the candor of youth, and he blurted out, "What about me?" Paley said, no, he knew Martin could handle the job, but the board would never accept it. Martin, so naive in the world of corporate decision-making, was baffled. "What's a board?" he asked Paley. The chairman laughed and carefully explained the power of the board of directors. Of course, since Paley controlled the board, it was unlikely that its members would reject any strong recommendation from the chairman. More likely Paley was concerned about appearances in the entertainment world, where a few gray hairs might inspire more respect.

Having been removed from consideration, Martin had no trouble suggesting a candidate to handle programming: Hubbell Robinson, who supervised program affairs at the Young & Rubicam advertising agency. In Martin's view, Robinson had the experience and the personality to succeed. Paley accepted his suggestion, scheduled a luncheon the next day with Robinson, Martin, Stanton, and himself, and within weeks, Robinson became the new vice president for programming. He, in turn, brought along his deputy at Young & Rubicam, Harry Ackerman, and the two men began a concerted drive to improve the quality of CBS programming.

As always, Paley remained the center of activity. He would guide the Program Board discussions, raise questions with Robinson, Ackerman, and other staff members, and carefully review the proposals they made. "He is the greatest question-asker I have ever heard in my life," said Robinson. "He can cut right through. He pushes and pushes and pushes. . . . You could never hide things from him. It didn't make any difference. If he wanted to find something out, he did. Just pry and pry and pry." But for all the questions, Paley did not interfere with his programming staff. "His greatest achievement," said Ackerman, "was to let the programmers alone. If they didn't perform, he fired them. But I have no memory of his dictating or masterminding programs."

Paley knew, however, that programmers alone could not develop programs that would enable CBS to surpass NBC. Stars, celebrities—they were the stuff of which good ratings were made. Unfortunately, most of the stars were with NBC, and there seemed to be little hope of persuading them to switch networks—until one day in the summer of 1948 Paley received a proposal from Lew Wasserman and Taft Schreiber, the president and executive vice president of the Music Corporation of America, the world's largest talent agency. They wanted to know if CBS would be interested in buying the "Amos 'n' Andy" show, which had been running on NBC radio for nineteen years and had consistently remained one of that network's most popular shows. The proposal revolved around money. Under the then-current tax laws, taxpayers had to give the government 77 percent of all income over $70,000. For entertainers and other high earners, the law was completely offensive, since it meant that most of their labors were for the benefit of the government rather than for themselves. Some clever schemes had been devised to avoid this result, and one of them required performers to organize themselves into corporations whose earnings could be taxed as capital gains at the much lower rate of 25 percent.

Paley would have taken "Amos 'n' Andy" under almost any scheme. He had known Freeman Gosden (Amos) and Charles Correll (Andy) for many years, and he had repeatedly tried to persuade them—without success—to come to CBS. In the early 1930s he had walked into Gosden and Correll's office, introduced himself, and made his first proposal. "I don't know what you're getting at NBC," said the young CBS president, "but I think you've got a terrific future. Whatever you're getting here, I'll just give you twice as much." The startled performers replied that they were very flattered by Paley's offer, that they would have liked to accept, but that they had just signed a long-term contract with NBC. Paley had never given up hope, and now there was no contract with NBC to stand in the way. In September 1948 CBS announced, to the industry's surprise, that "Amos 'n' Andy" was moving over to CBS.

The acquisition coincided with Paley's changing notions about the CBS program schedule. Until then, the conventional wisdom, initiated and preserved by NBC, dictated that each evening's fare should be a balance of different programs—comedy, drama, suspense, musicals. Now Paley proposed to deviate from that practice. He would use "Amos 'n' Andy" to build Friday nights into an evening of all comedy.

Paley's plans received a boost when Wasserman telephoned to ask whether CBS might be interested in buying Jack Benny's program. There was no question as to what Paley wanted to do. Benny had been the king of radio for sixteen years, the mainstay of NBC's domination of the ratings. As always, the only issue was money. Benny had organized his activities into a corporation called Amusement Enterprises, Inc. Like other stars, he was tired of working for the government, and he was willing to put his corporation on the bidding block. Wasserman and Paley negotiated a price and finally reached a tentative agreement for CBS to buy Amusement Enterprises for $2.26 million. And then Wasserman called to say that the deal was off, that NBC had gotten wind of the CBS negotiations and had dispatched its president, Niles Trammel, to California with orders to reach an agreement to keep Benny at NBC.

Paley was crushed. He knew that NBC could have known about the negotiations only through Wasserman, a disclosure that Paley considered to be a breach of good faith on Wasserman's part. But principle was the least of it. Paley wanted Benny, and Bill Paley was used to getting what he wanted. Something had to be done. And then it hit him. He had been dealing with Wasserman. He had never talked with Benny himself. Personal contact. Charm. That was the way to put the deal back together.

So he put in the call to Benny and was told that Benny was having dinner at George Burns's house. Paley reached him there. He explained his great interest in bringing Benny into the CBS family. Benny was encouraging, telling Paley that he should come out to Los Angeles and adding, much to Paley's excitement, that other NBC comedians might follow Benny's lead. "I can bring the boys," said Benny.

Paley grabbed CBS's outside counsel, Ralph Colin, and flew to California immediately, setting up house at the Beverly Hills Hotel. Ironically, David Sarnoff was in the same hotel with his outside counsel, John T. Cahill. And both network chiefs were in pursuit of the same goal: Jack Benny. Sarnoff, now chairman of the giant RCA corporation, had more money at his disposal, but Paley had something more powerful—a willingness to spend it.

Although fierce competitors in the same field, Sarnoff and Paley were extremely different in lifestyle and outlook. Sarnoff was an austere man in appearance and personality. Balding and very overweight, he cut the image of a corporate chieftain, with his three-piece suits and the gold chain across his vest. He earned a handsome income but did not live lavishly. He favored the more traditional values where money was spent on necessities and otherwise saved for later years. At the same time, he seemed to be insecure with this posture and would frequently (and indiscreetly) complain to people that Bill Paley had made so many millions more than he had even though he was not nearly as important. The RCA chief similarly deplored the extravagant excesses of the Hollywood movie colony, with its wild parties, its ostentatious homes, and its glittering lifestyles. He recognized of course that entertainers were essential to NBC's survival, but he had no interest in socializing with them, no matter who they were. In all his years at NBC, for example, Jack Benny had never met Sarnoff.

Not surprisingly, Sarnoff placed restrictions on how much he would spend to recruit or retain performers for his network. Benny wanted millions for his show, and Sarnoff wasn't willing to give it to him. Sarnoff himself didn't make that kind of money and, as one NBC vice president observed, he was not about to give exorbitant sums to someone like Benny, who, for all his success, was "just" an entertainer. There was also the legal side to the whole transaction. "Sarnoff was a man of strict propriety," said Mike Dann, an NBC executive who talked with Sarnoff at the Beverly Hills Hotel, "and Cahill told him—incorrectly as it later turned out—that the IRS would rule against the deal being proposed by MCA." When all was said and done, Sarnoff put his faith in NBC's technical facilities. The programs, he felt, would take care of themselves. It was an understandable but fatal mistake in judgment.

Paley soon found out, however, that it was not enough to convince Jack Benny. His sponsor, the American Tobacco Company, also had to be persuaded, because they had a contract with Benny that gave them the right to choose the network on which he appeared (the very kind of contract that Paley wanted to eliminate). After reaching agreement with Benny, Paley rushed back to New York to seal the deal—only to discover that no one would listen to him. To the people at American Tobacco and their advertising agency, Batten, Barton, Durstine & Osborn, it was ludicrous to think that Benny should move from NBC to CBS. After all, NBC had the more powerful and more attractive stations under its wing, and hadn't Sarnoff demonstrated that quality signals were the key to big audiences? It was a stonewall that Paley could not breach—until he made a stunning proposal. At a meeting with representatives from American Tobacco and BBD&O, Paley said CBS would compensate the sponsor for every ratings point that Benny might lose while at CBS. Vincent Riggio, by then president of American Tobacco, concluded the meeting quickly after the offer was made, saying, "The matter's settled."

In November 1948 it was announced that Benny would move to CBS. Industry observers later speculated that he had switched networks because Sarnoff had personally snubbed him, or because Sarnoff's lawyer, John Cahill, had, in his earlier career as a government lawyer, prosecuted Benny on a minor indiscretion (failing to pay a duty on imported jewelry). In truth, money was the only real consideration. "Jack left NBC because Paley offered him more money," said George Burns, Benny's colleague and close friend. "It was as simple as that. Even if Sarnoff had called him, it wouldn't have made any difference—unless Sarnoff offered him more money."

True to his word, Benny also brought along almost all of the NBC comedians, including George Burns and Gracie Allen, Red Skelton, and Edgar Bergen. It became commonplace to hear a comedian on NBC one week and the next week on CBS. NBC's vulnerability became a standing joke. In closing his January 23, 1949, show on NBC, Fred Allen told his audience, "I'll be back next week, same time, same network. No other comedian can make that claim."

In contrast to Sarnoff, Paley was not only willing to spend money to recruit stars; he was also willing, indeed eager, to spend time with them, to hear their complaints, to share their frustrations, to enjoy their company. In his view, the performer was the center of the broadcasting universe, the key to building an audience and keeping it. "Paley was by all odds the best executive in show business," said Ackerman, who could look back on more than thirty years of experience. "He cherished his relationships with show business people. And he was always ready to listen to those of us in programming, always indulgent of our needs and opinions."

Paley did not confine his programming inquiries to Manhattan. Every six months or so he would travel to California to review progress on new CBS programs being developed there and meet with the network's more important stars. Ackerman would brief Paley on the more pressing problems. Paley would then visit with the performers, using his charm to let them know that the people at the top cared. But it was not all business. Many of the performers were entertaining in private, and on that score, few gave Paley more pleasure than George Burns.

On radio Burns played the straight man to Gracie Allen's bizarre character, and audiences had little exposure to his talents as a comedian. In Hollywood, however, his skills were widely known and admired. Benny himself regarded Burns as the country's greatest comedian, and after spending time with him, Paley agreed. On his trips to Los Angeles he would usually make it a point to have dinner with Jack Benny and his wife Mary Livingstone and Burns and Allen. (Burns could not help but notice that Mary always seemed to have her eye on the debonair CBS chairman.) Their dinners were always full of jokes and laughter, and no one enjoyed a good time more than Bill Paley. Harry Ackerman would sometimes accompany Paley, and one night at Romanoff's remained particularly clear in his memory. "George had Paley laughing so hard he couldn't breathe," said Ackerman. "Finally, he stood up, gasping for air, and had to go to the men's room to regain his composure." For his part, George Burns enjoyed the CBS chairman's company as well. He and Gracie would often visit the Paley apartment in New York (sometimes with Jack and Mary) to play pool. "I would see him at parties, too," Burns recalled. "And every time he saw me at a party he would ask me to sing. And I did. Because I like to sing."

The fun was a bonus for Paley's efforts to recruit NBC's stars. But the real dividend was in the ratings. By 1949 CBS had twelve of the top fifteen radio shows, and the industry generally agreed that the "Paley raids" of 1948 were a turning point in CBS's fortunes.

Paley himself saw the raids as having a significance beyond the 1949 broadcast season. At one point during the turmoil, Jack Gould, the media reporter for *The New York Times,* had called Paley at his vacation retreat in Jamaica to ask whether the raids were, as NBC claimed, a vehicle to perpetuate a tax-avoidance scheme. Paley exploded, saying that his only goal was to improve CBS's long-term ratings position. Years later, he still adhered to that view, claiming that the raids on NBC had given CBS the strength and confidence to compete in television. "At that time," he observed, "I was not only thinking of radio, where I wanted to bolster our standing and please our audience; I knew that television was right around the corner. I wanted people who I thought would be able to transfer from radio to television. That gave us a very good start in television and a big advantage, indeed."

However great his faith in the performer, Paley recognized that the introduction of television required decisions, fundamental decisions, on the kind of technology CBS would pursue. The company would have to decide whether it wanted UHF or VHF stations, black-and-white or color transmissions. Paley made no claim to understand the technical aspects of these matters. Engineering details made him feel awkward, uncomfortable. It was a world alien to his real interests. Others at CBS sensed Paley's fear of technology, and a standing joke at the company had it that any new invention would break as soon as it was placed in his hands. But Paley, to his credit, did not pretend to be something he wasn't. He would not try to impose his technical opinions, such as they were, on the network. He would rely instead on CBS engineers and technical craftsman, and of those, no one inspired more respect from Paley—or more disdain—than Peter Goldmark.

Goldmark was a scientist of uncommon brilliance and exuberance, an inventor full of ideas and enthusiasm—and questionable business judgment. Born in Budapest in 1906, he had received his education at some of the finest institutes in Europe. In the early 1930s he decided to study television, a technology that had actually been inaugurated with the discovery of the cathode-ray tube in 1897 and largely ignored since then. The opportunities for research were limited in Eastern Europe, so Goldmark booked passage for New York, arriving in September 1933. Through a friend he met CBS's premier political commentator at the time, Hans V. Kaltenborn, and by 1936 Goldmark was settled into 485 Madison Avenue, working under the direction of Paul Kesten.

Kesten told Goldmark that Paley was interested in pursuing television, but the Hungarian scientist could see little evidence of that himself. Paley's office was on a different floor, and he remained largely unseen by the research staff. No matter. Goldmark had his own lab and the support of one of Paley's chief lieutenants. It was enough to keep him happy and optimistic. And then in 1940 Goldmark saw the movie *Gone With the Wind*—in color. Something clicked. Then and there he decided that he would develop color television for CBS.

Goldmark had great faith in himself, and it was rewarded at the end of the year. At an industry meeting to discuss standards for black-and-white television, Goldmark stood up to announce that CBS was prepared to deliver color. Shock and disbelief filled the room, but Goldmark made good on his word. A demonstration was held before the FCC, and in the summer of 1941 the commission authorized CBS to move forward with the development of color television. CBS, the junior network in technology, was about to beat NBC at its own game—until Germany and Japan decided that American broadcasting would have to give priority to other matters. The FCC suspended its authorization of color television for the duration of the war, but CBS did not remain inactive. Goldmark was recruited for a special wartime project at Harvard University, but he spent at least one day a week at the network. By the time the war ended, he was full of new ideas and enthusiasm for the establishment of a color television system.

Upon his return Goldmark told Kesten that the future lay in UHF stations. Although UHF stations (channels 14 through 83) were not nearly as powerful as VHF (channels 2 through 13), they were more plentiful and seemed to possess the technical characteristics compatible with the technology that Goldmark had in mind. Kesten was swept up by Goldmark's euphoria and involved Stanton in the discussions. It all seemed so clear. CBS, the stepchild to NBC in technology, would still be able to be the pioneer in the most advanced system in the newest medium of broadcasting.

Goldmark's proposal was not without risk—in fact, serious risk. By 1945 the FCC had already authorized the establishment of black-and-white television systems, and many manufacturers—RCA being among the largest—had already begun to sell their black-and-white sets to the public. Moreover, these black-and-white systems were for use on VHF stations, not UHF. Consequently, Goldmark's grand scheme ran counter to existing realities in the worlds of business and politics. But Goldmark was now on a roll, with Paley's two senior aides behind him. The only remaining question was the CBS chairman. No decision on a matter of this magnitude could be made without him.

In the winter of 1945 Kesten, Stanton, and Goldmark met with Paley to determine whether CBS would take the chance of becoming the pioneer of color television or play it safe with black-and-white VHF stations. It was the first time that Goldmark had spent any time with the CBS chairman, and the meeting left an indelible impression on him. "Paley struck me as extraordinarily handsome," said Goldmark; "boyish in face and manner, he sported a suntan even though it was winter. From that time on I don't think I ever saw Paley without a suntan, which may account for the nickname he got around CBS of Pale Billy."

Paley, of course, recognized the risks inherent in Goldmark's proposal. The FCC was then issuing licenses for VHF television stations, and CBS, which already had one in New York (WCBW, which would become WCBS-TV), was entitled to four more in major markets. If Paley endorsed

Goldmark's plan, CBS would, as a practical matter, have to abandon its opportunity to acquire more VHF stations and throw its hat in the UHF ring. And since RCA and other manufacturers were already selling their black-and-white systems for VHF reception, CBS might find itself in the position of having UHF television stations that no one could watch.

According to Goldmark, Paley listened intently to his presentation and expressed enthusiasm for the project. Paley himself disagrees, saying that he felt obligated to accept his staff's recommendation. It all came down, he claims, to a question of supporting subordinates. Effective delegation of authority required confidence in those assigned the work. And so, says Paley, "I could not see my way clear to countermanding Kesten and Stanton. It would be in effect a vote of no confidence in them and in all their work during the years of my being away in the war. As an article of faith, I had to go along with them."

With this rationalization, he was later able to absolve himself of responsibility for the disastrous consequences that followed. In September 1946, CBS asked the FCC for authority to develop a color television system on UHF stations. As a show of support for its own proposal, CBS refused to apply for the valuable VHF stations that the FCC had made available. After all, CBS could not be taken seriously if it endorsed UHF with one hand and accepted VHF stations with the other. However consistent this approach, it doomed the network to failure. RCA and other television set manufacturers—with millions of dollars already invested—pressured the commission to reject the CBS proposal. The FCC eventually bowed to the pressure, and the suspension order was issued in March 1947. For the moment, at least, CBS's bold adventure appeared to be dead.

All was not lost, however. Goldmark's enthusiasm remained undiminished, and Paley, for all his disappointment, allowed him to continue his pursuit of color television. No doubt Paley's support reflected an acknowledgment that, for all his mistakes, Goldmark was capable of significant achievements. And few gave Paley more satisfaction than the development of the long-playing 33⅓ record album.

RCA owned the Victor Phonograph Company (which Arthur Judson had tried to acquire at one point shortly after forming UIB) and was generally recognized as the leader in record technology and marketing. Although it could not match RCA's resources or experience, CBS had entered the record marketplace in 1938 with the acquisition of the American Record Corporation, whose primary asset was the Columbia Phonograph System—one of the early investors in United Independent Broadcasting and the source of CBS's name. Sentiment had had nothing to do with the purchase, however. Paley was convinced that records would become vastly popular (a judgment that time proved absolutely correct).

After losing $73,000 in its first year of operation, the company, renamed Columbia Records, began to generate profits that seemed to escalate every year.

Everyone in those early years relied on records that spun at 78 revolutions per minute—a speed that made the records large, bulky, and scratchy. Goldmark, ever on the lookout for scientific progress, created a new system where the record would proceed at the much slower speed of 33⅓ rpms, with much less bulk and higher quality sound. Given RCA's domination of the industry, CBS's achievement seemed especially remarkable, and Paley meant to take advantage of it.

Although their personalities and lifestyles were polar opposites, Paley could never disregard the presence of David Sarnoff. His stature in the industry exceeded Paley's—a distinction that enabled Sarnoff to secure an appointment as a brigadier general during the war even though Paley, who never rose above the rank of colonel, served longer. And it had to rankle that forever thereafter the RCA chairman was referred to as "General" Sarnoff. Bill Paley wanted to be recognized as number one, and such nomenclature made the task that much more challenging.

Goldmark's discovery of the 33⅓ LP gave Paley a chance to cast doubt on the General's status as the premier broadcaster. On the one hand, Paley had to feel somewhat tentative about his judgment in a technical matter like records, especially given the debacle at the FCC over color television; on the other hand, he was shrewd enough to know that Sarnoff would not take CBS's accomplishment lightly. The General prided himself on his technical expertise and was not shy in claiming to be superior to the CBS chairman in such matters. He would not be happy to learn that CBS had discovered a more efficient, higher quality record than the one produced by his own company.

Paley decided to exploit his advantage to the fullest. He invited Sarnoff to come to CBS for a preview of Goldmark's invention, and, while Sarnoff and his entourage of engineers listened, Goldmark demonstrated the superior qualities of his LP. Sarnoff was visibly shocked but remained sufficiently in control of his emotions to be gracious, telling Paley, "I want to congratulate you and your people, Bill. It is very good." Paley was gracious in response, offering Sarnoff the opportunity to produce the new LP as a joint RCA–CBS venture. Sarnoff said he would think about it, but Paley knew that pride would win out over practicality, and a short time later Sarnoff telephoned to say that RCA would go its own way. For Paley, it was a tacit admission that he, not Sarnoff, had paved the way to new accomplishments in the record business.

The CBS LP was marketed in June 1948. By the end of the year Paley had Benny and other NBC stars in the CBS fold. Sarnoff could no longer claim to be the industry leader on all fronts. And Paley was not about to concede victory in color television either. The battle would have to be renewed at the FCC, with Paley more determined than ever to prevail. Only this time he would not be alone. He would be entering the fray with a new partner.

CHAPTER NINE

Babe

For all their collaboration on the production of radio programs, Ernie Martin knew that he and Bill Paley lived in different worlds. Martin had grown up in the less populated areas of California, where social distinctions were not very visible and where people made few demands on life. Martin carried that perspective with him to Hollywood, and, while he worked for a national radio network in the exciting arena of entertainment, Martin retained his "down home" approach to life, an outlook in which social stature and sophistication were commodities of little consequence. After a few visits to CBS headquarters in New York, however, he could see that his chairman's social environment was not at all the same. And nothing made that more clear than the women Martin would occasionally bump into as they exited Paley's large office. Their dress, their bearing, their beauty. It was a new experience for Martin. "They were really high society women," he later remarked, "and I had never seen women like that before."

For Paley, it was not at all new, but it remained exciting. His separation from Dorothy had given him the freedom he wanted, and he enjoyed his single status, as he did most things, with unbounded enthusiasm. New York had come alive in the immediate postwar years with new night clubs, new plays, new restaurants, and Paley meant to take advantage of them all. But he was not a person who enjoyed solitude, and he intended to experience these opportunities in the company of beautiful women. There was little problem filling that need. He was handsome, charming, and the chairman of a prominent radio network—a combination that few women could resist.

Helen Sioussat would occasionally see her boss after hours, and she would sometimes act as an intermediary, introducing Paley to women who wanted to meet him and vice versa. One woman who longed to meet Paley at the time was Kitty Carlisle, the beautiful actress and singer who later acquired national fame as a panel member on the television show "What's My Line?" Carlisle made her desire known to Sioussat, and one evening Helen persuaded Paley to stop off at a party where she knew Carlisle would be waiting. But Paley had little interest and the relationship was not pursued. Judy Holliday was another story. Paley very much wanted to meet the well-known actress, who happened to be a friend of Sioussat's. So one evening Paley accompanied Sioussat backstage after a performance of the Broadway play *Bells Are Ringing,* in which Holliday had a leading role. "Paley really fell for her," Sioussat remembered. But Holliday did not make the introduction easy for Helen. "I said, 'Judy, I'd like you to meet Bill Paley, who's the chairman of CBS.' " Holliday, who had never seen Paley before, gave a look of disbelief, convinced that her friend was playing games. "Sure he is," responded Holliday, "and I'm the Queen of May."

None of Paley's relationships evolved into anything serious—until he met Barbara Cushing, the youngest of Dr. Harvey Cushing's five children and known as "Babe" to friends and family. Everything about Babe seemed so perfect. She was uncommonly beautiful, with auburn hair and sparkling brown eyes. She looked like the kind of picturesque woman whose photographs graced the pages of magazines such as *Vogue* (where Babe was then working as an editor). But Babe's real appeal lay in her manner. Because her beauty was so arresting, people expected her to be cold and aloof. But the opposite was the case. Babe possessed a warmth that seemed genuine. Her smile was quick, her desire to please evident. She seemed to care deeply about people and would, with softness and subtlety, engage companions in animated conversation on almost any topic.

This charm was not entirely happenstance. From early childhood Babe had been raised to be sophisticated and attractive. It was, after all, the Cushing way. Her father had grown up in an affluent home in Cleveland. From the start he did well in school, eventually earning an undergraduate degree from Yale and a medical degree from Harvard. In 1901 he joined the teaching staff at the Johns Hopkins University Hospital in Baltimore and quickly established a national reputation in brain surgery, a field where patient deaths were common and pioneers desperately needed. "By devoting his life to neurological surgery and its problems," concluded Cushing's biographer, "he made operations on the brain of little more hazard than those involving the abdomen, and this of itself has assured him a place for all time among the great contributors to the science of medicine."

Cushing's interests, however, ranged far beyond the practice of medicine. He had a love for books. He read them, talked about them, collected them, and finally wrote one—a two-volume biography of a well-known medical colleague—that earned him a Pulitzer Prize. Cushing also liked to draw, and he spent much of his free time making sketches of anything and everything, from people to flowers to scenery.

Harvey Cushing was also a man of iron discipline. He practiced in a field where death was the usual outcome, survival an unexpected blessing. It was not the domain of the fainthearted, and Cushing learned to keep a tight rein on his emotions. There was the time in 1924 when he learned that his eldest child, twenty-two-year old Bill, had been killed in an automobile accident. Cushing walked into his study to be by himself for a few moments and then went to the hospital to proceed with a delicate operation on a woman who had been victimized by sudden blindness. He was so immune from emotional distraction that he could also operate on his own family members, and on one occasion he performed a procedure on fifteen-year-old Babe to remove a growth on her neck near her jugular vein.

Cushing tried to impose discipline on his children as well, but his other interests left him little time for the task. As a result, most of the children's education was supervised by their mother. Katharine Crowell had been Harvey's childhood sweetheart in Cleveland and had qualities that mirrored her husband's. As one of the Cushings' friends explained, "Kate helped Harvey . . . by being just as decided as he was. . . . I suppose it *was* a fault that he was so absorbed by his work, that although he loved his children he had little time to take responsibility for them, and I believe he leaned on Kate far more than she did on him." Kate Cushing took her duty to heart and tried to impress upon the children, especially the three girls, that they were Cushings, that they had a certain stature in the world, and that they should pursue education and personal relationships with an eye toward preserving their social status. "Babe's mother was a woman of great social organization," said one of Babe's later acquaintances. "She wanted to make sure her daughters married well, that they knew how to find the right man and take care of him." Another friend agreed, saying of Babe, "There was a driving ambition there and a mother who taught her what to say, how to do these things, and how to run a house."

For all this instruction, Babe remained unpretentious and down-to-earth. Even as a teenager she had a special quality that made her unique. Marietta Tree, whose grandfather was Groton founder Endicott Peabody, remembered meeting Babe at social affairs at Groton, a prep school located about forty miles northwest of Boston, where the Cushings had moved in 1912 after Harvey accepted a teaching appointment at Harvard Medical School. "Babe was, by far, the most glamorous girl in the group," Tree recalled. "Everyone was in love with her. She was so beautiful, so sexy. And there was such a soothing manner about her. I was a little younger and was usually very nervous at these affairs. Babe was very sensitive to these anxieties and would be very comforting."

None of this meant that Babe was indifferent to her social status. In 1930, when she was only fifteen, her older sister Betsey married James Roosevelt, the son of New York's Democratic governor. The Cushings were conservative Republicans and could not have been entirely pleased with the choice. But at least the Roosevelts were aristocrats, of that there was no doubt. Babe's other sister, Minnie, wound up marrying Vincent Astor, scion of the wealthy New York family and someone else who carried the right social credentials. Babe was not about to depart from tradition, and shortly after her father's death in 1939 she married Stanley Mortimer, Jr., a wealthy New York investment banker with an "appropriate" background. Babe and Stanley had two children, Stanley III (whom everyone called Tony) and Amanda. But the marriage did more for Babe than expand her family. It also brought her to New York in the early 1940s and gave her the social recognition that Mrs. Cushing always wanted for her daughter. Babe met all the right people and quickly made a reputation as a woman of beauty and taste (being added to the list of the nation's best-dressed women and heading the list in 1945). But all the parental hopes and plans in the world could not guarantee a good marriage. By 1946 Babe was divorced and living with her widowed mother on East Eighty-sixth Street in Manhattan.

She met Bill Paley at a small dinner party, and their attraction to each other was immediate. Babe had everything the CBS chairman could want in a wife: beauty, intelligence, and social stature. All that was important to Paley. He always wanted the best of everything, and Babe was clearly in a league by herself. "Paley knew what was a hit," one of his CBS colleagues later commented. "He didn't pick the programs. He picked the stars. He didn't make Jack Benny a star, but he knew he was one. He didn't make Babe Cushing the best of the beautiful women, but he knew she was." More than that, Babe had the kind of social credentials that he lacked. The Cushing name carried weight in Republican WASP circles— the kind of people who did not easily accept Jews whose lineage could be traced back to Eastern Europe. Paley wanted that acceptance, however. The war had given him a new sense of his own stature, and he now wanted a social recognition equal to that stature.

He and Babe began to date regularly, but the foundation for their relationship solidified when Babe became hospitalized a short time later with phlebitis. Bill visited her every evening, and each night was made special by the dinner he brought with him. Every day he would go to one of his favorite restaurants (of which there were many) and carefully select a dinner he could carry to her in the hospital. She, too, appreciated good food, and the dinners in her hospital room gave them uninterrupted time to learn about each other. Shortly after she left the hospital, Babe and Bill decided to get married.

There was one impediment. Paley was still married to Dorothy. A settlement was quickly arranged for a reported $1.5 million, and Dorothy went to Lake Tahoe, Nevada, with Jeffrey and Hilary for the necessary six-week stay and a final divorce. (Ironically, Marietta Tree was also staying at Lake Tahoe with her daughter Frances for the purpose of getting a divorce from her husband, Desmond Fitzgerald, and Tree remembered that she and Dorothy and their children had "a very pleasant six weeks together.") Paley's divorce became final in the early summer of 1947, and on July 28 of that year he and Babe were married at her mother's summer home on Long Island. It was a small gathering with only the immediate family and a few friends (including Ed Murrow). The couple then left for Manhattan and a boat trip to Europe aboard the *Queen Elizabeth*.

Although Paley did not want his personal life publicized, his marriage to Babe Cushing attracted widespread media attention, including a major article in *Life* magazine. The text of the article was not entirely flattering. "Last week," it began, "as William Paley, the millionaire president of the Columbia Broadcasting Company, sailed for a wedding trip to Europe with his bride, a new chapter was added to the fabulous story of a fabulous family of sisters." The article then recounted the various marriages of the three Cushing sisters to some of the country's most affluent men, noting that Betsey had divorced James Roosevelt and in 1942 married John Hay Whitney, "a socialite, horseman and heir to more than $27 million." The story also mentioned Minnie's marriage to Vincent Astor, who, it was said, "has just as much money to spend on yachts as Whitney has to spend on horses." In concluding, the article observed that "the three daughters of Harvey Cushing are married to a total fortune of $125 million" and that "the only dull period for the sisters in the last 17 years occurred in 1940 when for a period of fully five months between divorces and weddings none of them had a husband." To give readers the full flavor of the sisters' success, there were photographs of their several husbands, including a large one of Paley and Babe as they set sail on the *Queen Elizabeth*.

Bill and Babe spent almost two months in Europe, traveling to Paris, the French Riviera, Monte Carlo (where Paley enjoyed some success at the baccarat table), Switzerland, and Italy. But the sweetness of the journey was soured by the *Life* article, which had been sent to them while they were abroad. Paley was appalled, and he vented his anger and frustration on C.D. Jackson, his wartime colleague at the Office of War Information, who had returned to an executive position at Time, Inc., publisher of *Life*. On their return trip on the *Queen Elizabeth*, Paley wrote a letter to

Jackson, thanking him for his letter of congratulations and for making a
Time car available for Paley's use in Paris. But the real point of the letter
was to complain about the *Life* article. "Really, C.D.," Paley lamented,
"how could Time have stooped to such a low order of journalism? It took
a decent and useful family and deliberately insulted and belittled it.
. . ." Paley had complained about *Time*'s coverage of him in the past, "but
I want you to know that my resentment then was of no account compared
to what it is now." The letter closed with a warning to Jackson: "Prepare
for more when I see you."

Jackson was disturbed by Paley's letter and immediately directed his
staff to review past *Time* articles and comments on Paley. Contrary to the
CBS chairman's impression, the results showed that *Time*'s coverage had
been generally complimentary, calling Paley at various points "experienced
and earnest," "earnest, boy-like," and "smart." Jackson saw Paley in the
fall of 1947 and made amends anyway, later writing Paley a letter saying
that he "was delighted that the Paley/Jackson misunderstanding is completely cleared up." Jackson playfully added that the letter should be
considered "a formal declaration of love, in which I will be delighted to
have you include your wife, unless you think that is inadvisable."

In the meantime, the newlyweds had begun to set up house. Although
they maintained an apartment at the St. Regis Hotel in Manhattan, they
spent most of their time at Kiluna. Paley continued to have considerable
affection for his Long Island estate, and for Babe it was a delight to be
in the country where she could pursue her interests in gardening and, like
her father, in sketching. Babe also wanted to have more children—as did
Bill—and they were soon blessed with a son, whom they named William
Cushing Paley, whom everyone called Billy, and a daughter whom they
named Kate, after Babe's mother. Babe's children from her first marriage
also lived with them at Kiluna. Jeffrey and Hilary stayed with their
mother but would make periodic visits to the Long Island estate. So the
Paley household now included four children at all times and six on special
occasions.

Bill of course loved the children, but it was not the kind of relationship
where the kids would scramble all over their father in the rough-and-
tumble atmosphere found in some families. Bill Paley was too aloof to
engage in that kind of play. "The words were warm in the family," said
one visitor to Kiluna, "but there was no touching, no spontaneity." It was
not only a reflection of Paley's personality, but an indication of his priorities. He did not want the children underfoot all the time, and there were
always plenty of butlers and servants to make sure they did not interfere
with the efficiency that Paley preferred in the management of his household. And more than that, he did not want the children's presence to

disrupt his social life, which continued to be of substantial importance to him.

As expected, Babe's presence at Kiluna expanded Paley's circle of social acquaintances, and on that score none proved more significant than his relationship with his new brother-in-law, John Hay Whitney, whom everyone called Jock. Although the two men were contemporaries (Jock being only three years younger than Bill), and though they had much in common, Jock Whitney came from a world that was light years from Sam Paley's cigar factories.

The Whitneys could trace their lineage back to the early days of America, and Jock's grandfather, John Hay, had gained fame as Abraham Lincoln's secretary and later as President William McKinley's secretary of state. The Whitneys were also among the most affluent families in the country. Jock's father, Payne Whitney, left an estate of $179 million upon his death in 1927. Indeed, looking back upon a long life at the age of seventy-five, Jock Whitney would say that there was no material thing that he had ever craved that he could not have because of the price.

Still, Jock Whitney did not settle for a life of inactivity. His wealth represented opportunity, and he meant to take advantage of it. After graduating from Yale in 1926, he pursued a broad array of interests that brought him into contact with some of the country's more enterprising talents. Among them was David Selznick, who was trying to become an independent Hollywood producer in the mid-1930s. Jock had met David on his travels to the West Coast, and, like Paley, had become enamored of Selznick's creative mind, boundless energy, and sense of fun. By 1935, Whitney was chairman of the board of Selznick International, a position and investment that brought Whitney prestige and profits when *Gone With the Wind* premiered in 1940. Whitney spent much of his free time playing polo, raising and racing thoroughbred horses, and developing the Museum of Modern Art in New York.

Despite his wealth and business success, Whitney, like Paley, remained somewhat shy and often had difficulty dealing directly with conflicts, whether at home or in business—perhaps a reflection of a childhood where he was overweight, awkward, and prone to stutter. No matter. Jock Whitney developed the same kind of zest for life that distinguished Paley, and, as a young man, women were attracted by his charm (and in some cases, no doubt, his wealth as well). In 1942, after divorcing his first wife, he had married Babe's older sister, Betsey, and life would have continued in the style to which Jock Whitney was accustomed if it had not been for the war. He had the money and clout to avoid the draft, but Jock Whitney had a high sense of duty. He enlisted in the Army and soon afterward went overseas as a captain.

Unlike Paley, Whitney became involved in combat and was taken prisoner in 1944. Not one to place his fate in the hands of others, he made a dramatic escape, finding refuge in a home in the French countryside. He eventually returned to the United States and resumed the many activities that had occupied him before the war.

Whitney and Paley knew each other only casually at that point. Their paths had crossed on a number of occasions in both New York and Hollywood. They were also neighbors on Long Island. Greentree, the Whitney estate in Manhasset, was located next to Kiluna. The two men did not socialize, however. In fact, a large fence separated the two properties, and each pursued life independently of the other. Bill's marriage to Babe changed everything. The fence came down and a connecting road between the main houses was constructed (which the two men decided to name Baragwanath Boulevard in honor of John Baragwanath, a mining engineer who had been a frequent guest at both homes). The Paleys and Whitneys now saw each other regularly. They would have dinner together, relax around each other's pools, and go boating on Whitney's yacht in Long Island Sound. Bill and Jock would play tennis on occasion, but their real love was golf. They would play almost every chance they got, and for Paley, it became a passion. Jock shared Paley's love for the game and, like his new friend, pursued it with enthusiasm, devoting considerable time to the pursuit of the right set of clubs. "Every couple of weeks he'd get a new set and then have a pro come and give him a special lesson with them," Paley remembered. "I once wandered into a back storage room at Greentree where Jock kept just some of his golf clubs and saw twenty-five or thirty sets."

Very little of Paley's contact with Whitney involved business, but they did share one memorable trip together to Camden, New Jersey, on Whitney's private plane. As the two men were driving to the Camden airport for the return trip to Newark, Whitney casually said to Paley, "You know, my pilot's my valet, too." "You mean you took your pilot and made him a valet?" asked an incredulous Paley. "Oh no," said Jock. "I made my valet a pilot." The conversation must have remained fresh in Paley's mind as they flew back, because the pilot soon became lost in the foggy weather. When Paley awakened from a short nap, he saw the pilot with his head out one window and Jock with his head out the other, both searching for evidence of Newark airport. Finally the pilot cried, "I see it! I see it!" They landed and a thankful Paley soon emerged from the plane—only to discover that they had landed at Floyd Bennett Field on Long Island.

Babe was pleased by the strong friendship that developed between Bill and Jock. She had an unshakeable belief in family unity—another product of her mother's teachings—and the relationship made it that much easier to remain close to Betsey. That proximity was important to Babe, because sometimes she needed someone to talk to when her marriage encountered difficulties.

Babe wanted the marriage to succeed and tried to accommodate her husband's needs and wishes. One of the first rules concerned Paley's work. He did not bring his work home with him, and he made it clear from the beginning that his home life was to be kept separate from business. Babe respected that separation, and no one, not even children and other family members, were allowed to question Bill Paley about CBS's radio or television programs—unless he sought their opinion on a particular matter, which happened only rarely.

Another issue concerned Babe's appearance at home. She had come to Bill Paley as a person of taste, a beautiful woman who had consistently ranked among the nation's best-dressed women. Babe learned that her husband always wanted her to look the part. They had separate bedrooms at Kiluna, and one of the advantages, for Babe at least, was that she could use the privacy to make sure that she had the right makeup on at all times so that Bill would never be disappointed by what he saw.

Babe also catered to her husband's interest in food. They discussed the day's menu at home and experimented with new restaurants when they went out. Paley's passion for food remained undiminished, and he welcomed the opportunity to share his interest with Babe. She, in turn, made sure the Kiluna kitchen was well stocked for almost any kind of meal at any hour. Paley also maintained a kitchen off of his bedroom, and one of his many pleasures was to be able to fix a late-night snack, and of those, scrambled eggs and knockwurst were favorites. Friends continued to be amazed at the quantities of food he could consume and still stay in shape. Marietta Tree remembered the time she and her husband vacationed with the Paleys in Barbados. "Even with three square meals a day," said Tree, "Bill would always be dodging into the kitchen to get a banana or a sandwich—and trying to do it in a way to avoid detection."

Babe would usually travel with Bill on business trips, and even then food remained a top priority. Restaurants were reviewed and plans were scheduled to fulfill that need. Harry Ackerman quickly became acquainted with their culinary interests when Paley came to California to review CBS's new programs. "I often picked them up at the Los Angeles airport in a limousine," Ackerman commented, "and we always went immediately to the Beachcombers restaurant—even before we went to the hotel. They had really developed a taste for the Polynesian food served at the Beachcombers, and that was more important than getting unpacked."

In all of this Babe seemed ever the congenial companion, sensitive to her husband's wants and reluctant to impose on him her own preferences. Friends took note that the relationship provided a striking contrast to Bill's first marriage. "The two Mrs. Paleys couldn't have been more different," observed Irene Selznick, who became close to both of them. But however accommodating on the surface, Babe Paley had her frustrations, and she would frequently take them to Betsey, and many times there were tears. Bill was strict with her about the money she could spend, the people she could hire to help her run Kiluna, even the magazines she could order (one of Paley's objections being that some were received at the office). And then there were the other women. "Bill was very flirtatious," said one friend, "and Babe worked hard at keeping a good relationship." But her hard work was not always rewarded, and Babe began to sense that her husband was not always faithful. She had married him despite some reservations from her family. He was, after all, not the kind of aristocrat that the Cushings had had in mind for their daughters. Now Babe began to have reservations of her own, sometimes feeling that she had been charmed into marriage only to become one of Bill Paley's acquisitions.

It was not a good feeling, and in her frustration Babe turned to someone who was willing to listen, who would understand, and who, most especially, would keep her confidences: Truman Capote. He was, by any account, a most unusual confidant. Small, cherublike, with a high-pitched voice and darting eyes, Capote seemed out of place in the Paleys' world of high fashion and café society. But through literary achievement and personality, he was able to ingratiate himself with almost everyone of importance in the worlds of publishing, entertainment, and politics.

Capote's beginnings were as distinct as his personality. He had been born on September 30, 1924, in rural Alabama and christened Truman Streckfus Persons. His mother was only sixteen at the time, having married a traveling salesman who did not have any interest in changing his habits, and by the time Truman was four his parents were divorced. It was not a good development for Truman. His mother was too young and restless to be tied down with a child, and Truman grew up with four relatives—three elderly ladies and an elderly uncle—in rural Alabama. "By and large," Capote later reminisced, "my childhood was spent in parts of the country and among people unprovided with any semblance of a cultural attitude."

Capote's escape route was his intelligence. A team of psychologists working with the Works Progress Administration came to Monroeville, Alabama, to perform intelligence tests and were reportedly overwhelmed by young Capote's scores. They sent him to Columbia University for further testing, and in later years Capote would boast that he had had the highest IQ of any child in the United States. Capote had begun to write even then, and he quickly discovered he had a natural talent for the written word. By his early teens he was producing articles and trying to write books, sometimes finding newspapers or magazines that would publish his work.

By 1939 his mother had moved to New York and married a Cuban businessman named Joseph Garcia Capote, who adopted Nina Persons's fifteen-year-old son. Truman completed his high school education at various boarding schools and Greenwich High School, finally landing a job at *The New Yorker* in 1941. By 1943 he had won the coveted O. Henry Memorial Award for one of his short stories, and by 1948 he had received national attention with the publication of his novel, *Other Voices, Other Rooms* (with the back-cover photograph of Capote lying suggestively on a divan). Other short stories, novels, plays, and screenplays followed, with his career reaching its zenith with the publication of *Breakfast at Tiffany's* in 1958 and *In Cold Blood* in 1965.

By then Capote had earned a reputation as a "madcap social butterfly" who seemed to know every celebrity's sexual habits and inner secrets. Amidst all this knowledge of others, there remained a certain confusion in public over Capote's own background. He told different stories to different people, and it was often difficult to say where the truth lay. This uncertainty was perhaps captured best when David Frost interviewed him on television. Frost began to ask Capote whether he had been, as claimed, a tap dancer on a Mississippi riverboat at the age of fifteen, a speechwriter for a Southern politician, and an artist who could paint imaginary flowers on glass. The ensuing dialogue was pure Capote:

FROST: You wanted to be a tap dancer? [Laughter]

CAPOTE: Oh, that's just something I put in *Who's Who.*

FROST: It's not true?

CAPOTE: No. You know, they just send you these forms to fill out, what you wanted to do or be in *Who's Who in America,* and I just sent them back a sort of joke thing. I said that I painted on glass and wrote political speeches and wanted to be a tap dancer, but it was none of it true.

FROST: Well, how do we know that the other story you just told us is true?

CAPOTE: Maybe it isn't. [Laughter, applause]

Later in the same interview Capote told Frost, "I don't care what anybody says about me as long as it isn't true."

Despite the mystery of his own background, Capote seemed to have a fix on others'. He was knowledgeable, perceptive, and, most of all, entertaining. One of those who succumbed to his charms was David Selznick. Capote and Selznick saw each other frequently, and on one occasion Selznick invited Truman to join him on a trip to the Caribbean. It would be enjoyable for Selznick, and it would give Capote an opportunity to meet the other friends who would be traveling with them—Bill and Babe Paley. When the Paleys arrived at the airport and saw Capote, Bill decided at once that he did not look like the kind of person he wanted to be seen with, and he mentioned his objection to Selznick. But David held firm, saying, I'm paying for his ticket and he's coming with us. Besides, Selznick no doubt knew that Paley's concerns would fade after he spent some time with the writer. And they did. By the end of the trip Paley agreed that Truman Capote was indeed a delightful companion.

The Paleys saw Capote frequently after that. He would visit them at their homes, drop in on Bill at his office, and sometimes meet Babe alone as well. And in those visits with Babe, Capote learned of the frustrations she sometimes experienced in her marriage, the feeling that Bill did not really care, that she could easily be replaced. Capote advised Babe to hold on, to master her frustrations by thinking of it as a job, the position of being Mrs. William S. Paley. People could do far worse.

Babe did hold on, working to keep the relationship alive. For his part, Bill spoke of Babe in glowing terms, taking her on business trips, summer vacations in Europe, winter ones in the Caribbean, and giving no hint of any rift in their marriage. But whatever he may have felt in his heart, Bill Paley was not the kind of person to speak freely to others about such private matters. He had learned the dangers of that long ago, and he saw no reason to change his ways now. He of course knew that Babe had developed an independent relationship with Capote but Paley saw no harm in that. He was all for new relationships. In fact, while Babe was developing one with Capote, Paley was pursuing his own independent relationship with a person of even greater prominence.

General Dwight Eisenhower returned from the war a national hero, and Paley, for one, felt that the honor was well deserved. Although he was not in a position to critique the general's overall military leadership, Paley had seen Eisenhower at close quarters in Algiers, London, and on the Continent, and Paley was very much impressed with what he had seen. Eisenhower knew how to handle people and how to provide direction. They were qualities that Bill Paley appreciated, and he had fond memories of his time with Eisenhower in Europe (as well as the parties he sometimes arranged for him).

Paley could also see that Eisenhower's involvement with CBS could enhance the company's prestige (and also help the financially strapped general). So, a few days before his marriage to Babe, Paley wrote "General Ike" to inquire whether he would be interested in becoming a member of the CBS board of directors. Eisenhower was inclined to reject the offer, but he wrote Paley that he would at least like the opportunity to discuss it with him after the CBS chairman returned from his "personal" trip abroad for two months. (Paley did not feel comfortable enough with Eisenhower at that point to tell him that the "personal event" which would lead to a two-month absence was his marriage.) The two men did meet periodically over the next year to talk about Eisenhower's future, his possible role at CBS, and other ventures they could pursue together. By September 1948—after Eisenhower had passed over opportunities to run for president on either the Democratic or Republican tickets (no one being quite sure—or caring—what Eisenhower's true political inclinations were)—Paley offered the general an opportunity to do a regular series on CBS. "I want you to know," Paley told Ike, "that I have a sponsor who would be willing to pay a substantial sum of money for the privilege of sponsoring a series of talks by you." Paley urged Eisenhower to accept the offer, saying, "I feel strongly that you should have a regular platform for the discussion of some of the serious issues confronting the country and for the expression of definite ideas on these issues whenever you feel you want to express them."

Eisenhower was not about to be rushed into anything at that point, especially something as commercial as a sponsored program. He and Paley did keep up their correspondence and meetings, however, and Eisenhower began to ask for Paley's assistance with educational programs in which Eisenhower had become involved as president of Columbia University. Sometimes the favors involved use of CBS personnel, and on other occasions Paley donated funds through the William S. Paley Foundation, an organization he had established as a conduit to support charities and other non-profit projects.

His friendship with Eisenhower grew closer, each man now on a first name basis with the other. Eisenhower had come to respect Paley's talents and dedication, and by 1950 he had another proposal for the CBS chairman: an opportunity to become a trustee at Columbia. Paley was excited by the prospect, but Eisenhower said it would take some time, since he wanted Paley to replace an existing trustee who was on the verge of death. In February of that year Eisenhower sent Paley a handwritten note saying he had not forgotten the offer "but the former Trustee involved is so old and ill that we are proceeding as delicately as possible."

Within a short time the appointment was made, and for Paley it was very much appreciated. It gave him the kind of public recognition he desired and to which he thought he was entitled. But more than that, it gave him an opportunity to become involved in an activity outside of CBS. That was of no small importance, because Paley was still suffering from his postwar restlessness. There were, to be sure, major challenges confronting CBS in 1950—the most significant being the growth of television. But Paley wanted something else, something that would present a new challenge. He did not know what it would be, and he could not know that, when it finally arrived, it would take him away from New York.

CHAPTER TEN

Washington

I n 1971, Peter Goldmark, age sixty-five, was obligated to retire under CBS policy. Shortly before his departure, Goldmark was ushered in to see the CBS chairman, age seventy, to bid adieu. Much had passed between them in the preceding twenty-five years, and not all of it had been good. For his part, Goldmark felt that his skills and accomplishments had not been properly appreciated by the company. Bill Paley felt differently. Paley repeatedly told associates that, for all his intelligence and creativity, Goldmark's principal contribution to CBS had been heartache and financial loss, that they all should have known better than to give the Hungarian scientist so much leeway to experiment, that he was a dangerous man with an idea and a budget. Company officials quickly picked up on the chairman's feelings, and many would joke that Paley needed a vice president in charge of Peter.

Still, Paley was not prone to voice his true sentiments when Peter came by to say so long. Bill Paley could be charming when he chose, and he put his arm around Peter, saying that they had been through a lot together and that he would be missed at the company. Goldmark was past the point of succumbing to nostalgia, and the chairman's kind words did little to ease the bitter feelings he held inside. Peter Goldmark left CBS a proud but disappointed man, and few episodes had produced as much despair as CBS's failure to launch color television in the 1950s.

The issue had seemed to be resolved when the FCC ruled in March 1947 that CBS's color scheme for UHF television was imaginative but premature. Goldmark himself was prepared to accept that judgment until 1949, when Paley passed the word to Adrian Murphy, Goldmark's supervisor, that Goldmark's research labs were to be closed down—immediately. The instinct for survival took over. "The next few days and nights I prowled the laboratory like a caged animal," Goldmark remembered. "At night, before I fell restlessly asleep, I tore through the paraphernalia of my brain, seeking to press it for ideas that I could build confidence in, enough confidence to sell others and to save the laboratory from extinction." And then Goldmark struck pay dirt—or at least so he thought: color for VHF television. He had been experimenting with some innovative techniques on a small scale, and Goldmark felt sure they could be adapted for public use. And, since millions of American families now owned television sets that received VHF channels, the FCC could hardly claim that the proposal was premature.

Goldmark pleaded with Murphy, and Paley in turn was persuaded to give the CBS scientist one more chance. The chairman was not disappointed—at least initially. The FCC set up a demonstration for CBS's color system in January 1950, and, impressed by the results, the commission immediately inaugurated another proceeding to explore the merits of the issue.

RCA was not about to accept a CBS technological victory quietly. The giant corporation had been working hard to develop its own color system, and, according to RCA at least, its system had the edge over CBS's in at least one critical area—the RCA color system was an electronic one that was compatible with the millions of television sets then in use; the CBS system was a mechanical one that could be adapted to existing black-and-white sets only with the use of a converter, a piece of equipment that Goldmark "hoped" could be sold for as "little" as $100—a considerable sum in those days. RCA applied the full force of its power on the issue, with Sarnoff himself appearing at the FCC hearings in the spring of 1950 to explain the merits of his company's proposal as well as the defects of his competitor's proposal. "CBS has asked the commission to adopt a system which would saddle an all-electronic art with a mechanical harness," Sarnoff told the commissioners. "You are being urged by CBS to build a highway to accommodate the horse and buggy when already the self-propelled vehicle is in existence and has been demonstrated."

Sarnoff's argument had more than logic behind it. He also had the support of television manufacturers and distributors who had invested millions of dollars in the hopes of marketing black-and-white sets that utilized the electronic system. Their position was echoed in most of the trade publications as well. "The owner of *Television Digest* was very much slanted in favor of RCA," remembered Al Warren, one of its reporters at the time, "and every week the *Digest*'s stories would convey that slant. And whenever I brought copies of the *Digest* to the commission, Goldmark would invariably comment on the arrival of *'Television Indigestion'* and its wrenching stories."

For all its significance, the color-television war was conducted largely without the public presence of the CBS chairman. Paley had now settled into his backseat role, and Frank Stanton was asked to assume the burden as CBS's public spokesman. Stanton performed well, studying the issues intently and providing the kind of firm statements that were to become his trademark. But for all his skill, Stanton had to admit that it was "desirable" to have a color system compatible with existing black-and-white sets and that his company's system did "not fully satisfy this feature." In his own testimony, Goldmark said it was "extremely doubtful" that the compatible RCA system could ever be made practical.

Goldmark's observation gained credibility when the FCC conducted a demonstration of the available color systems in September 1950. CBS had cause for hope, because in a preliminary demonstration the RCA color broadcast had not performed well. The pictures of a bowl of fruit included green cherries and blue bananas. The defects were also apparent during the commission's demonstration, and the end result was captured best by the headline in the next day's *Variety:* "RCA Lays Colored Egg." In contrast, the CBS system, for all its incompatibility, was sharp, clear, and the colors true. It may have been a "horse-and-buggy" operation, as Sarnoff said, but at least it worked.

The FCC issued its decision approving the CBS system in October 1950, and Paley, for one, was both pleased and surprised to be on the verge of again surpassing the great David Sarnoff in a matter of technology. The euphoria was short-lived, however. Sarnoff refused to accept the decision, and he pursued every avenue of relief. He received some immediate, and unexpected, assistance from the United States government, which was then supporting a "police action" in Korea and concluded that cobalt and other significant resources could not be used in the manufacture of CBS's color television sets because they were needed to support the manufacture of military hardware. In the meantime, RCA filed a lawsuit challenging the FCC's decision, and by early 1951 the matter was being heard by the United States Supreme Court. At one point, Paley, Stanton, and Goldmark were seated in the pew right behind Sarnoff and his entourage, waiting for the justices to make their appearance. Before they entered the courtroom, Sarnoff turned to Paley and said, "Bill, we could have avoided this headache if I had hired Peter in the first place." By the time the issue was resolved, Paley probably wished he had.

The Court issued its decision on May 28, 1951, saying that the FCC had both the authority and the evidence to approve the CBS system. It was a Pyrrhic victory. Too much time had gone by, and too many black-and-white sets, which were incompatible with the CBS color system, had been sold. Moreover, CBS had no capability to manufacture its own television sets. RCA and its corporate allies made good use of the hiatus. They perfected their own compatible color system, and by the time the Korean War was drawing to a close, RCA was before the FCC again, urging that CBS's authority be rescinded and that the color system developed through the National Television System Committee be approved. By this time technology and logic were on the same side, and even CBS could see that there was no hope of preserving its license. Paley was very bitter about the reversal, a bitterness that was not relieved when RCA later decided to pay CBS a royalty to use a patent that Goldmark had secured for an advanced color tube. Bill Paley liked to win, and payments of royalties could not disguise the bottom-line conclusion: CBS had lost the color-television war.

CBS's defeat at RCA's hands was not the only frustration Paley had with the government process. By the time the FCC reversed its decision in 1953, the CBS chairman was experiencing a far more personal disappointment with the government, and one, ironically, that had its first roots in the battle over color television.

Shortly after the FCC announced its decision to approve the CBS color system in October 1950, Paley received an invitation for him and Babe to attend a party in November at Ed and Janet Murrow's farm in Pawling, New York. Paley always enjoyed weekends with the Murrows, but the strain of the FCC battle had taken its toll. "The going really has been rough," he wrote Ed, and he felt the best cure would be a vacation. He and Babe had already planned to be at the Pink Beaches resort in Bermuda on the date of the Murrows' party. So he would have to defer his visit to Pawling until later. Paley added that they didn't have to do any pheasant "shooting" to make it enjoyable.

The Bermuda resort was elegant, the weather perfect. But Paley's mind was not entirely free of worry. Having won at the FCC (however temporarily), his mind was now focused on a completely different venture, one that involved service in the federal government. The inquiry had come from Stuart Symington, a Manhasset neighbor and sometime golf partner, who was then chairman of the National Security Resources Board, an agency in the Executive Office of the president that supervised the preservation and use of resources for defense purposes. Symington, tall and urbane, had talked with President Harry S. Truman about the need for an updated study of the nation's natural resources, especially those needed for defense purposes. His experience on the National Security Resources Board had convinced Symington that the country could face shortages in a number of critical areas in the near future, and he felt there was a need to develop a better understanding of what those shortages might be and how they could be avoided. Truman agreed with the proposal. He also accepted Symington's recommendation of the person to head that long-range study: William S. Paley.

Symington mentioned the idea to Paley in the early fall of 1950. The CBS chairman could not have been less interested. Not only was he then embroiled in the color-television war with RCA; of equal, if not greater, significance, he knew nothing about natural resources and how they could be preserved. But Symington pressed him, telling Paley that his lack of knowledge was an advantage, not a defect—he would come to the issue with an open mind, using his obvious talents as an executive to marshal the facts and make sound proposals. Although Paley continued to resist, Symington could see a glimmer of hope, and he pressed on, urging Paley to give the matter serious consideration.

Paley was starting to weaken, and he raised the matter with Chester Bowles in Bermuda. Bowles had just been defeated in his bid for re-election as Connecticut's governor, and, like many defeated politicians in the Northeast, he had gone to the British colony to recover from the trauma of the campaign. In Paley's mind, Bowles was certainly an appropriate person to consult on the Symington proposal. The two men knew each other well, Bowles having founded a research marketing firm in the 1930s that had pioneered many techniques later used by CBS. He also had another important credential: he had been the director of the Office of Price Administration during World War II, a job that required him to supervise the activities of almost every major industry in the country. Because of that experience, Paley no doubt believed that Bowles would have some worthwhile advice on the nature and scope of the problems Paley would face as the chairman of a commission designed to study resource management.

Bowles said he would be happy to offer advice, but the person Paley really needed to talk with was Phil Coombs, an Amherst College economics professor who had served with Bowles at OPA and later as his economic adviser in the governor's office. Coombs, said Bowles, was the one who understood the dynamics of American industry. He would be able to provide the kind of advice Paley needed. And, as luck would have it, Coombs—equally tired from having worked on Bowles's recent campaign—would be his way to Bermuda the next day.

Coombs, a young man of medium height with curly hair, was flattered by Bowles's recommendation and said, why of course, he would be happy to meet with the chairman of CBS. So, Coombs and his wife, Helen, met Bill and Babe Paley for dinner that night at the Pink Beaches resort. A man of modest means, Coombs had some trepidation about meeting the millionaire broadcaster and his high-society wife. But Bill and Babe quickly put the Coombses at ease. "He was charming and affable and unpretentious," Coombs remembered. "He seemed to be a very unassuming guy and made both of us feel very comfortable." While Babe and Helen listened intently, Paley peppered Coombs with questions about Symington's proposal, focusing on the personal and political risks he might face.

The first problem, said Coombs, was the status of the commission itself. Symington had suggested that the study be conducted under the auspices of the board which he then headed, but Coombs thought Paley would be well advised not to take the job under those circumstances. "Who knew where Symington would be in the next year or even in the next few months," Coombs recalled saying. "And besides, for all his good qualities, Symington did not have the kind of prestige that the president had. So I recommended that Paley accept the position only if it were elevated to being a presidential commission that would report directly to Truman. If Paley was going to put all that effort into the study, he should at least have some real stature as well as a chance of the report being implemented." And, finally, said Coombs, Paley should not believe, as Symington had suggested, that the study could be completed within six months. That was a pipe dream. "Any job of that magnitude," said Coombs, "would require at least a year."

Paley listened intently but left dinner without indicating what he would do. It was all so new, so different. He needed more time to make up his mind. He consulted with other friends as well, but Symington knew that Paley needed a push in the right direction, and, on that score, few steps could be as persuasive as a visit to the White House. At 12:30 in the afternoon of December 13, 1950, Symington and Interior Secretary Oscar Chapman—who also had a vital interest in the project—took Paley to the Oval Office to see Truman, who apparently tried to impress upon the CBS chairman the importance of the mission. Symington also took Paley to visit with Senator Lyndon B. Johnson, a rising star in Congress and, not incidentally, someone who knew Bill Paley. Johnson had a small radio station in Austin, Texas, and he saw great benefit in an affiliation with CBS. Paley and Stanton were always eager for new affiliates, and when the lanky Texan came to CBS's New York offices in the late 1930s, Paley and Stanton were eager to accommodate him. Johnson was then a congressman, reported to be a favorite of President Roosevelt's, and who knew when CBS might need some additional political support. Johnson got his affiliation, and CBS developed an ally in Washington. Symington, of course, knew this history and no doubt hoped that Paley would listen closely if Johnson agreed, as he did, that Paley should accept Symington's offer.

By the end of December 1950, Symington's manipulation had born fruit. Paley agreed to accept the assignment—but only on the condition that it be, as Coombs had recommended, a presidential commission. On December 27 Symington wrote to Truman, endorsing Paley's condition and suggesting that the president send the CBS chairman a formal invitation to become chairman of the new presidential commission. Truman sent the letter on January 2, 1951, and Paley responded by letter a few days later, saying that he would "be happy to serve as Chairman of a Presidential Committee to examine all natural resources incident to the security and the economy of the United States. . . ." On January 11, 1951, Paley had another meeting with Truman at the White House, this time accompanied only by Symington. The president was enthusiastic about Paley's acceptance of the assignment and promised to give him whatever support he needed to complete the task. Elated but nervous, Paley left 1600 Pennsylvania Avenue with a new title and a sense of unease about the commitment he had just made.

The first priority was CBS. His new responsibilities would require Paley to spend most of the ensuing year in Washington, but he did not want to completely leave his company. So Paley made arrangements for Stanton to assume additional responsibilities, telling him that he would return to New York at the end of every week and be available for consultation by phone in the evenings.

The next priority was finding appropriate assistance, and on that score there was no one more suitable than Phil Coombs. Paley telephoned Coombs at his Connecticut home and asked him to come to Kiluna for a couple of weeks. Coombs was again flattered and, since he had not yet found a new job, left immediately for Long Island's North Shore.

Kiluna Farm was a new experience for Coombs. Upon arrival he was given a bedroom that included pink polka-dot sheets on the bed. Every evening he placed his order for the next morning's breakfast, which the butler delivered with six newspapers. Coombs was also given a private telephone, which the butler said he could use to call his "bride" every evening. No material comfort was spared, Coombs recalled, in an obvious effort to make his visit a pleasurable one.

After breakfast, Coombs would come downstairs to begin his daylong meetings with Paley. "Our first priority," said Coombs, "was to select the other members of the commission. We decided that it should be small in number so that it could be manageable. And we also wanted to make sure we didn't have a lot of liberals. The panel had to have the kind of stature that would impress the business community. Otherwise, its recommendations would not be taken seriously."

The first person Paley and Coombs decided upon was Edward Mason, a Harvard economics professor and former president of the American Economic Association. Paley and Coombs flew to Cambridge to meet with Mason, and, as always, Paley was charming and soft-spoken, explaining the commission's goal to Mason and why his presence was needed. "Despite his own standing, Paley was very deferential to Mason," Coombs recalled, "and he seemed to be genuinely interested in meeting someone of Mason's stature in a field so far removed from broadcasting." Mason quickly accepted, and Paley and Coombs then moved on to their next targets. Within a week, three other individuals had been recruited: Arthur Bunker, president of Climax Molybdenum Company, who also happened to be a former investment banker and a former CBS director; George Rufus Brown, a founding partner in the Texas contracting firm of Brown & Root and someone who had been recommended by Lyndon Johnson (and whom Coombs found to be "the nicest and most conservative guy I ever met"); and Eric Hodgens, a former managing editor of *Fortune* magazine who had achieved literary success with his novel, *Mr. Blandings Builds His Dream House,* and who satisfied Paley's insistence that the commission have at least one professional writer.

After selecting its members, Paley and Coombs spent many hours planning the commission's agenda and reviewing the methods by which its work would be accomplished. Almost all of this planning took place at Kiluna, with Paley making periodic calls to the office. Sometimes, however, Paley and Coombs would be driven to CBS headquarters in Manhattan so that Paley could attend various meetings. Coombs was surprised and impressed by Paley's office. It did not appear anything like what he had imagined. "It didn't look like an office at all," he remembered. "It looked like a Louis the Fourteenth hotel suite. There was no formal desk, only a table that seemed to serve the function of a desk. There were comfortable chairs, an old cigar-store Indian statue, and, in general, an atmosphere that was very warm and relaxing."

On one visit to Paley's office, the chairman surprised Coombs by saying, "Why don't you call Helen and have her come down to see a show?" Coombs quickly agreed, and Paley asked what show they would like to see. Coombs had an immediate answer. *South Pacific* was then the top show on Broadway, and tickets were virtually impossible to find. In other circumstances, Coombs would have been more realistic. But everything seemed attainable in Bill Paley's world, and so Coombs confessed his true feelings. Paley smiled, picked up the telephone, and called his friend Leland Hayward, who also happened to be the show's producer. Tickets would be waiting for Phil and Helen at the theater. Paley then told Coombs to have his wife meet him at the Paleys' apartment at the St. Regis Hotel, where they could order dinner before going to the show.

At first, Helen resisted the idea of driving down to New York from Connecticut, saying that she would not have time to do her hair. Phil told her not to worry, to put her hair in curlers and get in the car. No one would be able to see her, and she could do whatever she had to at the Paleys' apartment. With the prospect of a wonderful evening in the offing, Helen yielded and said she would be there within hours.

Her husband was already at the Paley apartment by the time Helen arrived. The picture remained indelibly implanted in his mind. "Babe Paley, dressed elegantly and looking beautiful, answers the door. And there's Helen," said Coombs, "hair in curlers with a cloth bag. She looked like she just got off the boat." But Babe took no notice. "She was very gracious and accommodating," said Coombs, "treating Helen like she was royalty." Babe then brought over a menu from a nearby French restaurant and, since neither Phil nor Helen spoke French, translated the various items so that the Coombses could order dinner.

After the show Phil and Helen were driven out to Kiluna, and each was shown to a separate bedroom. Phil and Helen did not appreciate that aspect of the Paleys' lifestyle. They were young, they had only been married a short time, and they had been separated for many days. As soon as the butler left, Phil walked across the hall to Helen's bedroom. The butler said nothing the next morning when he found Phil and Helen together, but the maid was aghast. The butler tried to explain that it was alright, that the Coombses were married, but the maid did not seem satisfied with his explanation.

The experience at Kiluna was only the first of many occasions when the Coombses and Paleys got together. Paley needed an executive director for his commission, and Coombs was finally persuaded to accept the job and join the Paleys in Washington. For their part, Bill and Babe took an apartment at the Shoreham Hotel until they could take possession of a rented house in Georgetown. At the end of January 1951, the five members of the newly named President's Materials Policy Commission, along with the new executive director and secretary, met with President Truman at the White House for a ten-minute pep talk. Afterward, Paley wrote to Ed Murrow, saying that "the project is one of the most interesting I have ever tackled." It was a new role and new environment for Paley, and he confessed to Murrow that, for the moment at least, he felt "overwhelmed."

One of the first things Paley decided to do was to meet with Tom Finletter, a high-ranking government official who had chaired another presidential commission that had just released its report recommending the creation of a separate air force. That report had been well received, and Paley thought he could benefit from Finletter's advice on how to make the Materials Commission a comparable success. So Paley and Coombs met with Finletter at the latter's Pentagon office in early February, and the advice could not have been more surprising. Finletter told Paley to begin writing his commission's report immediately. Paley protested that they hadn't even started the research, let alone decided upon recommendations. No matter, said Finletter, you should develop the broad outlines of the report now, because that would, in the end, prove to be the most formidable part of the task. On the ride back to commission offices in the Old Executive Office Building next door to the White House, Paley was very troubled. "How the hell do I start writing a report," he mumbled. "I don't know anything." He then turned to his young assistant, so able and so eager. "You do it," he told Coombs. The executive director nodded, and shortly afterward Coombs began drafting the commission's report even though he did not yet know what it would conclude.

In the meantime, Paley and Coombs began to recruit government officials for a full-time staff and outside consultants to conduct special research assignments. In each case the goal was the same: to hire the most talented people they could find. Paley knew that whatever he lacked on specific knowledge could be easily corrected with the right staff. Within months word had spread within the federal bureaucracy that only the most accomplished people could secure a job on the Materials Policy Commission, and Coombs was flooded with applications from able and dedicated civil servants. Within months the principal hiring had been completed, and a staff of approximately one hundred and forty crowded the commission's new offices at 1740 G Street, NW.

In supervising the commission's work, Paley decided to adopt the same role he had developed for himself at CBS. He read the memos and he attended the staff meetings, but he did not otherwise involve himself in the supervision of the staff's work. That job was left to Coombs. "Paley would attend the weekly staff meetings," Coombs remembered, "but I chaired them. He was not interested in running the staff. He saw himself as an auditor." At the same time, Paley did not refrain from participating in the staff meetings. "Paley asked pointed questions at the meetings," said Coombs, "but he wouldn't dig himself into any position. He had great respect for the facts and always kept an open mind on all the issues."

In June 1951 Paley wrote to Truman to advise him of the commission's progress. "My first comment," said the chairman, "is that the need for the study you directed us to make is far greater than anything I was able to comprehend when we began. It seems clear now that the materials requirements for a healthy civilian economy and for our military security over the long-range period (twenty to twenty-five years) will be far larger than any nation has ever before been called upon to meet." Paley then reviewed the specific research projects undertaken by the commission and the conferences it planned to hold. The only problem was the schedule. As Coombs had predicted, the work could not be completed within the six- to nine-month time frame set by Truman, and Paley asked for the president's approval to take longer. Truman responded two days later, telling Paley to "[t]ake whatever time is necessary to get the job done as it should be done."

As the work progressed, it became more and more evident that some of its recommendations would involve controversial matters. The commission itself met every month—Paley being the only full-time commissioner—and although everyone was congenial, the debates were spirited, each commissioner applying the perspective of his own training and experience. "That was the most impressive aspect of those commission meetings," said Coombs. "There was always plenty of room for debate, and not once did anyone mention partisan political considerations."

Eventually the commission prepared a report recommending, among other things, that natural gas be preserved by prohibiting its use in the manufacture of tires, that lead be preserved by prohibiting its use in the manufacture of gasoline, and that international arrangements be made to store grains for worldwide use. None of these recommendations, however, generated as much debate—either inside or outside the commission—as a fourth recommendation: elimination of the oil-depletion allowance, which allowed the oil industry to claim large tax write-offs for oil investments. The oil-depletion allowance was a much-used tax loophole, one deemed to be a "sacred cow" within the business community. Paley recognized its importance and was plainly nervous as the commission moved toward its recommendation on the issue. He knew it would attract attention and probably criticism. But Coombs had warned Paley that the commission's report would not escape some criticism if it did anything worthwhile, and, in the end, Paley had to concur. He was convinced by the commission's research that the nation faced a potential energy shortage by 1975, and Professor Mason argued eloquently at commission meetings that the oil-depletion allowance would make the problem worse, not better. In the face of this analysis, the chairman concluded that the president, and the nation, had to be given the commission's honest view—no matter who might be hurt in the process.

By June 1952—almost eighteen months after he had first met with Truman on the matter—Paley was prepared to issue the commission's report. As the day of release approached, Paley wrote a letter to Symington, who was then campaigning in Missouri for the United States Senate (a development that probably caused Paley to recall Coombs's initial comment about not placing too much reliance on Symington's continued tenure at the National Security Resources Board). "Well, the baby is being born," Paley observed, noting that the report would be released on June 23. He enclosed an advance copy, adding, "I hope you won't think I have let you down." Whatever Symington's reaction, however, Paley was satisfied that he had made the right decision in accepting the assignment. "I must admit," Paley explained to Symington, "that during the past fifteen months I have more than once regretted the day you talked me into this project. Now that it is almost over I feel that I wouldn't have missed it for the world. I know I will regard my work here as one of the most rewarding experiences I ever have had. It taught me a hell of a lot and I have hopes that it may do some good. So thanks, boy, for getting me into it," wrote the CBS chairman to his long-time friend, "and please take a big bow for having the foresight and imagination to know a long time ago that this job needed doing. I must say quickly that I am not sure that it has been done properly but that would not be your fault."

On June 23 Paley went to the White House with the other commissioners and Coombs to formally present Truman a copy of the report. The meeting had been scheduled to start at noon and was expected to take only ten minutes. Instead, Truman spent an hour with the group. The president, wearing his horn-rimmed glasses and dressed in a light-colored suit, was clearly in a light-hearted mood, joking with the reporters who kept pleading for one more photograph. ("That's the 'one more' crowd," he told his visitors.) For all his good humor, Truman was plainly interested in the commission's work, an interest that hardly surprised Coombs. He had been sending galleys of the report over to the White House for Truman to read, and the White House staff had repeatedly called him and asked that he not send over any more galleys because they couldn't get "the old man" to read anything else. Now, as the commission met with the president in the Oval Office, Coombs could see that the White House staff's concern had been well-founded. It was obvious that the president had indeed read the lengthy report.

The commissioners expected a few pleasantries, a warm smile, a photograph, and they would be on their way. Truman was gracious in his compliments, but the meeting was hardly ceremonial. The president got up from his chair, walked over to a large globe in the corner of the Oval Office, and, as he spun the globe around, gave the startled commissioners and staff a short lesson in world history, speaking of the birth of civilization and the need to give something in return for all we had inherited. The commission's work, he told his visitors, was a major step toward that goal. As the group walked out of the White House, Arthur Bunker turned to his colleagues and expressed a sentiment they all shared. "That," said Bunker, "was an astonishing performance."

The meeting with the president only reinforced Paley's view that the Materials Policy Commission had made a major contribution toward understanding the country's resource needs over the next twenty-five years—a view that was shared by much of the media. In a two-page editorial, *Life* magazine said the Paley report "could prove as important a guide to the next century of America's development as was Alexander Hamilton's great paper on manufacturers to the century in which we became the number one industrial nation." The *New York Herald Tribune* concurred, calling the report "a truly historical document" that represented "a summons to our leaders to save the nation and the western world from possible disaster."

However much he appreciated the praise, Paley was interested in action, and to that end he turned to his good friend Dwight Eisenhower. The general had been among those whom Paley had consulted before accepting Symington's offer. Ike certainly understood the value of public service, but he had warned the CBS chairman that the report would not have any credibility or serve any useful purpose unless the commission performed its work in a truly independent and nonpartisan manner. Paley felt that he had followed that advice, and he sent an advance copy of the report to Eisenhower in Denver, where the general was campaigning for the Republican presidential nomination. "I know you've got all kinds of time on your hands these days," Paley jokingly commented, "but since you were in on the beginning of this, and because of your interest in the subject, I thought you might want to give the material a quick glance." Ever the diplomat, Ike responded that he had, in fact, glanced at the report and that his friend should be congratulated "on a thorough-going, extremely useful piece of work!"

Paley took hope from Ike's response. Within weeks after Eisenhower's election in November 1952, Paley sent him a more detailed letter emphasizing the importance of the commission's work. In basic terms, said Paley, the country had entered a "new era" in which it could no longer efficiently produce all the resources it needed to serve its economy and defense. "I am not an alarmist on this question," he continued, "but I do like to generate real concern. I feel that if industry and government, principally industry, take appropriate steps to meet our future needs and keep on top of the problem as a continuing matter, this country will not suffer because of the lack of materials. On the other hand," said Paley, "if we trust to the accident of the future and fall back on the belief that somehow everything will work out all right, we might find ourselves in serious difficulty." Eisenhower was again polite in response, saying he had been "very much interested" in the commission's work and would pass its report on to his brother and appropriate members of his incoming administration. But the new president's interest ended there. Despite his continuing inquiries with government officials, Paley could not inspire any meaningful measures.

The government's inaction did not diminish Paley's enthusiasm for the commission's work or his pride in its achievement. To almost anyone who might be interested, whether a social companion, a CBS colleague, or an unfamiliar interviewer, Paley would recall his tenure with the commission as one of his most productive and enjoyable experiences. And when the country did confront an energy shortage in the 1970s, Paley would tell people that the Materials Policy Commission—*his* commission—had predicted the shortage more than twenty years earlier.

Although Paley was powerless to implement the recommendations of the Materials Policy Commission, he could and did take action on other matters that were being discussed in Washington. And of those, few proved to be as exciting—or frustrating—as CBS's venture into the business of manufacturing television sets.

During his time at the commission, Paley developed an incredibly hectic schedule. He usually spent Monday through Thursday at the commission's offices and then left for New York on Thursday evening or Friday morning, dividing the weekends between CBS headquarters and Kiluna. Even when he was in Washington, much of his evening was spent on the telephone with Stanton and other CBS executives, discussing programs, budgets, and other developments. Although he was physically removed from the scene in New York, no major decision could be made without Bill Paley's knowledge.

In the midst of the color-television war, many people at CBS began to give serious consideration to the acquisition of a business that would enable the company to manufacture and distribute its own television sets. To some extent, the considerations were based on experience. When CBS had produced its LP record in the late 1940s, for example, the joy of success was dampened by the realization that no one was selling record players that could accommodate this latest development in record technology. Stanton and others tried to interest some manufacturers in producing a new player, but all the efforts proved to be in vain. Finally, Stanton decided to be more aggressive. "I had to go down to Philco [in Philadelphia] and beg Philco to make . . . [record] players," he recalled. But Philco was not taking any risks. "We had to buy them in advance simply because we had no way of getting the thing going without a player," said Stanton.

Goldmark and his boss, Adrian Murphy, remembered this experience well, and they reminded Stanton of it in 1950 after CBS began to enjoy some success in the color-television war. Where will we be, they said, if we win with a system that is incompatible with existing television sets and have no vehicle of our own to manufacture television sets that are compatible? It was persuasive logic, and Goldmark and Murphy were encouraged to find the right opportunity.

Ironically, Paley was being pressed along the same lines by Phil

Coombs. The two men lunched together almost every day in Washington. Coombs could see that Paley was a man who loved food, especially Jewish food; while they would frequent a variety of restaurants, they invariably went at least twice a week to Duke Zeibert's, a large restaurant on L Street that was popular with Washington's powerbrokers and, in addition, served some of the best Jewish food in town. During those lunches the conversation ranged far and wide. Although reluctant to express opinions during staff meetings, Paley felt sufficiently relaxed with Coombs to speak his mind on issues of importance to the commission as well as those related to CBS. Coombs, accustomed to open debate in the classroom and in government, spoke just as freely, asking pointed questions about CBS policy. If Paley's answer seemed unsatisfactory, Coombs would, like any good academic, question its completeness and logic. Paley never objected to Coombs's challenges. In fact, said Coombs, he seemed to enjoy the verbal sparring.

As someone who had dedicated himself to education and public service, Coombs frequently complained to Paley that commercial broadcasters should be doing more to fulfill their public responsibilities. After all, he would say, broadcasters had received a government license for free. In return, it was only fair to expect them to use some of their profits to develop high-quality programming for different segments of the population. "Paley was schizophrenic at heart about that," remembered Coombs. "He had good tastes and seemed to feel the same way. He was very proud of the news group, and not just proud, but very interested. But he would say, 'This is a competitive business, and it's an expensive business, and we're in it to make money. We want to do what we can, but we can't afford to set aside time for high-quality programs for small audiences.' "

Their discussions invariably touched on the economics of the broadcast business, and economics was something that Coombs could debate knowledgeably. "You're a sitting duck," he told Paley at one of their lunches. "Look at RCA. They're a vertically integrated company. They produce programs, they broadcast programs, and they manufacture television sets for people to use in watching the programs. CBS," he added, "will always be behind RCA unless it diversifies to match their capabilities." Paley listened intently when Coombs made this pitch. Here was an independent voice echoing the same arguments he was hearing from Goldmark and Murphy and others at CBS. It provided confirmation that CBS should become a manufacturer of television sets.

There were voices on the other side of the issue, and one of them belonged to Ike Levy, who was still a major stockholder at CBS. Levy had also grown close to Sarnoff over the years—an intimacy that would raise suspicions and eventually cause open conflict at CBS. But Levy felt comfortable with the relationship, and he would often speak openly with the RCA chairman about his competition with CBS, and on one occasion Levy mentioned Paley's plans to enter the business of manufacturing television sets. Levy passed on to Paley Sarnoff's response: I'll "knock his brains out." Sarnoff was equally candid in one of his luncheon meetings with the CBS chairman. "I advised him bluntly to forget it," Sarnoff later recalled. But Bill Paley was not one to take directions from outsiders, especially when the outsider was his chief rival. He had been told to abandon many ideas in the previous twenty years, and he had frequently proved people wrong. He could do it again. "[W]e had an idea for a long time," Paley later remembered, "that CBS, being so successful in the broadcasting business, could do very well if it made the instruments as well, . . . and we thought the time was right for us to have some control over a manufacturing organization."

Paley's decision seemed inevitable in 1951 after the Supreme Court upheld the FCC order blessing the CBS color system. CBS might have authority to install a color television system, but the public had only black-and-white sets that couldn't use it. Someone would have to manufacture compatible color television sets, and that someone was not going to be RCA or any other major manufacturer. "The Supreme Court can't order me to make color sets for CBS," said David Sarnoff. Other companies adopted a similar posture, and the message was clear: CBS would have to rely on its own resources.

Three weeks after the Supreme Court decision CBS acquired Hytron Radio and Electronics Corporation, a company headquartered in Salem, Massachusetts, that manufactured television sets. Later, there would be many questions about who had had responsibility for making an investigation of Hytron's assets and finances, but in June 1951, everyone, including Paley, was convinced that CBS had entered a new era. The price for admission was $17.7 million worth of CBS stock—an astronomical figure in light of the fact that CBS had only $68 million in sales at the time. But no one batted an eye. The exchange made Hytron's owners—Bruce and Lloyd Coffin—immediate millionaires, but the return to CBS, it was believed, would more than justify the investment.

Paley and Stanton were fascinated with the new member of the CBS family, and they would frequently be driven out to Brooklyn to inspect the manufacture of television sets by Hytron's subsidiary, Air King. It all looked so efficient, so productive. But problems began to appear even before the excitement had worn off. Further investigation revealed that Hytron's inventory of vacuum tubes and television sets had been overvalued by millions of dollars. Doubts about the propriety of the Coffin brothers' management techniques also began to be raised, and some people at CBS began to ask questions, hard questions, that did not have pleasant answers. Ralph Colin remembered the moment when someone finally worked up the courage to present the unpleasant truth to Paley. "Three months after we bought [Hytron], I was at a meeting on the West Coast," said the CBS counsel, "and we told Paley that you've got to bounce the management of Hytron." Paley did not like to admit to mistakes at any time, let alone so quickly after the event. He balked. Peter Goldmark had investigated Hytron, he had recommended it. The acquisition was important to the company's future. They could not transform its management so quickly.

The situation went from bad to worse. CBS suspended its manufacture of color television sets at the federal government's request, thus eliminating the major reason for acquiring Hytron in the first place. Then CBS decided to abandon Hytron's established relationship with Sears, Roebuck and create its own distribution arm for television sets. While that move was consistent with Paley's desire for independence, it also eliminated a guaranteed market for CBS, no small matter in a field fraught with competition. And then, to seal Hytron's fate, its managers rejected Goldmark's suggestion that the company initiate research into the transistor, a device that would soon revolutionize the manufacture of television sets. In a meeting with Paley and the Coffin brothers, the Hytron engineer belittled Goldmark's suggestion, saying, "The transistor is a toy." Paley, still enamored with Hytron management, agreed with their assessment, much to his later regret.

In the meantime, CBS had begun to receive complaints about the quality of the Hytron television sets that were now being distributed under the CBS trademark. Paley did not like to receive complaints about quality, and he also did not like to take responsibility for them—especially when he was so tied up with the work of the Materials Policy Commission. He passed his concern along to Stanton, but, for all his intelligence and dedication, the CBS president was no engineer, and he blamed it all on Goldmark and Murphy. ". . . Goldmark and Murphy recommended" the Hytron acquisition "very strongly," he later recalled. "We were being pressed to make a decision, and we took their judgment on it. . . . I don't charge either one of them with having misled us deliberately. I just don't think they had as much information as they should have had."

By the time the ban on color television sets was lifted in 1953, the FCC had authorized the RCA system—which was compatible with the then-existing twenty-three million black-and-white sets. CBS now had to compete on RCA's turf, and, as Sarnoff had predicted, Bill Paley's company did not come out on top. By the mid-fifties Paley, frustrated with the poor quality and slow sales of CBS television sets, terminated that part of the business, and in 1961 he liquidated the Hytron subsidiary completely, taking the losses but relieving himself of a major headache.

In retrospect, Paley could see the roots of the failures. "I think what happened there," he later said, ". . . is that we didn't know very much about the manufacturing business, and much more importantly, we didn't care about it. You know," he added, "it wasn't our cup of tea. It just didn't sort of fit into our way of doing business . . . dealing with creative people most of the time. . . ." However accurate, this new insight (which would be disregarded when CBS made other acquisitions in later years) could not overcome the financial losses generated by the Hytron venture. They were staggering.

The company had given almost one-fourth of its stock to the Coffin brothers. When coupled with the monies that CBS had to pour into Hytron to keep it afloat, the total loss approximated $100 million by the time Paley ended the fiasco in 1961. The Hytron episode represented the worst corporate financial decision made by CBS, and some Wall Street analysts believed it was one of the worst corporate deals in modern American history.

The magnitude of the disaster was not lost on Paley. Before he liquidated the Hytron companies, he had been plagued with despair over its sinking fortunes. And for years afterward, he refused to be pushed into major decisions, especially financial ones that involved substantial sums. There was a skepticism, an uncertainty, that was so uncharacteristic of the Bill Paley who had transformed a struggling United Independent Broadcasters into an incredibly profitable enterprise. Ralph Colin, who had been with Paley since those early days, took note of the difference. "He has been totally unable to make up his mind," said Colin years afterward. "The fact that he made so costly a mistake has weighed on him all the time—forever uncertain. Now he makes a decision, and he overrules it, and then overrules it again—and the one thing he will always do is put something off."

There were some things, however, that Paley could not put off. And in the early 1950s, one of them was a decision as to how CBS would respond to the dark forces of McCarthyism.

CHAPTER ELEVEN

McCarthy

O ne day shortly before the 1948 presidential election, Lou Cowan had lunch with the chairman of CBS. The purpose: to talk about voter surveys in general and, more specifically, the use of polls in the network's coverage of the forthcoming election. Cowan's interest did not reflect an idle curiosity. His good friend Elmo Roper had recently established a survey firm, and Cowan hoped to generate some business for him. There seemed no better place to start than with CBS. After all, that network had revolutionized the world of audience-survey techniques with "Little Annie." Surely, Cowan thought, CBS would want to take advantage of advanced techniques in reporting the progress and results of a political campaign.

Bill Paley was indeed interested in new voter polling techniques, and he agreed that CBS should use them in its coverage of the presidential campaign. But there were limits. Paley "was very much opposed to broadcasting anything that forecast an election result," Cowan remembered, "because he said that he felt that this created . . . a bandwagon atmosphere" and "that what was likely to happen, because of the power of those [broadcast] facilities, would be to influence enough people for one candidate or another"—and that, said Paley, "would be improper."

For Cowan it was an insight into the management of a powerful medium of mass communications. For Paley it was simply a reaffirmation of basic principle. He had first learned it from Ed Klauber, but now it was a cornerstone of CBS policy. "This medium has to absolutely live on the basis of fairness and balance or else we're lost," Paley once told a CBS news reporter. "And this thesis was developed in the early thirties when I first realized at an early age that there were two forces we had to protect ourselves against. . . . One was the government. The other was broadcasters themselves, who had a lot of power [and were going to get] even more power. . . . And I saw in it a lot of good if it was used properly," Paley continued, "and a lot of evil if it was misused."

Paley's sensitivity on this issue did not mean that CBS had to remain neutral on controversial issues of public importance. When he returned from the war, he told his staff that he had done a lot of thinking and that it might be wise for CBS to begin airing editorials. Joe Ream remembered the discussions. "Paley said the network should have more clout," Ream recalled. "He said look at the newspapers. They're smaller than us but they seem to get away with more. They have more power. And part of that is because they editorialize—a point that politicians always take into account." Paley's words carried considerable weight with his staff, but most of them opposed his proposal. FCC policy prohibited editorials, they said. And besides, editorials would undermine the spirit of evenhandedness that Klauber and Paley had worked so hard to preserve.

There were voices on the other side of the issue, and none was more powerful than that of Edward R. Murrow. He shared Paley's view. In his mind, the expression of opinion was an integral part of good journalism. Indeed, like H.V. Kaltenborn and Elmer Davis before him, Murrow believed that a journalist had a responsibility to express his opinions on important public issues.

Murrow's support made the difference, and by 1948 Paley had decided that CBS should formulate a plan to force a change in FCC policy. Although he was then preoccupied with the recruitment of performers like Jack Benny, Paley played a central role in the staff's deliberations, at one point inviting the group out to Kiluna for an open-ended discussion of the options. By 1949, the policy had been hammered out: CBS would sponsor individuals to express opinions and offer editorials. As a matter of courtesy, Frank Stanton telephoned FCC Chairman Charles Denny, only to be told that the commission was about to change its policy against editorials. Paley and CBS had been upstaged. Within months the commission issued its *Report on Editorializing by Licensees,* which allowed, even encouraged, broadcasters to editorialize. The report also reaffirmed earlier commission policy, which became known as the "Fairness Doctrine," that a broadcaster should cover controversial issues of public importance and that, as Klauber and Paley had long urged, that discussion should be balanced with contrasting viewpoints.

The new FCC policy was not the only factor occasioning a change in CBS's coverage of current events. In 1949 the company acquired a new vice president for news and public affairs—Sig Mickelson, former news director at CBS affiliate WCCO in Minneapolis. Mickelson, a hard-working, soft-spoken man, was impressed with the CBS chairman from the start. "He was a no-nonsense guy," said Mickelson. "He didn't waste time on inconsequential matters." There was no evidence of the light-hearted banter and warmth that had become Paley trademarks. "Those were reserved for entertainers and the foreign correspondents," Mickelson remarked. But the new vice president did not take offense. He accepted

Paley's aloofness as "part of being a good executive." When Paley spoke, the staff knew he meant business. One occasion in particular remained clear in Mickelson's memory. "We were having one of those big executive luncheons in his office, with all the top staff seated around the table," Mickelson remembered. "Paley said we've got some big decisions to make here, decisions involving a lot of money. And I think one drink is enough. He was very affable in the way he said it," Mickelson observed, "but everyone got the point. And no one had that second drink."

From the beginning Paley made it clear to Mickelson that he was very proud of the CBS news organization and that, with the approach of television, he wanted it strengthened. Mickelson's first project was to review CBS Radio's feature news programs. The principal show was "The March of Time," a review of weekly news events. Although the program was informative, it lacked the realism that Paley wanted in his network's news operations. Because of the expense in making recordings that could be rebroadcast over the air, "The March of Time" relied on readings by individuals who assumed the roles of various public figures. It was a procedure that might have been acceptable to the public when broadcasting was in its infancy, but Paley knew that audiences would become more demanding with the advent of television.

Mickelson's study resulted in a long memo that he shared with Paley and Stanton. At a subsequent meeting to discuss his recommendations, Mickelson again took note of Paley's quickness in getting to the point. "He is," said Mickelson, "a good interrogator who wants to get to the bottom line." By meeting's end, Paley had agreed with Mickelson that the network should use sound recordings and film in covering current events. The days of fictional news were over.

Ed Murrow became the vehicle for CBS's transition to the new format. His return to broadcasting in 1947 had been well received. His weekly news reports contained the same insight and drama that had catapulted him to stardom during World War II. More importantly, Murrow's quest for realism was legendary. He was the one, after all, who had stood on London rooftops while Nazi planes buzzed overhead—all in an effort to provide listeners with the actual sounds of warfare. Many people, including Paley, thought Murrow had taken unnecessary risks, but few could doubt the benefits that accrued to his listeners.

There were times when Murrow's pursuit of the truth could cause conflict. In the summer of 1950, for example, he traveled to Korea to give an on-the-scene report of American combat troops in action. His interviews and inspections raised serious questions about the American military's management of the war. In a taped report sent back to the United States, Murrow commented that the American high command had wasted men and resources on an offensive in southern Korea "because, in the words of one officer who was in a position to know, 'we decided we needed a victory.' " According to Murrow, this meaningless gesture weakened the Americans' ability to withstand North Korean advances in more strategic areas. And then there were the moral underpinnings of American intervention. Murrow's tape raised questions about "when we start moving up through dead valleys, through villages to which we have put the torch by retreating, what then of the people who live there? They have lived on the knife-edge of despair and disaster for centuries. Their pitiful possessions have been consumed in the flames of war. Will our reoccupation of that flea-bitten land lessen, or increase, the attraction of communism?"

In the aftermath of Vietnam, these questions hardly seem excessive. But the Korean War happened during a different time, with different standards. Paley had acquiesced to the government's restricted rules on coverage of the conflict, and Murrow's broadcast plainly violated them by criticizing American conduct. "Everybody in the news department thought [the Murrow tape] had broken the rules," Paley recalled. "I thought they were right. Murrow came back and there were a dozen people waiting in line to tell him. It was a matter of honor—he knew the rules as well as anybody. . . ." Murrow did not agree that his tape had violated the government's rules and was livid when he learned that CBS, his own news organization, had refused to air the tape because it was too critical. He did not keep these thoughts to himself, and years later Paley would remark that his worst fight with Murrow concerned the Korean report.

The argument over the tape did not prevent Paley and Murrow from collaborating on the improvement of CBS news coverage. Indeed, Murrow was enthusiastic about Paley's decision to make all news shows more realistic. He also had a specific proposal to advance the cause. He had narrated two popular record albums that used recordings to review the events leading up to, during, and immediately after World War II. Murrow believed they could use the same format and title for a new radio news program: "I Can Hear It Now." And to help him produce the program, Murrow would be joined by the same person who had helped him produce the record albums: Fred W. Friendly.

A thirty-five-year-old war veteran, Friendly provided a stark contrast to Murrow. Everything about him seemed big, even overwhelming. He stood six feet four inches tall and had large physical features and expansive ideas. Murrow was a man of few words who tended to brood. Friendly wore everything on his sleeve. He was a constant whirl of energy and emotion, always talking, urging, cajoling, complaining. To be sure, he was also a man of considerable talent, but his volatile personality added a lot of baggage that colored his colleagues' reactions. "Often in error, never in doubt," said one CBS correspondent in evaluating Friendly. And years later, when Friendly was appointed president of CBS News, Harry Reasoner would remark to his new boss, "Well, I see that the lunatics have taken over the asylum."

Murrow had already urged Hubbell Robinson, his nominal superior, to hire Friendly (who was then working at NBC), and Mickelson agreed after meeting Friendly while Murrow was in Korea. Paley, of course, acceded to this collective judgment that Friendly should be hired to help produce the new program, whose title had been shortened to "Hear It Now." Friendly told Paley, as he had told Mickelson, that he wanted to do a *Life* magazine of the air. Paley loved the concept, and when Friendly explained that he and Murrow had proposed a half hour program, the CBS chairman responded, "Why don't you ask for a full hour?"

The hour-long program made its premiere on radio in December 1950. As Paley had hoped, the program was well received. Almost immediately after its opening, plans were formulated to make the transition to television. The use of a new medium required a new title, and "See It Now" (reduced to a half hour because of cost) premiered on September 18, 1951, with live pictures of the Atlantic and Pacific oceans to demonstrate—for the first time—television's ability to span the continent. Murrow, smoking his ever-present cigarette, was somber and, as always, understated. "This is an old team trying to learn a new trade," he explained. For most there was little doubt that the Murrow team would be able to make the transition, and the first programs only confirmed their confidence. Usually, the weekly program would focus on a single topic of current interest. Many of the programs touched on controversial matters, but for the first couple of years, Murrow did not broach the controversy that dominated all others: McCarthy.

Joseph R. McCarthy often gave different dates for his birth, but the records in Grand Chute, Wisconsin, show that he was born on November 14, 1908. He was the fifth of nine children born to Timothy and Bridget McCarthy, his father the native-born son of Irish and German immigrants, his mother an Irish immigrant herself. Life was not easy for young Joe. The family farm was located in an area known as "the Irish settlement" about one hundred miles north of Milwaukee and eight miles north of Appleton. There was little return on the family's hard labor, however. Young Joe could not afford to stay in school and complete his secondary education. Instead, at the age of fourteen he started his own chicken farm, which grew and prospered for years until the entire flock was wiped out by disease. At the age of twenty, Joe McCarthy enrolled in a program to obtain his high school degree and managed to compress four years of schooling into one. ("We never graduated a student more capable of graduating," said the principal.) From there McCarthy went on to Marquette University in Milwaukee, where he intended to study engineering. He soon switched to law and by 1935, at the age of twenty-seven, was able to open an office in Waupaca, Wisconsin, sharing office space with a dentist who did most of the business.

Of medium height, barrel-chested, and possessing an engaging personality, McCarthy apparently saw politics as a refuge from an otherwise bleak existence. In 1939 he was elected a circuit judge as a Democrat. Even then his career was marked by questionable conduct, including a refusal to honor certain laws or established procedures that stood in the way of his chosen end. Although exempt from the draft, McCarthy insisted upon enlisting in the Marines and soon found himself stationed in the South Pacific as an intelligence officer whose principal duty was to debrief returning bomber pilots. Such ministerial tasks were not the stuff of legends, and, upon his return to Wisconsin, McCarthy spread the word that he had really been a tail-gunner.

With truth a flexible tool in his hands, McCarthy switched parties to run for the United States Senate in 1944. Although he lost, his unexpectedly strong showing encouraged him to pursue his political ambitions. In 1946 he defeated Senator Robert LaFollette, Jr., for the Republican nomination—a victory that assured his election in November. In January 1947 Joe McCarthy traveled to Washington, D.C., to assume his new position as the junior senator from Wisconsin.

His service was anything but exemplary. Joe McCarthy had neither the intelligence nor the magnetism to attract respect or a following—until he decided that he needed a theme to help win reelection in 1952. After a dinner with some friends in early 1950, McCarthy decided that the widespread fear of communism might just be the vehicle he was looking for to propel him into another six years in the Senate. At a Lincoln Day celebration in Wheeling, West Virginia, McCarthy claimed to have in his hands "a list of two-hundred and five [people] that were known to the secretary of state as being members of the Communist Party and who nevertheless are still working and shaping the policy of the State Department." The speech generated headlines across the country. While he could never produce the list, and while the number of communists in the State Department was subject to constant (and unexplained) revision, McCarthy's charges were accorded respect by the media, much of the government, and a majority of the population. Fueled by this unexpected support, McCarthy was soon inventing other charges of communist infiltration into government. At times it seemed that the only limitation was his own imagination.

Murrow was not one to be swayed by demagogues. He had seen enough of them during the war. "The whole McCarthy business is squalid beyond words," he remarked to a friend in 1950. But challenging McCarthy on television was not as easy as condemning him in private. Other factors had to be considered, and they did not support a decision to confront McCarthy before millions of viewers.

Murrow was by then a member of CBS's board of directors, an appointment Paley had urged upon him in 1947. Public concern with communism was already spreading by that point, and the media was attracting much of the attention. Many people in and out of government were not interested in honest opinion. They wanted assurances of fidelity to the United States—at whatever cost. Congressman John S. Wood, chairman of the House Un-American Activities Committee, proposed, for example, that all broadcast stations disclose the birthplace, nationality, and political affiliation of all commentators. The suggestion was ridiculed by Murrow's colleagues at CBS, but he appreciated the danger it represented to a company that depended on licenses granted by the government.

Murrow's inner anger was tempered by his obligations, and he would, as a CBS vice president and then as a correspondent, write to FBI Director J. Edgar Hoover to advise him of CBS's new programs and invite his comments. He surely knew that Frank Stanton had sent Hoover a telegram along similar lines to urge the FBI director to listen to and comment on "Hear It Now." And, for all his support of free speech, Murrow acquiesced when Paley and the CBS board agreed that the network had to adopt more aggressive measures to erase any appearance of disloyalty within the company.

None of this was easy for Paley or his subordinates. "It was a subject that a lot of time was spent on," Stanton recalled, "and we tried to administer it about as fairly as we thought we could. We not only had trouble with the outside critics on both sides [of the issue], but we had trouble with our affiliates. . . . Tempers and feelings ran very high on this score. And we had affiliates who . . . wouldn't clear programs if certain people were on the programs." The network's response, distasteful as it might be, was simple. "When I got there in 1949," said Mickelson, "Stanton gave me a list of people I couldn't use. . . . Stanton just said this is something we've got to do. People were intimidated, and everyone accepted it as a matter of fact."

Even these measures soon proved inadequate, however. Shortly after the outbreak of the Korean War in 1950, an organization called American Business Consultants published a small book called *Red Channels.* The publication purported to list almost two hundred members of the broadcast industry—including CBS correspondents Howard K. Smith and

Alexander Kendrick—who were alleged to be communist sympathizers. Ted Kirkpatrick and other members of American Business Consultants began to make visits to companies that advertised on the networks, and their favorite topic was CBS. These new threats required a new response, and Joe Ream, a senior vice president by now, took the initiative. "On blacklisting," he later commented, "I'm the guy with the black hat." He adapted a loyalty questionnaire that had been prepared by the government and proposed to Stanton that CBS require all of its employees to complete it and assure the world that no employee had any suspect affiliations. "I didn't want to hurt anybody," said Ream, "but I thought our business was in jeopardy, and our first responsibility was to the company. I just wanted to get Kirkpatrick and those guys off our back."

Stanton discussed the matter with Paley and the board members, and in December 1950 CBS formally adopted Ream's questionnaire. To Paley it was an unfortunate but necessary measure. "A very small step," he said in later years, "compared to what most corporations were doing by way of protecting themselves against the onslaught of McCarthy and people of that kind." Perhaps. But many people, especially those working for CBS, the premier news network, had come to expect something more from it. This was the organization, after all, that had withstood all kinds of pressure from the highest levels of government in the past, and Paley himself would recite incidents to show that even presidents could not bully CBS into submission. The difference in this case, of course, was that a president, for all his influence, did not have the same impact on the network's income as advertisers and affiliates.

It was in the midst of this turmoil that Paley decided to accept Stuart Symington's offer to chair the Materials Policy Commission, a move that left Stanton the lion's share of responsibility in dealing with the pressures of blacklisting. By the time the commission submitted its report to Truman in June 1952, the public pressure for blacklisting and accommodation had only intensified. McCarthy seemed beyond criticism. "The truth is," journalist Richard Rovere later wrote, "that everyone in the Senate, or just about everyone, was scared stiff of him. Everyone then believed that McCarthy had the power to destroy those who opposed him, and evidence for this was not lacking."

Paley had to hope that a change in presidents could thwart McCarthy's power and, not incidentally, ease the pressures on CBS. Truman had been willing to challenge McCarthy in public, but Truman was a lame duck and, more importantly, a Democrat with little popular support. His criticism could not have any real impact on McCarthy's base of support. Conversely, a new Republican president would surely have more influence over a senator from his own party—especially if that Republican president

was Paley's good friend General Dwight D. Eisenhower. Many political
analysts shared this view. *The Washington Post,* for one, commented that
"McCarthyism would disappear if Eisenhower were elected."

By the winter of 1952 Ike had left Columbia University to assume
command of the Supreme Headquarters, Allied Powers Europe, commonly referred to as SHAPE. Although he now resided in France, Eisenhower had managed to attract enough interest and money to be able to
establish a strong presidential campaign, one that his supporters believed
would derail the momentum of the recognized frontrunner, Senator Robert Taft of Ohio, otherwise known as "Mr. Republican." By March 1952
these hopes were reinforced when Eisenhower defeated Taft in the New
Hampshire Republican primary without spending a single day campaigning in the state. Within a couple of weeks Eisenhower picked up unexpected support in Minnesota, and the proverbial bandwagon seemed to be
gaining speed.

"I can't begin to tell you how happy I am about recent events," Paley
wrote to Ike in March 1952. Eisenhower had passed word through a
mutual friend that he wanted Paley to visit with him in Paris to discuss
his political future. "Nothing would please me more, Ike," continued
Paley, "but I wonder if I could be helpful. As you know, I'm an amateur
in the field of political strategy, and I would hate to crowd in on your busy
schedule unless I thought I had something to offer." Having proclaimed
his "amateur status," Paley added that he did have some advice on the
key question then being debated among Eisenhower's campaign staff:
whether he should leave Europe to actively campaign in the United States.
"I'm on the opposite side from those people who are advising you to return
before the Convention," wrote Paley. "My view is that the Eisenhower
movement is based on a combination of factors—including your absence
because of heavy duties and responsibilities overseas—and that these factors have produced an end result which is working and working damn
well. Why change the formula, especially when I know it must be your
inclination to stand by your present job until the very last minute." But
Paley was not urging this view under any circumstance. He knew too well
that timing was important and that the dynamics of the situation could
change. "On the other hand," he continued, "if the political climate
should change . . . and your presence is required to counteract adverse
trends, I would strongly urge you to return." He closed by saying that he
would be happy to fly to Paris later in the spring if Eisenhower thought
he could be of help.

"You may be an amateur in the political field," Eisenhower wrote in
response, "but to my mind, you speak on the subject with the wisdom of
Solomon." Ike then related that, while he did not want to leave Europe,

events might force that decision upon him. As indeed they did. By June 1952 Ike was back in the United States, scheduled to commence his active campaigning with a speech and a press conference in his hometown of Abilene, Kansas.

Both events had been given extensive advance publicity, and Paley surprised Mickelson one day by suggesting that he arrange to cover the speech live. Mickelson explained that such coverage would involve thousands of dollars just to lease the necessary lines from AT&T, but Paley seemed unperturbed by the cost. "I'll call AT&T," he told Mickelson, "and you go ahead and do it." Mickelson added that they might as well cover the press conference, too, but Paley said nothing, a silence that Mickelson interpreted as a rejection. So arrangements were made to cover only the speech.

If plans went according to schedule, Eisenhower would open his campaign to the thunderous applause of 20,000 supporters jammed into an open ball park. Unfortunately, no one gave any consideration to the weather. The only thunder heard was the rumble of a major storm that swept through the park just as Eisenhower was mounting the rostrum. While the few strands of hair on his head stood on end, the general wrestled with pages of his speech as heavy winds whipped around him. The only sign of an enraptured audience were the waves of umbrellas spread before the rostrum.

To anyone eager for an Eisenhower victory, the speech was a total disaster. That night, as Mickelson was about to leave his office in New York, he received an unexpected call from the chairman. "Don't you think we should cover that press conference?" Paley inquired, as though Mickelson had never suggested it in the first place. Mickelson replied that, yes, of course they should. The next day the three chiefs of the major television networks—Paley, Sarnoff, and Leonard Goldenson of ABC— put in a conference call to Murrow to arrange for a "network pool" so that they could all share the use of a single set of facilities (instead of duplicating each other's lines). Despite some resistance from Eisenhower's campaign staff (who viewed television as a distraction rather than a benefit), the event went much more smoothly than the speech and enabled the general to recover the momentum that had been lost the previous day.

Paley's involvement with the campaign did not end with the opening coverage. It was not only his interest in Ike's future. Of equal significance, Jock Whitney was Eisenhower's finance chairman, and Paley always enjoyed the company of his brother-in-law, be it on the golf course or the campaign trail. Jock was full of ideas, energy, and fun. And, as the campaign progressed, another mutual friend joined their ranks—Walter Thayer.

Thayer was some ten years younger than the fifty-one-year-old Paley. In many respects, their careers could not have been more different. A 1935 graduate of Yale Law School, Thayer had worked with some Wall Street law firms and as an assistant United States attorney before becoming Averell Harriman's special assistant in the Lend-Lease Administration during World War II. Although he had spent most of the war in London, Thayer had never run across Paley.

Their first meeting involved a legal matter. Thayer, lean, enterprising, and ambitious, had started his own law firm in New York after the war. In the early 1950s Thayer was asked by Minnie Cushing, Babe's sister, to handle her divorce from Vincent Astor. In the course of that representation, Thayer had a few occasions to meet the CBS chairman, but their encounters were brief and the relationship casual. All of that changed in 1952 when Thayer became counsel to the National Citizens Committee for Eisenhower. He was now an integral part of the campaign, someone with authority to do things, and Bill Paley had numerous suggestions on how the campaign should be handled. "He always had a lot of ideas," Thayer remembered. "He would call me up at almost any time to throw ideas at me. Have you thought about this? And what about that? Not at all pushy or oppressive. Friendly and helpful." It was the beginning of a close friendship, one that almost rivaled the intimacy that Whitney and Paley had developed. "Bill was a great kibbitzer in those days," said Thayer. "Always curious and always a lot of fun."

Paley never saw any conflict between his company's news coverage of the Eisenhower campaign and his efforts to make it succeed. In his mind, the two activities were entirely separate. He was entitled to his opinions as a private citizen, and CBS, under his policies, would always be fair in its coverage of political issues. The incident with Mickelson, however, indicated that the distinctions were not always as clear as Paley believed, and in later years he would remove himself from any active involvement in political campaigns because the appearances plainly undercut the notion that CBS was truly independent in its news coverage.

None of those ethical concerns interfered with Paley's enthusiasm for Eisenhower, and on November 5, 1952, he wrote Ike a short note to tell him how "overjoyed" he was by the election results. The president-elect, looking for people to staff his new administration, tried to persuade Paley to leave CBS to become secretary to the cabinet, a position that would involve coordination of major government policies in almost every area. Although flattered by the invitation, Paley declined, believing he had provided enough service to government and that his company needed him once again.

The rejection did not prevent Paley from maintaining frequent contact with Eisenhower. They exchanged letters on a wide range of matters, from birthday greetings to review of the appointment of new commissioners to the FCC. On future occasions Paley would attend the formal stag dinners that Eisenhower periodically arranged at the White House. And sometimes Paley would accompany Thayer and Whitney to the president's Gettysburg farm, where they would talk and barbecue and laugh a great deal.

From this frequent contact, Paley knew that Eisenhower had nothing but contempt for McCarthy. But like thousands, if not millions, of his fellow citizens, the president did not want to express those feelings in public. Part of the reticence reflected Eisenhower's discomfort with personal confrontations; the other part reflected a recognition that McCarthy's power had been enhanced, not diminished, by the Republican victory. The senator from Wisconsin had been re-elected to the Senate, and while his margin of victory was not large, it was clear that McCarthy remained a formidable and unpredictable force. "In 1953," said Rovere, "the very thought of Joe McCarthy could shiver the White House timbers and send panic through the whole executive branch." If Paley and CBS were to overcome the public pressure generated by McCarthyism, they would have to do it without any assistance from the White House.

Murrow, for one, was becoming more and more inclined to devote a segment of "See It Now" to McCarthy. Murrow did not want to subject CBS to an unmanageable controversy that could lead to public attacks and diminished profits. But McCarthy's tactics cried out for a public response—one that articulated the thoughts and fears that so many people were keeping to themselves. Murrow also felt he had an obligation to the many friends and admirers who saw him as a moral crusader. In their minds it was only natural that he would do a program on McCarthy. Still, when people inquired about the prospect in the early fifties, Murrow responded that he had no plans for such a program. At first there was surprise, then frustration and disappointment. On one occasion a visitor suggested that perhaps Murrow was afraid to jeopardize the comfortable lifestyle that he then enjoyed. The CBS correspondent took a long drag on his cigarette and replied, "You may be right." But that was theatrics. In truth, Murrow's concerns extended far beyond his own well-being. He had his wife, a young son, and a company that he regarded as part of his family. Their fates had to be considered as well.

Soon Murrow realized the subject could not be avoided—no matter what the countervailing forces. His first approach to the problem of McCarthyism was from the periphery. A young Air Force lieutenant named Milo Radulovich had been discharged as a security risk because his father and sister were allegedly involved with communist organizations. Radoluvich was never given a hearing, and his accusers were never identified. Based on the investigation of reporter-producer Joe Wershba, Murrow concluded that Radulovich's case represented the kind of star chamber proceedings that were supposed to be characteristic of totalitarian dictatorships, not democracy in the United States of America. On October 20, 1953, Murrow devoted the entire half hour of "See It Now" to Radulovich's case, concluding with questions that had as much force as any speech. "We are unable to judge the charges against the father or the lieutenant's sister," said Murrow, "because neither we nor you nor the lieutenant nor the lawyers know precisely what was contained in that manila envelope [held by the government]. Was it hearsay, rumor, gossip, or hard, provable fact backed by credible witnesses? We do not know." The program attracted immediate and favorble attention for "See It Now" and its sponsor, the Aluminum Company of America. "The program marked perhaps the first time," Jack Gould wrote in *The New York Times,* "that a major network, the Columbia Broadcasting System, and one of the country's most important industrial sponsors, the Aluminum Company of America, consented to a program taking a vigorous editorial stand in a matter of national importance and controversy." Within weeks the Air Force reconsidered its position and withdrew the charges against Radulovich.

The response to the Radulovich program gave Murrow heart. But still, there was a world of difference between the power of the Air Force and the standing of Joe McCarthy. The Wisconsin senator would not yield so easily.

Paley saw Murrow almost every day, and he understood the dilemma that his vice president faced. Although he had tried to minimize the significance of the blacklisting at CBS, Paley was troubled by it, and years later he would confess that it had been a terrible mistake. Understandable perhaps, but nothing to remember with pride. But the CBS chairman would not tell Murrow what he should do—or could do. Murrow was, for all practical purposes, an autonomous entity within the network. Paley would listen to his comments, would make suggestions for him to consider, but Murrow alone made the decision as to what he would present on "See It Now."

The breaking point for Murrow finally came in February 1954 when he reviewed the transcript of an attack by McCarthy on Brigadier General Ralph Zwicker, a World War II hero. In Ed Murrow's mind, it demonstrated, more clearly then ever, that no one was safe from McCarthy's venom. Something had to be done. Something would be done. He told Friendly to put together reels of film of McCarthy's appearances. They would hang the man with his own words and conduct. That night Murrow walked into his apartment and said to Janet, "We're going ahead with the broadcast." Janet did not have to ask which one; she had been living with the tension for weeks. "It was a stressful time," she remembered. "But through it all, Bill stood behind Ed, giving him lots of support. And Ed appreciated that."

Paley vividly remembered those times as well. "Ed and I were terribly close before the McCarthy broadcast and after the broadcast," he later observed. But Paley did not want to become involved in the editing of the broadcast. In the past, he had occasionally previewed segments of "See It Now" and made suggestions to help improve the presentation. But not now. It was Ed's show—for better or worse. It was not only a matter of respect for Murrow's independence. Paley had to be free of any involvement if the the show generated too much criticism and required unpleasant decisions about Murrow or the series.

Still, Murrow asked Paley, as he usually did on important broadcasts, whether the chairman wanted to see the program before it was aired before millions of viewers. Paley replied by asking Murrow if he felt confident about the facts and the position he would take. Murrow answered in the affirmative. "In that case," said Paley, "I won't see it. I'll see it on the air like everybody else." It was a vote of confidence—at least for the time being—and Murrow accepted it as such. Paley had only one suggestion: that Murrow offer McCarthy time to reply. The senator would ask, indeed demand, that he be given time, and Murrow might as well defuse the pressure of the request before it was made. It was the time-honored principle of balance, one that Murrow fully endorsed. "It's a hell of a good idea," he responded. "Thanks very much. I'll do it."

Tuesday, March 9, 1954—the day of the broadcast. Murrow was anxious, tense, worried, smoking one cigarette after another. He, Friendly, and the rest of the production unit reviewed the final cuts of film, editing the script. Everyone knew that their prestige, possibly even their jobs, were riding on the outcome. In the early morning the phone rang. It was the CBS chairman, wanting to talk to Murrow. He, as much as anyone, understood what Murrow was going through. "I'll be with you tonight, Ed," said Paley, "and I'll be with you tomorrow as well." It was a sensitive gesture, and Murrow was moved by his friend's concern.

Murrow had a sandwich around eight o'clock that evening, reviewed the film one more time, and then moved in front of the cameras. As 10:30 approached, he took his usual last-minute sip of Scotch and moved into the broadcast, introducing clips of McCarthy's tirades, his badgering of hapless witnesses, his mindless attacks on people who dared to express dissenting views. Murrow's conclusion was simple but eloquent. "This is no time for men who oppose Senator McCarthy's methods to keep silent, or for those of us who approve," he warned. "We can deny our heritage and our history, but we cannot escape responsibility for the result. There is no way for a citizen of a republic to abdicate his responsibilities. As a nation we have come into our full inheritance at a tender age," Murrow explained. "We proclaim ourselves—as indeed we are—the defenders of freedom, what's left of it, but we cannot defend freedom abroad by deserting it at home. The actions of the junior senator from Wisconsin have caused alarm and dismay amongst our allies abroad and given considerable comfort to our enemies, and whose fault is that? Not really his. He didn't create this situation of fear; he merely exploited it, and rather successfully. Cassius was right: 'The fault, dear Brutus, is not in our stars but in ourselves.' " Then, forehead furrowed and eyes soulful, Murrow ended with the closing that had become his trademark: "Good night, and good luck."

Murrow slumped in his seat, sweating and unsure of the result. The staff shared his apprehension—until the phones began to ring with congratulations. One of the first to call was Babe Paley, telling Ed that he had given one of his most impressive performances. In the ensuing days, Murrow was approached by friends and strangers alike, all eager to shake his hand and tell him how wonderful he was, how much they appreciated what he had done. And yet, in the midst of all the good wishes, fear remained ever-present.

The day after the broadcast Murrow went to the airport to pick up Janet and his eight-year-old son, Casey, who had been sent to Jamaica for a "vacation" while Ed struggled with the program's production. Janet had been unable to get any news of the reaction to the broadcast until she arrived at the Miami airport en route to New York. The euphoria of the coverage was dispelled as soon as Ed greeted her, informing her of the threats he had received and warning her, she later remembered, that "the most important thing was never to let Casey out of my sight." Murrow shared his concern with Paley as well, and the CBS chairman said the company would provide him with bodyguards. Murrow rejected the suggestion out-of-hand, but Paley would not be turned aside—he arranged for the protection without Murrow's knowledge.

Paley had also tried to insulate Murrow—and CBS—from any interference by the federal government. Murrow, Friendly, Stanton, and even Paley had maintained their periodic contact with FBI Director Hoover and other Washington officials, advising them of the network's plans and asking for cooperation in developing programs (including an abortive attempt to do a series based on FBI cases). When Murrow and Friendly disclosed that they were going to do the McCarthy broadcast, a telegram was sent to Hoover, informing him of the broadcast and, as on other occasions, asking for any comments he might have.

Ironically, the only criticism from official Washington came from President Eisenhower. He had been talking with Paley's good friend Jock Whitney and had expressed surprise—and disappointment—that Paley would offer McCarthy free time to respond and, more than that, assume responsibility for up to $25,000 in production costs for the reply. Jock passed Eisenhower's concerns on to Paley, and in May the CBS chairman wrote a letter to Ike explaining his decision. "Because of the potential power of radio or television to do evil as well as good," said Paley, "we have always maintained a policy of fairness and balance in the treatment of controversial issues." The advent of television, he went on, added a "new facet"—cost. If the network used "an expensive production budget to present one side of a controversial issue," it was only right that they make those same facilities available to someone to respond. "I didn't think I would ever find myself in the position of defending an action which would work to the benefit of the junior senator from Wisconsin," Paley concluded. "However, I believe our policies are sound and essential to the maintenance of a free broadcasting system in America and, therefore, Senator McCarthy or no, we must stand by them and implement them." Ike responded with a warm note, saying that he was surprised that Jock had passed on his concerns but, having considered Paley's explanation, was impressed with "the very impartial, not to say high-minded, attitude" that CBS had adopted.

Although he believed in those high-minded principles, Paley had no expectation that they would be followed by McCarthy and his supporters. A couple of days after Murrow's broadcast, Fulton Lewis, Jr., used his radio program to ask McCarthy for his reaction. "I may say, Fulton," said McCarthy in his staged arrogance, "that I have a little difficulty answering the specific attack he made, because I never listen to the extreme left-wing, bleeding-heart element of radio and television." Paley knew otherwise. He knew McCarthy's crowd would be combing through Murrow's past, trying to find something, anything, they could use against the famous correspondent. Paley was determined not to let that happen. No effort would be spared to protect Murrow. He hired Cravath, Swaine & Moore, the prestigious Wall Street law firm, to make the necessary investigations and preparations for any legal action; he sent word to Howard K. Smith in London and other foreign correspondents to secure endorsements from Winston Churchill, Anthony Eden, and other foreign leaders who knew Murrow. And he made himself available to Ed whenever he could. "My God," he later recalled, "after the broadcast, he spent hours in my office every day, and we had to, you know, be very careful how we handled McCarthy." One of the first matters they had to consider was a response to McCarthy's public attacks on Murrow. He could not ignore them, but, on the other hand, there was no percentage in dueling with the senator in public. Murrow asked Paley: What should he say? "Why don't you say something along these lines," Paley suggested. "When the history of these times are written we'll know who served his country better, the junior senator from Wisconsin or Edward R. Murrow." Ed liked the suggestion, ultimately using it with only minor changes.

Paley had to accept an additional cost beyond his time and the expense of the McCarthy reply. It involved Don Hollenbeck, a savvy but sensitive correspondent who anchored the evening news on the network's flagship station, WCBS-TV, in New York. Hollenbeck's was the first face New York viewers saw after the McCarthy broadcast, and he did not mince words in telling his audience how he felt. "I don't know whether all of you have seen what I just saw," said Hollenbeck, "but I want to associate myself and this program with what Ed Murrow has just said, and I have never been prouder of CBS." Tragically, it was the beginning of the end for Hollenbeck. Much of the print media picked up on this uncharacteristic display of emotion and criticized CBS, and especially Hollenbeck, for the outburst. Jack O'Brian, a columnist with the Hearst newspapers, was particularly vicious and personal in his attacks. The pressure proved to be too much, and within weeks the young correspondent was found dead in his apartment, the victim of suicide.

Murrow and Friendly were overwhelmed by Hollenbeck's death. They took their concerns to Paley immediately. Many CBS programs, including "See It Now," depended on the Hearst organization's "News of the Day" to furnish film and logistical support, including cameramen, editors, and projectionists. But Murrow and Friendly said they no longer wanted to be associated with any element of the Hearst organization. They wanted to develop their own film unit. Paley listened intently. Cost could not be a factor and he didn't even inquire about it. He had only one question for his two employees: "How soon can you do it?"

Despite his support for Murrow and Friendly, Paley recognized that the final judgment was not yet in. CBS was a publicly traded company with outside directors and people who worried about the bottom line. They of course respected Murrow's courage, but they were also anxious to know how much it would cost the network in lost advertisers. For days Friendly and Murrow did not hear anything from anyone in the top executive echelon at CBS, and Friendly began to sense that the board was asking itself, "Why does Murrow have to save the world every week?" Some executives, including Stanton, began to wonder out loud whether the

McCarthy broadcast might not undermine the network's ability to survive financially.

It was a perilous time for Paley—weighing his instincts for honest expression against the need to satisfy the money managers. There were no easy answers, but, as always, he fell back on the basic principles of "fairness and balance" that Ed Klauber had instilled in him. And to reaffirm his own leadership on the issue, he traveled to Chicago in May 1954 to make a now-rare public speech to the National Association of Broadcasters. He did not mention Edward R. Murrow or the McCarthy broadcast, but they provided the unspoken backdrop for his remarks—especially when the CBS chairman explained that he wanted to speak about "the broadcaster's role and responsibilities in the field of news and public affairs." Of course, said Paley, radio and television had revolutionized politics. Despite that impact, broadcasting did not have the stature it deserved—and would not, he insisted, "until we have shown through clear performance that we have faced up to our opportunities and our responsibilities." He recognized that each station would have to make its own decision on how to fulfill its duties, but Paley thought (not surprisingly) that other broadcasters might benefit from knowing the policies followed by CBS. "In news programs," he said, "there is to be no opinion or slanting. . . . In news analysis, there is elucidation, illumination, and explanation of the facts and situations, but without bias or editorialization." The ultimate goal, in short, was "objectivity." "I think we all recognize," he added, "that human nature is such that no newsman is entirely free from his own personal prejudices, experience, and opinions and that, accordingly, one-hundred percent objectivity may not always be possible. But the important factor is that the news broadcaster and the news analyst must have the will and intent to be objective."

It was a rigorous standard—but nothing different than what Paley and Klauber had been preaching for decades. Still, executives and correspondents in the CBS news operation—which was soon organized into a separate department known as News and Public Affairs—took notice. To them it was no coincidence that Paley was emphasizing objectivity immediately after Murrow had made clear his own opinion of McCarthy. "Paley's 1954 NAB speech was a new edict," said Sig Mickelson, the first director of the News and Public Affairs Department. "We all snapped to attention with the new statement on objectivity. It became the catechism for us."

Not everyone accepted this new edict willingly or gracefully. Eric Sevareid was one who did not. A forty-two-year-old native of Velva, North Dakota, Sevareid had established a national reputation as one of broadcasting's most thoughtful and literate correspondents. After working as a reporter for the *Minneapolis Star* and the Paris edition of the *Herald*

Tribune, Sevareid had been hired by Murrow in 1939 at the then "staggering" salary of $250 a month. After serving in war-torn London, Sevareid became a war correspondent in China. Between the military advances of the Japanese and the conflicts among China's many hostile factions, Sevareid was kept very busy—and would have stayed longer if he had not been forced to bail out of a plane and trek to safety through the Burmese jungle to avoid capture by the Japanese. After a short recovery period, he returned to Europe to cover the last days of Hitler's Third Reich.

Sevareid devoted long hours to the preparation of his radio commentaries, and he was obviously pleased with the favorable reactions he received from Bill Paley and others inside and outside of CBS. From this experience Sevareid had developed some firm ideas about the radio commentator's role—ideas that differed greatly from Paley's views. The goal of objectivity without opinion, Sevareid believed, was "unworkable" and "unwise." As he once explained to Mickelson, "The whole public reputation of persons such as Murrow, Howard Smith, or myself rests upon our individual approach to events and our individual means of expression. A writer cannot be good and keep out personal opinion." H.V. Kaltenborn and Elmer Davis could not have said it better. But Mickelson was unmoved. Paley was the boss, and objectivity was the standard.

Sevareid did not try to hide his feelings from Paley—even after the 1954 NAB speech—and Mickelson could see the tension between the two men building quickly. Sevareid had a late-night slot to provide radio commentary, and he was not as objective in expressing his views as Paley would have liked. Paley kept telling Mickelson how he felt about Sevareid's broadcasts, and Sevareid kept telling Mickelson it was "ridiculous" for him not to take sides on important issues. Mickelson could not resolve the dispute and finally suggested that the chairman have lunch with Eric. Paley readily agreed, but the results were not what they had hoped. Sevareid pressed his point, but, as Mickelson recalled, Paley was "tough," telling Eric point-blank, "We're going to adhere to strict objectivity."

Sevareid left the luncheon in a hostile mood and called Bob Kintner, the president of NBC's news operation, to inquire about a job at the rival network. Kintner was interested, but, in time, Sevareid was not. Paley's approach was all wrong, he thought, but there was nothing to compare with the excitement and prestige of being with CBS. It was, after all, the network that had dared to confront McCarthy.

But nothing can endure forever. Even Murrow recognized that. The public's memory was short. McCarthy finally faced censure from his colleagues in the Senate and receded from public view, a broken, almost pitiful replica of his former self. Although blacklisting at CBS and elsewhere continued, the public's attention moved elsewhere. Entertainment had always provided an escape from the tensions of real life, and, as the turmoil of the McCarthy hearings faded from memory, CBS and other television stations began to introduce a new form of diversion: the quiz show. One evening in 1955, Murrow himself had occasion to watch the quiz program that immediately preceded "See It Now." Murrow was appalled. The program was mindless, totally devoid of any redeeming value—except perhaps in ratings. But that was enough, and he knew it did not bode well for "See It Now," which possessed one of the most important slots in the prime-time schedule. Murrow did not like what he saw, but he was a realist. He leaned over to Fred Friendly while the quiz program was in progress and said, "Any bets on how long we'll keep this time period now?"

CHAPTER TWELVE

Entertainment

For Harry Ackerman, it was an easy decision. Some six months after he joined CBS in early 1948, Bill Paley told him that he would have to make a choice. "He said," Ackerman recalled, "that I could head up television programming in New York or go to Los Angeles to be in charge of radio programming there." Ackerman liked New York. He had worked there for years, he felt at home in the city. But who wanted to be involved in television? "I saw that as a dead-end," he later recalled. So Ackerman gracefully accepted his new assignment, and within weeks he was on a train to the West Coast.

Paley, of course, saw things differently. He knew that television was not a passing fad, that it was only a matter of time before every home had one. None of which meant that CBS's success was assured. NBC already had several advantages that could make the competition formidable. The rival network had powerful VHF stations in large markets; as of 1949 it had a new, creative director of programming named Pat Weaver (who, like Ackerman and Hubbell Robinson, had also emigrated from Young & Rubicam); and, in those first days of television in the late forties, NBC had the unquestioned star of the medium—Milton Berle. The program format—which Weaver later refined with great success—involved variety, reflecting the then-prevailing notion that audiences wanted a little bit of everything in their program fare. Berle's hour-long program served that notion, but, above all, he provided the kind of zany comedy that still seemed to provide the best vehicle to high ratings.

As in radio, Paley spent much of his energy in television programming responding to NBC's initiatives. But in the late 1940s, there was no one who could compare with Berle. Paley only had Ed Sullivan, who had been selected as the temporary host for CBS's own variety program, "Toast of the Town." Few, if any, people expected Sullivan to be able to compete with NBC's master comedian. Sullivan's personality was wooden, he had no talent, and he conveyed a strange impression on the screen, with his bowed head and his stiff motions. (After the first few programs viewers started writing to CBS to ask what was wrong with Sullivan's neck.) But

he fooled everyone, including Paley. His first show in 1948 included the new comedy team of Dean Martin and Jerry Lewis, and, along with some other performers, it made a favorable impression on both the CBS brass and the audience.

Everyone expected Sullivan to continue this success week after week, and he gave it his best effort. But money soon proved to be a problem. Sullivan complained to Hubbell Robinson that he could not attract enough quality performers with a budget of only $750 a week. Robinson passed the complaint on to the chairman, and, after a lunch with Sullivan, Paley agreed to increase the figure to $2,000 a week. No one would be able to say that CBS had failed for lack of willingness to spend money.

Although Paley was happily surprised by Sullivan's success, he remained on the lookout for someone who could challenge Berle as the king of television comedy. And he finally appeared in the early 1950s in the guise of Jackie Gleason. An extremely heavy man in his mid-thirties, Gleason seemed to overflow with talent and ambition. He had grown up poor in Brooklyn. (After accumulating wealth beyond his wildest dreams, Gleason would frequently remark that "a buck never threw its arms around my parents.") His ladder out of poverty was comedy. He used his appearance and natural ability to pursue acting roles anywhere and everywhere, finally acquiring minor parts in movies and even a Broadway play. In 1949 he was given the lead role in NBC's "Life of Riley," a television serial that centered on the trials and tribulations of a hardworking man whose bad luck was more than offset by his good heart. The show was successful, but Gleason wanted more from his professional life. In 1950 he left the series (yielding the lead role to William Bendix) to star in his own variety program, "Calvacade of Stars," which he had sold to the DuMont Television Network, one of the few entities that dared to compete with NBC and CBS. The program enabled Gleason to introduce the many characters he had invented for himself, and it soon became apparent that no one could fault Jackie Gleason for a shortage of imagination.

Bill Paley was among Gleason's most ardent admirers, and he decided that he needed the "Great One" for his network. Once again, his weapons of seduction would be money and food. Paley invited Gleason and his agent to lunch at his private dining room to discuss a new contract for Gleason with CBS, one that would involve a substantial increase in money for the comedian. It was a memorable moment for Gleason—but not for reasons Paley had hoped. "I arrived with a terrible hangover," Gleason later remembered. But the young performer was not one to turn down a drink under any circumstance. "Paley and his programming people were there, tossing around some very big figures," said Gleason. "But I had a couple of Bloody Marys, and within a short time I was asleep." Gleason's agent later related to him what happened next. As Gleason explained it, "Paley looked over at me fast asleep in the midst of these heavy negotiations, turned to his programming people, and said, 'If that's the way he feels you better give him the money.'"

With a substantial financial investment at stake, Paley followed Gleason's progress closely. He attended the first few shows, partly out of interest and partly to let Gleason know how important the show was (a gesture that Gleason very much appreciated). And when Gleason encountered difficulties with the production staff, Paley promptly gave him a letter that ordered all production personnel to provide the star with whatever support he needed. Paley had no cause for regret about his personal and financial investment. Gleason's show was an instant success, and soon CBS could legitimately claim that it had someone who could challenge NBC's number-one comedian in the ratings.

For all these achievements in New York, Paley had already learned that Los Angeles would have to be the center of activity for planning new television programs. Writers, producers, and performers were largely congregated on the West Coast, and he meant to take advantage of that talent pool. By 1952 construction was completed on CBS's own Los Angeles studios, known as Television City. Hubbell Robinson, the network executive in charge of programming, remained in New York, but more and more the programs were produced three thousand miles away. And, as television began to eclipse radio, Harry Ackerman, who had left New York to escape television, now found it his principal preoccupation.

The transition was not nearly as painful as Ackerman had anticipated. The production process was far more complex (and costly), but many of his more successful radio ventures were easily transferred to television. Still, the new medium involved new problems, and one of the more delicate issues was how to handle Lucille Ball.

It all began in 1948. Ackerman had decided to recruit Ball for a new radio program that would be based on a book he had read while taking the train to his new home in California. The story line would provide a humorous look at the dilemmas and frustrations of an All-American couple. At first Ackerman was unsure of who would play the husband's role, but he knew immediately whom he wanted for the wife. He had seen Lucille Ball appearing at the Stork Club on a local television show, and he had been taken with her beauty and her talent. Paley agreed with Ackerman's assessment of Ball. She was, he later observed, "[t]he best comedienne I've ever known. . . ." So Ackerman made the show his first priority in Hollywood, and within a short time "My Favorite Husband"

William S. Paley making the contact that opened up the world's largest regular hookup of radio stations. *(UPI/Bettmann Newsphotos)*

Paley appearing before the Senate Interstate Commerce Committee in 1941. (*Broadcasting* magazine)

Mrs. Goldie Drell Paley, Bill Paley's mother. (*Broadcasting* magazine)

Samuel Paley, Bill Paley's father.
(UPI/Bettmann Newsphotos)

Paley and his bride, Dorothy Hart.
(UPI/Bettmann Newsphotos)

Paley meeting with Nelson Rockefeller in 1941. (*Broadcasting* magazine)

Paley speaking at the United Hospital Fund Drive Parade in New York in November 1942. Mayor Fiorello H. La Guardia is to his left. (*Broadcasting* magazine)

Paley as a colonel in the army in World War II. (*Broadcasting* magazine)

Paley and Jack Benny in 1950. (*Broadcasting* magazine)

Edward R. Murrow hosting "See It Now" in 1951. (*Broadcasting* magazine)

Paley presenting the President's Materials Policy Commission's report to President Harry S. Truman on December 18, 1952. (*Broadcasting* magazine)

Babe Paley at the WCBS studio. (*Broadcasting* magazine)

Babe and Paley attending a premiere in 1954. *(UPI/Bettmann/Newsphotos)*

Ed Murrow in his office at CBS. *(Courtesy Janet Murrow)*

Bill Paley and Paul Kesten.
(*Broadcasting* magazine)

Paley greets John F. Kennedy just before the first historic Kennedy–Nixon debate in Chicago on September 26, 1960. (*Broadcasting* magazine)

At the wedding of his daughter in 1964, from left to right are Bill Paley, Amanda Mortimer (Mrs. Carter Burden Jr.), Carter Burden Jr., and Babe Paley. (*Ben Martin/Time* magazine)

Standing from left to right, Fred Friendly, Dwight D. Eisenhower, Walter Cronkite, and Bill Paley during the preparation for the *D-Day Plus Twenty Years* special in 1964. (*Broadcasting* magazine)

Frank Stanton and Bill Paley at
an annual stockholders meeting.
(*Broadcasting* magazine)

Paley and CBS president Arthur R. Taylor, 1975. (*Broadcasting* magazine)

Frank Stanton and Paley outside the new CBS headquarters building, Black Rock, on October 23, 1964, just before the building opened. (*Broadcasting* magazine.)

Bill Paley in his office at Black Rock. (*Broadcasting* magazine)

The Order of Merit of the Republic of Italy is conferred upon Paley by Italian consul general Vieri Traxler. (*Broadcasting* magazine)

Paley dancing with Katharine Graham in 1978. (*Broadcasting* magazine)

John Backe, far left, and Paley at a CBS social function. (*Broadcasting* magazine)

Bill Paley with Henry Kissinger in 1982. (*Broadcasting* magazine)

Paley making his retirement speech at the annual stockholders meeting, 1983. (*Broadcasting* magazine)

Frank Stanton, Walter Cronkite, and Bill Paley. (*Broadcasting* magazine)

Thomas Wyman testifying before the Senate Commerce, Science and Transportation Committee in 1985. *(UPI/Bettmann Newsphotos)*

Paley enjoying a speech. (*Broadcasting* magazine)

Bill Paley and Laurence Tisch. *(Alex Webb/ Magnum Photos, Inc.)*

(with the husband played by Richard Denning) became one of radio's top-rated programs.

Both Paley and Ackerman wanted to transfer "My Favorite Husband" to television in the early 1950s. At first the only key question was who would play the husband's role; but eventually, the matter involved the issue of who would own the program.

As a successful band leader, Desi Arnaz did not need another job. But conflicting schedules had prevented him and Lucy from spending much time with each other. In fact, those long separations had been one of the reasons why Lucy had filed for divorce in 1944 (the other reason being Desi's roving eye). Desi had promised that the future would be different, and Lucy withdrew the request for divorce. But little changed. He was always on the road and she was always in rehearsal. They would give their marriage one more real chance, and that required them to be together. If "My Favorite Husband" was transferred to television, Lucy said she would stay with the show, but only if it included a part for Desi. She explained all this to the CBS chairman, but Paley was not very sympathetic. What part could Desi play? "My Favorite Husband" was about an American couple—there was no place for a Cuban band leader who spoke with a heavy accent. Paley tried to persuade her, but Lucy was insistent. She would rather leave broadcasting than lose Desi.

No one was sure what to do—except that Desi had to be kept in line until a decision could be made. Ackerman was given authority to hire Arnaz and told to do something, anything, to keep him on the team. Ackerman decided to take advantage of Desi's background. He took the format of a radio quiz program called "Earn Your Vacation" (hosted by a very young Johnny Carson) and changed it to "Your Tropical Vacation," with the host none other than Desi Arnaz. Every week three contestants would try to answer questions about music for the right to a two-week paid vacation in a Latin American country.

In the meantime, Lucy and Desi went to Ackerman and told him they were forming a production company and wanted a share of the television adaptation of "My Favorite Husband." Paley rejected the suggestion out of hand. He had just helped wean the industry away from a system in which advertisers owned the programs; he was not about to set a precedent that allowed performers to own programs—in either case the network would lose control. "Absolutely not," he told Ackerman upon hearing Lucy and Desi's suggestion. "We don't share ownership of programs." But Lucy and Desi remained adamant, and, after reviewing the pilot—which featured a young American woman married to a struggling Cuban band leader—Paley decided that the cost was worth the benefits. He knew a hit when he saw one, and he was not about to forgo the high ratings that were sure to follow.

Paley's instincts proved to be correct. "I Love Lucy," as the show was renamed, quickly became television's most popular program. In 1952 the American Research Bureau reported that "I Love Lucy"—broadcast every Monday evening from 9 to 9:30—had become the first television program to be seen by ten million homes. And one year later 68.8 percent of America's television homes tuned in to watch the much-ballyhooed program segment that focused on the birth of Lucy and Desi's son, Ricky.

For Paley and CBS, the success of "I Love Lucy" meant more than a profitable program slot. They also inherited a new partner in the production of other programs. Arnaz was, Paley later said, "the best situation comedy producer in Hollywood," and Bill Paley always wanted the best for his network. Within a short time CBS was using Desilu Productions—the company formed by Lucy and Desi—to produce other programs, including "Our Miss Brooks" with Eve Arden, "December Bride" with Spring Byington, and the "Danny Thomas Show." In all of this Arnaz proved to be as capable as Paley in driving a hard bargain. At one point, for example, CBS (unknown to the chairman) dropped the option for the radio program of "December Bride," and Arnaz quickly picked it up with the expectation that the program could be easily transferred to television. When he learned of the oversight, Paley was on the phone immediately to Arnaz in California, saying, "Chico, you are a crook. . . . You stole 'December Bride' from me." Arnaz did not want to offend his greatest benefactor, and he soothed Paley's ruffled feathers with a promise to sell him 25 percent of the ownership. Again, it proved to be a good bargain for both men—"December Bride" was in the top ten shows for five years during the mid-fifties.

In addition to these serials, CBS was also able to transfer many of its radio stars to television, although the transition was not always easy. Jack Benny resisted before he accepted Paley's overture to move to television, and, even then, Benny's initial contract only required one appearance every eight weeks. Still, he remained a master at timing and wit. True to form, his first line on television balanced his well-known vanity against his reputation for stinginess. "I'd give a million dollars," he said, "to know what I look like."

George Burns had his own difficulty in moving to television. Paley wanted the American public to get some appreciation of just how funny George Burns could be. On radio his role had been confined to straight lines in response to Gracie's humorous illogic. What could he do on television that would be different? At lunch one day Paley urged George to create a role similar to that of the narrator in the play *Our Town*.

George could stand off to the side and ad lib comments about Gracie's remarks and situations. Burns loved the idea and was soon making great use of it. For her part, Gracie found the weekly grind of television exhausting. "Every Monday night after a show we would drive home and I would hand her the script for the next week's show," Burns recalled. "But unlike my role, her part did not allow for ad libbing. She had to memorize all those crazy nonsequiturs, and it wasn't easy."

Despite the network's success with these new television ventures, few programs gave Paley as much satisfaction as "Gunsmoke." And once again, Ackerman was at the center of the development. NBC had had a radio program in the late forties called "Philip Marlowe," based on the adventures of the detective created by the mystery writer Dashiell Hammett. NBC dropped the program when its star, Van Heflin, was recalled to "movie duty" by MGM. Ackerman picked the option up for CBS and was able to make it successful with another actor in the lead role. Shortly afterward, Hubbell Robinson passed the word from New York that Paley wanted a Philip Marlowe radio program set in the Old West. "What Bill wanted," Ackerman later remembered, "was a series based on a lawman who was a rugged individual, a loner who could single-handedly take on the outlaws."

While Robinson was describing Paley's goal, Ackerman knew then and there that he would call the show "Gunsmoke." It just seemed to convey the right impression—no small matter in a medium that depended on people's imaginations. The voice of the lawman had to be right as well, and, after many auditions, Ackerman finally selected William Conrad to play Marshall Matt Dillon.

The show's success on radio guaranteed a spot for it in CBS's television schedule. Unfortunately, one key element had to be changed. However appropriate his voice, Bill Conrad did not look the part of Marshall Dillon. He was heavy and balding, not at all the kind of portrait that the radio program had tried to create. Ackerman was polite enough to audition Conrad for the television part, but he knew they would need someone else. During the auditions in the early 1950s, John Wayne approached Ackerman one day and said he had an actor under contract to his production company who would be perfect for the role: James Arness.

For Jim Arness it was another break in a long streak of luck. He had traveled to California from his home in Minneapolis in the late forties because he hated the cold and had a friend who had described Los Angeles as "Lotus Land" where the weather was always warm. "I had no driving ambition to be an actor," he later recalled. "I just sort of fell into it." Arness had the qualities Hollywood was constantly on the lookout for— tall, handsome, with a warm smile and an easy manner. Director Dore

Schary needed a young Scandinavian to play Loretta Young's brother in the movie *The Farmer's Daughter* at the time, and, driven by a lack of money rather than a thirst for stardom, Arness auditioned for the part and got it. He then had to hustle back home, only to discover his landlady had locked his apartment (with all his things in it) for failure to pay rent. Arness told her about his new job and persuaded her to let him back into the apartment so he could get his things and travel up to San Francisco for the filming.

Once on the set, Arness discovered that he loved being an actor—the parties, the dinners, the fancy hotel suites, the celebrities all around. "Once I got a taste of this," he said, "it was hard to go back." After *The Farmer's Daughter* he landed some minor parts, and then captured the role of the creature in *The Thing*. Although the role was a starring one, his face—and his name—remained anonymous to audiences. Still, John Wayne felt that Arness had considerable potential, especially since he was still only in his twenties. Wayne signed him up, with the hope that Arness could secure some attractive roles in Westerns.

Ackerman became very interested in Arness after his screen test. As the Duke had said, Arness was the ideal choice. The only problem was the young actor himself. "I didn't want to do it," Arness remembered. "The only Western television programs were 'Hopalong Cassidy,' 'Cisco Kid,' and other children's shows. I wanted to be seen by adults, and television did not seem the way to go." Ackerman persisted, utilizing all the pressure he could muster—including a chat with CBS's new president of the Television Network, Jack Van Volkenberg. None of it worked. Arness knew what he wanted, and it wasn't "Gunsmoke." Ackerman finally pleaded with Wayne to do something about the young actor. "And Duke did lay it on the line to me," said Arness. "He said the series would give me an opportunity to be in front of the camera and perfect my craft. It would give me exposure to millions of people. And so he said I'd better get my ass over there."

For Arness it proved to be the crowning touch of a blossoming career. "Gunsmoke" quickly became one of the top-rated television programs of 1955, and, as Arness himself observed, "overnight I went from 'who's he' to 'who's who.' " Paley also knew that the show had great potential, and he kept abreast of its progress. At one point he passed the word to Ackerman (again through Hubbell Robinson) that the role of Chester, the deputy marshall played by Dennis Weaver, should not have a limp, as Ackerman had proposed. Ackerman felt very strongly about that limp, and he pretended that he never got the message—an "oversight" that Paley himself forgave when the show took off after its debut.

From then on Paley made it a point to visit the "Gunsmoke" set at least once during the year to check everything himself. And on each visit he would stop by to say hello to Jim Arness, telling him how much he enjoyed the show and asking if there was anything he could do. "That really impressed me," said Arness. "I know that program executives are probably saying that kind of thing to all their star performers, but he seemed real genuine. I just got a feeling that he really meant it. Man to man." And although he never had need to call on Paley, Arness always appreciated the fact that the chairman of the network seemed concerned with his welfare.

To a large extent, Paley's interest in his star performers *was* genuine. He had great respect for their profession, he liked being around them, he wanted them to be happy, and he was prepared to do what he could to make them feel important—and wanted. If it was an actor, there would be invitations to lunch or dinner. If it was an actress, there would be flowers. (*New York Times* media critic Jack Gould once commented, only half-jokingly, that when Faye Emerson came to New York, there were so many flowers from Paley in her hotel room you could barely open the door.) In either case there were gestures, warm notes, and frequent phone calls. George Burns, for instance, remembered that Paley would call him from New York every six weeks or so to tell him how much he loved the previous night's show. Burns was not one to let Paley off so easily. "What about the other five shows?" he would invariably ask the CBS chairman. Paley would laugh and say he liked those as well. Jack Benny and other performers received similar calls, and all agreed that Bill Paley was a wonderful employer. "Bill Paley was always a fair guy," said Jackie Gleason. "Very generous, too. You always seemed to walk away with more money than you thought you would."

Of course, all these good feelings were premised on the performer's success with the audience. However much he may have liked them personally, Paley never forgot that he was running a business and that a performer's utility to the network ended when the ratings dropped. And when the ax later fell for Jack Benny, Jackie Gleason and other star performers of the fifties, Bill Paley was nowhere to be found.

Most entertainers understood the rules of the game and accepted their fate without personal bitterness toward Paley (especially since there was always someone else to communicate the bad news of a dropped show or canceled contract). Ed Murrow also knew the rules, but he had a much more difficult time abiding by them—particularly when he knew that the ultimate decision-maker was a good friend, the same person who had planned and schemed and partied with him in wartime London.

Part of the problem was the pressure for conformity. McCarthy's fall from grace did not end the blacklisting in the broadcast industry. Other people picked up where he left off, and few were as effective as Vincent Hartnett and Laurence Johnson. Hartnett had assisted Ted Kirkpatrick in the preparation of *Red Channels,* and Johnson was a supermarket owner in Syracuse, New York. The two men formed an organization called AWARE, Inc., a self-proclaimed protector of public morality. To that end, they would advise broadcasters whether certain performers were Communist sympathizers who should not be used. If the broadcaster resisted Hartnett and Johnson's advice, the two men would visit advertising agencies and sponsors, threatening adverse publicity and prolonged boycotts of the sponsor's product in supermarkets across the country. The ploy was very successful. Ed Sullivan, for one, refused to allow anyone on his show who had not won a silent vote of approval from AWARE.

Hartnett and Johnson did not appreciate challenges to their authority, such as it was, and they were particularly offended in December 1955 when John Henry Faulk, a popular entertainer on CBS's New York radio station, won the presidency of the performers' union, the American Federation of Television and Radio Artists, and promised to end AWARE's influence. Agencies and sponsors associated with Faulk's show began to receive telephone calls and visits informing them (falsely) about Faulk's long involvement with Communist-front organizations. Faulk started to lose sponsors for his program and, in another coincidence, his ratings began to fall as well.

Under other circumstances, the decision to keep or drop Faulk's show would have been made at the station level. After all, he was not employed by the CBS network. But Faulk's situation was anything but ordinary. The WCBS station manager took the issue to Frank Stanton, and the CBS president made the decision to terminate Faulk's show in the summer of 1957. From that point on, Faulk was unemployed—and unemployable. No one in the broadcast industry would hire him for anything—even as a panelist on a quiz program. Sig Mickelson, still CBS's vice president for news and public affairs, remembered that he once proposed using Faulk on a show and was advised that that was not possible.

Stanton says now that he alone made the decision to terminate Faulk's services and that he never discussed the matter with Paley. It is inconceivable, however, that Paley did not know of Faulk's plight. Charles Collingwood, one of the chairman's few close friends within the company, was one of the names on the AFTRA slate that AWARE was so vigorously attacking. And more than that, one of Faulk's key supporters throughout his long ordeal was CBS's most celebrated newsman—Ed Murrow.

The Faulk controversy was painful for Murrow. He was, or at least had been, a power within the CBS organization. He was personal friends with the chairman. And he was a member of the company's board of directors.

And yet there was nothing he could do for Faulk except give him $7,500 to pay for the lawsuit that Faulk instituted (and ultimately won). "Let's get this straight, Johnny," he told Faulk. "I am not making a personal loan to you of this money. I am investing in America."

Murrow's frustration with Faulk's situation only compounded the disappointments he was experiencing in his own ventures. Despite the awards and plaudits won for the McCarthy broadcast, "See It Now" soon fared a downward slide. The program continued to explore sensitive and controversial subjects, but one—a 1955 investigation into land-grant scandals in Texas—led ALCOA (then trying to expand its installations in the Lone Star State) to drop its sponsorship. That prompted a search for a new sponsor, but the success was short-lived, and by the spring of 1955 "See It Now" had no one to help defray the $100,000 cost per show (almost three times the cost of a half-hour entertainment program). At the end of the season, Paley summoned Murrow and Friendly to his office to review the situation. He knew that Murrow was wearing down under the strain of preparing for the program (as well as his other chatty interview program, "Person to Person"). A half hour really could not do justice to an important subject, said Paley. Why not reduce the number of shows but increase the length of each individual segment? Murrow and Friendly went along with the suggestion, not realizing that it was the first step toward the program's demise.

In the 1956–57 season, "See It Now" did five one-hour broadcasts and two ninety-minute broadcasts. Eight hour-long segments were scheduled for the 1957–58 season, and they proved to be the last. The telling blow came in March 1958 as a result of a program that did not, at least in the opinion of Murrow and Friendly, seem to be controversial.

The program concerned the issue of statehood for Alaska and Hawaii. The segment included interviews with people who supported and opposed the granting of statehood, and public response to the program, at least judging from the mail it generated, was muted—except for one letter from Congressman John Pillion of New York. The show had included an interview with Pillion saying that the grant of statehood to Hawaii would give union leader (and alleged Communist sympathizer) Harry Bridges control of Hawaii's congressional delegation. In response, Bridges had ridiculed the charge, saying that Pillion was "crazy." The exchange was a minor squabble involving only about a minute of the hour-long program. But Pillion was not happy. He had been attacked on national television, and he wanted time to reply. He couched his request in the right jargon, saying that the opponents of statehood were all "elderly genetlemen," thus conveying the impression that anyone who was young and intelligent supported statehood. Pillion wanted to provide a contrasting view.

The issue was debated at the weekly meeting of the Program Board, with Paley, Stanton, Mickelson, and others (but not Murrow or Friendly) in attendance. Paley was quick to say that he thought that CBS should give the congressman time to reply. Fairness and balance were the watchwords, and the "See It Now" episode had not been either. Its slant was clearly in favor of statehood, said Paley, and CBS had a duty to rectify the imbalance. Mickelson argued against giving reply time, saying the network should not feel obligated to give away free time whenever some government official complained. The debate continued for hours, but no one proposed that a vote be taken. There was only one real decision-maker. "Well," said Paley finally, "let's give him the time." The meeting was over, and Mickelson was dispatched to tell Murrow.

The famous correspondent did not take the news well. To him it was tantamount to a charge that this program, his show, had not been balanced, and Ed Murrow prided himself on being fair. He and Friendly marched up to the chairman's office. They would not accept this decision without a fight.

As always, Paley was prepared to listen. No one yelled or shouted, but the room filled with tension. The Pillion decision was unnecessary and unfair, said Murrow. They had already provided exposure to both sides of the issue. The company was sending the wrong signals by giving time to the congressman. Murrow assumed—wrongly—that Stanton had made the decision and complained that, for all his administrative talent, Frank Stanton had no feel for the news business (another judgment that proved to be wrong). Paley did not make any effort to correct Murrow on either score. Murrow was his friend, and Paley did not want to unnecessarily strain the relationship. Better that Murrow should blame Stanton for these kinds of decisions (which Murrow usually did) rather than the chairman.

At another point Murrow suggested that, at least for the future, he and Friendly should be included in any decision to give reply time in response to a "See It Now" broadcast. Paley quietly interrupted, saying, "But I thought you and Fred didn't want to do 'See It Now' anymore." The comment stunned both men. True, they had agreed to reduce the number of segments, but neither man wanted to end the series. "Bill," said Murrow, "are you going to destroy all this? Don't you want an instrument like the 'See It Now' organization, which you have poured so much into for so long, to continue?" "Yes," Paley replied. Then he put his hand on his stomach and added, "but I don't want this constant stomachache every time you do a controversial subject." "I'm afraid that's a price you have to be willing to pay," said Murrow. "It goes with the job." But Paley didn't agree, and "See It Now" was dead.

Murrow was disturbed by this turn of events. "He came home that night and exploded," said Janet Murrow. "He was scornful of Bill's stomach-ache comment. As if Ed didn't have pressures of his own." None of that changed anything. In the summer of 1958 Friendly was summoned to the chairman's office to discuss the final plans for terminating "See It Now." The decision was a foregone conclusion, but that was not going to stop Friendly. He let his emotions get the better of him, telling Paley how terrible the decision was, how he was dropping one of the network's few consistently good programs. Paley let Friendly talk for a while and then interrupted, saying, "Fred, you are speaking beyond your competence." Friendly fumed at the remark, turned on his heels, and stormed out on the chairman—or at least tried to. Unfortunately, Paley's office had two doors that looked exactly alike—one leading to the outer office and the other leading to Paley's private bathroom. Friendly chose the wrong door, losing all the drama of his exit (but providing Paley with a good story to tell at lunch).

On the surface, Murrow seemed to recover. He was given a new pro-gram, entitled "Small World," which enabled him to moderate interviews with the world's notables in any field of his choosing, from literature to film to politics. The guest list was impressive by any measure, and in-cluded David Ben-Gurion, John F. Kennedy, Edward Teller, and Darryl Zanuck. In addition, the program's intellectual depth contrasted sharply with Murrow's other popular interview program, "Person to Person," whose interviews usually focused more on social gossip with people like Marilyn Monroe. (Media critic John Lardner referred to the two pro-grams as "Higher Murrow" and "Lower Murrow.")

Still, Murrow hurt. "See It Now" had been important to him, and its termination was a blow to his pride. It seemed to the people close to him that the spark was gone, the dark moods more frequent. There were no outbursts, no speeches, but colleagues could see the difference. "Ed never recovered his stride after 'See It Now' was cancelled," said Howard K. Smith. And when David Schoenbrun suggested that Paley had become too cautious, Murrow just shrugged his shoulders and said, "He's got other interests now."

Murrow could not have been entirely surprised by this turn of events. As he had predicted to Michael Bessie years earlier, television would have to be focused on entertainment to a much greater degree than radio. That's where the money was. And those profits were not going to be jeopardized by controversy over a news program. The costs were simply too high. But Murrow had had great hopes for television, and he could not accept the necessity of all this. "Ed was continually deploring the fact," said Janet Murrow, "that television wasn't doing more in the way of education."

Murrow had never used his stature to preach outside of CBS circles, but now he began to change his mind. The issues were too big, too important, to be kept controlled within a private company. He wanted to speak out; he would speak out. The opportunity came with an invitation in the spring of 1958 asking him to address the Radio-Television News Directors Association, a prestigious group that was planning to hold its annual meeting in Chicago that fall. Murrow did not respond right away, but by the summer he knew what he wanted to do and advised the RTNDA that he would be happy to try his hand at a speech. Nothing was said to Paley or Stanton, and Murrow did not give either man an advance copy of the speech.

On the evening of October 15, 1958, Murrow walked to the podium at the Sheraton-Blackstone Hotel in Chicago dressed in a gray suit and looking handsome. Hardly the portrait of a radical. His words, however, stunned the crowd. "At the end of this discourse," he said, "a few people may accuse this reporter of fouling his own comfortable nest, and your organization may be accused of having given hospitality to heretical and even dangerous thoughts. But . . . it is my desire, if not my duty, to try to talk to you journeymen with some candor about what is happening to radio and television. . . ." It was not good, to say the least—especially for those interested in broadcasting as a medium of information and opinion. "One of the basic troubles with radio and television news is that both instruments have grown up as an incompatible combination of show business, advertising and news. Each of the three is a rather bizarre and demanding profession. And when you get all three under one roof, the dust never settles."

Part of the problem was the inherent limits of human energy and talent. However skilled they might be in generating revenues for their companies, said Murrow, the training and background of most broadcasters focused on advertising and entertainment. As a result, he observed, they frequently had "neither the time nor the competence" to make sound judgments about news and public affairs. But the principle cause of broadcasting's failures, Murrow continued, was money. The first and foremost consideration was almost always the need for profit and even more profit—a goal which invariably limited the scope and quality of informational programming that reached the public. "There is no suggestion here," the newscaster observed, "that networks or individual stations should operate as philanthropies. But I can find nothing in the Bill of Rights or in the Communications Act," he noted, "which says that they must increase their net profits each year, lest the Republic collapse."

A large group of CBS executives, including Paley, had gathered in the board room to review a copy of Murrow's speech—which had been circulated to the media in advance of its delivery. They were not happy with what they read. People started remarking that, as he had suggested himself, Murrow was indeed fouling his own nest—and one that had treated him very well besides. "He was a star in the CBS family," said one CBS vice president. "We all treated Murrow with a lot of respect and deference. And we felt that he shouldn't criticize the company like that." Others in attendance, including executives associated with the news department, agreed. But no one could have been as hurt and as angry as the chairman. "He was burned up," remarked one CBS executive. "Apoplectic," said another. It was not only the content of the speech that troubled Paley. Of equal significance had been Murrow's refusal to let him know that he was planning to do it. "He was talking about things that he didn't *like,* which were under my control," Paley later told Murrow biographer Ann Sperber. "So it was very much of a personal attack. Which I resented very deeply." But Paley would not give Murrow the satisfaction of venting his anger in person, and the two men, close friends who had shared so much, never discussed the subject.

On February 11, 1959, Murrow formally asked CBS for a leave of absence. In a letter to Stanton, Murrow noted that his contract allowed him to request a leave, and "any reporter or anaylst should take a year off somewhere around the age of fifty." Since Murrow was almost fifty-one, the timing was perfect. The tone of the letter was cordial, and the request was quickly granted. But Murrow would soon learn that he could not escape the reach of Paley or CBS simply by leaving New York.

CHAPTER THIRTEEN

Disenchantment

K idder Meade vividly remembered the experience with Sam Paley. Meade had been hired as CBS vice president for corporate information in 1957. The position required supervision of the company's public relations efforts, and Meade seemed like the right man for the job. A small man in his mid-thirties, Meade was tough-minded and politically savvy. A graduate of West Point, he had served in Europe as a battalion commander and had lost a leg in combat in Germany. For anyone, the loss of a limb is traumatic, but Meade learned to adjust. After the war he became special assistant to Secretary of State Dean Acheson, and when Eisenhower assumed the presidency in 1953, Meade moved on to the New York public relations firm of Earl Newsome & Company. One of the firm's clients was CBS, and in due course Stanton decided that the network could make better use of Meade's talents if he worked for the company on a full-time basis.

One of Meade's responsibilities was to arrange for photographs of CBS board members that would be included in the company's annual report to stockholders. For almost every board member, it was a simple task. But Sam Paley—who was still an active member of the board—posed special problems. He was now retired, living in Palm Beach on the monies he had accumulated from the sale of his cigar company. He sent Meade a photograph which showed him in one of those loud Hawaiian shirts that gave tourism a bad name. Not at all the right image for a CBS director, especially one who also happened to be father of the network's chairman. So Meade had an artist redo the shirt into a jacket and tie. "Sam roared with laughter when he saw that touched-up picture," Meade recalled. "He was a wonderful man. Old Mr. Sam was very relaxed about things. Not at all tense and intense like Bill."

Of course, Sam could afford to be relaxed. He did not have to shoulder the burdens inherent in the operation of a company that did more than $100 million in sales annually. Still, for all that responsibility, Bill Paley could focus his attention on other matters and be very effective. Meade learned that from the start.

His first project with the chairman involved Israel. The 1956 Suez War had been a serious drain on the young nation's treasury, and considerable effort was made afterward to raise money in the United States. Paley, like his father, was an ardent supporter of the Jewish state, having donated considerable sums to its cause and having served as a director of the Israel Overseas Corporation since the early fifties. After Suez, he had been asked to help in the fund-raising drive, and he was determined to make the most of his contacts. Meade was asked to help arrange a luncheon in the CBS boardroom. The guests included corporate magnates and other affluent individuals known to Paley on a first-name basis. At the appointed hour, the guests arrived, Paley explained the purpose of the lunch, and pledges were invited. "The first person started off with seventy-five-thousand dollars," said Meade. "Someone stood up to better that by promising a hundred thousand. The ball was rolling, and they raised a lot of money at that one lunch."

For Meade, the figures tossed about at that lunch were astronomical. It was a world of affluence beyond anything he had known. But for Bill Paley it was nothing unusual. It was his crowd, his milieu—that infinitesimally small group of people whose financial resources make anything and everything possible in the material world, where limousines and private planes are the accepted mode of travel, and where every convenience is accessible on command. "The Paleys were part of the super rich set," one social acquaintance observed. "They enjoyed that rare lifestyle known only to a select few." "It was," said one CBS colleague, "a life that very few people could comprehend."

It was, however, all done with extreme taste. The Paleys did not need to impress people with their wealth. They were beyond that point. Companions and guests were made to feel comfortable. This was especially true for anyone who visited one of the Paleys' four homes in the 1950s. Besides Kiluna Farm and the apartment at the St. Regis, they maintained a house at Round Hill in Jamaica and another on Squam Lake in New Hampshire (where Paley could race around back roads at 80 mph in his Facel-Vega sports car). Sumptuous meals and snacks were always ready to be served by ever-present servants; golf, tennis, swimming and other activities were within easy access; and for evening entertainment a current movie could be shown on a large screen that was well camouflaged in the decor. (At Kiluna, for example, the movie projector was concealed behind Paul Gauguin's "Queen of the Areois," which was set on a hinge and would swing to the side at the appropriate moment, and then the screen would drop from the ceiling.)

Few of these pleasures were enjoyed in solitude. Bill Paley liked to have people around at all times, and usually the more the better. And, as in earlier years, his social life was kept entirely separate from business. On occasion he might invite a CBS colleague to Kiluna or to the Bahamas, but for the most part Paley's social world was filled with people who were rarely, if ever, seen at CBS headquarters. Even the network's performing artists were generally excluded—Jackie Gleason, James Arness, George Burns, Jack Benny: these and other entertainers never received invitations to spend a weekend with Paley at one of his homes.

Although the acquaintance of many, Paley had few close friends with whom he could share his life of luxury. One of those few intimate friends was Thayer, and even he confessed that "Bill Paley is a hard man to know." For all his warmth and charm, there was something closed about his personality, an inner wall that shielded his feelings from outside scrutiny. "Bill is just a guy who's very much self-contained in figuring out his own problems," said Thayer. "A lot of people talk to other people about their problems and seek advice. Not Bill. He didn't ask his friends for advice. He might mention that something was bothering him, but he wouldn't ask for any help. He would just tell you I gotta work it out."

Even then, there were limits to how far Paley would go. With the occasional exception of Jock Whitney, Paley would never discuss his business problems with social friends. He might mention important (and usually publicly known) developments affecting CBS, but he would not review his thinking or possible solutions on CBS matters. And so, after more than thirty years of friendship, Thayer could say that, "if it's about business, you can assume we didn't discuss it." On one occasion, for example, Thayer and Paley spent three weeks traveling in Europe, spending some of the time observing the shooting of a special CBS project. "You would think," said Thayer, "that being so close for so long, having an opportunity to talk about anything and everything, business would come up at some point. But it never did."

To help insulate himself from the pressures of business, Paley liked to spend his leisure time socializing with people who were more interested in having a good time than in tracking developments in broadcasting. Two notable and frequent companions were introduced through Jock Whitney. One was John "Shipwreck" Kelly, a former professional football player many years Paley's junior. A person with an insatiable appetite for golf, practical jokes, and adventure, Kelly was a perfect companion for Whitney and Paley, and both men genuinely enjoyed having him around on those days away from the office. Whitney made it easy for all of them by allowing Kelly to live in one of the several guest houses at Whitney's Greentree estate in Manhasset.

One of the other guest houses was occupied by John Reagan McCrary, Jr., another favorite companion of Paley and Whitney's. McCrary, known to all as "Tex," was a self-proclaimed hustler and wheeler-dealer who seemed to know everybody who was anybody, from President Eisenhower on down. After graduating from Yale, he had parlayed a budding newspaper career into a vehicle for socializing his way to the top. He had met Whitney in the Army during the war, and the two quickly became fast friends. Upon his return to the States, McCrary had married Jinx Falkenberg, an attractive woman who was as enterprising as her husband. The two of them developed a radio talk show, using their impressive list of contacts to provide commentary on any number of topics. Like Shipwreck Kelly, McCrary was a gold mine of gossip and jokes, and that made him a favorite companion on Long Island, in the Bahamas, or wherever Paley might be.

As always, Paley continued to pursue his social life with the same zest he had brought with him to New York in the 1920s. Golf remained a special passion. "He wasn't very good," said Thayer, "but he was very enthusiastic." One companion recalled the vivid memory of Paley on the golf course. "I used to love watching him walking up the fairway," said this guest, "leaning forward and moving at a quick pace with those flashing eyes—like a man possessed."

Paley enjoyed the game wherever he went, but a favorite retreat was the Augusta National Golf Club in Georgia. The club, developed in in the 1930s by Bobby Jones and Clifford Roberts, two of the sport's more accomplished professionals, was home of the Masters golf tournament and a popular facility among the talented and the famous. Paley not only enjoyed the golf at Augusta; he also loved the constant bridge that was available. "Bill and Jock played for a penny a point as though it were a dollar a point," said Thayer, who often accompanied them and liked bridge himself. On other occasions, Paley, Whitney, and Thayer would go to Augusta with Eisenhower. But almost always they spent considerable time with Roberts, who would constantly tease Bill and Jock about their golf and their bridge, and, as Thayer recalled with a smile, both men "loved it."

For all his love of easy times and practical jokes, Paley also savored the company of high society, the glamorous people whose wealth equaled his. Special favorites were among Europe's aristocracies—Lord Victor Rothschild in England, Baron Guy de Rothschild in France, and Loel Guinness, who had a home in France and a large yacht that cruised the Mediterranean. They provided a stark contrast to the Shipwreck Kellys and Tex McCrarys, but it was that very contrast, that diversity, which made Paley feel so good about the way his life was organized.

All of this left little time for the children. Jeffrey and Hilary would visit Kiluna and sometimes go on other excursions, but they continued to spend most of their time with Dorothy. The other four children would join Bill and Babe at Squam Lake or in the Bahamas, but much of Paley's traveling—done during the school year when his children had other responsibilities—was without them (and sometimes even without Babe). Child care was of course no problem. There were always servants available to handle whatever needs the Paleys might have—an arrangement that suited their convenience but sacrificed something in warmth. Indeed, friends who visited the Paleys were barely conscious of the children's presence—a phenomenon that said something about Bill Paley's ability to separate his life into discrete compartments.

Babe no doubt understood her husband's approach to the management of family matters. Her own father had rarely been around to give his children direction, to hear their complaints, to resolve their problems. That had always been his wife's responsibility. She in turn had instructed her daughters on the "proper" role of a woman, and, although there were moments of frustration and despair, Babe Paley accepted that role. She would supervise the children's education and social growth, and no stone would be left unturned in that venture. She even retained a rabbi to come to the house to tutor Billy and Kate on the tenets of Judaism. Babe was Episcopalian, and neither she nor Bill went to temple or followed Jewish traditions. But the children needed to have some understanding of their heritage, and a rabbi seemed to be the best route to that orientation.

Although he did not have the time or interest to supervise the details of his children's upbringing, Paley had a different view when it came to CBS. He considered the network to be his real offspring, and he was prepared to give the company whatever time it needed, especially when it came to programming. And it was that attention to detail that finally enabled CBS to eclipse NBC as the number one television network in 1955. Although he had Hubbell Robinson, Harry Ackerman and other programming executives on the CBS payroll, Paley retained a central role for himself to discuss their proposals, review their pilots, and offer suggestions. At least twice a year he would travel to California to preview the programs for the fall season (beginning in September) and other programs that could be introduced in the winter season (beginning in January) or at any other time as a replacement for a show that did not measure up to expectations. Although there were exceptions (like "Gunsmoke"), most of the program concepts were generated by the programming staff, and the depth of Paley's interest expanded the limits of his patience. "Bill was always ready to listen to us, always indulgent of our opinions," said Ackerman. "Much more so than with the business executives. I noticed at meetings that he was much more stern with the business executives than with the programming people." But no one forgot who made the ultimate decisions. As one CBS program executive used to say, well, we have people who are experts in statistics, and we have people who have creative ideas and are experts in programming, and then they all call Mr. Paley and he tells them what to put on the network.

There was no magical formula which Paley applied in making all his programming decisions. In response to an interviewer who asked if it was all based on a "gut reaction," Paley remarked, "Well, that's the word we always use, a gut reaction; and if it's strong enough, you have enough conviction about it, you go with it; and there's no rule; there's no guidebook that says you have to do it this way or that way. Some of the biggest successes have come about through going against every rule that we used to live by."

A lot of money was riding on these "gut reactions." CBS had developed a thriving record division as well as a radio network and its separately owned radio stations, but the heart of the company was now the television division. By 1958 CBS had in place its five VHF television stations (most of which had to be purchased at considerable cost). The company also had a separate television network which was organized in largely the same manner as the radio network and which boasted almost one hundred affiliates by the late 1950s. Together these television operations generated the lion's share of the company's revenues and profits—a fact that Paley always remembered in planning the schedule or evaluating a program's progress.

Because of all this, few program details escaped Bill Paley's attention. If Jack Van Volkenburg, president of the network television division, wanted to spend money to develop a pilot, he would have to get the chairman's approval, which could often be memorialized on a piece of scratch paper. If a young actor named Clint Eastwood seemed to be using a minor role in the television program called "Rawhide" to overshadow the principal protagonist, Paley would suggest that something be done to prevent it. And if Arthur Godfrey's ratings were down in the late 1950s, he would listen to—and ultimately accept—one executive's argument that CBS should give Godfrey a second chance because his television and radio programs had generated so much revenue for the network. ("I want to call your attention," said the executive at a meeting attended by Stanton and Paley, "to how much money he has brought into this company," and how important it was, "consistent with decent business practice, to continue his functions.")

However much he trusted his own judgment on programming issues, Paley wanted to rely on others. That was, in his view, the privilege of being chairman. He could listen, he could suggest, he could criticize, but someone else would have to bear responsibility for the final recommendations.

Consequently, there was no substitute for having good people on board who understood the business, who were creative, and who knew how to plan schedules. "He would always say," said Mike Dann, a programming executive hired by CBS in 1958, "that you don't hire a good program executive when you need him; you hire him whenever you find him." All of which probably explains why Lou Cowan found it so easy to get a position with CBS in 1955.

Cowan had returned from the war to resume his program production activities, eventually forming Louis G. Cowan Productions, Inc. In the next few years, his company placed numerous programs with CBS, the most successful one first airing at 10:00 P.M. on Tuesday, June 7, 1955. "The $64,000 Question" was a hit right from the start, although the idea was not entirely original. There had been an early radio program entitled "Take It or Leave It" that required guests to answer questions of increasing difficulty, with the winnings starting at $2 and doubling with each right answer until the contestant reached the final plateau of $64 (introducing into everyday speech the cliché, "that's the $64 question"). Cowan took the concept and added three zeros to it (and paid a royalty to the originator of "Take It or Leave It"). Then he got Charles Revson to agree to have his company, Revlon, sponsor the show, and CBS could agree to air it with the assurance that it would generate money from the start.

Cowan was unsuccessful in his bid to have Johnny Carson be the master of ceremonies and finally had to settle for Hal March. When he previewed the program, Paley made only one suggestion: the number of levels of winnings should be expanded to make it more difficult to reach $64,000 and, at the same time, increase the drama of a contestant's march toward that goal. Cowan agreed, and the questioning started off at $64 for a correct answer and moved, ever so slowly, up the scale, requiring several appearances in successive weeks before the contestant could reach $64,000. To add to the program's appeal, Cowan sought out ordinary people who possessed a wealth of knowledge in unexpected fields. The first "hero" on the program was Gino Prato, a Bronx cobbler who was an expert on opera. Cowan was alerted to Prato by a letter from his daughter, who had written that "Dad is a handsome man with a lovely Italian accent, and he is humble & sincere. . . ." Prato finally reached $32,000 and, with the nation waiting expectantly, decided not to go for $64,000 because his elderly father in Italy told him he already had enough and he always listened to his father.

Despite his program's unbelievable success, Lou Cowan was not around to enjoy all the initial rewards. Within a week after Gino Prato had made his momentous decision, Cowan had started a new job with the Columbia Broadcasting System.

It was all part of Cowan's plan to have a greater impact on American life. He was, by his own confession, an "unashamed idealist"—an assessment perhaps confirmed by his willingness to spend most of 1952 trying to get Adlai Stevenson elected president. But his idealism extended to television as well. "I wanted to have an influence on what the American public was offered by television . . . ," Cowan later remarked. "From many disappointments as a [program] packager, I had learned that to exert that sort of influence one had to be on the inside, in the management of a television network. . . ."

There was no question as to which network. CBS was by then recognized as the premier network, Cowan respected Frank Stanton, and, of greatest importance, Bill Paley was its chairman. "I suppose I have never admired any man more than I admired Bill Paley," said Cowan, "who seemed able to do all the things I thought I could do, and so many other things beside." Cowan's admiration was based not only on his contact with Paley during the war and the success of CBS in the ratings war. Cowan had had other encounters which demonstrated that Paley was a man of principle.

In the early 1950s Cowan had been given a tape of songs sung by the incomparable Mahalia Jackson. Under normal circumstances, it should have been relatively easy to arrange for her appearance on radio. Jackson's voice was that extraordinary. But Jackson was black, and that made all the difference. Cowan took the tape to agency after agency, and in each case the answer was the same. Only one executive had the courage to admit that the decision was motivated by racial discrimination. Still, Cowan had faith that somehow, somewhere, he was going to get Mahalia Jackson on radio. He then brought the tape to Jerry Maulsby, a friend at CBS. Maulsby played the tape through an open doorway, and the reaction among the other CBS employees was almost magical. People started wandering into Maulsby's office, sitting on the floor, lounging by the doorway, all asking that the tape be played again. "By that time," said Cowan, "all work stopped on the floor, everybody came into that room, it was packed with people, and they applauded at the end because it was so beautiful."

Maulsby was of course enthusiastic, but he told Cowan, as the producer had already suspected, that only one person could bring Mahalia Jackson onto CBS radio. So Cowan made the appointment to see Paley and played the tape for him in his office on a Friday afternoon. Cowan could see that Paley was "deeply moved by what he heard," and the CBS chairman asked if he could borrow the tape to play it for his wife and his friends over the weekend. Cowan could not have said yes any faster, and by the following Monday Mahalia Jackson had an initial contract to appear on CBS radio for twenty-six weeks.

From these and other experiences, Cowan knew he could adapt to a job at CBS. He raised the matter with Frank Stanton at lunch one day and, as expected, Stanton suggested that Cowan speak to Paley directly. The chairman was of course flattered by Cowan's interest—especially since "The $64,000 Question" was eclipsing "I Love Lucy" as the network's most popular show—but he said that Hubbell Robinson, the network's chief of programming, would have to be consulted. Cowan was wary of that suggestion. He had had numerous interactions with Robinson and, like many people, found the lean, austere executive to be arrogant and unapproachable. But a few days later Robinson, having sensed the direction of Paley's leanings, invited Cowan to lunch where the only question was how much salary the producer wanted to join CBS (whatever you want to pay, replied Cowan).

Cowan joined CBS in August 1955, and by the spring of 1956 he was promoted to vice president for creative services. (When asked by his three children to explain the amorphous title, Cowan said it meant that he was in charge of the keys to the men's room.) From the beginning, it was clear that he was a man brimming with energy and ideas, constantly talking with people, writing memos, or urging some new approach to programming. CBS seemed well suited to his personality and goals.

Cowan's initial encounters with Paley inside CBS headquarters also indicated that the Mahalia Jackson episode had not been an aberration. Paley was indeed a man of taste, sensitive to the public's interests and conscious of the considerable power that CBS wielded in shaping America's entertainment. On one occasion, the network was presented with a pilot of "Whirlybirds," a helicopter adventure program designed for children; Cowan predicted that the program would be a hit, but he urged Paley to reject it because it was too violent for its youthful audience. Paley agreed, and the program never made it on CBS. Another instance involved "Playhouse 90," a dramatic series initiated in 1956 featuring plays written, produced, and directed by some of the country's best talent, including John Houseman, Rod Serling, John Frankenheimer, and Paddy Chayefsky. Cowan observed that the periodic commercials interrupted the flow of the drama, and Paley wondered out loud at meetings whether it might not be better to bunch the commercials at the beginning and the end of the show—a proposal that was eventually adopted.

Cowan was seasoned enough to know that the chairman would not accept all of his proposals. Still, he was impressed with the leeway which Paley afforded him. He had joined CBS to make an impact, and Paley was giving him the chance. And on that score, no opportunity provided a greater challenge than to develop a response to NBC's popular morning show, "Today."

CBS had experimented with any number of formats and anchors—from Walter Cronkite to Dick Van Dyke to Will Rogers, Jr.—in an effort to crack the rival network's dominance of the seven to nine A.M. weekday slot. Cowan wanted to fill the eight to nine slot with "Captain Kangaroo," an innovative approach to a children's program where the host was not animated and where an effort was actually made to reach the children on their own level. Although the show did not get a sponsor for its first three months, and although it generated almost no profits in its first few years on the air, Paley stuck by it, making it the only regularly scheduled children's network program that did not depend on cartoons. Later Cowan would jokingly remark that "the only thing that . . . kept 'Kangaroo's' air time [was] fear in the executive suites that if the the show were killed some prominent people would be strangled in their beds some morning by the mothers of America."

No such fears existed with respect to the seven to eight A.M. part of the weekday slot. Cowan proposed that CBS use that time to provide a detailed review of news. Paley was skeptical. "What can you show people," he once asked Cowan, "that they haven't already seen the night before?" Cowan persisted, saying that people's lifestyles were changing, that they wanted more in the morning than an alarm to wake them up, that the public's appetite for information was expanding with the new medium. Paley didn't agree, but he was receptive to Cowan's requests for more money, and in 1958 (much to everyone's surprise and delight), the CBS morning news program came within one-tenth of a rating point of "Today."

No one appreciated good ideas and success more than Bill Paley, and in early 1958 Cowan got his reward. The growth of the company required greater division of responsibility, and Paley and Stanton decided to separate the television division into two separate units—one to supervise the television stations that CBS owned, and the other to run the television network, which provided programs to the owned stations as well as affiliated stations throughout the country. The president of the CBS television network had to be someone who appreciated the dynamics of program production, and on March 12, 1958, Lou Cowan assumed the position.

There were, of course, calls of congratulation from around the country, and suddenly Cowan was besieged with invitations for lunch and dinner. To the outside world his elevation signified an increase in power. Inside the company, however, Cowan recognized that his power stretched only as far as Paley's tolerance.

To be sure, the chairman was still receptive to many of his programming proposals. But when Cowan tried to use his new position to expand the diversity of programming, especially in news and public affairs, he bumped up against Paley's perception of the bottom line. At one point Cowan urged that there be a five-minute mid-evening news program. The world could blow up between 7:30 and 11:00 P.M., he told the chairman, and no one would know. Paley understood the logic of the proposal, but he was not about to take time away from the affiliates or the network. Paley also rejected any suggestion that the network make use of Ian Fleming's stories about James Bond, believing that the American public would have no interest in the escapades of a British spy. And when Cowan advised the chairman that he was exploring the possibility of broadcasting the 1960 Winter Olympics from Squaw Valley, Paley expressed his disagreement. "Nobody wants to watch that sort of thing in the wintertime," he told Cowan. But the network president had already committed some money to the project, and it was allowed to go forward (eventually winning high ratings).

Cowan soon learned that his new position required more than creativity. Performers remained the center of CBS's universe, and he was expected to do his part to keep them happy. At one program meeting some executives began to complain about Jackie Gleason, saying that he drank too much, that he was irresponsible, and that would not always come to rehearsals or read the script before the shows. Cowan interrupted to say that, with all that, he still regarded Gleason as one of the great comedians and a major asset to CBS. "If you really think that," Paley responded, "you ought to drop him a line and tell him so." Again, the Paley approach. Flattery. Concern. It had worked for him, and it worked for Cowan. The network president accepted the suggestion, and within a short time Jackie Gleason regarded Cowan as his major contact at CBS. Every so often Cowan would receive telephone calls from Gleason at New York's famed watering hole, Toots Shor's, obviously drinking and explaining that he wanted to say something before he drifted off into "cloudland."

For all its quirks, the experience with Gleason was enjoyable. Cowan could not say that about all his efforts to accommodate CBS celebrities. Jack Benny was a case in point. Benny's transition to television had been as successful as Paley had hoped, and he remained a staple of American entertainment week after week, with his stinginess intact and his able servant Rochester at his side. But Benny coveted greater success, and one evening he telephoned the CBS chairman at home to say that he wanted the half-hour slot at 10 P.M. on Sundays—a prime time for anyone and one that Benny saw as particularly profitable for him. Paley wasn't about to say no to one of the network's principal investments, and he quickly agreed—even though Lorillard Productions had had that 10 P.M. slot under contract for years.

Paley broke the news to Cowan the next morning. "I've just promised ten o'clock Sunday night to Benny," Paley explained, "and you're going to have to get Lorillard out of there." Cowan protested that Lorillard had a contract for the time, but Paley was not phased in the least. "If you'll read that contract carefully," he said, "you'll see that we have the right to move them out at the end of any quarter." It may have been clear in Paley's mind, but Cowan did not look forward to the assignment. Lorillard had produced some of his programs when he had been an independent producer. He knew the people. He liked them. They were his friends. And he knew they would not be happy. Bud Gruber, Lorillard's president, could not believe that CBS would do that to his company, and, as Cowan remembered, Gruber "called me names no man had ever called me before." But the network president had no power to change the decision. He was nothing more than a messenger.

It was then that Cowan started thinking that, for all its possibilities, the job at CBS was not all that he thought it might be. True, you could shape what millions of Americans knew about the world and what they watched for entertainment. But, in the end, whatever influence he had was totally dependent on the whims and decisions of one man. He openly raised the possibility that he might resign, that he should resign. Stanton argued against it, saying that the company needed someone with Cowan's talent and integrity. Paley agreed with Stanton, but his key point was to suggest that Cowan at least develop a successor before he stepped down.

The chairman was not only thinking of his company at that point. He was also worried about himself. He had always believed in delegating responsibility, and now that principle became even more important. Because Bill Paley, the man who had nurtured CBS almost from birth, the man who had tied his life to this growing media conglomerate, had started to lose interest in its activities.

None of this was a conscious decision. In the early spring of 1959, Paley came down with a chest cold while attending a golfing party at the National Golf Links in Southampton. Paley was not one to dismiss any sign of illness. He visited his doctor, who took an X ray and saw a shadow on one of Paley's lungs. Paley knew what that meant: he smoked between four and five packs of cigarettes a day, often one right after the other. Friends and colleagues noticed the tension, one saying frankly that Paley was a "nervous smoker." The smoking was so constant that his fingers had yellowed with nicotine stains.

He did not take the news well. He felt ill, and the suggestion of something serious made it worse. He lost his spark, his enthusiasm, his zest for any and every pleasure. Marietta Tree, who was a frequent visitor at Kiluna, remembered those times. "He languished, laid around, and complained that he was terribly ill," said Tree. The practical jokes, the flirtations, the inquisitive questions were now much less frequent.

Paley continued to see doctors, finally going to a New York hospital for a complete physical examination which included a bronchoscopy—the use of a tiny lighted instrument to inspect the interior of the lungs. The doctor reported that Paley's lungs were dark and velvety rather than smooth and pink—the obvious result of his many years of smoking. Paley liked his cigarettes, but he treasured his health even more. He crushed out the cigarette he was smoking while the doctor explained all this and promised never to smoke again (a promise he has kept). But the commitment did not resolve his immediate problem or make him feel any better. The doctors said that, in all likelihood, the shadow on his lung was a benign phenomenon, but there were no guarantees. Paley was not the kind to take chances, and in June 1959 he underwent exploratory surgery, which revealed nothing more than an elevated diaphragm. There was no evidence of any cancer.

The results of the operation could not have been more positive, and everyone expected Paley to bounce back in no time. "[Bill] is still too groggy to write," Babe wrote to Ed Murrow in Europe on June 9. "The first three days are rough, as you know, but he's doing marvelously well, and I suppose it will be only too soon before I'll be having a rough time keeping him down." But Paley fooled everyone. He did not bounce back. He continued to suffer from depression, and while his physical health was pronounced good by the doctors, he could no longer generate the kind of energy or enthusiasm that he had always brought to his professional and social lives. "It was a very difficult time for him," Walter Thayer recalled. "He was very ill for a long time and had a long recovery period."

Paley rarely went into the office, and his telephone conversations with CBS executives were infrequent. Kidder Meade, who had been working closely with him before the operation, hardly saw him afterward, and the only extended telephone conversation he could remember having with the chairman during that period was when Paley called to talk about arrangements for the "coming out" party for Babe's daughter, Amanda. Paley did talk with Stanton, of course, and one of the subjects of discussion was another government position.

Paley had always admired his brother-in-law Jock Whitney. He had been born to wealth, and he seemed to be able to do it all—manage corporations, provide useful services through his foundations, collect art, master any number of sporting skills. The CBS chairman had much in common with Jock, and the two had continued to spend considerable time together. Friends could easily see the bond between the two men, although many felt that there was something in Bill Paley that made him want to emulate Jock.

At the time of Paley's surgery in 1959, Jock was the United States ambassador to England, one of the most prestigious posts in the diplomatic corps. Whitney had earned the assignment through his service as finance chairman in Eisenhower's two presidential campaigns. Paley had not held any formal positions in the campaigns, but he had contributed money and he had tried to make helpful suggestions whenever possible. Perhaps he too could get an appointment as ambassador. The post in France, coincidentally, was available. It would suit Bill Paley's image of himself, and perhaps it would also generate the kind of interest and enthusiasm he could not muster for CBS. And beyond all that, it would show Babe that he could be as accomplished as her sister's husband.

Although he and Eisenhower had grown closer over the years, Paley was not about to confront the president directly with his desires. More subtle techniques would have to be used. Friends were contacted, inquiries were made, and, for a time, it seemed like it might happen. But then matters stalled. Frustrated by the delay, Stanton telephoned Helen Sioussat, who was then working in the CBS Washington office and was well connected with the city's power structure. "Well, Bill talked about it," Stanton remembered, "and then nothing happened. And I didn't talk to him about it [further] because I didn't want to pour salt in the wound if there was some hang-up. And so . . . I asked [Helen] to find out what happened, or what's going to happen." The response was not encouraging. Sioussat found that there was considerable opposition among the diplomatic corps because it might appear unseemly to have two brothers-in-law in the two most prestigious overseas positions. Paley's political connections were not sufficiently strong to overcome those reservations, and the appointment never came through. Stanton tried to salvage something for his boss by telephoning a White House aide and recommending Paley as Secretary of Commerce, but that suggestion also proved unsuccessful.

However much he may have wanted to take his own sabbatical from CBS, Paley soon found that his input was once again needed to deal with yet another crisis, one that had broad implications for the entire broadcast industry. The seeds of the disaster had been germinated in the summer of 1958. A contestant on a CBS quiz program called "Dotto" alleged that the program was fixed. The company conducted an in-house investigation, concluded that the charge was justified, and cancelled the show. That was only the beginning. Other allegations were soon being raised. The most sensational—and most highly publicized—charge involved "Twenty-

One," the quiz program that NBC had patterned after CBS's "$64,000 Question." An early (and successful) contestant said that "Twenty-One" was fixed. The public could not accept the allegation. Charles Van Doren, the son of teachers, a man so scholarly in demeanor, had won the hearts and admiration of America with his wrenching moments behind the glass booth, trying to answer the most difficult questions that could be posed. He had seemed so genuine, so credible, so enjoyable to watch. The public did not, could not, accept the fact that it had only been a charade performed for their entertainment. Thankfully, Van Doren reaffirmed their hopes, issuing a statement to the public in the summer of 1958 that the charges against "Twenty-One," as far as he knew, were false. He repeated his claim to a grand jury that was summoned in New York to consider the evidence in the winter of 1959.

The grand jury did not have enough hard evidence to return any indictments, but the panel and its supervisor, District Attorney Frank Hogan, felt that there was enough information to indicate that the quiz programs were not as clean as Van Doren had suggested. For that reason, Hogan decided to give the information he had gathered to Congressman Oren Harris, chairman of the House Subcommittee on Communications. Harris's subcommittee was not restricted by judicial rules of procedure, and he soon convened hearings in which the various people involved were asked to answer questions they would rather have ignored.

There was no evidence that Lou Cowan had been involved in any wrongdoing, and there was no evidence that "The $64,000 Question"—or its sister program "The $64,000 Challenge"—had engaged in any kind of systematic deception. But there were some troublesome admissions given to the public. Charles Revson, the sponsor, had tried to dictate to CBS how the programs would be presented, from the wardrobe worn by Hal March to the kind of contestants the program should use. (Revson was particularly offended by Dr. Joyce Brothers, a psychologist-turned-boxing expert, whose success in answering questions was, in Revson's mind, matched by her lack of audience appeal.) To accommodate Revson and maintain the necessary ratings, the show's producers had (after Cowan had left his production company) offered "assistance" to various contestants. Most accepted it happily. As bandleader Xavier Cugat explained, "I didn't want to make a fool of myself."

CBS had not anticipated problems like these, and it had not been prepared to deal with them. The company was only just beginning to adjust to the financial and organizational growth spawned by television. There were few controls and almost no standards to govern the conduct and supervision of quiz programs. Paley, of course, was concerned. "We've got to set up a system that prevents this from ever happening again," he told Kidder Meade. But Paley was not about to do the work himself. Stanton convened a weekend meeting in the early fall at the St. Regis Hotel in New York. Every top executive attended. Stanton chaired the meetings, except for the limited time when the chairman was in attendance. The issues were debated endlessly, and people kept coming back to the view that the best antidote for this misuse of entertainment programs was to increase the quality and time for news programs.

CBS news programs had dropped from a high of 526 hours (representing 12.9 percent of the network schedule) in 1954 to less than 433 hours, or 9.9 percent of the schedule, in 1955. The company had not even come close to equaling the 1954 record, and many executives suggested that it was time to reverse that trend. Several suggested that CBS's fifteen-minute nightly newscast be increased to one half hour, and at one point it seemed that the proposal would be adopted. But the affiliate stations (who had to release the time for network use) were vehemently opposed, and that proposal had to be abandoned. Other measures would have to suffice, and CBS announced shortly afterward that it would soon inaugurate a documentary series called "CBS Reports," which would be produced by Fred Friendly.

Additional news programs would help alleviate the public pressure, but they could never be enough. CBS had to eliminate any and every appearance of impropriety. So the quiz programs had to go. "I wiped off ten hours of [weekly] programming in one day," Stanton later recalled. "Oh, it was a rough period."

Cancellation of existing programs, however, could not prevent the problem from arising again in other contexts. Definite controls had to be established and, once again, Stanton took the lead. On October 16, 1959, he went to New Orleans to address the Radio and Television News Directors Association, the same group that had heard Murrow a year earlier criticize broadcasting's retreat from controversy. Stanton faced the issues squarely, saying that, whoever might be guilty of misconduct on specific programs, the television networks themselves had to assume ultimate responsibility. CBS, he said, would not shirk that responsibility. The network would take "a fresh hard look" at all of its programs so that the American public would know that what they saw on their television screens would be "exactly what it purports to be."

Kidder Meade had distributed the speech to the press, and he made sure that *New York Times* media critic Jack Gould had seen it. Meade also gave Gould Stanton's telephone number in New Orleans and urged him to call the CBS president for an interview. No media issue was hotter at the time, and Gould did indeed call Stanton. And he could not resist asking the obvious question—would the new CBS policy apply to Ed

Murrow's "Person to Person," an interview program on which guests were given the questions they would be asked prior to the broadcast. Stanton did not hesitate in saying yes, the new policy applied to all shows, whether they were entertainment, news, or public affairs programs. That was news to Gould, and his front-page story the next day reported that CBS was going to eradicate all "deceits" in its programs, and one of the programs listed was "Person to Person."

Ed Murrow was then in London on his sabbatical, and he was not at all pleased by the stories that he read. Frank Stanton, his colleague and nominal superior, had accused him of deceiving the American public. "Ed was absolutely furious with Stanton's comment," remembered his wife. Murrow took considerable pride in his principles, and he waited for some word from Paley—or Stanton—or someone to explain that it was all a mistake, that the press had misinterpreted Stanton's remarks. But the call never came, and Murrow decided he had to do something. A few days later he issued his own statement to the press, saying that "Stanton must know that cameras, lights, and microphones do not just wander around a home. Producers must know who is going where and when and for how long. . . . I am sorry Dr. Stanton feels that I have participated in perpetrating a fraud upon the public. My conscience is clear," the newsman concluded. "His seems to be bothering him."

The story was carried on the front page of the Sunday *New York Times* underneath a searing headline: MURROW SAYS STANTON CRITICISM SHOWS IGNORANCE OF TV METHOD. On Monday morning Paley, Stanton, and outside counsel Ralph Colin met in Paley's office to discuss a response. Everyone was upset. Why hadn't Murrow at least called before issuing his statement? In any case, the matter would have to be resolved, and quickly. The network had enough problems dealing with the quiz scandal, and there was no percentage in a public debate between its president and its most celebrated newsman. Colin was dispatched to London with a conciliatory statement that Murrow and CBS could issue jointly.

Colin arrived in London on the evening of the Murrows' twenty-fifth wedding anniversary. He explained the purpose of his visit, and Murrow listened intently. "Ed liked Colin and realized that he was only doing his job," said Janet Murrow. But Murrow had a blind spot when it came to the CBS chairman, and he placed no responsibility for the incident on Paley's shoulders. "He was only angry with Stanton," said Mrs. Murrow.

Murrow's focus on Stanton was not at all surprising. The tension between the two men had been building since the 1940s when Murrow had been the only CBS employee invited to attend Paley's marriage to Babe. Stanton of course understood that Bill and Ed had become good friends during the war and that he could hardly expect to compete for Paley's affections in the same way. Still, he was now president of the company and Murrow was supposed to be his subordinate. That may have seemed logical in theory, but Murrow's stature as a celebrity and as Bill Paley's friend placed him outside the company's formal structure. He could see and did see the chairman whenever he wanted. Murrow had no intention of purposely snubbing Stanton, but he also felt no need to advise the president of his every contact with Paley.

Murrow's favored status was only the starting point for the tension that evolved between him and Stanton. The basic problem reflected a difference in perspective. Like Murrow, Stanton could be an articulate and dedicated defender of principle—a commitment that would become more clear in the 1960s. But Stanton also had to worry about managing CBS on a day-to-day basis. And he believed in using any and every modern technique to assist him in that role, including public opinion polls. To Murrow, Stanton's reliance on those polls was dehumanizing. It reduced people's fundamental concerns and feelings to cold, unthinking numbers. Not at all the right way to approach any discussion of social and political issues. Murrow wrote Stanton a nasty, gloating memo when Roper's polls for CBS in 1948 mistakenly predicted Tom Dewey's election as president. And when Stanton started openly to question the financial impact of "See It Now" and other controversial programs, Murrow would, in his laconic way, denigrate Stanton to colleagues as a "numbers counter" or a "pseudo-psychologist."

Paley of course recognized this tension but, as in his confrontation with Murrow over "See It Now," he showed no interest in eliminating it. He liked Ed, he wanted to be his friend, and he did not want the burden, or agony, of telling Murrow things the newsman didn't want to hear. In Paley's mind, that was one of the advantages of being chairman. Paley felt the same way about the company's response to the quiz-show scandal. He was available to review the decisions, but Stanton was going to have to bear the heat of any public explanations. And so Paley had no difficulty agreeing with Kidder Meade's suggestions that the network have only one public spokesman on the issue and that that spokesman be Stanton.

The most immediate concern was a scheduled appearance before Congressman Harris's subcommittee in Washington. Stanton would have to face some hostile questioning under the glare of intense media coverage. As always, Stanton devoted untold hours in preparation for the task. His reaction to the growing scandal would be viewed as a measure of the broadcast industry's sensitivity to the public's concerns. He could not afford to make any misstatements, however inadvertent.

The CBS president rose to the occasion. He frankly admitted that his network, and probably the industry as a whole, had been lax in supervising the quiz programs, and for that, he said, there could be no excuse. But he steadfastly maintained that, whatever its oversights, no one at the CBS network had knowingly sanctioned deception. He also added that there was no evidence that Lou Cowan had done anything wrong while he had been producer of "The $64,000 Question." "This is not the kind of producer that Mr. Cowan was then or is now," said Stanton. "Mr. Cowan's main role . . . has been that of an idea man, a creator. He has not been the man who has gone into the control room or into the studio and done the detail work. . . . I have no reason to question Mr. Cowan's integrity as far as the [show] is concerned while he was in charge of it."

For all these kind words of support, Stanton and Paley soon concluded that Cowan could no longer remain president of the CBS television network. The ostensible reason was Cowan's failure to appear to testify before Harris's subcommittee. He was, after all, the creator and original producer of "The $64,000 Question," and the congressmen were anxious to know what he knew. Cowan's health made that appearance impossible. Perhaps it was the pressure, which was considerable, or perhaps it was just a coincidence. His leg turned purple and became painful. Family and friends urged him to see a doctor, who immediately placed Cowan in the hospital with a severe case of phlebitis. Travel to Washington was out of the question.

The timing could not have been worse. The focus of the controversy was deception, and in many circles (including the twentieth floor of CBS headquarters) there was a certain skepticism as to whether Cowan was as sick as his doctor claimed. This skepticism could not be ignored. Stanton commissioned a public opinion poll that showed that 92 percent of the public was aware of the quiz-show scandal. Firm action had to be taken; the public had to be convinced that CBS had purged itself of all wrongdoing. And if he couldn't do it through congressional testimony, Cowan would have to do it through his resignation.

Even before the quiz-show scandal made the front page, Cowan had sensed that his days were numbered. Later he would say that he could pinpoint the moment when he knew he would have to resign as president of the CBS television network. In early 1959 Cowan had the supreme pleasure of informing the chairman that the network's profits in the preceding year had reached record heights. Unlike Paley, however, Cowan did not see those record profits as a new plateau to be bettered in later years. "I told him," Cowan recalled, "that of course we shouldn't expect to make more than that in 1959." Paley turned to ice. "Why not?" he demanded. Cowan answered that, "having made the network so profitable, we now had an obligation to spend some of those profits in the public interest, to experiment with new kinds of programs, [to] provide more news and public affairs and entertainment shows that would raise the level of cultural awareness in the American public. What was the point of being Number One," said Cowan, ". . . except to seize the opportunities that leadership offered?" Paley did not agree with his assessment and their discussion was abruptly terminated.

Still, Cowan believed the network would not force him to resign in the midst of the quiz-show scandal. It would create the wrong impression. It would suggest that, despite Stanton's kudos in public, Cowan was guilty of something. CBS wanted, needed, to preserve its reputation, but Bill Paley's company would not do something so unfair.

Cowan learned of CBS's change of heart in a most unpleasant way. While he was still in the hospital, Stanton and Ralph Colin went to his apartment and asked his wife to sign a letter of resignation for her husband. Polly steadfastly refused, pointing out that many of the statements in Stanton's letter were untrue. Within days Cowan returned home to continue his recovery. Stanton and Colin made another attempt, showing up unexpectedly at the sixteenth birthday party the Cowans were holding for their daughter Holly. "When they came with the letter of resignation," Holly later remembered, "my father was torn between integrity, honor, and loyalty. He didn't know what to do—but he knew he was being made the scapegoat."

Paley had remained removed from the scene of battle. He had never liked personal confrontations and had always made sure there was someone like Stanton to step into the breach. But he kept himself advised of developments. Kidder Meade had established a strong friendship with Cowan and was making periodic visits to the Cowan apartment to review the situation, discuss the alternatives, and offer whatever advice he could in a situation that was becoming more and more hopeless. "I had a lot of respect for Lou and his family," said Meade. "All of them—his wife, his three children, and he—would sit around the kitchen table talking about what they should do and how they should handle the situation. It was really a remarkable family."

By December 1959 there was nothing left to discuss. Cowan would not agree to sign any letter drafted by Stanton, but he also knew he could no longer continue as president of the CBS television network. He would have to resign, but he would explain it his way. In a "Dear Frank" letter released to the press on December 8, Cowan pointed out that Stanton and Paley had "expressed, both publicly and privately, your complete confidence in me and in the fact that I had nothing to do with the rigging of quiz shows. Nevertheless," the letter continued, "in spite of my record and your confidence in my integrity, you have suggested repeatedly, directly and indirectly, that I should resign." Cowan acknowledged that CBS was entitled to have a person of its own choosing as president of the network. All he wanted, said Cowan, was a letter of resignation that would be acceptable to him and the company. That had proven to be an impossible goal, mostly because CBS wanted to base the resignation on Cowan's health, and Cowan had insisted that his health was now excellent. "There is a limit to the amount of time that grown men can put in on such an effort," Cowan observed. "I see no point in further discussion. So let us leave it at this: you have made it impossible for me to continue as president of CBS Television Network. Accordingly, I resign."

At first, Cowan, like Ed Murrow, was prone to place all the blame on Stanton's shoulders. He had tried to reach Paley numerous times by telephone, but the chairman was said to be in Jamaica and unavailable for discussion. If only I could have reached Bill, Cowan would say to family and friends, none of this would have happened. To Cowan it was simply inconceivable that Paley could have sanctioned this kind of pressure to force his resignation.

Those inside CBS knew differently. "You must remember," Kidder Meade later explained to a visitor, "that no critical decision was ever made without Paley knowing about it and at least acquiescing to it. So you can be sure that he knew Cowan was going to be fired." In time, Cowan came to the same realization. Stanton would never have made such a significant—and well-publicized—decision unless he knew in advance that the chairman would support him. Cowan became even more embittered. Bill Paley, the man of principle for whom he had had so much respect, did not have the courage that Cowan thought he had. And so, in looking back upon the experience many years later, Cowan would say, yes, Bill Paley was indeed "a man of great charm and grace," but that "anyone who can do what Bill Paley does must also be cruel, willing to see other people pay any price so that his vision will be realized." It was a sad ending to an engaging and fruitful relationship. And it was only the beginning of a decade that would prove to be even more turbulent for CBS and its chairman.

CHAPTER FOURTEEN

Growth

For Richard Nixon, it may have been the decisive factor. He had entered the 1960 presidential campaign as the favorite. He was, after all, a two-term vice president who had served under one of the country's most popular presidents. But Senator John F. Kennedy, with his good looks, eloquence, and self-deprecating humor had demonstrated surprising strength among the electorate. There had been a dramatic shift of voter sentiment toward Kennedy after the first of the four televised debates. With a tanned face and a confident command of the facts, the forty-three-year-old candidate revealed unexpected poise in answering questions. Nixon, in contrast, appeared tired and nervous, with beads of perspiration evident on his face.

That first debate had been held in the studios of WBBM-TV, a CBS-owned station in Chicago. Paley had traveled there on the eve of his fifty-ninth birthday to witness the historic occasion in person—although his interest was as much personal as it was professional. He knew Kennedy's father from earlier days in broadcasting when the senior Kennedy had teamed up with David Sarnoff to form RKO studios. Over the years, Paley had developed an acquaintance with John Kennedy as well. Although years older than Kennedy, Paley had much in common with the Democratic candidate—the driving ambition, the love of laughter and good times, the fondness for women. But Paley was not supporting Kennedy. He had cast his lot with Nixon.

Many factors lay behind Paley's support of Nixon—his relationship with Eisenhower, the involvement of Jock Whitney and Walter Thayer in the Republican effort, and, not incidentally, a hope that the support would lead to appointment as United States ambassador to the Court of St. James. Paley gave $25,000 to the Nixon campaign, and, as with Eisenhower, he was prepared to give advice as well. But the Republican candidate was not receptive to Paley's most important suggestion.

The 1960 debates were a new phenomenon, made possible in large part by Frank Stanton's successful efforts to have Congress temporarily suspend the legal requirement that stations give all candidates equal opportunities (because no station would have carried the hours of debates if it meant that the many minor presidential candidates would have to be given equal time). Paley studied the ratings and polls, and he noticed that Nixon scored better with the public after each debate. To Paley's mind, the meaning was clear—Nixon should agree to a fifth television debate, one that would probably increase his public support and completely eliminate the advantage which Kennedy had secured in the first debate.

Paley intended to make his pitch to the candidate at a meeting that he and Thayer attended at New York's Waldorf-Astoria in October. That plan was frustrated when Nixon excused himself early. Paley waited until many of the other participants left, and then he advanced his suggestion to Bob Finch and Herb Klein, two of the key campaign advisers. They in turn passed the proposal on to Nixon, but there was no response by the time Nixon left New York for his next campaign trip. Thayer then made a request through the campaign staff for him and Paley to meet with the candidate upon his return to New York. The word came back from Nixon—I'd be happy to drive into the city from the airport with you, but there will be no discussion about debates.

It was a lost opportunity that might have altered the future of Nixon as well as Paley. Not that the notion of an ambassadorship was completely lost. Despite his support of Nixon, Paley's name was still considered when President Kennedy focused on the appointment of an ambassador to England. "Kennedy liked Paley and respected him," said Mike Feldman, the president's deputy counsel, "but he felt that the Court of St. James was the most significant ambassadorship and that it was important to have a career diplomat in the post." So the appointment went to David Bruce, a highly respected foreign service officer (who also happened to be a Paley friend).

Even that disappointment did not entirely close the door. Months later, Lyndon B. Johnson, the new vice president, called his friend Frank Stanton to ask for his recommendations for government posts that remained unfilled. Paley "was in a restless period," said Stanton, and he asked Johnson, "What have you got open?" Among the positions was the ambassadorship to Italy. Johnson explained that, because of campaign charges that he would be subservient to the Pope, Kennedy was particularly anxious to fill that position with someone who was not Catholic. Stanton called Johnson back the next day and said, "I've got somebody who's even better. He's a Jew." Kennedy later discussed the matter with Stanton also, but, in the end, the appointment was never made.

The frustrations with the political process only compounded the restlessness that Paley was experiencing at that point in his life. Although he had fully recovered from his 1959 operation, he could not shake the depression that had plagued him since. His confidence and enthusiasm had been displaced with uncertainty and confusion. And it not only affected his business interests. It was taking a toll on his family life as well.

On the surface, it appeared to be a story-book marriage. He was the well-known and much respected chairman of a growing broadcast empire, and she was, as *The New York Times* once observed, "the ultimate symbol of taste and perfectionist chic" in the world of fashion. People took note in the early 1960s when Babe Paley began to wear pants, leave her graying hair uncolored, and almost everyone could recall her comment that you could never be too rich or too thin. Beyond their public images, Bill and Babe had access to every comfort and pleasure, and, as one friend observed, "they did have a lot of fun." The only pressures Babe placed on her husband concerned his eating. The years had made it more and more difficult for Paley to continue his impressive consumption of food and still maintain a desirable weight. To help deal with the problem, Paley had started having a masseuse come to the apartment every week who would, as one friend commented, "massage, rub, and beat his body into shape." It may have helped, but it was not a complete answer, and Babe began to limit the kinds and quantity of food her husband could eat.

Paley appreciated his wife's concern, but he remained a hard taskmaster. "Bill demanded perfection from Babe in running the houses," said one friend. "He couldn't stand for anything less than perfection." Babe did what she could. She loved gardening and made Kiluna a treasure trove of flowers, finely shaped bushes, and manicured lawns. She also tried to make sure that the furnishings and meals and other household arrangements were suited to his tastes and desires. But physical accommodations alone could not satisfy the restlessness that plagued her husband.

It was the family that finally drew Paley back into the life that he had known and loved before his lung operation. In early 1963 Sam Paley had a heart attack. Although he was eighty-seven, the family was surprised. Ever the hypochondriac, Sam had taken every precaution to insure good health, from periodic visits to the doctor to good food to relaxation in the Florida sun. The family expected that Sam would, somehow, someway, beat the odds against death. But more heart attacks followed, and Sam Paley passed away on March 31, 1963.

For Bill Paley, his father's death meant more than the loss of someone he loved. Sam Paley had always remained his hero, perhaps the only person whose opinions commanded instant respect from the CBS chairman. Kidder Meade was among those who sensed the depth of Paley's loss, and he and one other CBS colleague urged their boss to create an appropriate memorial, one that would be equal to Sam Paley's stature and equal also to Bill Paley's creativity. The idea energized Paley. He thought about the notion, he discussed it with family and friends, and finally he decided upon the establishment of a small park in midtown Manhattan, a place that would have benches and trees and waterfalls and offer some refuge from the towering facades that dominated that city. He pored over architectural designs and landscape schemes. No detail was too small— even the vendors who sold hotdogs in front of the park on Fifty-third Street. After the park was dedicated in 1967, Paley walked up to the vendor and suggested that the hot dogs might taste better if they were cooked in a different way. The vendor, not knowing Paley's identity, said, listen mac, these hot dogs are made by special order of the chairman of CBS, and if you've got a problem, you'll have to take it up with him.

As Paley was planning the park for his father, another activity captured his interest and whetted his appetite for life. Although he had a home in Jamaica, he had started making visits to Eddie Taylor's resort complex on the tip of Nassau in Lyford Cay. Everything was so beautiful and so well maintained, and soon he initiated plans to build a home there. "Bill's house in Lyford Cay," said Walter Thayer, a frequent visitor, "was like everything else he does: perfect." As with the construction of the Manhattan park honoring his father, Paley left no detail to chance. He spent considerable sums to study the tides so that the house would be close enough to the beach for easy access but far enough away to avoid any risk of erosion. The driveway consisted of multicolored gravel imported from Miami; the large room in the center of the house conveyed a warm, open feeling, with comfortable couches and large pillows; and, like every house, good food and numerous servants were within easy reach. The home in the Bahamas soon became a special favorite of Paley's, and after it was completed he would go as often as he could, sometimes spending as much as two weeks a month there during the winter season.

Ironically, CBS did not falter in the early 1960s while Paley's interest in the company had waned. Quite the contrary. Profits soared to record levels. For those inside and outside of CBS, there was only one explanation for this phenomenon: James T. Aubrey, Jr.

Months before he was forced to resign, Lou Cowan had sensed that Jim Aubrey was slated to take his place as president of the CBS television network. When Cowan had first talked of resigning—after making room for Jack Benny on Sunday nights—he had told Paley that there was a man already on staff who would make a "splendid successor." Paley naturally asked who that was, and Cowan mentioned Dick Salant, the CBS general counsel. Paley just shook his head and said, "Not a money-maker." To Cowan, that left only one man in the running.

On the surface, Jim Aubrey seemed to have everything Paley (or any network head for that matter) could want in a program chief. He was smart, glib, handsome, and, most importantly, seemed to have an instinct for knowing what kind of programs would appeal to audiences. Indeed, there was reason to believe that his feel for programming was even better than Paley's. As a junior executive at CBS in the mid-1950s, Aubrey had teamed up with a friend to produce "Have Gun, Will Travel," a Western program series that revolved around a man who made his home in the refined society of nineteenth-century San Francisco but made his living as a hired gun for whomever would pay the going price. That show's success had led to an offer in 1957 to become ABC's vice president for programming in Hollywood. Other men, even talented men, might have languished in that job. ABC did not have the kind of performers or prestige or profits that were so evident at CBS. But Aubrey turned those weaknesses to his advantage. The young network was hungry for ideas, and Aubrey had plenty of them. Within two years viewers were flocking to ABC to watch "77 Sunset Strip," "Maverick," "The Rifleman," and "The Donna Reed Show."

There was little in Aubrey's background to suggest where he acquired his skill in program selection. He had grown up in Lake Forest, an affluent suburb of Chicago, had gone to Phillips Exeter Academy and then on to Princeton, where he majored in English, earned his varsity letter as an end on the football team, and fraternized with friends at the exclusive Tiger Inn Club. After Pearl Harbor he became a major in the Army Air Force. While stationed in California he met Phyllis Thaxter, a young and attractive actress under contract to MGM. They were married in 1944.

After leaving the Army Aubrey decided to stay in Los Angeles, ultimately getting a job as a time salesman for a local radio station. But that was only temporary. Jim Aubrey had self-confidence, ambition, and big plans. Within a few years he had risen to become the station's general manager. But that too was only a way station. He came to the attention of Harry Ackerman, and the CBS executive knew that Aubrey would be a good addition to his staff. "He was," said Ackerman, "the most charming guy I ever met outside of Paley."

By the time Aubrey had left CBS and achieved even greater glory at ABC, Ackerman had himself left CBS to become an independent producer. But Aubrey was not interested in Ackerman's job as a West Coast vice president. He wanted something bigger, and there was no shortage of offers from movie companies and advertising agencies. But Aubrey's agent, Ted Ashley, advised him not to accept any of them. "There's going to be something opening at CBS," said Ashley. "Cowan won't last long there, and you could become president of the network."

Ashley tried to push matters along by calling Frank Stanton directly and saying, "There's a guy who used to work for you who would love to come back." Stanton told Ashley to have Aubrey call him on his private line, and the connection was made within minutes. The two men later met for lunch in New York at the Century Club, a frequent meeting place for the literary and entertainment establishments. With a handshake it was agreed that Jim Aubrey would return to CBS in New York as vice president for creative services, the very job that Cowan had vacated in moving on to the network presidency.

Stanton was pleased with the appointment. Like a manager of any major league baseball team, he wanted to have a "farm system" that included a stable of executives who could be trained to assume higher position on a moment's notice. "Jim was a terrific administrator, a fantastic salesman," said Stanton. "He could charm the birds right out of the trees. Just an exceptional individual." Paley knew of Aubrey's success at ABC and was delighted to learn from Stanton that he would soon be rejoining CBS.

Aubrey's later appointment as network president in December 1959 was well received by the outside financial community, but many inside CBS were concerned. Ambition was not a scarce commodity at 485 Madison Avenue, but Aubrey's made everyone else's pale by comparison. He was, at forty-one, considered young for a position of that magnitude. True, Paley had taken over UIB at twenty-seven, and Frank Stanton had been made president at thirty-seven, but the stakes were much bigger now, the need for experience that much greater. There was also something about Aubrey's drive that was too disciplined, too perfect—almost inhuman. In the 1950s he decided that it would be advantageous for his business career to play golf. For six months he rose at five o'clock in the morning so that he could play eighteen holes before going to work. By year's end he was shooting in the seventies.

Many CBS executives were even intimidated by his appearance. He was a man who believed in physical fitness. At a time when yogurt was known more as a culture than a food, Aubrey was eating grains, wheat germ, and fresh vegetables, exercising every day, and maintaining the muscular look of a man many years younger. With his handsome face and steel-blue eyes, he had the kind of magnetism that drew instant respect.

There was also an intellectual side to Jim Aubrey. "Aubrey is one of the most insatiably curious guys I know," said CBS producer Dick Dorso. "He's got to know everything." Despite a hectic schedule at the office, he managed to read at least a book a week and keep current on major developments in the world of theater and film. Kidder Meade, who was climbing the corporate ladder to larger and larger positions himself, was among those who were impressed. "Jim was a very, very gifted guy," said

Meade. "And I thought to myself, this guy's got all the earmarks of being Stanton's successor."

Aubrey wasted no time in making his mark on the company. With Paley absent most of the time, and Stanton focused on the administrative side of network affairs, Aubrey felt free to exercise almost complete control over programming—and he was not afraid to make the decisions and to take the responsibility that went with them. He would listen to proposals, review pilots, and consider scripts. Decisions were made fast, usually before the presentation was even completed. "Jim didn't waste time on preliminaries," said Meade. "He was the kind of guy who could have invented the word bottom-line."

He was, in a word, the perfect kind of executive for Paley. Especially in those days of uncertainty in the early 1960s, Paley wanted someone who would have faith in himself, who would push for his ideas, and who would execute them with enthusiasm. It reduced the pressures on the chairman. He wanted to rely on people, and Aubrey made that easy.

The initial decisions also made it clear that Aubrey still had the right feel for popular programming. In the aftermath of the quiz scandal, CBS had decided that it would have to exert greater control over programming. No longer could the network trust an independent producer to guarantee the integrity of a program. Aubrey made the most of the new mandate. He decided that the country wanted, needed, light fare, programs that would fill the time without troubling the conscience. Everything would be bright, upbeat, happy. When someone suggested that CBS inaugurate a drama series with a television production of Tennessee Williams's *The Glass Menagerie*—which centered on a girl with an affliction—Aubrey's reaction was immediate: "You think I'm crazy? Who wants to look at that? It's too downbeat. The girl's got a limp." No, people would not tune into CBS-TV and be depressed. Aubrey flooded them with comedies, usually rural comedies that presented nonsensical situations. By the early 1960s viewers could watch programs like "The Andy Griffith Show," "Mr. Ed" (a talking horse), "Petticoat Junction," and "The Beverly Hillbillies."

His judgment appeared to be sound. The programs became hits almost overnight. By the 1962–63 season, CBS had eight of the top ten prime-time programs, and seven of them were comedies. Many people suspected that Bill Paley, a man of culture and taste, tolerated these silly rural comedies only because of the profits they generated for CBS. In truth, however, Paley was prepared to go along with Aubrey's judgments because he liked the programs himself. Those unfamiliar with the chairman's programming philosophy found it difficult to understand, but for Paley it was all very simple. "Very often, I'd be interviewed like this," he once told some journalists, "people would make some snide remark about 'Beverly Hill-billies.'. . .[T]hey regard me as a sophisticated man with good taste. . . . 'Gee, how could you put a program like "Beverly Hillbillies" on the air?' they'd ask." Paley's invariable response: "What's wrong with 'The Beverly Hillbillies'? . . . I like it very much. I happen to like slapstick comedy. It makes me laugh, it's very amusing. I thought it was very funny. I saw nothing wrong with it at all." Whatever the merits of "The Beverly Hillbillies" and other programs, one point remained clear. As in the case of Lou Cowan, Jim Aubrey's discretion extended no further than Bill Paley's tolerance. "I had a close relationship with Stanton and Paley," said Aubrey many years later. "And when we disagreed—which we some-times did—it was all out in the open and often became heated. But always, without exception, Bill called the shots. Because it's his candy store."

Despite Paley's faith in Aubrey's judgments, one area remained off limits to the dynamic programmer—news. In 1959 Paley and Stanton decided that the news operation should be shielded as much as possible from the rest of management. Whatever questions might be raised about entertainment programs, no one should be able to challenge the integrity of CBS news programs. A separate news division was duly created, and Sig Mickelson became the first president of CBS News. For his part, Paley started spending less and less time in the newsroom. When Mickelson first joined CBS in 1949, he would see the chairman almost every day; now he hardly saw him at all. In part, Paley's absence from the newsroom re-flected his general disenchantment with CBS. But part of the cause was the growing importance of television as a source of news and other infor-mation. The number of television sets in American homes was growing by the millions every year, and by 1963 public opinion polls would show that people regarded television as their primary source of news. That increased significance meant that CBS News would have to be insulated that much more effectively from corporate pressures—and watched that much more closely.

None of this signaled any change in Paley's long-standing view that the network had to abide by principles of fairness, balance, and neutrality. He had of course welcomed the FCC's change in policy allowing broadcasters to editorialize. But over the years the CBS network had not aired editori-als, except for an occasional one that directly affected broadcasting (such as when Frank Stanton urged the Senate to allow live broadcast coverage of proceedings to censure Senator McCarthy). In Paley's view, the net-work had too many affiliates and too many viewers with different opinions to risk any editorials on controversial topics. He had the same concerns about a newscaster who wanted to express his opinions in reporting current events.

None of this should have been surprising to anyone who knew Bill Paley or the history of CBS. But Howard K. Smith was a man who had firm views on good journalism—and he was not about to change them for the sake of Bill Paley or CBS tradition.

Part of Smith's dilemma was caused by his experience as a foreign correspondent. He had periodically prepared fifteen-minute commentaries from London and other European cities that included opinions and were broadcast without resistance from the CBS hierarchy. But Smith soon found that that freedom to editorialize was a function of his distance from the domestic scene. Americans had far less interest in foreign affairs, and Smith's superiors had far less concern that Smith's opinions might be creeping into his commentaries. It was entirely different when Smith transferred back to the United States in 1957 and began to prepare reports on issues of direct concern to his American listeners. And few reports generated more emotion from Smith—or more resistance from his superiors at CBS—than those concerning civil rights confrontations in the South.

Smith had been born and raised in Louisiana. He, more than most reporters, understood the history and social underpinnings of racial discrimination. But that background only made Smith more sensitive to the need for change—and the benefits of expressing moral outrage. "The first big story I covered in the United States," Smith later recalled, "was desegregation of public schools in Little Rock. Dick Salant, who was then CBS's general counsel, told me that Paley was very upset with my report and that Salant would have to review my scripts prior to broadcast from now on." Smith did not accept this new oversight graciously, and Salant had a tough time trying to keep Smith's reports within the confines of Paley's policy.

The breaking point came in 1961 when Smith delivered a report on racial conflicts in Birmingham, Alabama. *The New York Times* had published an article likening Birmingham to a totalitarian state where public authorities openly sanctioned harassment of blacks. Ed Murrow had returned from sabbatical and was preparing a documentary on Birmingham when the call came from president-elect Kennedy—he wanted Murrow to join his administration as director of the Voice of America. For Kennedy, the appointment would help diffuse campaign criticism that he had not displayed sufficient courage in challenging fellow senator Joe McCarthy. For Murrow, the appointment was, as his wife recalled, "a timely gift." Murrow had returned to a different CBS in 1960. Paley was distracted and often absent, the company chastened by the quiz-show scandal and cautious about its future. No one seemed interested in the kind of moral crusades that had made Ed Murrow famous. Indeed, Sig Mickelson had negotiated a new longterm contract with him and then searched in vain for some superior who would provide the necessary signature. To Murrow it was a telling signal, and he was prepared to leave the company that had been his home for twenty-five years.

Although he did not and would not discuss his contract with Bill Paley, Murrow did ask the chairman what he thought of Kennedy's offer. "Well, you know you have a home here as long as you want one," Paley said, "but if you decide to take it, I have some advice on the job and the conditions you should insist upon." They included, basically, a require- ment that Murrow be recognized as a member of the president's inner circle, someone who could participate in major foreign policy decisions. Murrow decided to take the job and to insist upon that condition. There would be some compromises to make, however. He had been critical of Kennedy during the campaign, and he told Smith, "I'll have to take back a lot of words." "I told him not to worry," said Smith. "People in Wash- ington were always eating their words."

His new job meant that Murrow would be unable to complete the Birmingham documentary, and he asked Smith to take it over. Smith was only to happy to accommodate his friend and respected colleague, and he left for Birmingham almost immediately. The Freedom Riders—the loose coalition of bus riders intent on desegregating public facilities in the South—were due to arrive in Birmingham, and Smith wanted to be there to cover any trouble. He was not disappointed. Smith was in the bus terminal late one evening when, on an apparent signal, all the police officers suddenly vanished. The only people left were men whom Smith recognized as members of the Ku Klux Klan. When the buses finally entered the terminal, the Klansmen rushed on board and beat up the riders, crippling one of them for life. As Smith watched in horror, one Klansman looked at his watch, gave a signal, and the group departed. Within minutes the police returned and acted out the final charade by interviewing the bloody and frightened riders.

Smith proposed to close his report on Birmingham with the famous quote from Edmund Burke: "All that is necessary for the triumph of evil is for good men to do nothing." Salant previewed the report and immedi- ately told Smith the quote would have to go. It went far beyond any description of the facts. Smith abided by that command in his television report, giving a long pause before he finally said, "Good night." But he could not resist including the Burke quote in his radio report on Birming- ham. The next day Blair Clark, deputy chief of the News Division, told Smith that he was suspended.

Smith accepted his fate without rancor, believing that it was only a matter of time before he would be back on the job. But then the word came down that the chairman wanted to have lunch with him to discuss the matter. Salant added that Paley wanted Smith to write down his view of what CBS policy should be so that he could review it before the meeting. Smith was happy to comply, saying he would welcome the chance to discuss the issue with Bill. Fred Friendly got wind of the meeting and telephoned Smith, telling him not to go, that Paley was looking for a showdown, that Smith should use any excuse, even make one up, to avoid the meeting. But that was not Smith's style, and he went to the chairman's office on the twentieth floor at the appointed hour. Dick Salant and Blair Clark were also there. After a drink and some soup, Paley pulled Smith's written comments from his jacket pocket and threw them across the table at Smith, saying, "I've read junk like that before. But if you want to do commentaries with opinions, you're not going to do it on CBS." Smith, soft-spoken and courtly, responded that he had nothing more to say, got up and walked out of the room.

Although he had difficulty finding a job with another network (had CBS put out the word on him, he wondered), Smith did not bear Paley any hard feelings. He was the boss and, however much Smith disagreed, he did not doubt that Paley's convictions were honest ones. Paley had an entirely different reaction. Loyalty was important to him, perhaps one of the most critical elements in maintaining the strength of his network. He had treated Smith well, he had given him national exposure over CBS facilities, and he expected Smith to be as compliant as Sevareid. Smith's tenacity was, in Paley's eyes, tantamount to treason and not easily forgiven. And so, years later, when Smith was an usher at funeral services for Ed Murrow, Paley walked past Smith without even a glance at his former employee, completely ignoring his suggestion for a seat (though Babe Paley would later return from her seat to tell Smith that she was sorry).

Smith was not the only casualty of CBS News in the early 1960s. Sig Mickelson found that the public's increased focus on television news also made his position that much more vulnerable. The deciding factor for him was the 1960 political conventions. CBS had tried to come up with a winning team of newsmen to cover the proceedings and garner high ratings. Murrow had just returned from sabbatical, and Mickelson decided that no one was better suited to provide political commentary. Two people were needed, however, and for the second slot Mickelson chose one of the company's rising stars—Walter Cronkite.

The forty-three-year-old Cronkite had made his way to the top through a combination of hard work and good timing, but mostly hard work. He had been born in St. Joseph, Missouri, then moved with his family to

Kansas City, and finally settled in Houston. Cronkite's father was a dentist, the family was not poor, and Walter had the opportunity to go to college. But after a few semesters at the University of Texas, Cronkite decided that academic pursuits were not to his liking and, in 1936, at the age of nineteen, he quit school to take a job with the *Houston Press.* Within a year he moved back to Kansas City to work for the United Press as a wire service reporter. The pay was meager, the hours terrible, the working conditions variable and often unpleasant—but Cronkite loved it. "It was a wonderful feeling," he later told an interviewer. "Here I was, just a kid, shaping the front pages of the small client newspapers in that part of the Midwest."

The outbreak of war soon led to a transfer to Europe and an assigment covering the hostilities for UP. The proximity of battle and the possibility of death only increased the excitement of the job for Cronkite. He flew in the cockpit with the bomber pilots, talked with field commanders about strategy, and interviewed infantry troops on the horrors of war. His concentration was so great, his intensity so high, that he sometimes ignored the obvious. There was the time when he accompanied General George Patton's army to the outskirts of Bastogne. The Germans were using their remaining resources to frustrate the Allies' drive to victory. Cronkite was eager to provide the soldiers' perspective of the combat. His jeep stopped, Cronkite got out, and started he crawling around interviewing soldiers in the trenches, finally reaching one GI, and, with pencil and pad in hand, asking, What's your name soldier, where are you from? The soldier was perplexed and said to Cronkite, You should already know that. Why? Cronkite asked. Because, the soldier answered, I'm your driver.

Cronkite bounced around after the war, finally creating a job for himself as a Washington correspondent for a group of Midwestern newspapers. It was then that Ed Murrow re-entered his life. Murrow had tried to hire Cronkite during the war. The young UP reporter did not have the sophistication or educational background of Howard K. Smith, Charles Collingwood, and other Murrow recruits; but Cronkite was plainly a good reporter, someone who could talk to people and uncover stories. Murrow made an offer of $125 per week plus commercial fees—an offer that would have tripled Cronkite's UP salary. But UP didn't want to lose Cronkite, and they offered him a small increase in salary. It was not nearly as much as Murrow had offered, but it meant more because UP was not very free with its money when it came to employees. So Cronkite turned Murrow down. They met again in Washington in 1950 and Murrow again offered him the opportunity to join CBS—this time covering the Korean conflict. Cronkite's adrenaline started to flow, and he was soon a CBS employee.

Cronkite's plans to go to Korea were ultimately frustrated by his family and his own skill. His wife Betsy was expecting a child, and so he asked Murrow if his departure could be delayed until after the birth. Murrow, of course, said sure, and Cronkite took up temporary residence at WTOP, CBS's television station in Washington. Mickelson decided to give the young reporter some experience before an audience and scheduled Cronkite to deliver the eleven o'clock news. The results were impressive. Cronkite was relaxed, down-to-earth, and capable of remaining in control while handling late-breaking stories. To be sure, Murrow's more celebrated colleagues, like Sevareid, Smith, and Collingwood, were equally sure-footed—on radio. But Mickelson did not feel they would adapt to television as easily as Cronkite. They were too polished, too sophisticated, too aloof for the vast majority of viewers. So Mickelson arranged for Cronkite to take on other assignments at WTOP, and the former UP reporter never made it to Korea. "I was madder than hell!" Cronkite later remembered. "I thought I had been sold down the river to a lousy local TV station, and I was ready to quit, right on the spot."

His ruffled feelings were soon placated by better assignments. One of the first was an opportunity to be an anchor (along with Robert Trout) of CBS's television coverage of the 1952 political conventions. Cronkite, after all, had been a Washington correspondent for several years; he had some feel for the political process; and he would do whatever was necessary to make sure his commentary was fair and knowledgeable. Cronkite confirmed the wisdom of the decision. He studied the candidates, the nomination procedures, the political circumstances. Although the audiences were small, Cronkite was superb. He was rewarded with a weekly network series called "You Are There," a stilted, almost juvenile, re-enactment of great moments in history, with Cronkite seeming to go back in time to interview key figures. (Later the technique was refined to include film of actual events and interviews with genuine participants in a program series narrated by Cronkite and called "Twentieth Century.") There were other news specials along the way, and by 1960 Walter Cronkite had established himself as one of the network's more experienced and more appealing newscasters.

Still, when it came time for Mickelson to choose someone to work with Murrow at the 1960 conventions, there was at least one other contender—Charles Kuralt. He too had earned praise from all quarters with his warm personality, his keen insights, and his hard work. The choice was Mickelson's to make, but Jim Aubrey let the news president know where he stood. Kuralt may be a good newsman, said Aubrey, but he doesn't have the right image. He was too heavy and too bald to win the kind of audiences the network wanted. The pressure from the top only made the choice of Cronkite that much easier.

However logical the choice seemed on paper, it did not work out in practice. For all his talents as a recruiter, Murrow was not a team player on the air. He had always been alone—in London, in his radio commentaries, on "See It Now," in "Person-to-Person." He never had to worry, did not want to worry, about developing any interchange with someone who would share the microphone. Murrow was used to being center stage by himself, and it was too late to change. "I thought it would be disastrous having Murrow and Cronkite together in the same room," Mickelson later remarked. "Murrow's strength was being alone, direct with the audience. Conversation was a weakness. I would have kept Murrow and Cronkite in separate rooms, but Ed kept coming into the booth with Walter."

Mickelson's observations were reflected in the ratings. CBS ran a distant second to NBC, and Bill Paley did not like being second. By early 1961 Mickelson had been replaced by Dick Salant. There was no farewell meeting with the chairman for Mickelson. There was not even a phone call.

Mickelson's departure did not affect Cronkite's future. Most—including Paley—seemed to feel that the failure at the 1960 convention was more a reflection of bad chemistry than poor journalism. Salant was among those whose respected Cronkite's talents, and his name was high on the list when Salant and his colleagues had to choose a successor for Douglas Edwards as the anchor for the fifteen-minute nightly news program.

Edwards had been doing the show for fourteen years, having fallen into the job in 1948 when no right-thinking newscaster wanted anything to do with television. Like almost everything in those early days of television, the news was primitive, with film being flown in from distant cities and being aired one day or more after the event. Indeed, during one economy move in the late 1950s, the news studios were closed on the weekends; as a result, the weekend newscast included film of Edwards that had been prepared the previous Friday. No matter. Edwards worked hard, and by 1955 it paid off—"The CBS Nightly News" (originally the "Douglas Edwards with the News"), sponsored by Pall Mall cigarettes, took over the ratings lead from John Cameron Swayze's "Camel News Caravan" (sponsored by Camel cigarettes). But the lead was short-lived. In 1956 NBC had asked two young, obscure reporters to cover the political conventions. Just another move in that network's efforts to overcome CBS's dominance in news and public affairs. In retrospect, it proved to be one of NBC's most rewarding decisions. Chet Huntley, the tall Westerner with the somber look, provided an enjoyable counterpoint to the Southern-born David Brinkley, with his staccato presentation and his dry wit. The ratings confirmed their appeal—and explained some of the pressures on Mickelson to devise a winning team for CBS's convention coverage in 1960.

Having discovered a winning combination, NBC promptly gave Swayze his walking papers, and by 1958 the Huntley–Brinkley evening news show had eclipsed Douglas Edwards's news program as number one. Edwards did not take the unrelenting pressures well. His lunches became longer, his drinking more serious. By April 1962 Dick Salant and his colleagues had selected Walter Cronkite as the new anchor for the CBS Evening News. The decision left many disappointed contenders, including Sevareid and Collingwood. Both men felt that they had earned the position through their association with Murrow, their many years of labor for CBS, and their considerable skills as journalists. But Salant concluded that neither was appropriate for the role. The news division president remembered the difficulties when Sevareid had been asked to anchor the eleven o'clock news on Sunday evenings. "[H]e had a terrible time," said Salant. "The words seemed to stick in his throat." And while Collingwood was much more relaxed in front of the camera, he had had no substantial experience as an anchor; and beyond that, he had an obvious sophistication in his manner that would have undermined his credibility with Middle America. Cronkite was a marked contrast to both Sevareid and Collingwood. The former UP reporter was experienced, down-to-earth, and plainly comfortable with the anchor position.

Paley believed that the selection of Cronkite was the correct decision. He knew as well as anyone that a newscaster's credentials could not assure high ratings. As in the case of all programming, the anchor for the evening news would have to make that mystical connection to the audience. He would have to have that certain something that would make him a credible conveyer of current events. For all his disappointment with the network's coverage of the 1960 conventions, Paley remained convinced that Cronkite could master the role. His years of service on the network had made his name and face known to viewers, but he was not another Ed Murrow. "I'm not an intellectual," Cronkite remarked with pride at one point. "I am not a brilliant analyst. But I have the capacity to pull things together." He had a straightforward style that masked personal opinions. Paley was not going to have to worry about reliving the constant battles he had had with H.V. Kaltenborn, Elmer Davis, and even Edward R. Murrow. Cronkite was comfortable, safe. There were not going to be any more stomachaches.

Cronkite's first year as anchor of the nightly news went as smoothly as could be expected—although Huntley–Brinkley remained number one in the ratings. Still, Paley liked what he saw, and he was willing to give Cronkite time to grow into the job. More than that, he was learning to appreciate Cronkite's skills—his hard work, his easy manner, his ability to draw people out. They were talents that were plainly evident when Cronkite had the opportunity to interview General Dwight D. Eisenhower for a program commemorating the twentieth anniversary of the D-Day landings of June 6, 1944.

The plan for the program had evolved from a suggestion that Fred Friendly had first made to Paley in 1960. Why not ask your friend if he would be willing to spend some time after he leaves the White House, asked Friendly, discussing his experiences as president? Paley jumped on the idea at once. He had tried without success to recruit Eisenhower as a commentator after World War II. Now the social benefits—and commercial value—of an Eisenhower commentary would be that much greater. And the prospects of getting him to agree had also improved. The CBS chairman had grown closer to Eisenhower over the years. In July 1960 the president had asked him to serve on the American delegation participating in ceremonies to honor the newly formed Republic of Congo. And after one of their breakfasts at the White House, the president had sent Paley a note saying, "For goodness' sake, never hesitate to let me have a message from you at any moment you have anything you'd like to communicate to me." Now was the time to take advantage of that offer, and Paley wrote the President on October 13, 1960, to ask if he would consent to "a simple conversation" that would give the public "your fresh recollections of those things that happened during your tenure of office and your ideas and impressions about the Presidency. . . ." Ever the salesman, the CBS chairman tried to impress the departing chief executive with some sense of the historical significance that such an interview could have. "[C]an you imagine," he rhetorically asked Eisenhower, "how vital and valuable a record of this sort would be, were such a document possible in the age of Washington or Jefferson or Lincoln?"

Eisenhower appreciated Paley's thoughts, and within a week he sent word that he would submit to the interviews. And so, over the first months after his departure from Washington, Eisenhower gave some informal interviews at his Gettysburg farm, talking about his experiences, his thoughts on the issues, his hopes for the future. But none of these conversations contained the excitement or the sentiment of Eisenhower's decision to go to Europe to relive the drama of the D-Day landings. The program would be produced by Friendly. The on-camera interviews would be conducted by Cronkite.

Paley had started to become more involved in the company again, and he decided to travel to Europe with Eisenhower, Friendly, Cronkite, and the production crew. He would not be involved in planning or supervising the program. He was there to be an observer, to watch an interesting program in the making and to have some fun. And to help maximize the enjoyment, he asked Walter Thayer to join him.

The journey occupied three weeks in August 1963, and for Thayer it was pure pleasure. "That trip was wonderful," he recalled. The weather was beautiful, the scenery was majestic, and the company was stimulating. The group started in England and moved across the Channel to France, and for Paley, that was the highlight of the trip—because he loved French food. "We ate our way through Normandy," said Thayer, and one day in particular remained particularly memorable for him. Toward the end of the trip he and Paley rented a car to drive from Normandy to Paris. Along the way they stopped at a four-star restaurant for lunch. Paley knew the route, he had done the research, and he had made the reservations. After finishing a sumptuous meal, Paley and Thayer were relaxing when the chef approached them. He had heard that Bill Paley, chairman of the CBS network, was in his restaurant, and he wanted to say hello. Paley could always talk about food. He was ecstatic about the restaurant, the atmosphere, the meal. The chef then asked, What did you have? After Paley and Thayer disclosed their choices, the chef shook his head. Too bad, he said. You should have had the duck. It's the house specialty. A long pause. Then Paley looked up at the chef. How long would it take to cook it? About a half an hour. Fine, said Paley, we'll wait. And so Bill and Walter had their second gourmet lunch of the day. But even that was not enough to satiate Bill Paley. The two men arrived at their hotel in Paris and went to their rooms, Thayer still not believing how much he had eaten for lunch. Around six o'clock that evening there was a knock at his door. It was Bill—where do you want to go for dinner?

However constant Paley's interest in food, life was full of change by the time he returned to CBS in September. And one of the more notable innovations was the introduction of a half-hour evening news with Walter Cronkite. Paley did not like being number two in the ratings, the pressure was building inside CBS to expand the news program and—perhaps of greatest importance—NBC was moving in that direction as well. The expanded news show was inaugurated on September 2, 1963, with Cronkite interviewing President Kennedy about the Vietnam War and his fears of American involvement.

However useful the additional time, Huntley and Brinkley remained number one. But Cronkite's reputation as a tireless and objective reporter mushroomed two months later, and, tragically, Kennedy again was a part of the story. Paley was in Europe when word of the assassination reached him. He and Stanton discussed the matter on the telephone, and the two of them decided that all regular CBS programming would be suspended and the network time turned over to the News Division. Cronkite remained at his desk for hours, covering every aspect of the events that ensued. "Iron Pants" they called him. He stayed with the story until it was done—no matter what the effort. No opinions, no editorials, just the facts. And just what Bill Paley wanted.

Although Paley's view of good journalism had remained unchanged, his involvement in the news process had. The company had grown and layers of bureaucracy had been created. Ed Murrow was now in Washington, and among the CBS journalists, only Charles Collingwood could call Bill Paley his friend. Still, he liked to keep in touch with the news people. He would attend weekly meetings with Stanton, Salant, and Salant's deputy, Blair Clark, to review news division problems and other media developments. Those in attendance noticed that the chairman was especially interested in gossip about other news organizations and the people who ran them. The same kind of interest was extended to foreign affairs. At least once a year Paley would travel to Paris, register at the Ritz, and arrange a lavish lunch for the CBS foreign correspondents, including Paris correspondent David Schoenbrun and others who would fly in for the day—Collingwood from London, Winston Burdette from Rome, Daniel Schorr from Bonn. "There was no directed conversation," said Schorr. "Just very relaxed, aimless talk."

However superficial his interest might have appeared, Paley still paid close attention to the News Division's performance. And while quality remained important, there was no substitute for high ratings. But Dick Salant, for all his dedication and skill, was not producing the kind of ratings Paley liked to see. Huntley and Brinkley's continued dominance of the evening news ratings plagued the chairman endlessly. CBS, after all, was supposed to be the premier news network—not NBC. Cronkite was the man on the screen, but Salant was the one who became expendable. "You don't fire DiMaggio if the team is doing poorly," said Bill Leonard, a senior member of the news division at the time and a sometime companion of Paley's. "You fire the manager. So that was the end of Salant." In February 1964, Fred Friendly became the new president of CBS News.

Cronkite's show remained number two in the ratings, but he was still the star of the news team. And when Friendly had to choose an anchor for the 1964 Republican convention in San Francisco, there was no question that Cronkite would get the nod. Paley decided to watch the proceedings in person, although his plans were made against advice from Stanton, who urged the chairman not to go. "Bill had a way of getting into things and really screwing up the works at the last minute," said Stanton. "I was afraid that he was going to make a shambles out of Friendly's operation out there."

Although he did not make a shambles out of the operation, Friendly, for one, would have much preferred if Paley had not been a constant presence in the control booth. Because the convention produced Friendly's first crisis as News president, and he would rather have handled it without persistent pressure from the chairman.

The issue involved a report by Dan Schorr from Germany. A conscientious and tenacious investigative reporter, Schorr had started his career as a stringer in Europe for *The New York Times* and other news organizations. He had joined CBS in 1953 and eventually worked his way up the ladder to become the network's correspondent in Bonn. As arch-conservative senator Barry Goldwater was receiving his party's nomination in San Francisco, Schorr, citing unnamed sources, gave a televised report from Bonn stating that Goldwater would leave California after the convention to vacation at a Bavarian resort Hitler had used and where Goldwater himself would "link up" with Germany's extreme right-wing groups. Goldwater was furious when he heard about it and he publicly attacked the report, saying that it was entirely untrue. Paley was even more upset. The integrity of CBS News had been challenged, and he didn't know whether Schorr could name his sources and prove Goldwater wrong.

Friendly was on the phone to Germany at once, asking, demanding, that Schorr identify his sources and clarify his report. Schorr responded that he could not provide a source who would confirm the charge of Goldwater "linking up" with the German groups. Still, Schorr insisted that the gist of the report was accurate, and he refused to go back on the air with a correction. Paley became apoplectic. As he later explained to Schorr, "You probably know as well as I do what pride I take in CBS News, and how I've worked for it and tried to develop it over a long period of years. And I take great pride in its accomplishments, its integrity, its honesty, and its willingness to make corrections when it does anything wrong. And this was the first example I'd come across, frankly, where I thought somebody made a misleading report who was unwilling to make amends or to correct it."

The chairman turned his wrath on Friendly. What are you going to do about this? How are you going to handle Schorr? Friendly interpreted the questions as a hope, a request perhaps, that Schorr be fired on the spot. Like Murrow, Friendly did not relish that prospect, and he pleaded with Schorr to do something to save both their jobs. Schorr finally acceded and aired an amended report, saying there would not be any "linking up" with right-wing German political groups, only a "gravitation" toward them. It was not the kind of correction Paley had in mind, and from that point on he remained skeptical about Schorr, telling colleagues that he could not be trusted.

Schorr was not the only problem that arose at the 1964 Republican convention. The other was Cronkite. He dominated the broadcasts, giving little air time to floor reporters. The people in the control booth, including Paley, began to question Cronkite's actions, openly suggesting that he had turned into an "air hog." Still, the situation might have been acceptable if the ratings had been good; but they were miserable. Huntley and Brinkley preserved their reputation as the frontrunners, and Paley demanded a change before the Democratic convention in Atlantic City in August.

Friendly was not eager to do or say anything that would upset Cronkite. After all, whatever mistakes he had made at the convention, Walter was still the company's best newscaster. Paley did not worry about people's feelings. He was concerned with the ratings and insisted that a change be made. He had had his eye on Roger Mudd, a tall, suave newcomer who had quickly established himself as a first-rate journalist with his marathon coverage of the 1964 Civil Rights Bill. To Paley, there was no doubt as to what the new anchor combination should be—Mudd and Robert Trout, the network's senior journalist. Youth and experience. It was a sure winner. But Paley would not actually make the decision. He just pressed his viewpoint with Friendly, giving him the idea and asking, pointedly, what he was going to do.

Friendly responded by telling Paley he could not remove Cronkite, that Walter would quit rather than accept the demotion. In Friendly's recollection, the chairman responded with words to the effect, Good, I hope he does. Paley disputes that he would ever say something so blatant to Friendly or that he wanted Cronkite to quit. Although the memories cannot be reconciled, it is doubtful that Paley would have been so direct on a personnel matter. It was not his style. He liked to have his opinions known and followed, but he rarely chose to make the decisions himself. In any event, Friendly flew to California, where Cronkite was vacationing, to explain the situation and offer a face-saving solution: Cronkite could have a role as a periodic commentator, a reduced role to be sure, but at least he would be involved in the convention coverage. Cronkite rejected the offer. It would be recognized by everyone for what it was. Better not to be there at all than to accept the humiliation of defeat on television.

As Paley wanted, Mudd and Trout became the anchors, but the results were hardly reassuring. Their ratings did not even match Cronkite's for the San Francisco convention. The only positive outcome was a demonstration of Cronkite's lasting popularity among the public. The network received hundreds of letters of protest, demanding an explanation for Cronkite's absence, a protest that was echoed in the columns of media critics. No one was more surprised than the chairman. "I never thought it would cause such a clamor," Paley remarked at the time. And so

Cronkite returned to the "Evening News" with his reputation and position more secure than ever.

Mudd and Trout were not the only fiasco for CBS in 1964. The New York Yankees were another. There was a major difference, however: it took Paley much longer to realize his mistake.

In November, CBS purchased 80 percent of the Yankees, with options to acquire the remaining 20 percent in later years. The purchase was the result of Paley's growing belief that CBS should broaden its interests beyond broadcasting and records. Despite the debacle with Hytron, there were still numerous opportunities for growth in other fields. Indeed, Paley decided that CBS would be more secure economically if 50 percent of its income were derived from non-broadcasting enterprises. That kind of diversity would protect the company against inevitable economic and regulatory cycles (although profits from broadcasting rarely dropped by any significant amount).

To pursue this goal, Paley and Stanton decided to appoint Michael Burke to the newly created post of vice president for diversification in 1962. Burke, a slim forty-four-year-old man of Irish descent, had a diverse background of his own. After graduating from the University of Pennsylvania (where he had been a star running back), he had parlayed his good looks, intelligence, and sense of adventure into a series of exciting jobs, first with the OSS in World War II, then as a sometime producer and occasional actor in Hollywood, then as an undercover agent for the Central Intelligence Agency in Europe, and finally as president of the Ringling Brothers Barnum & Bailey Circus. In 1956 the circus decided, literally and figuratively, to close its tents because of rising labor costs. Mike Burke needed a job, and broadcasting, unlike the circus, seemed like a field with a future.

C.D. Jackson, Paley's wartime colleague and a friend of Burke's, set up a luncheon with Stanton. The CBS president was always on the lookout for good executives (the "farm system" never had its fill of able recruits), and Burke was hired to work under Hubbell Robinson in programming. For months Burke did nothing but follow Robinson around, listening to telephone calls, going to meetings, and making observations. Then, in early 1957, Robinson invited Burke to go to Europe for a few years to develop programs from there. For Burke it was like going on an adventure, and he jumped at the chance. Burke loved the job, and the results reflected his enthusiasm. But after five years of living abroad, he was eager to return home, and CBS was glad to have him back.

From the outset Paley made it clear that Burke's primary responsibility as vice president for diversification was to recommend companies that CBS could acquire. But not just any company. It would have to be engaged in a field compatible with broadcasting (a broad notion that was interpreted to mean any form of entertainment). And more than that, they would have to be worthy of the CBS tradition. "Paley had a passion for excellence," said Burke, "and when we had discussions about acquiring companies, he always wanted to know whether they had the same passion for quality. He thought that was the most important trait." That may have been a sound principle for someone concerned with image, but a sound investment strategy probably would have emphasized other considerations. After all, a company with a passion for quality was likely to be successful and carry a high price tag. The point was not lost on Richard Jencks, who was executive vice president during much of the time when CBS was buying music companies, toy companies, and other enterprises. "Paley's strength became his weakness," said Jencks. "He wanted perfection, the best. So they didn't buy just any piano company. They bought Steinway. Not just any toy company. Creative Playthings. If it was for CBS, it had to be the highest quality. They made acquisition decisions like a consumer. But if you're thinking of investments," Jencks explained, "you don't always buy the best. You buy something that's in terrible shape and make something of it."

However clear this may have seemed in retrospect, it was not apparent to CBS management in the early 1960s. "We were just feeling our way, groping for a program of diversification," said Burke. He would meet with Paley and Stanton every Thursday morning at ten o'clock and on other occasions if necessary. From this frequent contact Burke developed a strong admiration for the chairman. "Paley's vigor and restless imagination led the way," Burke remarked. "He was an enthusiastic, acute, intellectually tough boss. With him you had to be thorough, precise, and accurate. Or you were lost. For me," Burke continued, "it was a disciplined, mind-stretching process, a tremendous learning experience." Burke learned from the start that Paley was a no-nonsense executive when it came to business meetings, always in a rush, always eager to get to the bottom line, and always ready to ask the kind of penetrating question that the staff often preferred to avoid.

Despite Paley's dominating presence, Burke soon realized that the chairman was usually prepared to support whatever recommendations he proposed. CBS had made millions of dollars because Paley had accepted a recommendation to buy 40 percent of *My Fair Lady* in the mid-1950s. Believing lightning could strike twice, Paley had told Burke to keep his eye out for promising Broadway plays. At one point Burke was asked to preview a play being produced by Paley's friend Leland Hayward. Burke did not like what he saw, recommended against it, and Leland's calls to Paley proved unavailing. On another occasion Burke rejected a music publishing proposal from the famous (and egocentric) composer Richard

Rodgers. Soon afterward Paley asked Burke to come to his office. Once there, Paley said that Dick Rodgers had just visited him to complain about the rejection. Burke explained the basis for his action and mentioned, in passing, that he was preparing to invest in another music publishing venture. Paley had only one question: "Is it a good deal?" When Burke answered in the affirmative, Paley was satisfied and closed the meeting.

The proposal to buy the Yankees came from a most improbable source: Frank Stanton. At lunch one day, Paley, Stanton, and Burke were tossing about ideas when Stanton raised the suggestion. "Terrific idea," said Burke. To Paley it also seemed to be a perfect fit with CBS. Major league baseball was just another avenue of entertainment, and no team played better than the Bronx Bombers. In the early summer of 1964 they were on their way to their fifth straight American League pennant and their fifteenth in the last eighteen years. Other benefits could accrue from the ownership. Paley always liked to look toward the future, and he was convinced that cable television was on the horizon. Ownership of the Yankees would give CBS some valuable programming rights to sell to cable operators. With all these potential rewards, there was only one question in Paley's mind—how to explore the proposal.

Burke immediately suggested that Paley call his friend, Dan Topping, who owned the Yankees along with Del Webb. Personal contact—it was the Paley way, and the chairman quickly agreed. A few days later he appeared in Burke's office after returning from lunch with Topping. The broad smile said it all. "He said yes," Paley reported. "I told him you would come around to his apartment this afternoon and start working out a deal."

The deal was closed within months, right after the Yankees had lost a seven-game World Series to the St. Louis Cardinals. But the deal was doomed even before the ink was dry. Paley, Burke, and Stanton had been blinded by their preoccupation with image. However glorious their past, the Yankees were on the verge of collapse. Superstar Mickey Mantle had had a good year in 1964, but he was now thirty-four and his legs, weakened by injury and disease, could not carry him much longer. Whitey Ford, Roger Maris, Bobby Richardson, and other Yankee mainstays were also nearing the end of their playing careers. It was obvious to baseball insiders that the team would soon lose the depth and strength that had carried it for so many years. In 1965 it finished sixth, and in 1966, the New York Yankees, the team of Babe Ruth, finished dead last. The team did not fare much better in the ensuing years, and in December 1972 CBS sold the Yankees to Burke and shipbuilder George Steinbrenner for $10 million—$3.2 million less than CBS's original investment (which included the exercise of options to purchase the remaining 20 percent).

All that lay in the future, though. In the fall of 1964 Paley had great expectations for the Yankees. They were a winning team, and he liked to be associated with winners. Which is why he was starting to have his doubts about Jim Aubrey's stewardship of the network's program schedule.

There could be no doubt that Aubrey had made a monumental contribution to CBS coffers. After five years of his leadership, network profits had doubled, approaching the $50 million mark. His golden touch was also recognized on Wall Street, where CBS stock had jumped from $17 to $40 a share. Still, there were rumblings inside and outside the company, and they did not bode well for Jim Aubrey's future at CBS.

There was, to begin with, his style of executing certain decisions. Aubrey was the one who had to deliver unpleasant news to a fired executive or a performer whose show had just been canceled—and he did not waste time with explanations or hopes for a better tomorrow. He conveyed the message directly, without any embellishment or sugarcoating, and there were many at CBS who began to feel that he enjoyed the task. The "Smiling Cobra," they called him. The most notorious example concerned the dismissal of Hubbell Robinson, CBS's long-time programming chief. Cowan had warned Robinson in early 1959 that Aubrey was likely to be Cowan's successor as network president. Robinson had known Aubrey from his first stint at the network and did not relish the prospect of reporting to his former subordinate. So he left for a job at MCA. But that opportunity had failed to match the excitement or prestige of CBS, and in 1962 Robinson had asked Paley if he could come back. Paley, who had great respect for Robinson, quickly agreed. But it was no longer the same company for Robinson. He did not fit into Aubrey's world of sitcoms, and the end came crashing down unexpectedly at a meeting where Robinson was outlining his proposals for the 1963–64 program season. Midway through the presentation, Aubrey said, ever so softly, "You're through, Hub." "Almost, Jim," said Robinson, thinking that Aubrey was referring to his presentation. "No," said Aubrey, "I mean *you're* through." Flustered, Robinson stammered that he would discuss the matter with the chairman. "I've already talked to Paley," said Aubrey. "I accept your resignation. *He* accepts your resignation."

Aubrey used the same direct approach with fading performers, and it did not enhance his reputation. Jack Benny's departure from CBS drew particular attention. By 1963 his ratings had dropped, and it became clear that Benny's perennial dominance of broadcast comedy had come to an end. When Benny finally left to go to NBC (where he lasted only a year), word spread throughout the broadcast industry that one day Aubrey had suddenly told him, "You're through." The actual scenario was far less dramatic but equally direct. Aubrey contacted Sonny Werblin, the head of MCA's New York office, to arrange a meeting to discuss Benny's contract with CBS. Since Benny was one of MCA's biggest clients, the meeting was quickly scheduled. Lew Wasserman and Taft Schreiber, MCA's two top men, flew in from Los Angeles, and Aubrey told them all that Benny's days at CBS were over. The MCA representatives protested the decision, but they all understood that it was beyond debate.

On another occasion Lucille Ball had to be told that her then-current program would have to be switched to a different time slot. Ball had been one of CBS's most profitable performers, and she expected to be accommodated. Aubrey flew out to Los Angeles to tell her otherwise. Ball did not take the news graciously and, as Frank Stanton recalled, she telephoned him immediately to say, "I can't live with this man."

To Aubrey it was the inevitable reaction of large egos being deflated. The hostility was to be expected. No one liked to receive bad news, especially when they had been told for so many years by the chairman how important they were to his network. "As you know," Aubrey remarked to an interviewer, "nothing was ever done at CBS—especially anything involving big stars like Jack Benny and Lucille Ball—without Paley calling the shots completely. The stars were very important to him. He had nurtured a very warm relationship with them over the years. But Bill is sentimental about the network," Aubrey went on. "And when the time came to tell these stars that they no longer belonged on CBS, he couldn't do it. So I was asked to implement these decisions." To Aubrey, there was no sense in trying to camouflage the truth. "I always tried to be nice and gentle," he remarked, "but I also felt that the most painless way to deal with these decisions was to be direct and honest." Of course, those on the receiving end had a different perspective. But however much they might protest, the stars did not call Bill Paley. And the chairman did not intervene to reverse Aubrey's verdict.

Paley probably could have lived with Aubrey's direct approach in handling these matters, but other developments raised more troubling questions. Aubrey had started to become arrogant, even cocky, and while Paley respected executives with confidence, there were limits. To be sure, Aubrey had reason to believe in his own infallibility. By the 1963–64 season CBS had the top twelve programs during the daytime schedule and six of the top ten prime-time shows. He had also purchased the rights to broadcast National Football League games on Sunday afternoons, and that, too, had become a big money-maker. With each success, CBS executives noticed that Aubrey became more and more patronizing toward the chairman. When Paley questioned him on some matter, Aubrey would say, with a slightly annoyed tone, Don't worry, Bill, I'll take care of that.

And when Paley would call at his office, Aubrey would wink at his visitor and say to his secretary, Tell the chairman I'll call him back later.

Paley never acknowledged any of this condescension, but he did take note of Aubrey's lack of preparation for the 1964–65 season. CBS produced only eight new pilots, as compared with twenty-five for NBC and twenty-seven for ABC. Aubrey also seemed to feel that his judgments were beyond reproach—no matter how unethical they might appear to others. In 1964 he purchased three pilots from Richelieu Productions even though he had not seen them and had not asked for input from the rest of his staff. As it turned out, the president of Richelieu Productions was Keefe Brasselle, a long-time friend of Aubrey's. Other conflict-of-interest charges began to be circulated—that Aubrey was being chauffeured around in a car owned by Richelieu Productions and that he was living in a Manhattan apartment owned by another production company that did business with CBS. Eventually, the Federal Communications Commission demanded an explanation. CBS's outside attorney, Ralph Colin, conducted an investigation and submitted a report to the FCC in October 1964 that predictably concluded that there had been no improprieties in Aubrey's conduct. Privately, however, Colin was outraged by what he knew and saw, and he urged Paley to fire Aubrey. Colin's advice was supported by another key executive: Frank Stanton.

Programming was Paley's domain, but Stanton could not help but notice that Aubrey's approach to program development was destructive. "Jim got completely out of hand with talent, with [affiliate] stations and with advertisers," Stanton later observed. "[H]e was brutal. . . . There are people today who still cringe at the thought of having to go into Jim's office. That's no way to run a creative business." The network's almost two hundred affiliated stations were of particular concern to Stanton. After all, they were the ones who had to clear time for network programs. Many of the affiliate owners complained about Aubrey, and Stanton vividly remembers one who told him, "You've got somebody here who's going to wreck the goddamn company."

Paley already had concerns with Aubrey's leadership. There was the meeting in 1964 when Aubrey had charts and projections to describe the growing network profits. At numerous points, however, Aubrey kept interjecting for Paley's benefit, "You can see, Mr. Chairman, how much higher our profits could have been this year if it had not been for the drain of news." Paley sat silently in the room of crowded executives until Aubrey had finished. He then complimented Aubrey on his presentation but added, very firmly, how offended he had been by Aubrey's negative comments about the news division. "It should not be forgotten," said Paley, "that news and public affairs helped build CBS and everything we are today." Aubrey did not appreciate the chairman's remarks and later complained to Friendly, "Look, Fred, I have regard for what Murrow and you have accomplished, but in this adversary system you and I are always going to be at each other's throats. They say to me, 'Take your soiled little hands, get the ratings, and make as much money as you can'; they say to you, 'Take your lily-white hands, do your best, go the high road and bring us prestige.' "

For all his criticism of Aubrey, Paley had to admit that the man was doing his job and making money for the network—lots of money. That was something to remember. Still, other factors had to be considered. Aubrey was the third man in the CBS hierarchy. If anything should happen to Paley and Stanton, Aubrey would be in charge of the entire network. Paley was not so sure that that was prudent planning. It was not only Aubrey's autocratic style. Paley began to worry that Aubrey did not have the right temperament and image to run a business that was regulated by the government. The press had begun to circulate stories about Aubrey's rough-and-tumble affairs with women. Having divorced Phyllis Thaxter in 1962, Aubrey had achieved instant recognition as one of New York's more eligible bachelors with his power, his high visibility, and his charm. But some of the stories were not pleasant, recounting incidents of women whose affairs with the CBS network president had ended with bruises. Some of those close to Paley speculated that Aubrey was having a nervous breakdown, speculation that gained credibility in Paley's mind when Stanton reported telephone calls to him at all hours of the night in which Aubrey had carried on wildly, making abusive comments to the CBS president.

It finally gelled in Paley's mind: Aubrey would have to go. So he gave Stanton the signal. There was no question as to who would replace Aubrey. Jack Schneider was already waiting in the wings, Stanton always making sure that there would be complete continuity in company operations.

Schneider, age thirty-nine, was then in New York as the general manager of the network's flagship station, WCBS-TV. He had spent his entire professional career with CBS, having joined its Chicago radio station in 1949. Virtually all of that career had been spent in sales not programming. But Schneider had made his mark as a savvy and aggressive executive, and Stanton felt that he should be brought to New York in a managerial role so that he could be groomed as Aubrey's successor under the watchful eyes of CBS's chairman and president.

On the afternoon of Friday, February 26, 1965, Schneider received a call from Stanton on his private line, asking to see him immediately. When he arrived at Stanton's office on the twentieth floor, Stanton explained quickly that Aubrey would be leaving the company and that Schneider would be made president of the television network—effective the following Monday. Secrecy was important. News of the impending transfer could send shock waves through Wall Street, where Aubrey was still held in high regard. Stanton told Schneider that he could report the news to his wife (on Stanton's telephone), but that he was to tell no one else and that he was to take the rest of the day off.

Later that evening—after the stock market had closed—Stanton reached Aubrey in Miami, where he had gone to attend a party to celebrate Jackie Gleason's forty-ninth birthday. Stanton told Aubrey to take a plane back to New York so he could meet with Stanton on Saturday morning, and if Jim could not get a commercial flight, they would send the company plane for him. No one had to explain to Aubrey what that meant. "I had an inkling that Paley was going to fire me," he later remembered. "When you work with people closely for years, you get vibrations of what is going on."

Aubrey showed up at Stanton's office the next morning, having survived some wild parties the night before. However much he expected the news, Aubrey was jolted by Stanton's explanation of the change of guard. "It was," said Stanton, "an emotional situation." But Aubrey didn't ask for any better treatment than he had given to others. When Stanton asked how they should handle it, Aubrey was quick with a recommendation. "Nothing can be gained by dragging it out," he said. "There will be no graceful exit, no world cruise for me. I'll just clean out my desk and not be here on Monday."

Aubrey then asked if Stanton would mind if he went to see Paley, who was then staying at the Regency Hotel while his new apartment on Fifth Avenue was being readied for occupancy. The CBS president called Paley and said, "Jim's here and he would just like to come by and visit with you." Paley did not want a confrontation and asked, "Does he know what the answer is?" "Certainly," Stanton replied. So Paley agreed.

Paley was then in bed in traction with a bad back. Aubrey was, as Paley later recalled, "magnificent" in defeat. He told the chairman that he wanted a second chance but knew he didn't deserve one. He just wanted to thank the chairman for the opportunity he had been given, adding his hope that they could meet again without any bitterness. And they did—on periodic occasions afterward, Aubrey would visit New York and have lunch with the chairman in his private dining room.

Aubrey's departure removed a heavy burden from Paley's mind. Even so, he was not about to break "tradition" and discuss a business matter with his family. Later that same afternoon he received a visit from his stepdaughter Amanda and her husband, Carter Burden. Amanda, called

"Ba" by family and friends, had her mother's beauty and charm. Now twenty-one, she had dark hair, almond-shaped eyes, and, as one writer later remarked, "the exquisitely featured, flawless face of a lady in a Whistler painting." She had met Shirley Carter Burden, Jr., a senior at Harvard, in her freshman year at Wellesley College. There was an immediate attraction. Burden seemed to be everything a girl could want—blond, handsome, smart, and very, very wealthy. He had grown up in Beverly Hills, living in a mansion once owned by Frederic March and surrounded by people primarily known through their appearances in movies and magazines. Carter was charming in his own right, and by 1964 Amanda had quit school to marry him, a decision that later caused some regret and seemed to be an inspiration for her pursuit of education and cultural sophistication through voracious reading and attendance at evening classes offered by the many colleges in New York City, where she and Burden went to live (primarily because he was then attending law school at Columbia University).

Amanda's stepfather was very impressed with Burden. He was articulate, ambitious, and blessed with appropriate social standing. Still, Paley did not feel comfortable discussing CBS affairs with either of them. They were part of his family life, an aspect of his own life he remained determined to keep separate from business. So when they dropped by the Regency to see how he was feeling, nothing was said about the CBS chairman's earlier visitor. After a few hours, they left the hotel and picked up an evening newspaper, which informed them for the first time—in banner headlines—that James Aubrey had just been fired that very same day.

Aubrey was not the only one to say his farewells to the CBS chairman. Within months, Paley lost two friends who had been a central part of his life. The first was Ed Murrow. His tenure as director of the Voice of America had been productive and exciting, and he had been especially impressed with the quality and dedication of the staff. ("If I could only use those people for another network," he told Janet.) But all his enthusiasm could not protect him against lung cancer. Ten days after it was diagnosed in the fall of 1963, Murrow had had one of his lungs removed. He and Janet were full of hope that the operation would prove successful, but there was to be no recovery.

Murrow resigned from his position with the Voice of America in January 1964, and he and Janet took a house in La Jolla, California, where the temperate weather would make life more manageable. Although there had been occasional communications and meetings with Bill while he was in Washington, Murrow's relationship with the CBS chairman had lost some of its special quality. The tensions that had driven Murrow from the network were never discussed. They remained an open sore, a wound that never healed properly. And so Murrow was very much surprised when Paley unexpectedly came to visit him in March 1964. "Ed was very glad to see Bill," Janet Murrow remembered, "and very touched that he took the effort to come." Paley was shaken by Murrow's appearance. He could see then and there that the prospects for recovery were not good. But he did what he could. He offered Murrow a secretary to help him handle the mounds of unanswered mail, and he later called periodically to consult with him about news decisions. When Murrow returned to New York months later, Paley visited him constantly to check on his progress and to talk about a new future at CBS that he knew would never be.

Ed Murrow died on April 27, 1965, a shell of his former self. Friendly produced a special television program in tribute, and Paley made one of his rare appearances on the CBS television network. "He was," the chairman said of Murrow, "a resolute and uncompromising man of truth. His death ends the first golden age of broadcast journalism. I shall miss him greatly, as will all of us at CBS. But one thing we know—his imprint will be felt by broadcasting for all time to come."

Sadly, Paley wrote other words of eulogy for another friend that spring—David O. Selznick. The 1950s had not been kind to the celebrated moviemaker. He had never come close to matching the success of *Gone With the Wind*. Later movies produced mostly debt. On one occasion Paley, knowing of his friend's plight, unexpectedly handed him a check for an enormous sum and refused to discuss it, except to say that it was not a loan (although David took much pride in being able to return the money within six months). Selznick's financial problems were further compounded by his deteriorating health. Excessive weight, excessive smoking, and a lack of exercise had taken their toll. He developed a serious heart condition, and by the early 1960s the slightest exertion could immobilize him. Nothing was said to Bill, however. As Selznick explained to his former wife, Irene (with whom he was still close), he did not want to "cast a pall on their relationship."

That silence created some agonizing moments for Selznick when Paley invited him to Kiluna for a weekend in the spring of 1965. On the day of his arrival, Selznick telephoned Irene in an excited state. His room was on the third floor, and what could he do? His former wife reminded him that there were landings on each level. He could rest at each one, and if he went up the stairs only once, he might avoid detection. Selznick followed the advice and later expressed great satisfaction at having been able to go through the entire weekend without raising suspicions about his illness. But it was only a temporary reprieve. Selznick died on June 22 at the age of sixty-three.

Paley, knowing nothing of Selznick's condition, was shocked. He immediately made arrangements to fly to California for the funeral. He also drafted a eulogy, delivered by Cary Grant, another close Selznick friend. Selznick's loss created a void in Paley's life, and years later he would still be touched as Irene Selznick recounted David's efforts to prevent him from learning the truth of his heart condition. But Bill Paley was someone who could appreciate a person's desire to withhold certain information from public scrutiny. It was a whole different matter, however, when the same was said about CBS.

CHAPTER FIFTEEN

Controversy

Don West remembered how easy it was to answer the question. The year was 1965, and he was then, at age thirty-five, managing editor of *Television* magazine in New York. "My father asked me one day what I would do if I could pick any job," said West. "And I replied without hesitation, 'Frank Stanton's assistant.' " West did not know Stanton personally, but he had covered the CBS president's activities for many years, and he was impressed with what he saw and what he heard. It might be Bill Paley's candy store, and Paley might be the one with the genius for programming, but everyone in the broadcast industry knew, or at least assumed, that Frank Stanton ran CBS.

These impressions were, in fact, well-founded. Paley had never liked the managerial side of the business, and, as the years went by, he shifted more and more of the responsibility to Stanton. By the mid-1960s, Paley rarely attended meetings or functions dealing with the administration of the company—even if the subject matter concerned news. In 1960 Stanton created a CBS News Executive Committee whose members included both corporate and news personnel and whose purpose was to provide coordinated oversight of major news problems. Although Paley was on the committee (along with Stanton), he rarely attended its meetings. He was content to make his views on these and other issues known through Stanton and other subordinates. The only general exception was entertainment programming, where he continued his close review of developments.

For most CBS employees, Paley had become a remote figure, a man whose presence was often discussed but rarely witnessed. The company's growth into a large corporate conglomerate only fueled the image of him as the distant ruler. Even the camaraderie with news correspondents had become a thing of the past. Bill Paley had become an insulated emperor, and most within the company felt that his every whim had to be satisfied, no matter what the effort or cost. Royalty deserved nothing less.

For Hughes Rudd it was an eye-opening experience. At one point during his tenure as the network's news correspondent in Moscow, he received word from New York that the chairman was planning a visit to Moscow and that Rudd would be expected to help make the trip an enjoyable one. Thus began a series of never-ending cables from New York, telling Rudd to have a car available every day, to make sure the chairman had access to Perrier, and to provide a variety of other physical comforts. Rudd wanted to be accommodating, but he thought the level of concern in New York had gotten out of hand. "So I sent back a cable," Rudd recalled, "saying that we were going to serve him a chili Mac and . . . meet him at the airport in Big Brother overalls and my wife's hair done up in curlers."

That ended the cables from New York, but it did not reflect a retreat on Rudd's part. When Paley finally arrived in Moscow, Rudd thought he heard the chairman say that he wanted a Hungarian salami—a request that presented considerable problems in a country where even the most basic consumer goods were often difficult to find. "My God," thought Rudd, "here I am in Moscow, and the chairman wants a Hungarian salami!" But Rudd did not let Paley know of his concerns. Instead, he hurried backed to his office, convened a meeting, and sent his staff in every direction in search of the salami. Prospects looked bleak until they reached a contact in the Kremlin, and word was passed along that a salami would be secretly conveyed if CBS sent someone (wearing a black hat for identification) to a specified lamppost the next morning at six. Rudd breathed a sigh of relief. His job had been saved. He rushed back to Paley's hotel and said, with great satisfaction, "Mr. Chairman, we haven't gotten the Hungarian salami yet. But we're going to get it tomorrow." Paley was perplexed. "What are you giving me a Hungarian salami for?" he asked. Well, Rudd responded, I thought that's what you said you wanted. No, said Paley, "I brought six of them with me. What I asked for was a board—a breadboard—so I could carve on it."

Rudd enjoyed the rest of Paley's visit, eating at various restaurants with the chairman and marveling at his enthusiasm for food and his insatiable curiosity about the Russian people. CBS executives back in New York rarely had that opportunity to enjoy the chairman's company. For them, an encounter with the chairman was almost always a somber affair, sometimes heightened by a fear that the chairman's demands could not be satisfied. "Paley had a way of displaying his anger with staff that was really unsettling," said Richard Jencks, who rose to become general counsel and president of the Broadcast Group during the 1960s. "He would raise a problem and ask what you had done about it. And after you had outlined what you had done, he would repeat the question: 'But what have you done to resolve this problem?' " These and other experiences led Jencks to conclude that, for all his famed geniality, Bill Paley was "cold, calculat-

ing, controlled." As far as Jencks could tell, Paley had "no apparent
interest in ideas, no wit. If these were there," Jencks added, "he saved
them for his jet-setter friends."

Bill Leonard, another CBS executive who had frequent contact with
Paley throughout the 1960s and 1970s, agreed with at least part of
Jencks's assessment. "He would rarely raise his voice," Leonard said of
Paley, "but he was very persistent, even about little things. If he got
something into his head, you couldn't turn him around. It was like a dog
shaking a bone. If he didn't get the answer he wanted, he would never let
go."

Stanton cut a completely different impression among the staff. "He held
people to him by his quiet civility," Jencks recalled, "and by the depth of
his curiosity about what you were doing. If you presented to him a paper
for discussion, you always knew that he had read it. If the time for a
meeting with him had to be changed, it was not Winnie [Williams, Stanton's secretary] who called you, but Frank himself, asking quietly if you
could make the changed time and sounding grateful if you could." To the
staff, Stanton's patience and courtesies seemed all the more remarkable in
light of the breadth of his focus. It seemed that no detail was too small
for him. He worried about whether the men's room doors should have just
an *M* or the words *Men's Room* on them; he had fun trying to select a
general CBS telephone number that would be easy to dial (and finally
settled on having the numbers "4321" added to the exchange number);
and he even devised a special system so that a light would go on in his
office whenever his secretary left her chair. Bill Leonard, who ran CBS's
election unit in the News Division in the 1960s, remembers that the team
would create special booths for election eve, and "we would always do
something wrong for Stanton to spot and correct."

Despite the breadth of his concerns, Stanton never seemed to tire or
complain. And that, in the end, is what made him so valuable to Bill Paley.
The chairman could count on him to do anything and everything. The
matter could be trivial—Dan Schorr remembers that he first met Stanton
in Paris in 1953 when the CBS president's mission was to buy a car for
Paley. More often than not, however, the chairman would rely on Stanton
to perform chores of direct concern to the company. In either case, Stanton would be there. He might raise questions or suggest another option,
but once Paley's wishes were known, there would be no protest about the
merits of the matter, no resistance in executing the decision. Dick Salant
was a case in point. Stanton had great respect for Salant and was primarily
responsible for his selection as News Division president in 1961. When
Paley suggested in 1964 that the evening news' low ratings required a
change, Stanton urged that Salant be retained, that the ratings were bound

to improve. Paley disagreed, and Stanton was the one who had to confront his protégé with the bad news. When Salant asked if the change had been Stanton's idea, the company president looked him in the eye and said, "Yes." All very efficient, all very clean. Bill Paley would not have to worry about Frank Stanton undermining a decision or giving the chairman a bad name.

Stanton's willingness to accommodate was complemented by a refusal to ask for anything for himself. He went on, year in, year out, doing the job (and making considerable money for himself in salaries and in stock options). But he did not, would not, request any special rewards or considerations from the chairman. He would do as much or as little as he was asked and be back the next morning to ask for more. On one social occasion a CBS correspondent found himself engaged in conversation with Babe Paley, and the topic turned to Frank Stanton. He's a puzzle, the correspondent said, so colorless, so yielding. "Yes," said Babe, "that's true, he's that way, but he's taken a lot of the load off of Bill."

By the mid-1960s Paley began to wonder himself why Stanton assumed all these burdens without protest, without demand. He raised the question one day with Mike Burke. "What the hell does Frank want?" Paley asked. Although a relative newcomer to the CBS family, the issue posed no mystery to Burke. However silent Stanton might be on his own wishes, it was easy to imagine what they were as Paley moved into his mid-sixties and approached the expected age of retirement. Stanton had the title of president, but he was not the company's chief executive officer. That title and responsibility belonged to Paley, and it remained the last brass ring within Stanton's possible grasp. So Burke had no difficulty answering Paley's question about Stanton's motivations. "He wants to be named the chief executive officer of CBS," said Burke. "And he wants that more than anything in the world." Paley was incredulous at first. "Why, for God's sake? He is the president. Everybody thinks he runs the place anyhow. He's always running down to Washington to testify before some damn committee," Paley went on. "Always running off to meetings of the Business Council or whatever. Why does he want to be called the chief executive officer?" At that point Burke suggested that Paley ask Stanton himself.

It was not an easy subject for Paley to broach with Stanton or anyone else. Retirement. The word had had a nice ring to it when he was eighteen years old and "retirement" represented fun, women, and lazy days in the sun. But retirement at the age of sixty-five—which would hit Paley on September 28, 1966—held a very different meaning. It would signify—to others but most especially to Paley himself—that he had lost some vitality, some opportunity to participate. Of course, it was all a question of attitude. Theoretically, the loss of the chief's title would mean a reduction in responsibilities and an increase in free time to travel and play golf. But Paley had already delegated to Stanton whatever tasks he didn't want, and he was already taking whatever vacation time he desired. And more than that, he would still be the chairman of the board; he would still be the company's largest stockholder (with almost 9 percent of the millions of outstanding shares); and he would still be *the* power to be reckoned with.

These realities could not overcome the tremendous psychological barrier that had been erected in Paley's mind. He recalled conversations with his father in the 1930s when Sam considered the prospect of retirement. Bill had argued against it, telling his father that he would be restless, that he would lose the compass that gave his life meaning. Sam took a different view and retired at the age of fifty-eight in 1934. But he did not lie around waiting for things to happen. "He was very methodical about his retirement," said Paley, "and worked very carefully to schedule himself to do whatever he wanted. . . . He could tell you three months in advance where he would be every single day and what he would be doing." For all that, Bill Paley thought his father had made the wrong decision. "You know," he told Burke at one point, "my father made a fortune, lost a fortune, made a fortune again, and then he made a great mistake—he retired." For anyone interested in the direction of Bill Paley's thinking, it was a clear signal.

Still, Paley began to believe that maybe he should allow Stanton to succeed him as chief executive officer. The company did have internal rules (proposed by Stanton) that required all employees to retire at sixty-five, and maybe he would be making a mistake himself by trying to evade them. So he raised the question one day with Stanton in October 1965. The two of them happened to be in Paley's office on a Saturday afternoon, watching a college football game and the World Series on a split television screen. "As I was leaving his office," Stanton recalled, "he said did I have a minute? He said he had been thinking about whether he should retire at sixty-five. And I told him," said Stanton, "that it had never occurred to me that he was going to cut out at sixty-five. Because of his dominant stock position, and [because] it was his life." Paley responded that, Well, he had given it some thought, and maybe they should discuss it some more at a later point.

Despite the contrary impressions of his colleagues, Stanton now insists that the notion of being chief executive officer did not mean that much to him. "[L]et's just reason that out for a bit," he said to a visitor at one point after his own retirement. "I knew as well as anyone could know . . . that this was central to Bill's life—being chairman of that board. Whether he was chief executive or I was chief executive wasn't going to make any difference. . . . I wouldn't have acted unilaterally on anything as chief executive. I would have talked with him just as I did when I was president."

While all that might have been true, there was something to the title. Paley might have remained a force in the company, but being chief executive probably would have given Stanton that much more discretion in shaping the company's agenda and in selecting the people to implement it. Certainly that was the impression Stanton gave Don West when the journalist interviewed with the CBS president for a job as his assistant. About a year after his father had asked him to identify his ideal job, West had gathered up the courage to call Stanton and ask for an appointment. Stanton knew West by reputation and immediately agreed to see him. The two men talked in January 1966, and two months later Stanton made it clear that West's wish could be realized—he would be hired as assistant to the CBS president. "Stanton explained that he would soon be the chief executive officer," said West, "and that he and I would revolutionize the industry." For West it was an opportunity beyond belief, and he anxiously waited for Stanton's next call to finalize the arrangements.

Other developments at the time had to make the prospect of becoming chief executive officer that much more exciting for Stanton. The company had just completed construction in 1965 of a new building for its headquarters in midtown Manhattan. Stanton had first advanced the idea in 1958. "Bill was ambivalent," said Stanton, "but it didn't take much to convince him." All Paley had to do was review the physical accommodations at the company's existing headquarters at the time. As one long-time employee remembered, "At 485 Madison Avenue, the urinals stank, the toilets hardly ever flushed, and there was no air conditioning." Beyond that, the space was simply too small to handle the growing organization. Employees were spread among several buildings throughout the city (and even after the construction of the new building, the news studios and offices would remain in another building on the West Side).

On November 21, 1958, Paley and Stanton had lunch with Eero Saarinen, one of the country's most respected architects. After many meetings with the two men, he proposed a sleek, simple skyscraper made of granite. In the meantime, Paley and Stanton had to find an appropriate location for the new building. At one point they considered buying some property from the Catholic Church (which had a large cathedral on Fifth Avenue), and at another point they considered buying a square block on Park Avenue. (In fact, construction was actually initiated on the Park Avenue site, but Paley changed his mind and the excavated crater—which filled with water—became known as "Paley's Pond.") Paley finally settled on a parcel of land located on Sixth Avenue between Fifty-second and Fifty-third Streets—a central location that was even more accessible than Madison Avenue.

Paley and Stanton spent years poring over designs and mock-ups. Saarinen unexpectedly died of a heart attack in 1961 at the age of fifty-one, and the debate shifted to whether the company should retain a new architect. Stanton liked the simplicity of the Saarinen design and reminded Paley that the new CBS headquarters would be the only skyscraper designed by Saarinen. That fact struck the right chord with Paley, and he agreed to continue with Saarinen's firm. After many unsuccessful pursuits, the firm finally found an appropriate granite in Quebec—a black rock that seemed to have just the right texture for Saarinen's original design. By 1965, the new building, informally christened by the broadcast industry as "Black Rock," had been completed and the staff relocated.

Stanton had spent hours reviewing and planning the interior design of the building. Consistent with his own taste in art, the furnishings and fixtures reflected a sleek, modern look. Glass, chrome, and modern paintings dominated the interior space. Even the location and quantity of plants received careful consideration. The only exception to the master plan was Paley's office. It continued to reflect his own (and very different) tastes. The French gaming table remained as his desk, rich paneling still adorned the walls, comfortable couches were placed strategically, exquisite paintings hung on the walls, and various artifacts—an old CBS microphone, the cigar-store Indian, and later a photograph of Edward R. Murrow—all helped to provide a warmth that seemed even more pronounced because of its stark contrast with the rest of the building.

Aside from his office, there was only one other aspect of the headquarters that captured Paley's undivided attention: the development of a new restaurant on the ground floor. The notion of owning a restaurant had always appealed to Paley, especially as the years went by. Decades of culinary experience had only added to his knowledge and heightened his interest in planning a restaurant. It would, of course, have to feature the best in everything—from its design to the food to the service. Friends noticed the considerable energy he put into the restaurant—picking a name, shaping the decor, and planning the menu.

Paley eventually chose a name that was both descriptive and simple: The Ground Floor. The interior design also complemented the exterior of the building, a move that Jerry Brody, the restaurant's first manager, regarded as counterproductive. He felt that the building was too cold and stark for a restaurant. Then there was the cost of the fixtures. Bill Paley wanted the best, but the cost made it that much more difficult for the restaurant to show a profit. All of which might have been overcome if the restaurant became popular, but Bill Paley's zest for food was not matched by his success as a restaurateur.

Brody proposed that the restaurant be a northern European steakhouse, but Paley rejected that proposal. Not the right image. He wanted French cuisine. He went to France almost every year, knew the food, and it would draw the right kind of customers—sophisticated people, those who appreciated the finer things. But all these plans and hopes and expectations could not guarantee results. No matter how much time Paley spent in the kitchen tasting the soups and other fare (which he did almost every day), The Ground Floor did not produce the business that Bill Paley wanted, that he felt he deserved. It was a never-ending source of frustration. He knew food, he knew New York City, and yet he could not make the kind of mystical connection to customers that he had made with his programming. And those who confronted him with the obvious truth proceeded at their peril.

There was the time, for example, when Stanton, Fred Friendly, and Bill Leonard met with Paley one afternoon shortly after The Ground Floor had opened. As soon as he walked into the meeting, Paley asked the three executives if they had eaten at the restaurant. In fact, they had all just eaten there—and thought it was terrible. Neither Stanton nor Friendly dared to speak the truth, though. They mumbled that it was fine, just fine. But Bill Leonard loved food as much as Paley, and the two of them had spent many occasions passing away hours discussing food. Leonard could not compromise the truth on so important a matter, and he blurted out, "It was awful. The food was terrible. Fred had a fish dish and got sick. The service was bad and the prices were way out of line." As Leonard continued, on and on, the color started to drain from Stanton's face, and the effect on Paley was obvious. "It was as though I had said his mother had been caught with a young man," said Leonard. The meeting ended more quickly than anyone had anticipated, and the phone was ringing for Friendly almost as soon as he and Leonard returned to the news offices on West Fifty-seventh Street. Friendly reported that it was Stanton with a message for the deputy news chief. "Tell Leonard," said Stanton, "that he has just set the News Division back ten years. He's wrecked everything. All Paley can talk about now is the restaurant."

Paley's displeasure with Leonard's comments eventually faded. His concern with the News Division did not. But none of that concern could be laid at Leonard's door. However muted he might be in discussing food, Fred Friendly was not the kind to suppress his feelings about the News Division's coverage of current events. And as the 1960s progressed, no issue generated more debate in the CBS newsroom than Vietnam.

When President Kennedy had answered Walter Cronkite's questions about Vietnam in September 1963, few people could have predicted that the conflict would soon require a massive American military presence. Gallup did not even conduct a single opinion poll on Vietnam while Kennedy was in the White House. And when Undersecretary of State George Ball tried to warn the president that his policies might eventually mean the dispatch of 300,000 American troops to Southeast Asia, Kennedy had laughed and said, "George, you're crazier than hell."

All of that changed in Lyndon B. Johnson's presidency. The alleged attack on American ships in the Gulf of Tonkin had produced a congressional resolution that authorized Johnson to do whatever was necessary to repel the Communist foe, and by 1966 thousands and thousands of American troops were wading through Vietnam's jungles. The rapid deployment of America's military machine had caused many within Congress—and most especially Senator J. William Fulbright, chairman of the Senate Foreign Relations Committee—to raise questions whether they had known the real truth about the Gulf of Tonkin incident and whether Johnson was abusing his congressional resolution to pursue a war that did not make sense and could not be won. To help educate Congress and the public, Fulbright scheduled hearings before the Senate Foreign Relations Committee in the winter of 1966. Although the witnesses would include both advocates as well as opponents of American involvement, the real purpose of the hearing was to provide a legitimate forum for the airing of questions that Fulbright had begun to ask himself. It was no small step in those pre-Watergate days. The country did not often see public challenges to a sitting president's conduct of a war that was said to involve the country's very security.

CBS News reports had helped to fuel the debate. In 1965 a young reporter named Morley Safer sent back film of an American GI using a cigarette lighter to set fire to the thatched roof of a home in a Vietnamese village. The graphic pictures did more to undermine the moral base of American participation than hundreds of congressional speeches. Friendly understood the significance of the report from the start. He remembered being awakened in the early morning to be told what Safer's report would include, and Friendly's first reaction was fear. The broadcast of Safer's report to millions of American homes on Cronkite's evening news would generate instant and immense pressure from the White House (Friendly knowing about Lyndon Johnson's special relationship with Stanton and CBS). After satisfying himself that Safer's report was accurate, Friendly agreed that it should be broadcast. The News Division president then sat at the phones himself to help handle the avalanche of protest as people called to complain about a news report that surely had to have been fabricated. Advertisers and affiliates also registered their complaints with the network, and, as usual, Stanton was the one who had to bear the heat. Friendly remembered a meeting with representatives of Proctor & Gamble—one of the network's largest sponsors—as particularly impressive. Although he had initially expressed his own concerns about the truthfulness of Safer's report, the CBS president deflected hostile questions from the audience with firm, unwavering support of his network's news division.

Friendly had appreciated Stanton's support, knowing that it necessarily reflected Paley's support as well. However large it might become, CBS was not going to abandon the principles and tradition that had been set in place by Ed Klauber. And so Friendly proposed to provide gavel-to-gavel coverage of the Fulbright hearings in February 1966. The American public would have a full opportunity to hear seasoned diplomats and military leaders debate the wisdom of American involvement in the Vietnam war. Friendly was particularly pleased that CBS had provided live coverage of testimony from Lieutenant General James Gavin, whose critical comments on February 8 provoked sharp and illuminating interchanges with the Senate panel.

Ironically, Friendly's decision to cover Gavin's testimony had been accepted only reluctantly by Stanton. By preempting regularly scheduled programs, the News Division was charged with the cost of the $175,000 in lost advertising revenue, and Stanton cautioned Friendly that the News Division should not deplete its budget with continued coverage of the Fulbright hearings. Friendly was not about to be deterred, however, and he came back to Stanton on February 9 to discuss the News Division's live coverage of another important witness: the venerable George F. Kennan, a career foreign service officer who had played a critical role in shaping President Truman's policy of containment against communism. Kennan was scheduled to appear the next day, and Friendly wanted CBS cameras to be there.

Other events had converged to make Friendly's request more significant than he could have anticipated. When Friendly reached the president's office on the thirty-fifth floor of Black Rock, Stanton explained that the board of directors had approved a reorganization that would promote Jack Schneider from Television Network president to the newly created position of Group Vice President for Broadcasting, which would vest Schneider with authority over all broadcast divisions, including news. Schneider, in short, would have to be the one to approve Friendly's decision.

Stanton also explained to Friendly that the board had asked Paley to remain as chairman past his sixty-fifth birthday, a development that was no surprise to anyone. (Stanton, in fact, had arranged for director Joe Iglehart to offer the resolution at the board meeting, and Iglehart had performed wonderfully, saying, "Bill, this sixty-five-year-old rule is silly.") In his conversation with Friendly, Stanton did not say anything about the chief executive position, but, as he talked with the News Division president, Stanton fully expected that the post would soon be his. Paley had drafted a memorandum describing the transfer of power and had given it to Stanton for his comments before the board meeting. Stanton had made some changes and returned the memo to Paley with a request to discuss only one aspect of it—salary. Paley never responded to the request, and Stanton raised it again as the two men were about to walk into the boardroom. "[B]efore we went to the meeting," Stanton recalled, "I said one thing we hadn't discussed was salary. What the salary situation was going to be. And I had some ideas about that. And Bill said, 'Gee, there isn't time to talk about that now. Let's talk about it later.' " Stanton was a patient man. He had already been waiting twenty years. Another few weeks wouldn't matter.

Friendly, in contrast, had little patience for any delay—especially when it concerned news. Decisions were made quickly and positions were aired vociferously. "Friendly," a colleague had once told the News president, "you'll never have a nervous breakdown, but you sure are a carrier." And one of Friendly's first decisions after hearing about the corporate reorganization was to tell Stanton how much he objected to it. He had been hired, he said, with the understanding that he would have direct access to Stanton and Paley. And now Stanton was telling him that Jack Schneider, a time salesman with no experience in news, would be evaluating his news recommendations. Unless the arrangement was changed, said Friendly, he would have to consider resigning.

Upon further reflection, Friendly decided to give Schneider at least one chance. He wrote the new group vice president a memo, congratulating him on his appointment and then requesting approval to cover Kennan's testimony live. The memo was not well received. Schneider did not have much faith in Friendly or his proposal. In Schneider's view, it was "ridiculous" to provide live coverage of the testimony. There could be no anticipation over what would be said, and the viewing public might have to watch hours of testimony of little value and no interest. That, in Schneider's view, was not the function of a television news department. "The job of the media," he later recounted, "is to distill all the information into a digestible report and interpret it—not give it to the public in its raw form." So Schneider made a counterproposal to Friendly: the News Division could present a special program every evening between 7:30 and 8:00 that would review the highlights of the Fulbright hearings. But that was not what Friendly had in mind, and he was quick to let Schneider know it. "He said that I would have to give him the live coverage or he would quit," Schneider remembered.

Schneider knew of Friendly's volatile temper. "His method of management," said the group vice president, "was to turn everything into a crisis." Still, Schneider had been on the job only a day, and he was not about to risk everything in a confrontation with the president of CBS News. So he went to see Paley and outlined the dilemma.

Ironically, Paley was sympathetic to Friendly's desire to air criticism of President Johnson's Vietnam policies. The News Division president had earlier arranged a luncheon for himself, Paley, and Walter Lippmann, the venerable columnist who had been one of Johnson's most vigorous—and respected—critics. Much of the discussion had focused on Vietnam, and Paley repeatedly expressed his agreement with Lippmann's views, saying that the policy was a mistake, that the best course in business and in politics was to admit a mistake and move on. "If you are losing on something and things aren't working out, you should get out," said Paley, "and, Mr. Lippmann, that is what the president should do about Vietnam." But Paley was not going to let those personal opinions interfere with his philosophy of how to manage a large corporation. Schneider was now the man with the authority, and the chairman was determined to support his executive staff. "Whatever you think, Jack," said Paley when the group vice president asked what he should do. "You're in charge. But for what it's worth, I think you're right." Schneider's doubts were eliminated. He had the authority he wanted. Paley was prepared to see Friendly resign rather than challenge the wisdom of Schneider's judgment.

Friendly went to see Paley by himself and appealed the merits of Schneider's decision. It was a lost cause even before Friendly uttered a word, although none of that prevented Friendly from arguing his point at great length and with much emotion. By then it was already February 10 and Kennan was in the witness chair. NBC was providing live coverage; CBS was airing reruns of "I Love Lucy" and "The Real McCoys." Still, the hearings would continue, and Friendly wanted some avenue of appeal to Paley and Stanton. The thought of having to pass all these news decisions through Schneider rankled him. But Paley was not about to express his own views on the merits of Schneider's decision. He simply urged Friendly's cooperation with the new structure. "Fred, I don't want to judge this one decision," said the chairman. "In this case [Schneider] could be wrong or right, but he's new at the job and he'll learn." It was not the answer Friendly wanted to hear, and he again mentioned the likelihood that he would feel compelled to resign. Paley suggested that Friendly try to work it out with Stanton, and, if an accommodation could not be reached, then Stanton would know how to handle Friendly's resignation in a mutually satisfactory manner.

Paley was about to depart for his home in Lyford Cay for an extended stay, and he wanted only one assurance from Friendly before he left. Cowan's public outburst had hurt Paley, and he didn't want any more of those. He wanted a departing executive to follow Jim Aubrey's lead—no substantive comment to the public, no charges against CBS. Paley expressed his wish when Friendly mentioned the possibility of resigning. "I told him," Paley later remembered, "I hoped he didn't [resign], but if he did, that it would be an amicable separation. He agreed that it should be and promised me he'd have nothing to say except that we had a split on a matter of differences on policy or something to that effect." That was Friendly's last conversation with the chairman as a CBS employee.

By February 15 Stanton and Friendly were independently drafting alternative resignation statements that could be released to the press. Stanton's statement reported that Friendly had resigned because of disagreement with Schneider's decision not to allow live coverage of Kennan's testimony. The statement praised Friendly's contributions to CBS over the prior sixteen years and expressed the company's regret over his departure. Friendly's letter—addressed to both Paley and Stanton—was many times longer, much more detailed, and far more emotional. He was resigning, said the letter, because he "was convinced that the decision not to carry [the Kennan testimony] was a business, not a news, judgment." That decision, the letter went on, "made a mockery of the Paley–Stanton crusade of many years that demands the broadest access to congressional debate." The letter recited the discussions Friendly had had with Paley and Stanton and reiterated his opposition to a reorganization that vested Schneider with such broad power over news decisions. "My departure is a matter of conscience," Friendly explained in the letter. "At the end of the day it is the viewer and the listener who have the biggest stake in all this. Perhaps my action will be understood by them. I know it will be understood by my colleagues in news, and I know Ed Murrow would have understood." And for those who doubted the basis for that last comment, Friendly's letter quoted at length from Murrow's 1958 speech to the Radio and Television News Directors Association in which he had criticized CBS and the other networks for shirking their responsibilities for news and public affairs.

As Friendly well knew, his quotation of that speech was not likely to endear him to Bill Paley. On the other hand, Friendly was not the kind of executive to leave quietly without a word of explanation to the public. So when Stanton inquired whether he planned to release the letter to the press, Friendly replied that he was not sure, that he might regard it as necessary to insure accuracy in reporting his reasons for leaving. But Friendly did not dwell on the issue for long. Moments after Stanton's statement was given to the press, *New York Times* media critic Jack Gould called Friendly for a comment, and the former CBS News president released his letter.

Stanton later told Friendly that he had read the letter to Paley over the phone and that the chairman wanted to talk with him. Friendly placed the call to the Bahamas, but it was not productive. "I told him," Paley remembered, "that Stanton had read his letter of resignation to me and was he keeping his word in not voicing his resentment to the outside world. His answer was, 'Yes, I'm not telling anyone about it. The only thing I've done is send a copy of my letter to *The New York Times.*'" Paley was not pleased. "I blew my top and told him what I thought about him," said Paley. "He had broken his word. He had made a public issue of something that should have been a matter kept within the family. In breaking his word he lost a great deal of my respect. He decided to make this a cause célèbre, get as much publicity as he could out of it, hoping that [it] would advance his own position in one way or another."

Friendly did feel some remorse—more that he had made the promise to Paley than that he had broken it. But he pushed on and gave a farewell speech to the assembled News Division, which gave him a long standing ovation when he had finished. (Not everyone accepted the drama at face value; as Bill Leonard remarked, "Friendly always walked close to the edge of the cliff, and it was only a question of whether he would jump or be pushed.") After the meeting with the news staff, Friendly flew to Washington to brief the CBS news people there. By the time he had returned to clean his desk out the next day, his departure was front-page news on *The New York Times* and carried by all the other major media.

In the heat of debate, however, little attention was given to the real issue: whether the News Division should have been placed under the authority of the Group Vice President for Broadcasting. That question of corporate structure was not likely to generate much interest among the viewing and reading public. Instead, the media focused on the merits of Schneider's decision not to allow live coverage of Kennan's testimony, and many public leaders wondered out loud and in the press whether CBS, the network that had supported Ed Murrow's challenge to McCarthy, had lost its resolve, whether the financial pressures of running a big business had eroded its moral courage. "The question remains," said Senator Ernest Gruening on the Senate floor. "What lies behind this attempt to keep from the American television audiences the true facts about our involvement in Vietnam."

Although he was "sore as hell" at Friendly for the furor he had created,

Paley could not stem the criticism. True enough, his power had expanded with CBS's growth. But, in a perverse sort of way, that growth had also diminished Paley's ability to control what was said about him and his company. Television had become a vital factor in shaping the country's political and social agenda. It was expecting too much to believe that the company could escape public comment on the actions it' took. And this applied as well to the issue of whether Bill Paley would, as he had promised, bestow the title of chief executive officer on Frank Stanton.

Even as they were reporting Friendly's departure, Jack Gould and other media critics were expressing their own expectations, fed by the CBS publicity machine, that Stanton would soon be assuming responsibility as the CBS chief executive officer. After all, that was the real message of the corporate reorganization that had led to Schneider's elevation. Paley was moving out. Younger people were moving up. Certainly Stanton had that view. When he met with Don West in February 1966, he said that their discussion about West's employment would have to be deferred while he handled Friendly's resignation; but there was no doubt in Stanton's mind that the plans were still on track, that he and West would still have the opportunity to revolutionize the broadcast industry.

As the board meeting for March approached, Stanton felt even more secure about the future. The contracts had been drafted. Kidder Meade had prepared the press releases for the media. The board meeting was the last step before the world could know, officially, that Frank Stanton would indeed be CBS's next chief executive officer. Dick Salant, who had been appointed acting News Division president upon Friendly's resignation, was the board secretary, and that meeting in March 1966 remained vivid in his memory. "The entire board had gathered, waiting for the meeting to begin—only Paley was absent," Salant recalled. "Stanton's secretary came into the board room and whispered to Stanton. Stanton left the room. He returned some minutes later—looking even paler than usual—while we waited. Paley then came in and the meeting got under way. The issue of the new contract making Santon the new CEO never came up, nor was it discussed." And all because Paley had changed his mind. Paley had asked to see Stanton moments before the board meeting only to tell him that he could not go through with it—however reasonable it might appear to others, he could not relinquish the title of chief executive officer.

After the board meeting, Kidder Meade went to see Paley. Like most senior CBS executives, Meade had been hoping, "rooting," as he later explained it, for Stanton's appointment. But now Paley told his public relations adviser that it was not to be. "Frank will be made chief executive," said Paley, "but not yet. I can't do it now." Meade went immediately to Stanton and repeated the conversation. "What the —— does this mean?" he asked the CBS president. Stanton looked stoically at Meade with his cold blue eyes. "You know what the —— it means," he replied.

Stanton now insists that he never felt any disappointment in the lost appointment, and few within the company can recall him saying anything that directly conveyed disappointment. That silence, however, is not as significant as it might otherwise appear. Stanton was and is an extremely disciplined person, and he was not the kind to share his inner feelings with other employees—all of whom were subordinate to him. "I was sort of a closed-mouth guy when it came to inside things," Stanton recently remarked, "simply because I found early on that if you expressed yourself about what you were feeling about any issue it somehow went down through the organization. And there are enough problems in an organization without letting that kind of thing go on. Now some guys work that way. I didn't work that way."

Still, virtually everyone around Stanton noticed a change after the board meeting in March. He was there every day, doing his job, putting in the long hours. But the spirit was gone, the spark that had made him so attractive to so many was no longer there. Don West was among those who noticed the difference. He had finally joined the CBS payroll as Stanton's assistant, and he had had great expectations about the role he would be playing in shaping the company's future. But all that changed after the March board meeting. "After that," said West, "the heart went out of him, the absolute heart went out of him." West also remembered the evening that he and Stanton were flying to Washington in the company plane. It was the end of a long day, Stanton was relaxed, and he began to reflect on what had happened to him. "He said Paley had essentially been gone for twenty-five years with his friends in New Hampshire, Nassau, Paris," West remembered. "Then Paley turned around and walked back into the company saying, 'I want to play.' " It was obvious to West that his boss felt a certain betrayal after all his years of hard work, for all those moments when he had stepped into the breach and taken the heat.

The matter was not entirely closed, however. Paley continued to debate the issue with himself, and by 1969 it appeared that he was finally willing to pass the CEO title on to Stanton. Jack Schneider had been performing well in his new position (which had been retitled President of the Broadcast Group). The ratings had kept CBS in the number-one spot, the company seemed free of turmoil, and the transition could take place without disruption. Paley also seemed comfortable with Schneider. He had invited the CBS executive to his apartment for dinner on several occasions, and whenever Schneider vacationed on the Bahamian island of Eleuthera, Paley would send word for him and his family to fly to Lyford Cay for the day. They were enjoyable times, and Schneider even remembered the day his seven-year-old daughter got a little tipsy from some wine she had sipped. ("A little wine wouldn't hurt her," said Babe.)

It all seemed so harmonious, so appropriate. Not surprisingly, Schneider had high expectations when he discussed the matter with Stanton. The CBS president would become the chief executive officer, and Schneider would be appointed to the newly created position of executive vice president of CBS, Inc., the new corporate name for the company. Schneider would thus step into Stanton's shoes as the company's chief operating officer, handling day-to-day management, while Stanton focused on broader matters of policy. Schneider went to the board meeting in February 1969 filled with exhilaration. He would, at the age of forty-three, become the "crown prince," the annointed successor to Stanton, the person who would eventually assume the reins of power that had been held by William S. Paley for forty years.

But it was not to be. As the board meeting opened, Joe Iglehart, the director who three years earlier had made the motion for Paley to continue as chairman past his sixty-fifth birthday, again took the lead. "Bill," said Iglehart, "you've been the soul of this place, and I don't see why you should have to step down." Leon Levy, who was still a member of the board, chimed in, saying that he would second a motion calling for Paley to remain as chief executive officer. The other board members quickly rallied around the motion, and Bill Paley was still the chief executive officer of CBS, Inc. "I looked across the room at Frank," said Schneider. "We had just been had in one of the great double-crosses of all time."

Few historians would agree with Schneider's broad pronouncement, but his disappointment was certainly understandable. And while Stanton could not recall the incident when asked about it many years later, there were many inside and out of CBS who believed that Paley's failure to relinquish the CEO title was a personal tragedy for Stanton—as well as a disaster for the company. "I was disgusted that Stanton was not made chief executive officer," said Kidder Meade. "He deserved it. And from the company's long-range perspective, I had to worry about Wall Street and how they would react to any succession of power. And I knew that Stanton's appointment would be well received. It would have been very professional and would have appeared to be an orderly succession, which Wall Street likes." Even Paley's friends felt he had made the wrong decision. "Bill made a terrible mistake in not making Frank chief executive officer," said one friend involved with a large media company. "Frank knew the business, he knew the company, and he commanded wide respect."

These comments fail to take into consideration the psychological forces that shaped Paley's perspective. Age had not diminished his zest for life.

If anything, the added years had made him that much more intent in the pursuit of life's pleasures. He would beat the odds against the aging process. His father, after all, had remained active and alert well into his eighties. However much time he spent away from the company, CBS was still the focus of Paley's universe, the home to which he could always come back. He was not about to yield even an inch of ground that might suggest otherwise.

Then there was the company's future. True, Stanton was the perfect manager, an executive who could watch over every detail, no matter how vast the CBS enterprises. Stanton could also fulfill the role of public spokesman, issuing firm statements before congressional committees and other forums about the importance of free speech or about the network's service in the public interest. But for all his virtues, Stanton was not a programming executive. He had not played any significant role in the development of entertainment programming, he had not nurtured the kind of warm relationships with performers that were the mainstay of Paley's professional world, and there had to be a fear on Paley's part that CBS would be a far different company if Frank Stanton had control over everything. "Paley wanted his successor to be a Paley man, not a Stanton man," said Bill Leonard, who spent increasing amounts of time with the chairman throughout the 1970s. "If Stanton became chief executive officer, Paley might have had difficulty molding his successor in his image." As later events would show, Paley would have that difficulty anyway. But Bill Paley had had so much control over so much of his life. As 1970 approached, he no doubt expected he would have little problem finding the perfect successor, the person with the right mixture of flair and strength to oversee the complex demands of a vast entertainment empire.

Part of Paley's confidence reflected a belief that he had an ability to find people to whom he could delegate almost any task. "I think I am a pretty good selector of people," he once commented to an interviewer. That faith not only gave him hope in finding an appropriate successor, it also enabled him to spend much of his time involved with activities unrelated to CBS. So when Senator Robert Kennedy came to lunch one day in 1967, Paley was willing to accept his offer to become a director of a nonprofit corporation that would try to revitalize the Bedford-Stuyvesant section of Brooklyn. Although he did not know the younger Kennedy, Paley did know that his son-in-law, Carter Burden, was a member of the senator's New York office staff and a major participant himself in the Bedford-Stuyvesant project. And beyond that, Paley knew that the Bedford-Stuyvesant project was the kind of high-visibility venture worthy of his involvement. As civil rights protests had erupted throughout the 1960s, public attention had more and more been focused on social planning. "If you're not part of the solution," ran the ads for the Urban Coalition, "you're part of the problem." Paley had a sense of social justice, no doubt formed in part by the anti-Semitism he had experienced, and he was receptive to Kennedy's plea for help. He "opened my eyes," Paley later explained, "to just how desperate things were in Bedford-Stuyvesant." He became committed at once, devoting many hours and many days to the Bedford-Stuyvesant venture. "Paley worked very closely with the people who were interested in and working on education," recalled Benno Schmidt, Sr., another member of the board. "And he also worked with the people who were trying to develop a television program for Bedford-Stuyvesant and those who were considering possibilities of cable television in Bedford-Stuyvesant." Before long it became a top priority for the CBS chairman, and he later estimated that at one point he was spending twenty-five percent of his time on the project. "Whenever I called him," said Frank Thomas, the organization's executive director, "he called me back the same day."

However deep his commitment to Bedford-Stuyvesant, Paley did not give it as much energy and attention as the Museum of Modern Art. The collection of art had become an increasingly important hobby over the years, and his talent was soon evident to those who visited the Paley homes. "They were not just good paintings," said one friend, "they were truly great art." Paley also had remained a trustee of the museum over the years, and he decided to become more active in the museum's affairs as he emerged from the despair that had settled on him after the lung operation. As with almost every nonprofit organization, there was almost always a need to raise more money, and on that score Paley thought he knew just the right person for the task.

Walter Thayer had spent much of 1965 raising considerable sums as finance chairman for John Lindsay's mayoral campaign. One day after the election, Thayer received a call from his friend Bill, who said that he and David Rockefeller wanted to see him on an important matter. When the two men arrived, they complimented Thayer on his successful campaign effort, and then they raised the purpose of their visit. "We want you to become a trustee of the museum," said Paley, "and we want you to head up a fund-raising drive to raise thirty million dollars for the museum." Thayer balked. That was no small challenge. Paley and Rockefeller agreed, but they quickly added that it was an important job as well. Thayer said he would have to think about it, and the two visitors left without an answer. After a few days Thayer went to see Paley and said, "Bill, I've thought about this and I'll do it on one condition." Paley was all smiles. Sure, Walter, whatever you want. "I'll direct this fund-raising drive," said Thayer, "if you and David each donate five million to start the ball rolling." Paley gasped—and said okay.

The $5 million was plainly a tremendous sum—although one that Paley could easily afford. Still, the donation reflected the depth of his feelings about the museum's work. And it also helped to explain the pride he took when the board asked him in 1968 to become its chairman, a position that would make him the museum's chief executive officer. It was work he loved and prestige he coveted. He could not know, however, that the responsibility would eventually cause one of his very few personal confrontations with a member of the CBS team.

The controversy centered on the museum's executive director, Bates Lowry. He was the one charged with the day-to-day operation of the museum, and however respectable his skills as a curator, Lowry had not provided the kind of management the board expected. Paley heard the grumblings from the other board members, but he was not going to fire Lowry on his own initiative. He wanted to know beforehand that his action would have the support of the board. So he consulted with the past presidents and board chairmen of the museum, who also comprised a majority of the board's executive committee. They all agreed that Lowry had to go, and Paley and David Rockefeller offered Lowry the opportunity to resign. Telegrams were then sent to the other board members advising them of the action.

The other board members accepted the decision without protest—but Ralph Colin, CBS's long-time outside counsel and Paley's personal attorney, objected to the procedure. He, too, had been a long-time member of the museum's board, and he felt that all of the board members were entitled to know about Lowry's forced resignation before it became an accomplished fact. Colin did not share these concerns with Paley in the confines of a private meeting. He openly raised them at the board meeting, and Paley, for one, was not pleased. To begin with, he felt the procedure had been appropriate. "The problem of procedure in arriving at such unhappy decisions is always difficult for those responsible for the governance of institutions," Paley later explained. But he felt that he had used an appropriate approach in consulting only a select few of the forty-member board. The smaller the group, he said, "the better it usually is for both the institutions and the individuals involved."

But the merits of Paley's procedure had been eclipsed, in his mind, by the procedure utilized by Colin to voice his complaint. To the CBS chairman it was an act of treason. Colin had tried to humiliate the CBS chairman in an open forum. That was unacceptable, and on the morning of May 16, 1969, the day after the board meeting, Colin was summoned to Paley's office, where the chairman quietly and quickly told Colin that he was no longer going to be Bill Paley's personal attorney. And after Paley left for Lyford Cay, Colin received word that, after forty-two years, he was no longer outside counsel for CBS. The chairman, he was told, had finally decided to accept a long-standing request by the CBS legal department to find a new counsel.

Colin had his own idiosyncracies, but he was proud, and he was not about to ask Paley to reconsider. He already had the stature he wanted in New York's legal community, he already had position in society, and he certainly did not want for money. But he did not like the discomfort he felt, and he did not want to feel awkward when he encountered Paley at museum functions or social gatherings, encounters he knew were inevitable. So he went back to Paley with a simple request: for the sake of friendship, they should put aside their past differences. Neither should feel awkward at later meetings between the two of them. Paley did not share that view. He could not, would not, put aside his feelings. Colin had turned on him—in public no less—and that was not easily forgiven. So Paley had a quick answer for his former attorney: "Ralph, we were never friends. You were my attorney."

Paley later denied that he used those precise words, but he did not quarrel with the message. Ralph Colin was no longer a welcome presence. Colin remained forever bitter, and years later, when an interviewer asked his widow about Bill Paley, all she would say was that what Bill Paley did to her husband was "disgusting."

Paley's distaste for confrontation and controversy extended to the way in which he made programming decisions as well. He did not like it when executives or producers raised their voices and used strong language. The quiet approach was much more preferable. If a person lowered his voice, Paley was more likely to focus on the comments. And in no event did he want to hear program executives pat themselves on the back. That was rarely productive. " 'Don't tell me the good things,' " Mike Dann would remember Paley constantly saying. " 'Tell me what's wrong.' And the more you worried," Dann continued, "the more interested he became. He wanted to get his hands dirty in programming."

Ratings had now become the focus of almost all programming decisions. Dann had pushed A.C. Neilsen and Company to develop overnight ratings, and Paley was always available, day or night, to talk about a program's performance. "There was no time I couldn't call him to talk about a program and ratings," said Dann. "Sometimes I would call him at eleven o'clock at night to talk about a program that had just aired. Or sometimes we would talk at nine o'clock on a Saturday morning to review the previous day's ratings. He watched all the programs closely. Even the soap operas."

Paley wanted to avoid controversy in his network's programming as much as he tried to keep controversy out of his personal life. At one point in the late 1960s Dann developed two versions of a program similar to NBC's "Laugh-In," a popular comedy show that was not afraid to use off-color jokes and poke fun at current events. Paley didn't want that kind of program on his network, and Dann's proposals never saw the light of day. As media critic Les Brown observed, CBS was a little too formal, a little too polite, to let anyone use its facilities to say, "Go look that up in your *Funk and Wagnall's.*" All of which made Robert Wood's proposals difficult for Paley to accept.

After spending his entire career at CBS, Wood had, at the age of forty-four, become president of the CBS Television Network at the same time that Schneider was made executive vice president. Like many programming executives, Wood's background seemed totally alien to the programs he proposed for his company. Born in Boise, Idaho, he had moved with his family to the sunny and affluent environs of Beverly Hills (a background that eventually led him to become a trustee of the University of Southern California and a member of the Southern California WASP establishment). After service in the Navy during World War II and receiving his degree from the University of Southern California, Wood began a steady progression up the CBS corporate ladder, starting with a job at the network's Los Angeles radio station, then as general manager of the CBS television station in Los Angeles, vice president of the Television Stations Division in New York, and finally the network presidency.

Wood studied the ratings as closely as Paley, but he drew entirely different conclusions from them. To be sure, the network's entertainment programs still attracted the most people, but the demographics of CBS audiences were disturbing. Most of them were either very young or very old. Almost half the people who watched "The Red Skelton Show," for example, were over the age of fifty, and much of the remainder was probably under twelve. The network had little strength among people in the eighteen-to-forty-nine-age group, the fastest growing and—for advertisers—most important segment of the viewing population. If CBS wanted to retain its number-one status, changes would have to be made. Big changes.

The moment of decision came at a meeting to plan the 1969–70 program season. Red Skelton and Jackie Gleason were both asking to have their contracts renewed for three years with substantial increases in compensation. To Wood it made no sense to agree to the proposed contracts. Neither Skelton nor Gleason was generating much profit for CBS. The former represented a mere $25,000 gain, and the latter a $300,000 *loss.* Even more important, neither Skelton nor Gleason was in step with the times. The country was at war, cities were being burned to the ground, hundreds of thousands of people had taken to the streets to protest—Skelton and Gleason were not relevant to that environment, and that, in turn, would mean a continuing loss of viewership.

In addition to Paley and Wood, the programming meeting was attended by Schneider and Broadcast Group President Dick Jencks—both of whom were Wood's superiors and both of whom agreed with Wood's perspective. That staff support carried a lot of weight in Paley's mind as Wood made his argument. "Mr. Paley," said Wood, "you can sit on your front porch on a rocking chair collecting your dividends on what you've created. A parade will be coming down the street and you may watch it from your rocking chair, and it will go by you. Or you might get up from that chair and get into the parade, so that when it goes by your house you won't just be watching it, you'll be leading it. Mr. Paley," Wood concluded, "CBS is falling behind the times, and we have to get back in step." Gleason and Skelton would have to go and be replaced by something more attuned to the younger generation.

There were dissents to Wood's proposals. Mike Dann had spent more than ten years with Bill Paley and CBS television programs. He, more than most, appreciated Paley's reliance on performers, the stars who packed them in week after week. Whatever Wood's arguments about demographics, the fact remained that Skelton's program was among the top ten, and Gleason was always capable of a big draw with the right show. But Paley prided himself on being farsighted. He liked the stars and he understood their value to the network, but he was not going to cling to them for the sake of nostalgia. He had sacked stars like Jack Benny and he could do it to Gleason and Skelton. So he accepted Wood's proposals.

Paley left for Lyford Cay immediately after the meeting, but he was not sure that the right decision had been made. No doubt he was plagued by Mike Dann's arguments. CBS had been built on the star system, and Skelton and Gleason, unlike Benny, still had the power to attract large audiences, even if they were too frivolous for Wood's tastes. Paley would not overturn the decision by himself, though. He began calling Wood back in New York, asking, pushing, Are you sure? Do you think we're doing the right thing? Wood kept responding, Yes, Mr. Chairman, you're doing the right thing, you won't be disappointed. "Hell, I didn't know any better than he if we were right," Wood later confided to a friend, "but I knew I couldn't waver with Mr. Paley. . . . If I'd shown the least sign of indecision or doubt, Skelton and Gleason would have been back in the schedule the next day."

Thus began Wood's crusade for programs relevant to the changing times. And one that he grew increasingly excited about was a pilot that had been rejected by ABC. The plot line revolved around a bigoted but lovable middle-class man in Queens. It had been developed by Norman Lear, and it was entitled "All in the Family."

The original idea for the pilot was not actually Lear's. In 1965 the British Broadcasting Corporation had aired a program series called "Till Death Do Us Part," the story of a middle-aged bigot named Alf Garnett who lived in a home with a very liberal son-in-law. The program had attracted the attention of ABC and CBS, but the rights for an American production were sold to Lear and Bud Yorkin, a creative team that had written and produced a number of television specials and movies, including "Come Blow Your Horn" and "Divorce: American Style." For Lear, the BBC program had special meaning. Alf Garnett reminded Lear of his own father, a middle-class man who had dominated the Lear household in Bridgeport, Connecticut. Lear himself had become involved in many progressive causes as a youth in the 1940s, and he remembered the arguments he had had with his father, how difficult his father could be, and how easily his mother could disregard his father's foibles.

Lear negotiated a contract with ABC for the production of "All in the Family." The first pilot was not accepted, and Lear produced another. ABC still refused to schedule the program, and Lear decided to market it to another network. Sam Cohen, Lear's agent, telephoned Mike Dann one day in 1968 and said he had a business project to discuss. Cohen had picked his target well. He and Dann were both Democrats and both eager to focus public attention on the political and and social issues then confronting the nation. "I want you to see a program," Cohen explained to the CBS executive, "and tell me why it can't get on the air." Dann reviewed the pilot and was immediately ecstatic. "I thought it was sensational," he remembered. "One of the funniest things I had ever seen." Dann then made arrangements for the pilot to be seen by Wood, Schneider, Jencks—and Paley.

The chairman did not like the program at all. It made "Laugh-In" look subdued by comparison. Schneider agreed. "I hated it," he remembered. "I sided with Paley that it was too coarse and too vulgar." But Wood felt differently. "He took after it like a dog with a bone," said Schneider. Wood's enthusiasm for the program was all the more remarkable because of his background as a true conservative, a certified member of the WASP establishment. But Wood had promised to drag Bill Paley and CBS into contact with contemporary society, and Lear's program did it with both humor and poignancy.

Archie Bunker, the protagonist, was a bigot who freely used words like *coon, spic, kike,* and other epithets to describe those with different ethnic backgrounds. But he was also a man of sensitivity—as later displayed on the occasion when his daughter Gloria bought him an anniversary card to give to his wife Edith; by mistake, Edith picked up the card and read it aloud, and Archie, thinking it was for him, cried. (Edith stole the show with her next line, "And, ooh, it's almost a Hallmark.") As Charlie Brown might have said, Archie Bunker was a person who hated mankind but loved people.

Some aspects of the first program did trouble Wood, however. There was the scene in which Mike, the son-in-law, walked down the stairs on Sunday morning, zipping up his fly after having made love to Gloria. ("Eleven o'clock on a Sunday morning!" Archie cried out upon realizing what had happened.) Wood wanted to be adventuresome, he wanted to reach the youth of America, but he didn't want to lose all of CBS's affiliates in the process. We have to go slowly, he told Lear. We can't overwhelm affiliates and audiences with everything at once. Lear resisted. "We gotta get our feet wet," he responded. If they decided to move incrementally at the start, said the show's creator, they might not move at all.

Paley was not directly involved in this process. He had always relied on his programming executives in the past, a reliance that had only increased with the years. This had become especially true under Aubrey's regime. Paley had refrained from aggressively pushing programs that Aubrey opposed. "The Defenders" was an example. An intelligent show about a father-and-son lawyer team, it dealt with controversial social issues like abortion. But it did not fit into Aubrey's world of rural comedies, and the program did not make it into the schedule until a replacement was needed in mid-season. A similar phenomenon occurred in later years when Dann and other programming executives proposed cancellation of "Gunsmoke." Paley loved that program—it had been one of his most profitable initiatives. He wanted, somehow, some way, to keep it on the air, but he ultimately acquiesced to Dann's decision. Later he asked Dann how the replacement shows were doing, and when Dann reported mixed results, Paley suggested that they put "Gunsmoke" back on the air at a different time when it might have a better chance of attracting a larger audience. The ploy worked, and "Gunsmoke" enjoyed five more years as one of the nation's top ten programs.

But all of this was behind the scenes. Paley believed in delegation. He would make his views known, but he respected the program executive who could tell him no. So, while his objections to "All in the Family" were strong ones, he allowed himself to be worn down by Dann and Wood and their associates. "All in the Family" was finally aired as a replacement program in January 1971. It soon became the network's number-one show and the source of various "spin-offs" that benefitted both CBS and NBC (when CBS refused to take them all).

Paley's approach to news programming was even more removed. He had insulated the News Division and given it the freedom he thought it needed. He would, if need be, make his views known, but he now wanted the machine to run without his involvement. For the most part, he did not even watch the evening news anymore. It did not fit in with his schedule. He generally left the office around five o'clock and went home to enjoy an early dinner with Babe at their Fifth Avenue apartment or, on some occasions, they might dine at the homes of friends. There was little of the late-night carousing that had been a central part of Paley's life before the war. Nor was there any need for a valet to drag him out of bed in the mornings. He woke up early, had his breakfast and the morning newspapers brought to his room, and then watched "The CBS Morning News." He had now accepted the wisdom of Lou Cowan's earlier observation about the need for an early morning news program, and he was full of suggestions for Dick Salant on how the program might be improved (and later, after the debacle with Sally Quinn, Paley suggested to Salant that he not worry about glamour and glitz and ratings but focus instead on using the network's resources to develop a good, hard-hitting news show).

However distant he might seem from most of the news programs, and however independent Dick Salant and the News Division wanted to feel in making decisions, there was no escape from the fact that, when all was said and done, it was still Bill Paley's company. And so the staff was eager to know the chairman's reaction to Vice President Spiro Agnew's blistering attack against the networks in November 1969. It was not a matter of curiosity, however. To the people in the News Division, it was a question of survival.

The vehicle for Agnew's attack was an evening speech in Des Moines. The vice president was vicious and colorful, calling the networks "nattering nabobs of negativism." And, while his complaint seemed to be with all the networks, CBS drew special attention. It was still viewed in some circles—especially Republican ones—as the most prominent media outlet for liberal opinions, and Agnew charged that a liberal bias had infected CBS's coverage of President Nixon and his administration.

Agnew's criticism attracted instant attention throughout the country (in part because the networks had decided to provide live coverage of the speech). Experienced observers sensed that Agnew's comments were just the beginning of Nixon's new war against the press. He had never liked the media. In his mind, they had always been his adversary. He believed that they had tried to force him off the Republican ticket in 1952 (pressure he had surmounted by a direct appeal to the electorate in the infamous "Checkers" speech), that they had hounded him during the Eisenhower years, and that they had sided with Kennedy in 1960 because of the

Democratic candidate's glamour and wit. The media had written Nixon off after his 1962 defeat in the California gubernatorial election; and he had returned to Washington—to the White House no less—in spite of their political obituaries. And now he would have his revenge. Or so seasoned journalists surmised as they listened to Agnew's attack.

There was a certain irony in Agnew's focus on CBS. After all, Bill Paley had been a confidant of Eisenhower's, a sometime golfing partner of Nixon's, and someone who had made concerted efforts to help Nixon defeat Kennedy in 1960. Paley had also suggested that Nixon not run for governor of California in 1962, because a loss would damage his political standing (a suggestion that was quickly rejected by Nixon advisers—how could the former vice president possibly lose, they asked).

All that was in the past, though. Paley did have several dinners and meetings with Nixon, Thayer, and others in 1967 and 1968, and some observers even thought that he would finally secure the coveted ambassadorship to the Court of St. James. But Paley was not among Nixon's supporters in 1968. "I was a Rockefeller man," he later explained. He and the New York governor had been friends since the 1930s, and it was only natural for Paley to want to see Rockefeller sitting in the Oval Office on January 20, 1969. It all may have seemed logical to Paley, but he suspected that Nixon saw it differently. "I don't think he ever forgave me for that," said the CBS chairman. And so, despite the long association with Nixon, Paley understood why he received no phone calls from the new president, no requests for private meetings, and no personal correspondence.

Paley also could have predicted Agnew's attack and Nixon's unhappiness with CBS. "Listen," he later told Dan Schorr, "I've been in this game for forty-eight years, and I've had to deal with presidents of all kinds. And very few have been happy with broadcasting, and very few have been happy with the press." Because of this perspective, the CBS chairman bristled at any suggestion that he would succumb to pressure from the White House, or try to shape the news to accommodate a specific political viewpoint. "Well, if I started to worry and took any action accordingly, I wouldn't be worthy of holding down this office, would I?" he rhetorically asked Schorr in that same conversation. " . . . Talk about Nixon, there were guys before him who were much more vicious in the way they talked. And they didn't have any effect on me at all. I realized very early in the game that we were not going to make everybody happy. And most of the time we used to get as many criticisms from the left side as from the right side. And that sort of proved to me," he continued, "that we were maintaining a very good balance. I believed and still believe that our greatest protection against government in any form or any administration is to maintain this fair position about everything of a controversial nature. And I'm more sensitive about that than about anything else."

For all this courageous talk, Paley was not on the firing line in deflecting the pressure. And there were moments when he began to believe that there was some merit to the complaints registered by Nixon and his supporters.

The doubts emerged during the controversy over the CBS News documentary entitled "The Selling of the Pentagon," which had been aired in February 1971. Relying on the techniques that Murrow had used to great effect against McCarthy, the News Division employed the Pentagon's own films and spokesmen to expose the questionable practices used by the military to publicize its views of war and peace. The bitter debate over the Vietnam War only made the program that much more controversial. And tempers became even more inflamed when it was learned that CBS had employed some questionable practices of its own in preparing the program: in editing an interview of a Pentagon representative, the producer had spliced the film so that the response to one question was seen by viewers as a response to an entirely different question. The technique may have facilitated the production, but it also created an erroneous impression about the spokesman's remarks.

Congressman Harley Staggers of West Virginia, chairman of the House Commerce Committee, was one of those most offended by CBS's editing process. His committee had jurisdiction over the FCC, and he was not about to stand by while a major television network deceived the public. So his committee issued a subpoena to CBS President Frank Stanton to appear before the committee with all the "outtakes"—the film that had been excised from the broadcast.

Kidder Meade was at home when he received an evening phone call from journalist Tac Nail telling him that two committee staff members would deliver the subpoena the following morning. Meade immediately telephoned Stanton at his townhouse, and, after consulting CBS's Washington attorneys, the two men plotted their strategy. It all revolved around a defense of freedom of the press.

Stanton had by now developed firm opinions about the role of journalism in a democracy. He believed it was critical for the press to remain free of government oversight, no matter what its sins. His feelings were so deep, so strong, that he sometimes took positions that surprised even the most ardent advocates of free speech. There was, for example, the well-publicized robbery at CBS's television station in Philadelphia. Stanton refused to provide details to inquiring local reporters. "To his mind," said CBS broadcast president Dick Jencks, "you couldn't release any information without compromising your First Amendment rights. He likened it to a journalist revealing his confidential sources."

Stanton would be equally adamant in refusing to honor Staggers's subpoena for CBS outtakes. So when the two staff members delivered the subpoena, Stanton entertained them with danish and coffee while Meade put the finishing touches on a press release attacking the committee's request as a threat to the First Amendment rights of CBS and every other broadcaster. "The fact that television and radio stations are licensed by the government," Stanton later observed in testimony before Staggers's committee, "does not deprive the broadcast press of First Amendment protections. . . ."

Staggers and other committee members were not happy with this response. They asked Stanton to reconsider his position. And if he did not, they promised to cite Stanton and CBS for contempt of Congress—a threat that carried the prospect of jail for the sixty-three-year-old CBS president. But Stanton would not bend, and on June 30, 1971, the Commerce Committee voted 25 to 13 to hold Stanton and CBS in contempt. The matter was sent to the House floor for a necessary vote by the entire membership. Although Democrats controlled the House, the outcome was by no means certain.

For the most part, Stanton, Meade, and News Division president Dick Salant struggled with the problem alone. As Salant later recalled, "Paley had no role in it, as far as I was aware, until the very end. I never dealt with him about it, and I did not know whether or not he took a position on any aspect of it." As it turned out, Paley was gone most of the time, traveling on vacation and business. But he was not indifferent to what was happening in Washington. In fact, he was extremely disturbed by developments.

To begin with, he was not at all pleased with the production techniques that had been used in "The Selling of the Pentagon." Years before he had expressed shock and disappointment when Dan Schorr had explained the News Division's use of "reverses" in television interviews. Because a reporter had access to only one camera, it was focused on the person being interviewed; after the interview was completed, the camera was used to take film of the reporter asking the questions, and then the two sequences were spliced together to create an impression that there had been two cameras operating during the interview. Paley had not previously known of this practice, and he finally asked Schorr, "Isn't it basically dishonest?" Schorr tried to explain that "reverses" were necessary unless the network wanted to give each reporter two cameras. Paley was not satisfied with that answer, and he directed the News Division to terminate the practice.

Paley must have reflected on these earlier concerns when he learned about the splicing used in the production of "The Selling of the Pentagon." He treasured CBS's reputation for integrity, and he was extremely disturbed to learn that the company, his company, had used a production technique that raised questions about the truthfulness of the broadcast. The merits of Staggers's position only made the likelihood of his success on the House floor that much more probable. Many congressional members already felt that CBS was too arrogant, and they would welcome an opportunity to humiliate the network. As Paley told Walter Thayer at lunch one day at New York's "21," his mind was preoccupied by one problem, and it was spelled S-t-a-g-g-e-r-s.

Despite these concerns, Paley agreed with Stanton that the government should not be allowed to review and evaluate the editing process. A news organization, even one that had broadcast licenses, had to have complete control over its own operation. That was what the First Amendment was all about.

However much he agreed with Stanton on the principle, Paley was not happy with the role the CBS president had assumed in articulating it to the public. True, Paley had never really liked being the public spokesman in earlier years, and he had welcomed Stanton's willingness to assume the position after World War II. But Stanton was attracting considerable attention in the media because of his courageous defense of the First Amendment. He was the one out front, the one risking jail. CBS was Bill Paley's company, but his name was rarely mentioned in all these glowing tributes to the network's willingness to fight Congress. Jock Whitney began to needle his good friend, asking, demanding, to know why the public had heard nothing from him on this important issue.

At one point Paley summoned Meade to his office and confessed his frustration. The CBS vice president tried to explain the decision to have only one spokesman (an approach Paley had endorsed in handling the quiz scandal and other controversies). Perhaps the choice of a spokesman could have been different, but Paley was out of the country when the subpoena was delivered and, in any case, the name on the subpoena was Stanton's, not Paley's. Paley was not satisfied with that answer, and Meade could see the anger mounting. "I almost lost my job over that one," he later recalled. Finally it was agreed that Meade would draft a memo that Paley could send to the entire CBS organization before the vote. The chairman was mollified, and the memo went out on July 7. Any compromise in yielding to Congress's demands, said the memo, would "go against every principle that CBS has stood for and fought for since its founding."

On July 13, the House of Representatives rejected Staggers's contempt citation by a vote of 226 to 181. Although Paley had allowed the full use of CBS's considerable resources in the fight, Stanton, for one, gave much of the credit to Wilbur Mills, chairman of the House Ways and Means Committee. After a presentation by CBS counsel Lloyd Cutler, Mills went to the floor and used his substantial influence to urge defeat of Staggers's proposal. Stanton was gratified and later commented that Mills was the "man who saved my neck."

Charles Colson, Nixon's infamous special counsel, had a different view. He later claimed that Stanton was spared a jail sentence by a White House directive to House Republican leader Gerald R. Ford to help defeat the Staggers motion. Colson would later say that he expected CBS to reciprocate the favor with more positive coverage of the Nixon administration. No one at CBS could remember making such a commitment, and the network's coverage of Watergate one year later made it clear that no such promise had been made.

In the beginning, *The Washington Post* was the only major media outlet to devote substantial resources to unraveling the intricacies of the break-in at Democratic Party headquarters. As the *Post*'s almost endless revelations moved the conspiracy closer and closer to the White House, other newspapers, including *The New York Times* and the *Los Angeles Times,* picked up the banner. But not the television networks. They confined their coverage to sporadic reports of major developments—until Walter Cronkite decided that CBS had to do something more. "The story wasn't getting out in the daily papers," said Cronkite later, "and *we* weren't covering it right. Revelations were dropping out every day, but nobody was pulling them together." And so Cronkite, managing editor of "The CBS Evening News," decided to provide his viewers with a detailed explanation of the various allegations, their origins, and their significance.

The final product was too long to be aired on one evening newscast, which only allowed for about twenty-two minutes of actual news (the remaining time being used for commercials). The presentation would have to be divided and offered on two separate shows.

The first segment aired on the evening of Friday, October 27, 1972. The show generated attention even before Walter Cronkite appeared on the screen. Colson had heard from newly appointed Attorney General Richard Kleindienst that Cronkite was planning a special on Watergate, that CBS had already tried (without success) to obtain a sponsor for the program, and that the program was Cronkite's vendetta against Nixon for having refused an earlier Cronkite request for an interview to talk about the issues. Colson was anything but timid, and he made a telephone call to Stanton that morning to ask if there was any truth to Kleindienst's reports. "I just absolutely denied [them] out of hand," said Stanton. "We were not doing any specials, and, if we were, we wouldn't be showing them to prospective advertisers." Colson was not satisfied with that answer. "He swore up and down that I didn't know what I was talking about," Stanton recalled.

Colson must have felt a certain sense of vindication when he watched

Walter Cronkite open that evening's broadcast by saying, "At first it was called the Watergate caper. . . ." Stanton was having drinks with a friend in his private dining room when the first "feed" of the Cronkite show came on the monitor at 6:30 P.M. He was surprised—and concerned. It was not the content that troubled him. It was the length. The Watergate presentation occupied about fourteen minutes—almost two-thirds of the air time devoted to actual news. Cronkite added at the end that a second half would be presented the following Monday. That was an inordinate amount of time to devote to one subject on a news show that was designed to cover news events all over the world. Then there was the timing. Within a few days the country was going to cast its votes for president, choosing between Nixon and his Democratic challenger, Senator George McGovern. There were likely to be strong protests of bias from the Republican camp, which was no small matter given the likelihood of a Nixon victory and his administration's entrenched hostility toward the press in general and CBS in particular.

As soon as the Watergate presentation was finished, Stanton excused himself, went to his office, and used his private line to call the CBS chairman at his apartment. He told Paley that he should be sure to watch the Cronkite program, which was aired at 7:00 P.M. on the network's New York station.

Paley remembered being "very upset" when he saw the presentation. "Not because the information wasn't important, not that we doubted the accuracy of it," he observed, "but this was a half-hour program that was supposed to cover the news of the world [and] this kind of information should have taken place in a half-hour special or something of that kind." The chairman was also concerned that the presentation was not as fair and balanced as it should have been. CBS had asked the White House for reactions to some of the charges, even though denials had already been published in the *Post* and other periodicals. The White House refused to accommodate CBS, and Cronkite refused to note in the broadcast that the charges had already been denied. "I thought that was a little high-handed, you know," said Paley. The chairman also felt that the average viewer would have difficulty distinguishing between "what we called facts and what we called allegations"—a critical point that led Paley to conclude, overall, that "this wrap-up could not be classified as completely objective, that it did show bias against the administration."

Paley did not keep these thoughts to himself. He telephoned Stanton immediately after the broadcast and relayed his concerns. He also suggested that Stanton contact Salant to advise him of Paley's feelings and suggest that, in the remaining days of the campaign, the News Division should "insist on a balance which would be fair to both sides."

The next morning Colson spoke with Nixon about the broadcast as the president was about to depart on a campaign trip to Ohio. Colson, as was usually the case, would be the one to execute the president's will on a matter relating to the television networks. After speaking with Nixon, Colson placed a call to Stanton at his New York townhouse, only to learn that the CBS president was not home and not reachable. That left only one alternative, and Colson telephoned Paley at his apartment.

Colson and Paley were not strangers. They had spoken on the phone numerous times over the preceding four years, and they had had one memorable meeting on September 23, 1970, right before the midterm elections. On that occasion Colson had come to Paley's office with some documents to prove his charges that CBS news coverage was unfairly slanted against the Republicans. While Stanton sat by primarily as an observer, Colson continued his harangue, referring to the papers he had brought to confirm his claims. Colson commented, as he usually did, that he knew Paley was not to blame, that it was the fault of the "leftists" and "pinkos" in the News Division. Paley responded, as he usually did in these kinds of sessions, that he had great confidence in the News Division, that CBS tried to abide by its long-standing policies of fairness and balance, and that the network would make corrections whenever they were warranted. But Paley would not give Colson the satisfaction of asking to see the documents that the White House counsel had brought with him. "I was so proud of Bill," Stanton later remarked, "because he didn't do what I thought maybe he instinctively would do, which is to say, 'Can I have a copy?' " Finally Colson offered them, saying to Paley, don't you want to see the documents I brought?

Colson left that meeting without getting any satisfaction of his demands (although he later wrote a memo for White House consumption indicating otherwise). And when CBS coverage of a Nixon speech on October 7 was not what the White House wanted, Colson called Paley the next day to repeat his complaints about CBS's Democratic bias. Paley again listened patiently and again repeated his standard line that all people, including reporters, have certain biases and that CBS would take appropriate action if those biases were reflected in newscasts.

Paley was receptive and polite when he took Colson's phone call on the morning of October 28, 1972. He listened as the president's special counsel repeated the allegations he had made the previous day to Stanton—that Cronkite was out to "zing" the president for refusing him an interview and that CBS had unsuccessfully tried to sell the Watergate program as a special to an advertiser. Colson added that the program was completely one-sided, having repeated false accusations about the Republicans without saying anything with respect to existing allegations of misconduct by the Democrats. On and on he went, repeating himself and finally concluding that, if Nixon were re-elected, "it would be very hard for them to establish good relations with [CBS]."

Paley did not like these kinds of personal confrontations, and Colson's pointed remarks added to his discomfort. The CBS chairman generally regarded Colson as a "monster," once commenting that it "was amazing that a person could be as evil as I think he was." True to form, Paley thought that Colson was "pretty vicious" in his remarks about the Watergate broadcast. Still, he told Colson that he had his own doubts about the program's length and fairness. He knew nothing about the program being planned as a special, and when Colson was unable to give him the names of any advertiser or agency that had rejected the program for sponsorship, Paley said only that he would check the matter out with Stanton. But the CBS chairman did not have to investigate Cronkite's motivations. "I told him," Paley said of his conversation with Colson, "from my own observations and knowledge of Cronkite, he was a very objective person, and I was sure that in no way would he allow his feelings or emotions to have any effect on the selection of a story or how he reported it."

Paley did talk with Stanton later that Saturday afternoon, and the CBS president soon reported back to the chairman that there was no truth to Colson's claim that the program had originally been planned as a special. Although that answer confirmed Paley's own expectations, it did not put the matter to rest. The Watergate program troubled him, Cronkite had said another one was scheduled for Monday, October 30, and Paley decided that he wanted to express his views in person.

The top CBS news executives gathered in Paley's office on the morning of Monday, October 30, 1972. In addition to the chairman, the group included Stanton, Salant, Jack Schneider, (who had been reappointed as president of the Broadcast Group), and Arthur Taylor, the newly appointed president of CBS, Inc. With Stanton's retirement approaching, Paley had decided to search for the appropriate successor to his long-time colleague and, at some point in the future, himself as well. At one point it had appeared that Jack Schneider would be that successor. After all, the company had created the position of executive vice president to give Schneider the stature and experience to become an appropriate heir. But Paley had developed second thoughts about Schneider. He was too glib, too wise-cracking, and, of perhaps greatest importance, too indifferent to Paley's suggestions for programming. Paley of course believed in delegating authority, but when it came to programming, he wanted to know that his opinions would be given close consideration. Schneider did not give the chairman any confidence on that score. Too often Paley's suggestions for new programs or new approaches would go unanswered, usually because Schneider did not think much of them. "If we put out a fishnet over Sixth Avenue and took in the people walking in the street," Schneider later remarked, "they would have been more helpful in programming decisions than Bill Paley." Schneider remembered the time when another network had a popular program set in San Francisco, and Paley asked Mike Dann how many programs CBS had set in San Francisco. "Four," Dann immediately responded, and Paley seemed satisfied—even though Dann's response was a total exaggeration (a point that Schneider and Dann joked about at a later lunch at "21"). On another occasion, Paley sent Schneider a memo commenting that the set on NBC's local news program—which had higher ratings than CBS's local news program—was brown and asking when CBS was changing its set to brown as well. Schneider refused to respond to the memo, even after Paley's secretary called to inquire when the chairman could expect a reply. ("How do you respond to that kind of nonsense," Schneider later commented.)

After a couple of years, Schneider became a marked man, and later CBS presidents had to spend much of their time rebuffing Paley's repeated requests to dismiss him. When the end finally came in 1977, Paley tried to turn on the charm, placing his arm around Schneider and saying that they had lived through some interesting times together. But then the anger seeped through: "You never answered my memos or my telephone calls. You ignored me."

Paley was not going to take such chances with his successor. To be sure, he wanted someone who was smart, shrewd, and a good manager. But he also wanted someone who would show more respect for his views and opinions on programming. And to find that kind of person, Paley decided that he would have to look outside of CBS.

Rumors circulated about the search for a new successor, and some within CBS assumed that Paley was trying to recruit Walter Thayer for the job. After all, Paley's respect and fondness for Thayer were well known, and it seemed only natural that he would want someone who was a known quantity. But there was no truth to the rumors. Paley did not intend to draw his friends into his business life, and he and Thayer did not even discuss the subject of replacing Stanton, let alone Paley's retirement. "Let me assure you," Thayer later told a visitor, "that Bill Paley never tried to convince me to take Frank Stanton's job."

Instead of looking to his friends, Paley had CBS hire an executive search firm. Stanton screened the prospects, and in July 1971 he sent Charles T. Ireland, Jr.—"Chick" to his friends—to speak with Paley, who was then vacationing in Europe. To all appearances, Ireland had the right qualifications. He had held an impressive series of positions in top corporate management, from president of the Allegheny Corporation to chairman of Investors Diversified Services to vice president of International Telephone and Telegraph, the country's largest conglomerate. But, of perhaps equal significance, Ireland had no background in broadcasting. Paley could train him, implanting the ideas and perspectives of one lifetime in someone who had no preconceptions, no bias, that might resist the teachings of the CBS chairman.

On October 1, 1971, Ireland assumed the role of CBS president. Stanton was elevated to the position of vice chairman of the board. Paley genuinely liked Ireland and was hopeful that the fifty-one-year-old executive would prove to be a worthy and acceptable successor. But Ireland foiled those hopes. Eights months after taking the job he unexpectedly died of a heart attack. As the CBS plane was flying to Maine to bring Ireland's body back to New York, Paley was reviewing a list of possible successors with Stanton.

Through the use of the executive search firm, Paley finally selected Arthur R. Taylor, a thirty-seven-year-old vice president with International Paper, a Fortune 500 company. A native of Rahway, New Jersey, the tall, darkly handsome Taylor was a man of keen intelligence and driving ambition. After getting his doctorate in history from Brown University, he had landed a job at the prestigious investment house of First Boston, where he stayed for ten years. International Paper was one of the firm's clients, and they soon persuaded the dynamic financial whiz to join their firm as its chief financial officer. His youth and management skills were appealing, but, as in the case of Ireland, Paley was no doubt also attracted by Taylor's lack of experience in broadcasting. Another clean slate on which to write.

In the summer of 1972, Paley had invited Taylor and his wife to Kiluna for a leisurely Saturday afternoon. After lunch, Paley and his guest strolled the grounds, with the white-haired chairman speaking of his hopes for the future and his plans for the new president of CBS. "He said he was interested in bringing modern management techniques to CBS," Taylor remembered. "He wanted to enhance the company's financial position and prepare for broader diversification." Paley also spoke of his own status, saying that Stanton would be retiring in 1973 and that he had not made up his mind as to what he would do. "He was the founder of the company," Taylor recalls Paley explaining, "and he was not sure whether he would go out with Stanton." In the meantime, arrangements would be made for Taylor to become president of CBS, Inc.

Taylor had only been on the job a matter of months when the top CBS executives assembled in the chairman's office to discuss the Watergate broadcasts. The new president was to get one of his first lessons in crisis management at a television network. Unfortunately for Taylor, the significance of the Monday morning meeting could not be fully appreciated without an understanding of the complex forces that could have been evident only to those who had had a longer association with the chairman.

On the surface, there was no need for the meeting. Paley had already instructed Stanton to convey his concerns to Salant, and that directive should have sufficed. But Paley had second thoughts about relying on Stanton on a matter as important as these broadcasts appeared to be. The controversy over "The Selling of the Pentagon" was still fresh in Paley's mind. He had allowed Stanton to lead the defense on that issue. He was not about to make the same mistake twice. If there was to be any leadership here, Bill Paley was going to be the one to exercise it.

Those attending the Watergate meeting heard the chairman make an off-hand remark about "The Selling of the Pentagon" as he discussed the problems with the more current broadcast. And while Stanton sat by quietly, Paley dominated the discussion, telling the group, and especially Salant, that the Watergate segment was longer than any other he could remember on a single subject on the news program, that the segment had not adequately distinguished between substantiated fact and unproven allegations, and that the segment was a departure from the network's sancrosanct policies of fairness and balance. Salant tried to defend the segment, but it was a losing cause. Paley had viewed the broadcast himself, and no amount of argument could change what he had seen and what he now felt. Questions were asked about the second part of the Watergate presentation—scheduled for broadcast that evening—but no directions were issued to Salant. That was not Paley's style, and, in any event, it would have been foolish for the CBS chairman to cancel that broadcast after Cronkite had already announced it (no matter what Paley's true feelings, everyone would have attributed the decision to White House pressure as soon as Colson's call was disclosed). Neither Paley nor Stanton said anything at the meeting about Colson's phone calls. Both executives regarded themselves as "buffers" who would shield the News Division from the political pressures inherent in running a news department (although Colson's call and indirect threat to Paley was news in itself and would have added a new dimension to Cronkite's broadcast if it had been disclosed).

Salant returned to the News Division offices on West Fifty-seventh Street a very shaken man. He had never had an encounter like that with the chairman. Nobody had given him instructions, and he knew he alone would have to make the final decision. He also knew, of course, that the chairman would closely review the second part of the Watergate broadcast and that Salant's job might hang in the balance. But Salant did not want those thoughts to shape his news judgment. He wanted to do what was fair and appropriate. It would not be easy, but Salant decided to screen the second part again, hoping that he could separate concern for job security from his independent judgment as a newsman.

After a lengthy debate among his colleagues, most of it heated, Salant decided to shorten the segment to eight minutes, eliminating material that had been repeated in the earlier broadcast or that were unnecessary to the presentation. Although he had originally proposed the Watergate show, Cronkite remained distant from the scene of battle. He could sense the direction of the decisions, and, unlike Ed Murrow, he was not about to risk his standing with a personal and probably unproductive confrontation with the chairman.

Because of the additional editing, the second part aired on Tuesday, October 31. Despite the changes ordered by Salant, Paley was "very unhappy" with it. He continued to believe that it was too long for a news program designed to cover world events, and he still felt that the presentation was biased against the administration, creating confusion among the viewers between proven facts and unsubstantiated charges. The next morning he vented his feelings in a memo to Salant, saying that the broadcast "seems to me unworthy of our fine traditions and ought not to be practiced. I hope very much," he added, "that it will not be repeated." Salant did not let the matter rest there. He submitted a memorandum in defense of the broadcast, and later he and Paley met for several hours over lunch to discuss the issue. The chairman was not convinced by Salant's arguments. The Watergate broadcasts were unfair and should not become a standard for the future. "He wasn't angry," Salant later said of Paley's attitude. "Just critical and firm."

Weeks later, *Washington Post* publisher Katharine Graham met her friend Bill Paley at a party in New York. For so many months, the *Post* had been there alone, making the charges, taking the heat, and wondering whether they could survive politically if Nixon were re-elected. Cronkite's broadcasts on Watergate had given the story the kind of national exposure it needed, the kind that only a television network could provide. And that, more than anything, had helped to legitimize the *Post*'s gamble. So Graham approached Paley happily, telling him, "Oh, Bill, we're so grateful for what you've done." Paley said nothing of his call from Colson, his meetings with Salant, or his disappointment with the broadcasts. He smiled and said, Yes, we did take you national. CBS had made its mark despite the reservations of its chairman. But if Bill Paley had any hope that he could reap the reward without challenge, he was soon to be disappointed.

CHAPTER SIXTEEN

Frustration

J ack Loftus was a young journalist who had been hired to help Kidder Meade in the corporate information office, and his first experience with the CBS chairman in 1973 was not as enjoyable as he had hoped it would be. Paley was scheduled to deliver a speech before the national Boy Scouts organization at the Waldorf-Astoria in Manhattan, and Loftus had been asked to make sure that the chairman's appearance went smoothly. The young executive was waiting at the hotel when Paley's limousine pulled up. He gave Paley a copy of the speech, escorted him into the ballroom, and took a seat in the rear to listen to the remarks that he had helped draft. Everything seemed to be very much in order until Paley neared the end of the speech. He started to fumble a little and discreetly picked up the written draft in an obvious search for the last page, which was apparently missing. Not finding it, Paley finally set the document down, made some humorous comment about preparations going awry, and ad-libbed his closing.

Loftus was embarrassed about his oversight and anxious to put the incident behind him. Knowing of Paley's aversion to crowds, Loftus had already tipped the bell captain $20 to rope off the freight elevator so that he and Paley could leave unnoticed by a back route. Loftus directed the perplexed chairman onto the freight elevator after his speech, but instead of going down to the lobby on the first floor, the elevator went up and opened on a kitchen. Loftus was now frantic and decided not to take any more chances. He hustled Paley through the kitchen toward a regular elevator, which they took down to the main lobby. They then pushed through the crowds, out the front door, and toward the waiting limousine. After the chairman got in the car, Loftus was about to close the door when he saw Paley's arm reach out to pull him into the car. The two of them rode the short distance back to Black Rock, Paley pleasantly inquiring about Loftus's family and background. They then got into the elevator together at CBS headquarters, and as Loftus started to get off at his floor (below the chairman's office on the thirty-fifth floor), Paley said, "Oh Jack, by the way"—and Loftus knew, here it is, I'm about to be fired—

"thanks very much for helping out today." "At that point," said Loftus, "I would have done anything for Bill Paley."

For Loftus the experience at the Waldorf-Astoria was a momentary setback. For Paley the episode seemed to exemplify, in some small way, the turmoil and disruption that beset him throughout the 1970s. He was a man who liked to be in control, and he had reached the stage in life where that seemed to be an attainable goal. He had access to the prestige and resources of a media empire that now generated more than $1 billion in revenues and represented approximately 20 percent of the total pretax income in all of broadcasting. His name was known and respected in the highest councils of society and corporate management. He could and did enjoy any and every material comfort that he wanted. And yet he could not master his personal and professional environments to his satisfaction. It seemed that he was constantly moving from one crisis to another.

Some of his worst fears concerned President Nixon's reelection in 1972. However much he anticipated criticism of CBS's news coverage, Paley recognized that the Nixon administration would probably present difficult problems. The threats and badgering of Colson and other White House aides were unrelenting and often mean-spirited. "The startling fact of this administration," Paley observed at one point after Nixon's reelection, "is that, virtually from its inception, it has launched a systematic effort to discredit both the objectives and conduct of those journalists whose treatment of the news it disapproves."

As always, Paley was willing to use personal charm to help deflect the attacks. When Colson called to complain again in December 1972, Paley responded with a promise to see the White House special counsel on his next visit to Washington, a promise which Paley kept. And in March 1973, Paley took the initiative to stop by at the White House to meet H. R. Haldeman, Nixon's chief of staff. For over an hour the two men talked, Haldeman expressing his concerns and Paley asking questions, explaining his commitment to fairness and balance and offering to review specific allegations. "It was a get-acquainted meeting," Haldeman remembered. "He was very personable and we seemed to get along well. I also wanted to make my points about bias in CBS News. He didn't say to me I was right in my criticisms. He just said I had some legitimate concerns and that he would look into it."

One of the areas of agreement between the two men concerned CBS's "instant analysis" of Nixon's addresses on prime-time television. After each speech, various CBS correspondents—Sevareid, Cronkite, Dan Rather, Roger Mudd, and whoever else might have expertise in the particular subject matter—would offer reports and opinions. The White House deplored the practice, arguing that it was often biased against Nixon and something that inherently detracted from the importance of the president's message. Paley did not share those concerns, but he did have reservations of his own. He believed it was expecting too much to ask reporters—no matter how experienced—to listen to a speech and immediately provide a thoughtful analysis. "I was personally very impressed by Eric [Sevareid]," Paley said later, "who was charged with the responsibility of doing it very often. [Sevareid] said, 'It's not fair. I can't do a good job.' " Paley recognized that an instant analysis might be possible where the president's speech was made available to the media hours before its delivery. "But very often," he explained, "you didn't get it at all [or] you got it a few minutes before the broadcast. And I thought, 'My God, that's not doing a good job or serving the American people.' "

There was no doubt in Paley's mind that there had to be some kind of analysis of the president's remarks to the nation on an important issue. The only question involved the mechanics of who would do it and when they would do it. At one point in the 1950s Stanton had proposed that the company institute a format called "The Loyal Opposition." Every time the president spoke, the other party's leader would be given an opportunity to reply. While the proposal was still under discussion, Stanton raised it in a meeting he was having in Washington with Democratic senators Johnson, Mike Mansfield and Stuart Symington. They all wanted to know who the Democratic spokesman would be. To Stanton the answer was obvious: the party's most recent presidential nominee. "Well, Stevenson," he responded. No one liked that idea. Johnson, who was then the Senate majority leader and fancied himself a future presidential nominee, walked over to Stanton, poked him in the shoulder, and pointedly said, "He isn't the opposition." Stanton knew then that his idea would involve constant bickering between the network and partisan leaders over who should be the spokesman, and the concept of a "Loyal Opposition" was buried.

Despite his unsettling experience with Johnson, Stanton remained convinced that the idea had merit. It was all a question of waiting for the proper environment. In broadcasting, as in most things, timing was key. And that moment seemed to arrive in 1970. In June of that year the FCC ruled that President Nixon's five prime-time television speeches in defense of his Vietnam policy required the networks to provide an opponent with one half hour of uninterrupted time in which to present a contrasting view. Otherwise, said the commission, there would be an imbalance in the information and opinion being made available to the public—a result that would fly in the face of the agency's Fairness Doctrine.

CBS was of course prepared to honor the commission's directive, but the network also wanted to establish a framework that would minimize the likelihood of further FCC review of network decisions. To achieve that goal, Stanton offerred a revised version of his "Loyal Opposition" concept. The opposing party's governing body—which under Nixon's presidency meant the Democratic National Committee—would periodically be given free time to speak on issues of importance to the country. Implementation of the proposal would insure balanced coverage of controversial issues and, at the same time, avoid the kind of confrontation that Stanton had had years earlier with Johnson. As Stanton explained in a July 1970 speech to the National Broadcast Editorial Conference, "the one place in which logically to put responsibility for speaking for the opposition party—or for deciding who should speak for it—is that party's national committee." Any complaints about the selection of the spokesman would have to be addressed to the committee, not CBS.

However logical it may have appeared to Stanton, Paley held a very different view. The "Loyal Opposition" policy was instituted while the chairman was away on vacation, and he was "very upset" when he re- viewed the format upon his return. In his eyes, the "Loyal Opposition" represented an abdication of the network's "editorial responsibility and judgment to a political party." That was unthinkable, said Paley.

The first experience with the "Loyal Opposition" in the summer of 1970 seemed to confirm Paley's concerns. Larry O'Brien, the Democratic Party chairman, used his half hour to review a variety of issues and solicit funds for his party's coffers. The presentation was too rambling and disjointed to sharpen the debate on Vietnam policy or any other issue. Paley's dissatisfaction was compounded when the FCC subsequently ordered CBS to provide additional reply time for the Republican Party—even though O'Brien's time was intended as a response to the Republican president. CBS ultimately succeeded in having the FCC's decision over- turned in federal court, but by then there was nothing left to consider. The "Loyal Opposition" series was dead.

CBS continued to rely on instant analysis immediately after the presi- dent's prime-time television speeches until the spring of 1973, when Paley began attending meetings of the CBS News Executive Committee. In June he "persuaded" the committee to replace instant analysis with a policy of providing reply time to an appropriate spokesman selected by CBS. But the response would not be aired immediately after the president's speech; instead, it would be broadcast a day or more later. With this change, Paley regarded the new policy as much more effective in providing the public with access to contrasting views.

Most of the public did not agree. Editorial opinion throughout the country was almost uniformly negative. White House pressure on the networks was a matter of common knowledge, and most people seemed to feel that CBS's new policy was designed to accommodate the Nixon Administration rather than enlighten the public with thoughtful opposition opinions. The CBS chairman was totally unprepared for all this criticism. "I was amazed," he remembered. Still, he clung to the new policy for several months, until he had dinner with Averell Harriman one evening in the fall of 1973. Of all the damn foolish things to do, said the elder statesman, was to cancel instant analysis. Shortly afterward, Paley went back to the CBS News Executive Committee and said, "Boys, it isn't working. . . . I think people expect some reaction right after the president's speech, and I think we have to change the policy." Instant analysis was back.

All of this back-and-forth transpired after Frank Stanton had retired, and many within the company thought that instant analysis never would have been dropped in the first place if Stanton had still been CBS vice chairman. He had supported the concept, had fought for it, and many believed he would have prevailed in any discussion on the issue with the chairman. They took note, for example, that Paley did not attend meetings of the CBS News Executive Committee with any regularity until after Stanton had left. And many network executives—especially those in the News Division—saw the abandonment of instant analysis in June 1973 as an effort to "de-Stantonize" the company.

These reactions were fueled in part by the growing and obvious disharmony that had developed between Paley and Stanton in the previous few years. Virtually everyone attributed the disaffection to Paley's failure to appoint Stanton chief executive. They knew how much time Stanton had given the company, how he had seemingly sacrificed almost all his leisure time to advance CBS interests. He had no children, he did not socialize with CBS colleagues, and no one knew if he had any friends beyond the small terrier he sometimes brought to meetings. He did not even have time to read books, relying instead on his wife to provide him with written reviews so that he could keep abreast of developments in the literary world. Colleagues who went to lunch with Stanton expecting to discuss a matter of network policy might instead be treated to a long recitation of the vice chairman's complaints about the chairman. On other occasions Stanton might recall the opportunities he had passed up to remain with CBS—undersecretary of state in the Kennedy and Johnson administrations, president of the University of California, even a chance to run for the United States Senate. This obvious rumination about the past created a jumble of emotions that disrupted his relations with Paley, and shortly after his retirement Stanton would tell Dan Schorr that he and Paley "weren't seeing eye to eye on very many things" in 1973 and that the decision to drop instant analysis after his departure almost could have been expected.

Paley offered to honor Stanton with an appropriate reception upon his retirement, but the long-time CBS executive declined—probably because, for all his achievements and recognition, he had failed to secure the one honor that apparently meant the most to him: the title of chief executive. On Friday, March 30, 1973 Stanton spent most of the day traveling with Paley back and forth to Miami to attend the funeral of Niles Trammel, a friend and long-time president of NBC. Upon his return late that afternoon, a few colleagues stopped by Stanton's office for a drink and fifteen minutes of nostalgia. Late that evening, Frank Stanton, age sixty-five, placed his keys on the desk, walked out of Black Rock, and retired from CBS.

Stanton's departure cleared the way for Arthur Taylor to assume, in a very real sense, the role of Paley's successor. No matter what the titles, no matter what the expectations, Stanton's presence had cast a shadow over CBS that had prevented the new CBS president from exercising the prerogatives to which he thought he was entitled.

There were some similarities between the two men. Like Stanton, Taylor developed a deep interest in preserving the independence of CBS News, and he earned Dick Salant's respect by publicly endorsing a proposal to expand the "Evening News" from one half-hour to one full hour—a change very much opposed by CBS affiliates (who did not want to give up time used to produce local revenues). And while CBS executives initially joked about Taylor's seeming pomposity (including the Homburg hat he wore to work), many later believed that he was a good manager of people who might soon earn the reputation attained by Stanton. But for all these parallels, Arthur Taylor was a very different man.

The most obvious and dramatic difference was in his relationship with the chairman. Stanton had been soft-spoken, almost deferential, never resisting a decision once Paley had made his wishes known. Taylor was not so accommodating. He argued with Paley long and hard about any number of matters—and many of them, in Taylor's view, were too picayune to warrant the time of officers of a major media conglomerate. But like other CBS executives before him, Taylor soon discovered that the chairman was a hard man to shake loose once he had set his sights on some goal. Unlike executives in earlier days, the new president found that the chairman was very capable of raising his voice and demanding obedience to his wishes. Taylor responded in kind, and on one Friday afternoon he stormed out of Paley's office, slamming the door so hard that some plaster came loose from the wall. That stunned the chairman. He became concerned that the incident would trouble his president over the weekend. He walked over to Taylor's office, saying that they should put the argument behind them and not let it spoil their relationship.

For all their arguments, Paley continued to express satisfaction with his selection of Taylor. "He's dedicated. He's very bright; and he caught on very quickly," Paley told an interviewer from *Broadcasting* magazine after working with Taylor for more than three years. "And he's won the confidence and respect of the organization. And I look to him. He's got leadership qualities. . . ."

Leadership. It was a mixed blessing for a CBS executive. On the one hand, Paley expected his views to be accepted if he felt strongly about an issue; and executives who took actions inconsistent with those views might never be forgiven. One of Jack Schneider's unpardonable sins was to sell CBS's movie production arm because of antitrust concerns raised by company lawyers—a move that startled and upset the chairman, who was intent upon remaining in the movie business. On the other hand, if Paley was not already committed to a particular position, he derived enormous pleasure from executives who were prepared to take a stand without knowing the chairman's views on the issue.

There was the occasion when Paley asked Lou Dorfsman to prepare some new graphic designs for the "Evening News." Dorfsman was CBS's creative director and successor to the gifted Bill Golden—the man who had designed the CBS "eye" and who had helped promote CBS as the network with class (the "Tiffany Network" insiders called it). Dorfsman was a talented designer in his own right, and he had great respect for the CBS chairman. "He made you do it better," Dorfsman observed. "He kept saying, 'We're going to make money and do good stuff.' It was the Paley credo." So when WINS successfully competed in the crowded New York radio market as an all-news station, Paley suggested that CBS's radio station also consider an all-news format. Some executives said, well, WINS is already doing that. So what, Paley would say, we'll do it better. And when Paley asked Dorfsman to prepare designs for the "Evening News" that would have the modern look captured by NBC's evening news graphics, Dorfsman protested at first, saying he didn't want to play "catch-up ball." Paley had the same answer: "So what, we'll do it better."

Dorfsman put considerable energy into the project, and he soon developed various alternative designs, some of them involving animation. Before the scheduled meeting with Paley, Dorfsman called Schneider, who was still president of the Broadcast Division and Dorfsman's ostensible superior. "You better come down here and look at these," Dorfsman told Schneider, "because you're going to be at the meeting and you're supposed to know what's going on." Schneider came by Dorfsman's office and was full of enthusiasm for the designer's work, saying, "This is absolutely terrific stuff." He then made a proposal to Dorfsman: "You should show them all to the chairman and then ask, which one do you like, Mr. Paley?" Dorfsman quickly replied that he was going to do no such thing. "I know more about this than he does, and I'm going to tell him which one I recommend," said the designer. "And besides, that's what he wants. He doesn't want the burden of making the decision, and I'm going to take it off him."

The presentation before Paley and Taylor could not have been more successful. While Schneider helped with the equipment, Dorfsman ran through each proposal. Paley's excitement was visible to all, and at the end, Dorfsman remembered, "I made up some reason for recommending the one I liked the best, and he accepted it." After Dorfsman returned to his office, he received a telephone call from Taylor, who was full of praise and quick to add, "You just made that old man happier than if you had come in with twenty million dollars' worth of new business."

These and similar experiences convinced Taylor that Paley would support executives who took the initiative and performed well. And so he decided to take some initiatives of his own in the area of entertainment programming. Not that he would usurp the chairman's prerogatives. When it came to making choices for new programs and new schedules, network president Bob Wood (Taylor's nominal subordinate) and Paley would make the final decisions. It was Paley, for example, who decided— unilaterally—that CBS would not go forward with a scheduled broadcast of Joseph Papp's television production of *Sticks and Bones,* the story of a Vietnam veteran who returns home blind and embittered. At one point the father becomes so exasperated that he hands his son a razor and suggests suicide. The show would have been deemed controversial under any circumstance, but Paley was not pleased to learn that the play would be aired on March 9, 1973, the very day that American prisoners of war would be returning home from Vietnam. So he cancelled it.

Taylor was not involved in that decision or the multitude of other decisions concerning the specific programs that would grace CBS's schedule. But there were other aspects of programming that were open to his involvement, and one concerned the growing level of sex and violence on television.

For all his ambition and success, Arthur Taylor was, at bottom, a family man who enjoyed the weekends with his wife and three children at his home in suburban New Jersey. And like many Americans, he was becoming more and more concerned about the flagrant displays of sex and violence on television, especially in early evening hours when young children were glued to their sets. Gone were the days of Ozzie and Harriet when couples, even married couples, had to have twin beds and could never, absolutely never, be shown in bed together. With the political and social explosion of the 1960s, American television had dropped many of its inhibitions. Producers and program executives now openly solicited shows with more "T & A," a less-than-oblique reference to a woman's anatomy. Other programs were equally uninhibited about violence. While many Americans seemed to enjoy that fare, the United States surgeon general issued a report saying that television violence had an impact on younger minds, especially those of children in inner cities, where violence was often an everyday reality.

Taylor shared many of the report's concerns. He prided himself on having a social conscience, and it was no coincidence that one of his heroes was the late Senator Bobby Kennedy. And like Kennedy in the late 1960s, Taylor believed he was in a position to do something about an emerging issue. So he began making suggestions at planning meetings to explore ways in which CBS could reduce, or at least control, the amount of sex and violence on television. It was no small task. Such programming appealed to millions of viewers, and they, in turn, attracted the advertisers who filled the coffers of CBS and its almost two hundred affiliated stations. Taylor was undaunted, however. He had faced large challenges before, and he was happy to pursue this one with vigor. "I saw it as a confirmation that broadcasters are ethically responsible for the impact of their programs," he later explained.

Taylor's efforts received an unexpected boost from Congress. The surgeon general's report, as well as media attention on the issue, had generated hearings in Congress, where senators and congressmen kept badgering FCC Chairman Richard E. Wiley to tell them what his agency intended to do about this problem. Never mind that broadcasters had their own First Amendment rights, and never mind that the FCC had only limited powers to shape network programming. Congress wanted action, and Dick Wiley, whose commission was subject to congressional oversight, wanted to give it to them. So he convened a meeting in his office in the fall of 1974 with Taylor and representatives from ABC and NBC to explore the matter. Taylor, for his part, quietly and almost cryptically responded that he had been working on the issue for a couple of years and that CBS would develop its own policy—without FCC assistance.

Dick Wiley had no pride in authorship. He wanted something, anything, to show Congress, and after the meeting he called Taylor frequently in New York to inquire as to how his plans were progressing. Taylor would say very little, except that they were moving forward. The CBS president felt he could afford to be optimistic. He knew, even then, that the chairman would probably support his initiative.

From the beginning Paley was sympathetic to the project. He had always prided himself on being tasteful, and, as evidenced by his rejection of "Whirlybirds" in the 1950s and "Sticks and Bones" in 1973, he was not eager to foist too much violence on CBS audiences. The same caution was exercised with respect to sex. "We have always been quite restrained," he told an interviewer in the 1970s, "never using sex or violence, except for the purpose of advancing the story, so to speak." And even then the network would proceed gingerly. "The greatest writers of all time had to [use sex and violence] in order to make things real and interesting," Paley observed in that same interview, "and that's just the nature of storytelling, the nature of drama, the nature of the theater, and also the nature of television; but I think you have to be conscientious. I think you have to know when you go too far."

By December 1974 Taylor had decided that the best course was to propose that all television stations voluntarily agreed not to air suggestive or violent programs between seven and nine P.M., the hours when young children were most likely to be among the audience. The "Family Viewing Hour" it would be called. And to insure industry-wide acceptance, Taylor proposed that the policy be made a part of the television code sponsored by the National Association of Broadcasters, the industry's premier trade association. In an earlier meeting with Jack Schneider and Kidder Meade, Taylor had explained the benefits of the proposal to Paley—the value to CBS consumers, the importance of easing congressional pressures, and the wisdom of making FCC Chairman Wiley look good. Paley assented then, and later, before sending his letter to the NAB, Taylor asked the chairman and other key executives to attend a meeting to air whatever comments or criticisms they might have. "And I went around that table," Taylor later recalled, "to ask if anyone had any objection. And everyone agreed with the proposal."

Taylor sent the letter to the NAB, which had already been alerted, and the association asked its members to vote on whether to incorporate the CBS proposal into the NAB code. To Taylor's great satisfaction, 94 percent of the members agreed. ("They never had a higher acceptance on any other proposal," he later boasted.) Paley was also pleased with the reaction—because he sensed that it was something the public wanted. "Between seven and nine it wasn't easy for the mother to sit in front of the television set with [her] children," the chairman commented, "because too many things were on that embarrassed them, and provoked questions that they found it difficult to answer."

The difficulty of communicating with your children. The CBS chairman could relate to that. He had had his own problems trying to understand his children, problems that were not easily resolved. One point of disagreement was the sexual revolution of the 1960s and 1970s. Women had always been an integral part of Paley's life. He was handsome, charming, and powerful. Women often threw themselves at him, and he did not always duck. They might call him at his office, but it was discreet, shielded from public view. The younger generation was more open, more willing to dispense with the charades, and Paley for one felt uncomfortable when he learned that any one of his unmarried children was living with someone of the opposite sex.

The difference in attitudes toward sexual relations no doubt reflected, in part at least, the broad gap in ages between Paley and his children. He was now in his seventies. Kate and Bill were in their twenties, with the other children ranging in the thirties. Paley was still full of zest, still eager to make the most of his life, but there was no getting around the fact that he was the product of a very different generation. These age differences might have been overcome by constant communication, but Bill Paley was not able to give his children the same attention that Sam Paley had showered on his son. Sam had groomed young Willie to be a businessman who could some day take over his cigar business. As a youth Bill Paley had swept the floors, ordered the tobacco, and negotiated the contracts— all under the constant tutelage of his father. The close contact with Sam had not only fueled Paley's ambition and skills; it had also fostered a mutual respect and affection that would last their entire lives.

None of Paley's children could look back upon a similar experience. While CBS might be Bill Paley's candy store, he had one strict rule that applied to all executives, including himself: no nepotism. The principle had been ingrained in CBS policy by Ed Klauber, who was extremely sensitive to any suggestion that an employee had been hired or promoted on the basis of family connections. There was only one easy way to avoid that kind of issue, and Klauber had made it clear that no relatives would be hired. So no consideration was ever given to hiring any of Paley's children, and few CBS executives even knew what they looked like.

The policy might have preserved the company's integrity, but it did little to expand the quantity and quality of time Paley spent with his children. While they were growing up in the 1940s and 1950s, CBS was still a company struggling to overcome NBC's competition, and Paley devoted much more time to it in those years than later, after it had established itself as the premier network in news and entertainment. Other interests—including a constant preoccupation with his social life—made it that much more difficult for Paley to give the children more of his time. The older ones, especially Hilary and Amanda, felt frustrated, wishing they could be closer to the aging patriarch. Kate and Billy, members of the "baby boom" generation, were resentful. For a long period in the

1970s Kate wouldn't even talk to her father. And Billy, torn by the social and political trauma of the 1960s, could not decide who he wanted to be or what he wanted to do. He drifted from job to job, served in the military during the Vietnam years and then he opened a restaurant on Capitol Hill in Washington. It was the kind of vacillation that was alien to his father. Bill Paley had been so single-minded in his pursuit of success at CBS—he found it difficult to relate to people, especially his own children, who lacked direction.

For all their arguments and problems, the children were of one mind with their father on one issue: the desire to insulate their lives from public scrutiny. Like Paley, the children appreciated the value of their privacy and jealously guarded it. Although their father was the head of a major media empire, and although their mother was one of the most preeminent role models in society and fashion, the children escaped with barely a mention in the press.

The exception was Amanda. As a young married couple she and Carter Burden threw lavish—and very public—parties at their apartment in the Dakota, one of the more prestigious apartment buildings on New York's Upper West Side. They seemed to invite everybody who was anybody. The parties received coverage in the society pages of *Vogue, Cosmopolitan,* and other periodicals. They were, as one reporter observed, "truly spectacular," and in some circles it was almost a sign of social acceptability to have been invited (or at least attended) one of the Burden's parties.

Their social life began to change after Carter graduated from law school and took a job with Senator Robert Kennedy's New York staff. They began to have second thoughts about the image they had created for themselves. They moved to the East Side and adopted a lower profile— until Kennedy was assassinated and Burden decided to embark on a political career of his own. His first goal was election to a seat on New York's City Council. He shed some weight, adopted an aggressive, almost populist approach to campaigning, and, much to his surprise, won handily. Because of his electoral strength, his background, and his dashing appearance, Burden soon attracted considerable attention in media-hungry New York. A 1971 article in *The New York Times Sunday Magazine,* for example, said about Burden that, "in an age of politics by electronics, when the race is just about always to the wealthiest and most telegenic candidate—he has virtually every qualification necessary to end up ultimately in residence at 1600 Pennsylvania Avenue."

The honeymoon with the media did not last as long as Burden would have wished. Although he won reelection to the City Council, he was later defeated in his bid to win a seat in the United States House of Representatives. By then, his storybook marriage to Amanda was over. She had asked for a divorce amid rumors that she was involved with Senator Edward Kennedy and other high-profile celebrities.

Paley was no doubt disappointed by the loss of Carter Burden as a son-in-law. He had always liked Burden's background and respected his intelligence and ambition. Indeed, years later, after Burden had remarried, he would receive frequent invitations to dine with Paley and his friends at the Fifth Avenue apartment. The CBS chairman obviously was not going to let his stepdaughter's decision stand in the way of his social enjoyment.

At the same time, Paley was not one to maintain a social relationship at any cost. That became clear to Truman Capote in the fall of 1975. Prior to that, Capote had continued to be a regular guest at the Paley homes. He always seemed so knowledgeable, so full of gossip, so entertaining. Both Paleys enjoyed his company, and at one point in the early 1960s, Babe had introduced him to Katharine Graham, saying, "I want you to meet the most wonderful person." *The Washington Post* publisher still remembers her first meeting with Capote, a lunch at a New York restaurant with Capote, Babe, and the writer Harper Lee. It was obvious that Capote was a special person in Babe Paley's life. And then *Esquire* published his article on "La Côte Basque" in November 1975.

The article recounted the dialogue of two women having lunch at a fashionable restaurant in New York called La Côte Basque. Much of the conversation centered on the story of a Jewish corporate magnate who tries to make love to the governor's wife, only to be foiled at the last moment and then find his body and sheets covered with the woman's menstrual blood. For those who traveled outside of New York's exclusive social circles, it was an innocuous piece of fiction. But others readily recognized the frustrated lover as the CBS chairman himself. Capote later insisted that Paley himself used to tell the story to friends—a claim that Paley denied and that seems totally inconsistent with Paley's personality. In any event, neither Bill nor Babe was pleased to see the story in print. To them, its publication represented betrayal of a trust. "It was savagery," said one friend about the article, "and both Paleys were outraged. After that they never talked with Capote again." It was indeed an unsettling experience. But it was nothing compared with the frustration and anger Paley soon felt toward David Halberstam.

Everything about him seems larger than life. He is a tall man, approaching six feet four inches, with a face that seems chiseled from granite and a baritone voice that conveys confidence and conviction. He can be charming and entertaining, but if there is one trait that best characterizes David Halberstam it is self-assurance. No doubt, no uncertainty, a man of firm judgments—even if the subject is other people. "David divides the world into two groups: the good guys and the bad guys," one friend observed. "I don't think there are too many people in between for David. . . . He doesn't forget if you're one of the bad guys. But he doesn't forget if you're one of the good guys, either." All of which was unfortunate for Bill Paley, because in the early seventies Halberstam decided to write about CBS, and his research had convinced him that the network's chairman was one of the bad guys.

Halberstam's decision to focus on a major media company was a natural outgrowth of his career. From the beginning, he had wanted to be a journalist. Not just any journalist, however. The best. That ambition had been fueled at Harvard College, where he had been an editor on the *Crimson,* the student-run newspaper. After graduation he pursued jobs at various newspapers, first with a small paper in Mississippi, then with the *Nashville Tennessean.* While working at the Nashville paper, he also wrote some articles for *The Reporter,* a small but influential national periodical. James Reston, *The New York Times'* Washington bureau chief, liked what he saw, and in 1960, David Halberstam, age twenty-six, joined the *Times'* staff in the nation's capital.

Halberstam was an aggressive reporter, unrelenting in his search for the facts and unafraid to speak the truth as he saw it. After a brief tenure in the Congo, the *Times* dispatched him to Vietnam in 1962. Most of the American government's attention in Southeast Asia was focused on Laos, but the Vietnam conflict seemed to be widening every day. While President Kennedy insisted otherwise, more and more observers were starting to wonder whether the American involvement might eventually require the introduction of large contingents of American combat troops.

Halberstam soon joined the ranks of the skeptical. He did not trust the reports fed to the press by the American embassy and the military command in Saigon. He traveled the countryside, speaking with guerrillas and peasants and soldiers and anyone who might have some sense as to what was really happening. And he became more and more convinced that the government's portrait of Vietnam was less than accurate. Although the Kennedy Administration wanted the world to believe otherwise, President Ngo Dinh Diem did not have the support of his people, and he was unlikely to survive protracted civil war.

Halberstam's reports began to appear regularly on the front page of the *Times,* and many people did not like what they read. Diem, for one, was worried that the foreign correspondent might be undermining the American support that he so desperately needed. "Halberstam should be barbecued," said Diem's sister-in-law, Madame Nhu, "and I would be glad to supply the fluid and the match."

Another unhappy reader was President Kennedy. Halberstam's reports were raising doubts about American policy, and Kennedy didn't like it. At a White House meeting, he pointedly suggested to *Times* publisher Punch Sulzberger that Halberstam be moved to a new post, one far removed from Vietnam. Although many *Times* editors had their own doubts about the accuracy of Halberstam's reports, they were not about to yield to such blatant pressure from the government. (Later, after he had won a Pulitzer Prize for his reporting, which had proven to be prophetic, the *Times'* editors were pleased with their willingness to stand behind Halberstam.)

It was all an instructive experience for the young journalist. He wrote a small book about the Vietnam conflict (*The Making of a Quagmire*) and a biographical essay (entitled *Ho*) about Ho Chi Minh, North Vietnam's venerable leader, but the subject of Vietnam could not be dismissed so easily from his mind. By 1969 he was working at *Harper's* magazine and preparing an article on McGeorge Bundy, national security adviser to Presidents Kennedy and Johnson and one of the major architects of American policy in Vietnam. But that was not enough to satisfy Halberstam. There were too many things he didn't know about Vietnam, too many things that required explanation. The article soon evolved into a book. "The question which intrigued me the most was *why*, why had it happened," he later explained. "So it became very quickly not a book about Vietnam, but a book about America, and in particular about power and success in America, what the country was, who the leadership was, how they got ahead, what their perceptions were about themselves, about the country and about their mission." *The Best and the Brightest* was published in 1972 and quickly became a best-seller. It was reviewed, analyzed, and debated, more for what it said about the men who made the war (there were very few women in the higher councils of government then) than for its explanations of why the government's Vietnam policies had failed.

The book made Halberstam's name a household word in the worlds of journalism and government. He had made his mark—not as a writer of cold, detached analysis, but as a reporter filled with passion. Some challenged his methods, saying that he often failed to cite sources, asking readers to accept his anecdotes and descriptions on faith, even as he was criticizing government officials for accepting too much information in the same manner. Other critics attacked his style, saying he was long-winded and far too repetitive. (There was the notorious *Doonesbury* cartoon that had Halberstam responding to a question about how he liked his coffee, saying, "Black, Joanie, very black, utterly without cream and sugar.") But for all the criticism, there was almost universal recognition that David Halberstam was a tenacious researcher and a powerful writer.

As he was basking in the success of *The Best and the Brightest,* Halberstam decided to do a book on CBS and the presidency. Watergate was starting to unfold, the Nixon administration's principal adversary in the media was CBS (who could forget Dan Rather's televised confrontation with President Nixon at the 1974 National Association of Broadcasters Convention in Houston), and Halberstam was fascinated by the exercise of power. Although the book was later expanded to include a review of three other media companies (*The Washington Post,* the *Los Angeles Times,* and Time Inc.), CBS and presidential politics remained a principal focus.

Halberstam was not the kind to spend hours in a library reading scholarly treatises and historical documents. His principal tool was the interview, and he took almost five years to talk with hundreds of people about politics and the media. And many of those interviewed had some connection to the CBS empire.

Paley was wary of the project from the start. Halberstam was unpredictable. There was no telling what he would find or what he would say about CBS and its chairman. Paley was too powerful and too conscious of his image to let fate take its own course. Plans would have to be made and, most importantly, Halberstam would have to be watched closely.

Halberstam learned about Paley's strategy in Tulsa, Oklahoma. After he had given a lecture at a local college, Halberstam was approached by a young man who introduced himself as a "stringer" for CBS. I don't know what's going on, said the stringer, but CBS has asked me to follow you everywhere and tape everything you say. Halberstam was no babe in the woods, but he was shocked and appalled by the young man's disclosure. "I had been a reporter in Poland covering a Communist government," he later remarked. "I believed my phone had been tapped, and I knew what it was like to live in a closed society and be monitored by an unfriendly government. But I felt that CBS was watching me more closely than any other institution I had ever covered."

Halberstam did not keep these thoughts to himself. He raised the issue when he interviewed the CBS chairman in his office in 1975. Paley had submitted to the interview in the apparent hope that he could influence Halberstam's view of history. Charm was Paley's great strength, and he began the meeting by complimenting his visitor's skills as a writer. Halberstam made it clear immediately that that ploy would not work. He described the incident at Tulsa, bluntly telling Paley that he should be ashamed of himself, that the monitoring was a crude tactic and something unworthy of a network that employed journalists like Dan Rather.

Paley became unglued at once. He had had friends and colleagues call Halberstam to find out what he was doing and whom he was interviewing.

Their reports gave little comfort. And now Halberstam's open challenge on the Tulsa incident. Bill Paley was not in control, and the experience was unsettling. "That first visit was one of the most neurotic performances I'd ever seen," Halberstam later said of Paley's reaction to the interview. When Halberstam tried to ask him normal questions about his background, Paley turned him aside, saying, "I've led a good life, but you're out to get me."

Before long Halberstam tried to raise the issue of CBS news coverage and the company's relationship with the Nixon White House. Halberstam did not fence with Paley. He pointedly revealed his own impression that the news operation had become a source of discomfort to the CBS chairman. Paley retreated to the past to prove otherwise. He spoke of Murrow, of his support of the McCarthy broadcast, and of how he tried to deal with Murrow's deep depressions. And in an effort to dispel "rumors" that there had been a rupture in his relationship with Murrow at the end, Paley had his secretary retrieve some letters that Janet Murrow had written to him, thanking him for his support. None of Paley's comments or letters dissuaded Halberstam from what he knew—that Murrow had felt some bitterness toward and disappointment with Paley years before he died. Nor was Halberstam persuaded when Paley spoke of CBS's contribution to the breaking of the Watergate story. "And here was clearly a man," said the journalist, "who seemed to have forgotten that he in fact was furious when CBS took up what *The Washington Post* had been doing." When he saw Halberstam's skepticism, Paley became defensive, again saying that he was an honorable man, that he had led a good life, and that Halberstam was out to get him.

After numerous interchanges like this, Halberstam finally got Paley to discuss specific people and episodes in CBS history—Ed Klauber, Elmer Davis, Murrow's broadcast from Korea (which Paley refused to air), the McCarthy broadcast, and similar matters from the more distant past. As Paley talked, Halberstam noticed that "there's a kind of nostalgia as he talks about it—that it was an exciting time; everything was brand new. . . . Now it's all formalized . . . and it's all kinds of layers and it's all too structured." But then the conversation switched to the present day, and Paley took the offensive against his interviewer, claiming that Halberstam and other members of the liberal-intellectual establishment were all against him.

By the time he left the chairman's office, Halberstam was very frustrated. It had not been a productive interview—at least not in terms of exploring CBS's past. "All of Paley's paranoia—of which there is a lot— came out and flourished." Halberstam attributed Paley's reaction to the lack of control. The CBS chairman had friendly relationships with almost every media organization. There was always someone he could call to ask for assistance in making sure the story was reported the way he wanted. "And suddenly," said Halberstam, "I think he is confronting somebody who worked very hard and about whom he can make no phone calls." Although he had almost twenty years of experience as a reporter and author, Halberstam recounted that he had "never seen anyone so defensive in all the people I've interviewed in my life."

Despite the frustrations, Halberstam asked to see Paley again, and the CBS chairman agreed. The second interview some weeks later started off differently than the first. Paley began by reviewing the history of the company—Jerry Louchheim's approaches to his father about United Independent Broadcasters; Paley's encounters with George Washington Hill; Murrow's rise to fame in Europe; the development of independent production facilities after World War II; the "raids" to acquire Jack Benny and other NBC radio stars in the 1940s, and other matters from the distant past. At one point the discussion turned again to Watergate, and again Paley expressed his satisfaction with the role played by CBS. Halberstam knew of Colson's telephone call to the chairman after the first Watergate broadcast, and he expressed his view that that call had had an impact on Paley's decision to become more involved in shaping the second Watergate broadcast. Paley disagreed vehemently, saying that "Colson never had any degree of influence over CBS News," and that his reaction was formulated independently of anything Colson had said.

Although there was no agreement in assessing the Watergate broadcasts, Halberstam came away concluding that his second session with Paley was much more productive. But overall, the impression formed in Halberstam's mind was not favorable. "You could ask him questions," Halberstam later said about the interviews, "but he had an emperor's memory. He remembered what he wanted to, and he remembered that very well. He had a 'moat memory.' He would let down the drawbridge into the castle of his memory when he wanted, but not otherwise. He was okay if you asked him about stories of the distant past, but anything relating to current controversy was difficult."

The first products of Halberstam's efforts were published as two articles in *The Atlantic Monthly* in January and February 1976 under the title "CBS: The Power & the Profits." Although Halberstam gave Paley credit for developing the programs and the structure that had evolved into the CBS empire, he also painted a portrait of a man and a company that had become obsessed with profits—even at the expense of maintaining an independent news organization. Halberstam did say that "[o]f the three networks, only one covered Watergate with any enterprise or effort, and that was CBS." But he went on to describe the sequence of events following Cronkite's first Watergate broadcast, concluding that Paley's discussions and meeting on the subject "had been precipitated by one call from the White House."

These and other comments about Paley's professional and personal lives had the predictable effect on the thirty-fifth floor of Black Rock. Two anecdotes related by Halberstam were especially painful to Paley. At one point Halberstam wrote that as he got older and richer and more powerful, Paley was prepared to abandon his Jewish heritage for the WASP connections offered by Babe Cushing. As evidence, Halberstam observed that only members of Babe's family had attended their 1947 wedding. In fact, it was not so, and Paley would repeatedly explain the error to visitors, offering a photograph that showed his parents and sister were very much in attendance.

The other issue concerned Paley's decision not to invest in the hit Broadway play *Fiddler on the Roof,* a poignant musical about a Jewish family that wrestles with pogroms and cultural changes in Russia at the turn of the century. Mike Burke, then in charge of diversification, had previewed the show and recommended that CBS participate in the venture. But Paley did not share his subordinate's enthusiasm. "You really like this, do you?" asked the chairman after reading the script. "Very much," Burke replied. "And don't you think it's too depressing," asked Paley. "No, in what sense?" came the response. "Well, the poverty. The pogroms," said Paley. Burke tried to explain that it was really a funny, uplifting story, a "triumph of spirit." But Paley didn't see it that way. Burke, Irish Catholic, began to sense that Paley felt uncomfortable with the play and responded that he had not made any commitments and that they did not have to go forward with any investment if Paley did not want to do it. "I'd rather not," the chairman said in a matter-of-fact way, and the proposal was dropped.

Halberstam recounted much of the discussion in his articles, adding a comment from another source who quoted Paley as saying, "I couldn't do it—it's the story of my own family." All of which, in Paley's mind, suggested that he was somehow ashamed of his family and uncomfortable with his Jewish origins. That angered the CBS chairman. He adored his father and had emulated Sam's generous support for Israel. Indeed, in February 1975—months before the publication of Halberstam's articles—Paley had announced that the William S. Paley Foundation would fund the construction of a new art center in Jerusalem that would be dedicated to his mother. "He talked incessantly about his mother at the time," said Kidder Meade. Goldie had taken up painting after her eightieth birthday, and Paley was impressed by her drive and proud of her accomplishment (and even hung one of her paintings in his office). "She's a spunky old

lady," he told Meade, "and she's part of where I am today." Because of
his mother's active support for Israel, Paley wanted to do something in
her honor in the Jewish state. John Minary, executive director of the Paley
Foundation, remembered the key role played by Teddy Kollek, Jerusalem's mayor. "Kollek tried to persuade Paley to build the art center in his
city," said Minary, "and Kollek can be *very* persuasive."

Unfortunately, Goldie died shortly before the dedication of the art
center in January 1978. But Paley was very pleased with the idea and
happy with the pleasure it had given his mother. And now Halberstam
threatened to destroy all that with comments that Paley regarded as
totally untrue. The CBS chairman was equally disturbed by Halberstam's
rendition of his conversation with Mike Burke about *Fiddler on the Roof.*
Paley insisted that he had decided against the investment because he did
not like the ending.

Paley was so troubled by Halberstam's description of the *Fiddler* incident that he had his lawyers contact the writer and threaten a libel suit.
Halberstam was not one to be intimidated so easily. He telephoned Mike
Burke in London to receive confirmation of the story's accuracy, and the
threat of a lawsuit evaporated. Still, Paley could not put the Halberstam
articles out of his mind. They gnawed at his insides, diverting his attention
from almost every other matter. Something had to be done, something
would be done. And in trying to formulate a response, Paley turned to the
one man who had the perspective of an historian and the loyalty of the
most favored CBS employee—Arthur Tourtellot.

He was a most unusual man. Then sixty-three, Tourtellot had joined
CBS in 1968 after a long and successful career as a scriptwriter and public
relations executive. But he did not go to CBS to promote himself to higher
office. (Indeed, he turned down a corner office because he knew it was a
sign of prestige that might provoke rivalry with other CBS executives.)
Nor did he go to CBS to pursue any particular project. His only responsibility was to be available to advise the chairman on any issue Paley chose,
and for Tourtellot, that was enough. "He was happy to be near Paley and
the center of action," one of Tourtellot's sons later recalled. "He liked that
because he felt he could have an impact on history."

For Tourtellot, that was no small consideration. He was a man with two
separate careers. He maintained an apartment in Manhattan for ease in
commuting to Black Rock and his other city endeavors, including an
involvement with Paley on the Museum of Modern Art. On the weekends
Tourtellot would return to his family at their home in Westport, Connecticut, and devote his free hours to writing history books. In a sense, that
was his first love, and if he could have earned enough from his books, he
might never have divided his time with other employment. But what he

lacked in revenue he made up in enthusiasm, concentrating his writing projects on English and American history in the seventeenth and eighteenth centuries (and also a work that catalogued the American presidents' view of the presidency).

Tourtellot had a personal style that was all his own. He was a fastidious dresser and, being an Anglophile, emulated the best in British fashion, from cutaway suits to loud striped shirts with detachable collars. His personality suited his clothes. Always smiling and upbeat, he seemed to be totally devoid of conceit and guile—something that Paley knew to be rare for anyone working near the top of the corporate world.

Tourtellot and Paley respected and enjoyed each other enormously. They would have lunch every Wednesday and, depending on the pending problems, would meet and talk on the phone many times during the week. "He was able to defuse Paley and reason with him and calm him down and make him laugh when he got angry," said one CBS executive who knew both men. Paley appreciated the importance of that role. "It's not easy for me to talk about Arthur," the CBS chairman commented at Tourtellot's funeral in October 1977. "He was close to me both in matters concerning business and in matters concerning my extracurricular activities as well as my personal life. In all these areas," Paley added, "he was a perfect man to have by my side. His judgment was excellent and his advice always of great value. My relationship with him was a matter of great comfort to me." And nowhere was that comfort needed more than in determining what Paley should do about David Halberstam in the spring of 1976.

Paley's instinctive reaction was to take control, and to that end he repeatedly suggested to Tourtellot and others that they buy *The Atlantic Monthly.* That approach was hardly productive, and Tourtellot proposed instead that they try to cooperate with the famous author in an attempt to correct the record so that Halberstam's imminent book—eventually entitled *The Powers That Be*— would be more to Paley's liking. Paley and Tourtellot enlisted the help of Kidder Meade, who was still vice president for corporate affairs and the executive with principal responsibility for public relations.

Meade was an eager participant, because he believed that Halberstam's articles were very unfair to his boss. "Halberstam painted the wrong Bill Paley," Meade later observed. "He painted a picture of Paley as scheming and apprehensive about his public image and so selfish as to have no interest except for the image he projected. Paley is not perfect," added Meade, "and he can be arrogant, but that portrait does a disservice to him and what he has accomplished." Meade used every resource at his command to develop some memos that would identify every error, no matter how insignificant, that the CBS group perceived in Halberstam's articles. Jack Loftus was a member of Meade's staff, and he remembered that "the activities of the Corporate Information Office came to a virtual standstill so that we could collect material to be used in responding to the Halberstam articles."

On June 16, 1976, Paley sent a letter to Halberstam, enclosing two long memos that detailed, by page, paragraph, and line, the errors that CBS saw in *The Atlantic* articles. "Despite the many complimentary things that you had to say about me in your two-part article," Paley wrote, ". . . and because it was described by the editor as 'part of a larger work in progress,' I call your attention to the fact that the piece contains numerous errors, some of them central to your thesis and many of them resulting in untruthful, unfair and undocumented allegations against CBS, several of my colleagues in the management of the company and myself as its chief executive officer and, though they have no bearing on CBS or its operations, me as an individual." Paley added that he would "be happy to arrange a meeting" if Halberstam thought further discussion might be helpful after he reviewed the enclosed materials.

Halberstam responded by letter on September 18, telling Paley that he had a responsibility to be accurate but that he found most of the material in the Paley memos to be unconvincing. The frustration was evident in the CBS chairman's response to the writer one month later. "I put a lot of time and effort into the material sent you on June 16," Paley told Halberstam, "and my staff and I went to great lengths to insure that it be wholly factual and accurate. I think we have the right to expect that it be judged seriously and with an open mind." Paley reiterated, in a last plea, that he "would be happy to meet" with Halberstam to review the memos in detail.

Halberstam was willing to change certain items where he could see that errors had been made. But he was not willing to accept CBS's view on matters of interpretation and judgment, and for that reason, he saw no point in further meetings.

Paley anticipated Halberstam's refusal. If something was to be done, other avenues would have to be explored. One of them was to prepare a history of CBS News that could be distributed with the CBS annual report to stockholders—and which would, not incidentally, demonstrate that Halberstam was wrong in some of his characterizations of CBS and its chairman. To achieve that objective, the company turned to Martin Mayer, a talented writer who had written a book and numerous articles about broadcasting.

"They called me in and asked me to prepare a pamphlet of about twenty-five thousand words that could be given to the stockholders," Mayer later recalled. He was given access to CBS records and, most importantly, the chairman himself. Mayer spent time with Paley in his office, in his apartment, and even driving back and forth with him in his limousine, trying to recapture the history of CBS news operations since the 1930s.

From this frequent interaction, Mayer quickly developed a sense of the strengths and weaknesses in Paley's character. "He was a warm person, with a good intellect and very goal-oriented," said Mayer. "But he also had this incredible self-image of sweetness and generosity, and he always seemed surprised when it was said that someone didn't like him." Part of this protective self-image reflected the CBS chairman's view of his past. "He really seemed to restructure the world for himself," Mayer observed. On numerous occasions Mayer would listen to Paley's rendition of a particular incident and then find a document in CBS files that provided a different version. "And I would always show him the document," said Mayer, "and he would invariably say, 'I don't remember it that way.' Maybe he's unconscious of it," Mayer continued, "but he's got an awfully selective memory."

For all the time they spent together, Mayer could not always get Paley to focus on the history of CBS news operations. Not that the CBS chairman had lost interest in challenging Halberstam. Few things were as important as his public image. But Halberstam's book would not be published for at least a couple of years, and in the meantime, Paley had to confront a more immediate priority.

It was Babe. During a trip to China in 1973 she had developed pneumonia. She had been placed in a hospital and, upon her return to New York, she had undergone a complete physical check-up, which revealed a spot on her lung. As one CBS colleague said later, "Babe was a lovely, beautiful, and gracious woman who had only one bad habit—cigarettes." The tumor on her lung was removed immediately, and although it was malignant, her doctors gave her hope that everything would be fine. But that proved to be unduly optimistic. Two years later another tumor appeared, and this time the doctors felt compelled to remove an entire lung. At first Babe seemed to recover from the operation, but by 1976 her health began to deteriorate rapidly. Chemotherapy and radiation did not appear to be effective, and it was obvious that more drastic measures would have to be taken.

Paley did not want to lose his wife. Like many married couples, they had had their problems, their differences, their disappointments. But she had been the mainstay of his home life and his social activities. He knew he would be lost without her, and it was inconceivable to him that something could not be done. He had so much power, so much control (Halberstam aside)—there had to be an answer somewhere that would let Babe live. He would not accept anything as inevitable. "He used to bring in doctors from all over the world to meet and brainstorm," Marietta Tree recalled, "to see if they could collectively come up with a solution they couldn't reach individually." Mayer also remembered the attention and energy that Paley devoted to Babe's medical problems. "Her illness dominated the conversations," said Mayer. "The treatments, the doctors, how brave she was. It was never far from his mind."

Frustration had now become a daily staple of Paley's life. Halberstam. His wife. And there was more. In February 1976 former CBS News President Sig Mickelson disclosed that Paley had had a secret relationship with the Central Intelligence Agency during the height of the Cold War in the 1950s. According to Mickelson, he had attended a meeting in the CBS chairman's office in 1954 during which two CIA representatives had revealed that CBS press credentials had been given to Austin Goodrich, a man purportedly working for CBS but, in reality, a CIA undercover agent. Mickelson added that Paley—who was present during the meeting—seemed to know all about the CIA connection.

Mickelson's disclosure was big news. (William Safire of *The New York Times* called it Paley's "big secret.") Watergate had awakened the country to the misuse of power by government intelligence agencies, revelations that had led to articles, books, lawsuits, and congressional investigations. Now a former CBS executive was saying that one of the government's intelligence agencies had used a CBS reporter to perform undercover work—with the apparent knowledge and cooperation of the network's chairman. No responsible news agency could ignore the story—and that included CBS News. CBS correspondent Bruce Morton interviewed Mickelson in Washington with the expectation that the tape would be used on that evening's broadcast. But the Mickelson interview never made it on the air.

Paley knew about Morton's interview with Mickelson, because the CBS News bureau chief in Washington had called for the chairman's reaction. "Totally untrue," said Paley. Mickelson, however, refused to concede any doubt in his recollection, and Kidder Meade soon called to ask if the former CBS executive would meet with the chairman to discuss the matter. "It was a pleasant meeting," Mickelson later recalled, "with Paley asking questions, probing my memory," and finally yielding, saying to his former employee, "well, perhaps your memory is better than mine."

Although he could not recall the Goodrich meeting, Paley did later acknowledge that he had had what he called a "personal" relationship with the CIA during the 1950s. "I was approached as somebody who could cooperate with them to their advantage," Paley explained to Daniel Schorr in 1977. "And this was back in the early fifties when the Cold War was at its height and where I didn't hesitate for a second to say, 'Okay, it's reasonable. I'll do it.' " The requests were varied. On one occasion the agency wanted to use the chairman's personal nonprofit corporation, the William S. Paley Foundation, as a vehicle to transfer funds to support a research project that could not be identified in public with the CIA. On other occasions Paley allowed the agency to buy CBS outtakes (film that was never broadcast), to interview foreign correspondents upon their return to the United States, and to use the CBS control booth at the United Nations to read the lips of Soviet representatives while Soviet Premier Nikita Khrushchev delivered a speech.

As later news reports revealed, Paley was not the only media executive to cooperate with government intelligence agencies during the Cold War. But he was sensitive to any allegation that seemed to cast doubt about the independence of CBS and frustrated when stories insinuated that he and his network had been compromised by the CIA connection. Of particular concern was Daniel Schorr's book *Clearing the Air*, which was scheduled for publication in 1978 and promised to discuss the Paley–CBS–CIA relationship in detail. To defuse any further controversy, Paley directed the CBS public relations office to issue a press release in September 1977 describing—and justifying—the relationship.

Paley's frustration with CBS programming could not be alleviated so easily. In retrospect, the problems seemed to start with the departure of Fred Silverman. He had been recruited to CBS in the 1960s by Mike Dann, and by the early 1970s, Silverman, only in his thirties, had established himself as a major contributor, if not *the* major contributor, to CBS's long domination of the ratings war with NBC and ABC. Silverman's success was not accidental. He was a driven man, totally preoccupied with programming. He seemed to spend every waking second planning shows, reviewing pilots, and evaluating their performance. A standing joke at Black Rock had it that if Fred Silverman went to China he would have the overnight ratings delivered by bicycle.

For all his enthusiasm and success, Silverman felt very unappreciated. True, his annual compensation was $140,000, but he was only a mid-level executive. Other members of the CBS team had much higher salaries, many more privileges, and far greater access to the chairman. Silverman wanted more recognition for his achievements, and Network President Bob Wood urged Paley to give it to him—a limousine, a $50,000 bonus, his own dining room. Paley resisted, saying that Silverman was not that special, that it would set a bad precedent for other mid-level executives. In May 1975, Silverman jumped ship to become chief of programming at ABC—a switch that Paley would later regret.

The loss of Silverman was followed by a very disappointing fall season.

Ratings dropped for CBS's perennial hits such as "All in the Family" and "The Mary Tyler Moore Show," and none of the new programs made any lasting impression on viewers. And of all the failures, none was more discouraging to the CBS chairman than the fate of "Beacon Hill."

The program was fashioned after the popular PBS series "Upstairs, Downstairs" and featured an affluent family in Boston during the 1920s. Over one million dollars was spent to develop sets, costumes, and dialogue that had the ring of authenticity. Paley proclaimed it "one of the best-produced shows that we ever put on." The series represented high-quality cultural fare and was sure to set the new standard for excellence in commercial television.

None of these dreams were realized, because the show flopped after a short run. Later Paley recognized his mistake. "Jack Benny used to say to me," he remembered, " 'You know, I only have about one good show out of five. . . . But people are interested in me, and they want to know what I'm doing. And sometimes what I do is very, very funny, and sometimes what I do is only mildly funny. But I know that they want to find out what Jack is up to, or Rochester, or Mary, and all the other people in the cast.' " "Beacon Hill" did not hold the same interest for mass audiences. "Here was a rich family in Boston," Paley observed, "eight or nine servants, living the life of Riley, and it was too foreign to those things that they knew about, and therefore . . . [they] couldn't develop a special interest."

These and other disappointments were compounded by a further depletion of CBS programming executives. With Silverman gone, some executives began to question the network's commitment to program development. By early 1976 the network had lost Perry Lafferty and Frank Barton, two long-time employees who had supervised program production in Hollywood. And then Bob Wood, anxious to leave the grind of corporate politics for the safer haven of an independent production company in his native California, also resigned, leaving the company with no one to pick up the fallen mantle; Frank Stanton's farm system was now a thing of the past. So the company turned to Robert Wussler, a forty-year-old producer who had worked his way to the top after nineteen years of service—from mailroom clerk to head of the News Division's election unit to station manager and then director of sports programming—but someone who had no experience in entertainment programming. "They were bankrupt in people," Wussler later commented, "and they had nowhere else to turn."

Wussler's promotion did not mean that Paley was willing to abandon the program philosophy that Bob Wood had urged on him seven years earlier. Paley was now firmly committed to programs that were topical and would appeal to the youth of America. He was not going to sit in his rocking chair and watch the parade go by. As he explained to an interviewer in 1976, "You know, the younger audience of America is becoming more and more important." For that reason, he remarked, CBS was going to rely on younger men (no women) "who have a good feel for what their younger audience wants." It was the only way to remain vibrant. "We never let the old minds predominate," said Paley.

To anyone unacquainted with the CBS chairman, the comments revealed an aging executive prepared to walk away from any involvement in program decisions. But Wussler knew otherwise. Programming was still Paley's first love, the one part of CBS that never bored him. He could not, would not, let go. Sometimes Paley's secretary would telephone Wussler to tell him that the chairman was on his way to the conference room where the network schedule was laid out on large boards denoting the programs being aired at every time slot on every day of the week. "And I would wander over there," said Wussler, "and find Paley, all by himself, moving the boards around, obviously trying to think of ways to improve the schedule."

Wussler found his interaction with the chairman to be very productive. "The guy was seventy-five years old, he needed his naps, and he was not always sharp," said Wussler, "but he was knowledgeable, he was interested, and he always had a good suggestion up his sleeve." And Paley was not shy about communicating those suggestions to the new network president. He would call him anywhere, any time, to ask a question or advance a proposal. "He especially loved finding me on Friday nights," said Wussler, "because he knew I would be out." Paley would contact Operator 51 at Black Rock—the one person who always knew where every employee was— and she would invariably track down the network president at some restaurant or a friend's house. To Wussler it was all an enjoyable game. "High fun," as he called it. When he finally got Wussler on the phone, Paley would say, "we gotta do this" or "we gotta fix that." One of the more memorable proposals concerned Linda Evans, then a co-star in a CBS series called "Hunter" (and later the popular co-star of ABC's "Dynasty"). Paley found Evans very appealing, and he would repeatedly say to Wussler, "Roberto, we gotta get that Evans woman in her own show." On another occasion Paley asked Wussler what he thought about "Charlie's Angels," the new hit show on ABC that focused on the looks and bodies of three beautiful women. "And I told him," said Wussler, "that we can do something like that without all the T and A." To which Paley responded, "Terrific. Go find it."

For all his involvement, Paley would let others take final responsibility—if they wanted it. At one program meeting in the fall of 1976, Paley began to express concern about the network's low ratings. It was time, he said, to start thinking of moving some programs to new time slots and finding replacement shows for those that were not doing well. Bob Daly, an experienced programmer and one of Wussler's key assistants, disagreed. "We always start off poorly in the fall," he said. "We don't have the World Series, and it sometimes takes audiences a while to recover from the summer and get into their normal viewing patterns." Paley was skeptical. "Are you sure?" he asked. Daly was quick to ease the chairman's mind. "Don't worry," he said. "We'll be fine. If we're not number one by January first, you can fire me, or I'll resign, but don't change the schedule." Paley loved that, and the schedule remained unchanged.

Daly's assurances did not eliminate all of the chairman's programming concerns. Whatever the appeal of the current schedule, the future did not look bright. "It had taken management six weeks to replace Lafferty and Barton in Hollywood," said Wussler, "and those are jobs that shouldn't be vacant for six days." Without any experienced programmers on the West Coast, the network had fallen behind in developing new pilots. The program development process was further compromised when the budget for new pilots was slashed to $15 million.

Then there was the lawsuit by Norman Lear and other producers challenging the networks' adoption of the Family Viewing Hour. The producers had reason to be concerned. The new policy limited the time slots that would be available for many of their programs—a matter of prime importance, since, as in the earlier case of "Gunsmoke," scheduling can have a critical impact on a program's performance. "All in the Family," for example, had been deemed unsuitable for impressionable children; consequently, it had been moved from its slot at eight o'clock on Saturdays—where it had become the number-one prime-time show—to nine on Mondays, where its ratings began to fall. With millions of dollars hanging in the balance, producers argued that the Family Viewing Hour amounted to government censorship (because it was adopted in response to pressure from Congress and the FCC) and that the court should declare the policy a violation of the producer's constitutional right to free speech. In the meantime, implementation of the policy did little to enhance CBS's relations with producers. As Bob Wood later observed, "It went down the creative community's throat like a chicken bone sideways."

Paley laid all of these problems at Arthur Taylor's doorstep. He was the one, after all, who had ultimate responsibility for filling executive vacancies on the West Coast and for preparing the budget. And while Paley had initially endorsed the concept of the Family Viewing Hour, he now told Taylor that it was "opportunistic" and unsuited for CBS.

Under other circumstances, Paley's growing frustration with Taylor's leadership might have evaporated over time without impairing their relationship. But the problems ran deeper than any specific decision or policy. It was a matter of personality and perspective, and it did not bode well for Arthur Taylor's future at CBS.

To begin with, the two men disagreed over the proper approach to management. Paley believed in delegating responsibility. A person with intelligence and initiative could rise to the top very quickly in CBS—as long as he did well. But any signs of failure could be disastrous. There were no performance evaluations to identify areas of possible improvement. The first indication of the chairman's displeasure was often a demotion or a dismissal notice. In Taylor's mind, the results were usually counterproductive for both the employee and the company. "People worried to death that they would be wrong and that Paley would criticize them for it," he observed. Taylor recalled that on several occasions he had to soothe executives who began to cry because of anxiety over a forthcoming meeting with the chairman. (One CBS executive remembered an emotional meeting with Taylor himself that raised a question whether the CBS president wasn't also troubled by the pressures of Paley's approach.)

Taylor eventually began to speak of Paley in disparaging terms, referring to him with a roll of the eyes as "that crazy old man." He was not as discreet as he should have been, and his comments were soon circulating back to the chairman himself. All of which reinforced Paley's view that Taylor was, as one CBS executive commented, "taking over too much too fast." Taylor was making decisions on the budget, on corporate structure, and even on programming, without consulting the chairman. Paley wanted Taylor to assume responsibility for managing the company, but he didn't want the CBS president to forget that Bill Paley was still around. For Paley, the breaking point probably came when he happened to be in the Washington corporate offices and saw the opulent suite that Taylor had designed for himself. As Paley told Bill Leonard, the CBS president "was too big for his britches." Despite all the earlier hopes and expectations, Arthur Taylor was not going to replace Paley as chief executive officer and chairman of CBS.

By the summer of 1976 Paley was already thinking of a possible replacement for Taylor. This time he would not use an executive search firm. He needed someone who had worked at CBS, someone who appreciated the stature and privileges of its chairman. Only one qualification would remain unchanged. It would have to be someone who had no prior experience in broadcasting, someone who would respect Paley's special role in programming, and, eventually, someone who would hopefully embrace Paley's views of programming.

One Friday evening in September John Backe received a call from the chairman inviting him and his wife to join Bill and Babe for dinner at their Fifth Avenue apartment the following Monday. As president of the CBS Publishing Group, Backe had met the chairman on many occasions. But Paley had never displayed much interest in the publishing house of Holt, Rinehart & Winston or the other activities of the publishing group, and Backe did not socialize with Paley outside of CBS. Still, he was not about to say no. He and his wife dutifully appeared at the appointed hour.

Shortly into the dinner Paley cryptically said to Backe, "I find our lives are inextricably intertwined." And then Paley showed his hand. He said that Arthur Taylor was going to be leaving the company. Paley further explained that he had already talked with the board of directors, and they wanted Backe to assume the position of CBS president—with the understanding that Backe would become the company's chief executive officer at the next annual stockholders meeting in the spring of 1977.

To all appearances, Backe seemed like the perfect choice. Only forty-four, he had already established himself as a good negotiator and an aggressive manager. A native of Akron, Ohio, he had received a degree from Miami University at Oxford, Ohio, then became a bomber pilot with the Strategic Air Command, and, upon leaving the service, had joined the General Electric Company in Cincinnati. His talents as an executive were readily apparent, and before long he had become president of Silver Burdette, the textbook publishing subsidiary of General Learning Corporation, which in turn was a joint venture of GE and Time, Inc.

His success in that position had brought him to the attention of CBS, which was looking for a new executive to head its languishing Publishing Group. After meeting with Paley and Taylor, Backe had told them that he was happy where he was and had no interest in leaving. Taylor would not accept no for an answer. He kept calling Backe, asking, pushing, urging him to change his mind. When the pressure failed to work, Taylor finally said, "Well, if you won't take the job, will you at least take a look at our publishing operations and advise us how they can be improved?" "That sucked me in," said Backe, and in March 1973 he joined the network as the new president of the Publishing Group.

Backe's impact was felt almost immediately. Profits in each of the divisions started to soar, and, to Paley's surprise, Backe was able to purchase the paperback house of Fawcett for only $50 million, several million dollars less than the authorization he had received from the company. Paley felt sure that Backe would make an appropriate successor. "I had had my eye on John Backe for some time," he later observed. "From the day he came to CBS, I had been impressed with the caliber of his work, and, seeing him several times a week in meetings and conferences, I came to like and admire him personally."

Although flattered by Paley's offer at dinner that September evening, Backe resisted. "I don't even know what a chief executive does," he told Paley. "All they seem to do is give speeches and sit on the dais." Backe was also concerned about a potential clash of styles with the chairman. "You and I are strong personalities," he said. "We'll run into each other." None of these protests dissuaded Paley. He was going to retire, he said, and Backe was the man to fill his shoes. Backe left the dinner without yielding, but Paley was used to getting his way. He telephoned Backe almost every day, pressing him to take the job. "I'm going to retire," Paley kept saying. "Give it a shot." Within weeks the CBS chairman finally got the affirmative answer he wanted. "He wore me down," Backe later said.

On the evening of October 12, 1976, Paley hosted a dinner at his apartment for the board members who were not CBS employees. The board was scheduled to meet the following day, and Paley wanted to advise the outside directors that Backe had accepted the job and that Taylor could be fired. Paley had already informed the board members who worked at CBS (minus Taylor), so there would not have to be any discussion at the meeting. Backe could simply be introduced as the new CBS president.

On the morning of October 13, 1976, Taylor was making final arrangements for a trip to Moscow to negotiate television rights to the 1980 Olympics. He received an unexpected call informing him that the chairman wanted to see him immediately. When Taylor walked into Paley's office, he knew there was trouble. The chairman was standing there flanked by two outside directors, Roswell Gilpatric and Henry B. Schacht. Paley told Taylor that the board wanted his resignation. The CBS president was completely surprised by the request. For all his criticism of Paley, and despite all their arguments, he had no sense of any deterioration in their relationship. So he told the chairman and the two board members that he would think about it. "No," said Paley, "we want your resignation this morning." Taylor was even more stunned. The company had more than $400 million in cash in government securities and in bank accounts—no small achievement, and one that gave Taylor enormous satisfaction. He could not accept the chairman's request without some explanation. Why, said Taylor, the company's in great shape. "I know," said Paley, "but . . ." At that point Gilpatric interrupted, saying, "Bill, you don't have to answer that, and I don't think you should." With that, the meeting was concluded. Taylor hurried back to his office and began making calls to the other directors. Most told Taylor that they were appalled by Paley's decision, some adding, "But you know Bill."

The trade press was startled by Taylor's abrupt dismissal. As *Business Week* commented, "CBS prospers, but Paley wields the ax." None of the criticism gave Paley any second thoughts about the wisdom of his decision. He remained confident that he had finally settled on an appropriate successor, someone whose presence would allow him to plan his retirement with the knowledge that the company's future was secure. It was indeed a grand feeling—but one that would not withstand the test of time.

CHAPTER SEVENTEEN

"Retirement"

D avid Sonenberg was sitting in his Upper East Side office one afternoon in February 1978 when his secretary told him that Walter Yetnikoff, president of the CBS Records Group, was on the phone. Sonenberg, a thirty-year-old Harvard Law School graduate, had forsaken a traditional law practice to manage singers and other members of the creative community. Some of his clients had contracts with CBS Records, and of those, none was more successful than Meat Loaf—the three-hundred-pound rock singer with long stringy hair and a Texas drawl. Meat Loaf's album, *Bat Out of Hell*, had skyrocketed up the charts, and Yetnikoff was now calling Sonenberg to say that "the chairman" would like to meet Meat Loaf, and could he be available at 2:30 the following afternoon?

From years of contact with CBS, Sonenberg did not have to ask who "the chairman" was. Although rarely seen, Paley was a constant topic of conversation at Black Rock. So Sonenberg was full of excitement when he passed the word to Meat Loaf. They were going to meet the man who had assumed almost mythic proportions in company gossip. Meat Loaf had only one question for his manager: Do you think it's for lunch? Sonenberg said he was not sure, but Meat Loaf was not one to take chances on such an important matter.

When he showed up at Yetnikoff's office the following day, Meat Loaf was dressed in his concert attire—black tuxedo, ruffled shirt with an open collar, and a large gold medallion hanging conspicuously around his neck. None of that was unusual. There was, however, something distinctive about the brown shopping bag that he held in his right hand. Despite repeated inquiries from Yetnikoff and Sonenberg, Meat Loaf refused to identify its contents, saying only that he was ready to meet Mr. Paley. So the three men proceeded to the thirty-fifth floor, through several outer offices, and finally into the richly paneled, warmly decorated office of the CBS chairman. Paley, dressed in the usual dark suit, white shirt, and wide tie, got up from behind his gaming-table desk and walked over to greet his three visitors. Yetnikoff dutifully introduced Sonenberg, who shook

Paley's hand, and then Yetnikoff said, "Mr. Chairman, this is Meat Loaf." Since his right arm was drapped around the brown paper bag, Meat Loaf did what only seemed natural—he grabbed Paley's outstretched hand with his left hand and cheerfully said, "Yo, Bill!"

Paley smiled broadly and directed his guests to a comfortable couch. As they all sat down, Meat Loaf pulled out a six-pack of beer from the bag and asked "Bill" if he wanted one. Paley gamely said yes, and as they started sipping at their beers, Meat Loaf pulled out a package of Jarlsberg cheese from the bag, asking "Bill" if he wanted to try some. "I had some of this Jarlsberg cheese the other day," said Meat Loaf, pronouncing the *J,* "and it was great." Paley again said Sure, and from there the conversation never dragged. Paley was obviously amused by Meat Loaf's lack of inhibition, and the singer was mesmerized by Paley's story of how he had built CBS into a sprawling empire.

By 1978 the CBS Record Group was a major part of that empire, but it had occupied little of the chairman's time over the previous decades. In the early days of radio he had had a good appreciation for the kind of music that would do well on his network, but he had not tried to use that talent to manage the company's record business. Instead, he relied on the skills of his executives—and they did not disappoint him. Shortly after purchasing the Columbia Phonograph Company in 1938, CBS began to reap ever greater profits almost every year. And before long, it was clear that much of the credit belonged to Goddard Lieberson.

Paley was very fond of Lieberson. There was something very refined about him. He was soft-spoken, polished, and engaging, and by the 1960s Lieberson had become one of the very few CBS employees who socialized with the chairman. Nothing could have seemed more improbable when Lieberson first joined CBS in 1939. Then twenty-eight, he was a struggling songwriter who came to New York because "as a composer, I thought that was the thing to do." After being hired for the modest sum of $50 per week, Lieberson and Columbia Records president Edward Wallerstein began a drive to find artists and market their records. Their eventual success reflected good taste, abundant energy, and, on occasion, daring imagination. With the introduction of the LP in 1948, Lieberson proposed to Paley that they form a record club comparable to the Book-of-the-Month Club. At first Paley laughed at the notion, but Lieberson remained convinced that the proposal was sound. After further meetings with book club executives and record wholesalers, Lieberson devised a format that Paley could accept—much to their later satisfaction.

Paley's involvement with the record club typified the extent of his contact with the planning and management of the record business. He was available to consider major proposals, but the selection and marketing of talent was generally a decision for Lieberson and his colleagues. After he had been named president of the CBS Record Group in 1966, Lieberson explained to an interviewer that neither Paley nor Stanton would interfere with an artistic judgment. "I tell them what I'm going to do, that's all," he said. "They never question a . . . decision of this kind."

The same comment could not be made about broadcasting. It seemed that Paley was always there to review a pilot, make a suggestion, or perhaps impose a decision. But when he met Meat Loaf in the winter of 1978, he didn't even have much time for broadcasting. Other matters were dominating his life.

His principal occupation had now shifted to the preparation of an autobiography. Martin Mayer had completed his history of CBS news operations and thousands of copies of the pamphlet had been produced. But at the last minute Paley had decided against distribution of the document. Although no official explanations were offered, Kidder Meade told Mayer that "Bill's problem with the piece is that there isn't enough of Bill in it." While he could and did suggest changes, Paley could not force Mayer to make them because, as part of his contract, the writer had insisted on final editorial control. So Paley changed formats. Instead of a pamphlet authored by Mayer, he would hire Mayer to help him write his memoirs.

Over the years Paley had received repeated requests from authors and publishers who wanted to write a book for or about him. All inquiries had been turned aside. Bill Paley did not like to dwell on the past. He focused on the future, on the challenge that remained ahead. And more than that, any review of his life might only remind him of his own mortality.

Paley's attitude started to change in the early 1970s, and he signed a contract to do an autobiography for Doubleday & Company. He would not shunt the task off to some writer, however. He was determined to provide the gist of the story himself. But the project proved to be a struggle. He was a decision-maker, not a writer. He hardly ever read books. (When asked by one interviewer to name his favorite authors, Paley drew a blank.) And he had never previously written anything of any length. The appearance of Halberstam's articles in *The Atlantic* gave him the incentive to push ahead, and Mayer would provide the writing skills he lacked for himself.

There was one obstacle to the plan. Mayer had already agreed to help Lou Cowan write his autobiography, and Mayer said he couldn't do both. Meade told Mayer not to worry about it. Lou's much younger than Bill, he said; he'll certainly release you from your contract (especially since Paley was offering more money). Meade said he would make the necessary arrangements with Cowan, and Mayer went ahead with a couple of planning sessions with the CBS chairman. "You'll have to spend a lot of time with me," Paley said. "You'll have to go with me to Long Island, the Bahamas, and in New York, to understand my lifestyle." Mayer was prepared to undertake the work and travel but, despite Meade's assurances, wanted to contact Cowan himself to make sure the former network president had no objections.

Cowan was completely surprised by Mayer's inquiry. No one had told him about Paley's offer to Mayer. And although he was a low-key person who usually thought of others first, Cowan was not willing to accommodate the CBS chairman in the preparation of his memoirs. Cowan had not forgotten his experience at CBS, and he remembered that little time had been spent considering his feelings. "Normally my dad would have said, sure, no problem," his son Geoffrey later explained. "But when Mayer raised the issue, my father said no. He said he was not going to let Bill Paley have his way on this one." And so Mayer excused himself from Paley's project.

Other writers were hired, but the chairman was not willing to depend on them for the facts that would be the heart of the story. He began spending days, even weeks, at Kiluna and in the Bahamas trying to organize his recollections so they could be transformed into a finished product by an accomplished writer. "He was gone for a month or two at a time," remembered Backe, "working on his book. He would call from wherever he was, say he would come in, and then never show." Walter Thayer also remembered that period. "I used to see him with page after page of lined yellow paper," said Thayer. "He really seemed to be working hard at it."

Paley did not have the luxury of missing deadlines. Halberstam's book was due out in the spring of 1979, and he wanted his memoir to be published around the same time. When the manuscript was at last completed, he asked Backe to review it, and the newly appointed CEO was appalled by what he read. "Paley took credit for everything and blame for nothing," said Backe. "Paley's view of history was whatever made him look good." Unfortunately, critics had the same reaction after the book was published in March 1979. "There's no new insight, just a reshuffling of facts to fit his version of events," said one reviewer. "He savages [Daniel] Schorr and David Halberstam in a particularly underhanded fashion, but in no way discredits the latter's 1976 *Atlantic* series . . . which, for the moment, has the real story." Les Brown, reviewing the book in *The New York Times Sunday Book Review,* reached a similar conclusion: "[A]lthough William Paley's take-my-word-for-it approach may suffice for those who work for him at CBS, it does not represent gospel to outsiders, especially in the context of a book that is otherwise short on candor."

The book's harsh reviews and limited sales compounded the despair and frustration Paley was already enduring. It seemed that he was caught in a whirlwind of forces that he could not even influence, let alone control. In time, he could and would overcome the disappointment with his book. The same could not be said about the other focus of his life.

Babe's health had deteriorated progressively through 1977 and '78. When chemotherapy and radiation proved ineffective, Paley turned to experimental drugs, hoping that there was some way his wife could be saved. "He became frantic about it," said Backe, who was often with Paley when the doctors' calls were put through. "He was spending almost all of his time on the phone with all kinds of doctors offering all kinds of treatment." The futility of it all began to wear on him. Bob Wussler remembered the time he had to go to the Paleys' Fifth Avenue apartment to meet with the chairman. "Babe opened the door," said Wussler, "looking very emaciated and not at all well. A few minutes later Paley came into the room, and there were tears in his eyes." Paley openly discussed his frustration with Wussler a few days later when the two men were traveling to a meeting on the company jet. "He went on and on," Wussler recalled, "saying what a terrible thing it was to see such a wonderful woman go through something like that."

Babe appreciated the energy her husband devoted to her medical problems. At a lunch with Janet Murrow, who could empathize with the Paleys, Babe kept saying "how wonderfully supportive Bill had been during the illness." For her own part, Babe tried to be stoic, but the horror of the disease was plainly evident. "Babe was as brave as anyone could be," said Katharine Graham, who saw her in those last days. "But it was painful to see. She was so short of breath that she would gasp for air with even the most minimal exertion."

To the last, Babe remained a woman of style and consideration. When she realized the inevitable, she prepared instructions for the funeral reception that would be held at Kiluna. Even in that moment of grief she would take care of her husband and family. The end finally came at their Fifth Avenue apartment on July 6, 1978, the day after her sixty-third birthday. With her husband and all six children beside her, Babe Paley closed her eyes for the last time. The funeral service was held on Long Island. The children, especially Hilary, made an effort to comfort their seventy-six-year-old father, but, as one friend commented, he was committed to showing "a stiff upper lip."

Babe's death drew appropriate recognition from the media. "Mrs.

Paley's sense of elegance set a standard for style-conscious women for three decades," said *The New York Times.* "Her approval lent an immediate cachet to almost anything in the world of fashion, beauty and decor, and her appearance at a public event was a signal for the kind of attention accorded such women as the Duchess of Windsor and Jacqueline Onassis."

However strong he might appear in public, Paley was very shaken by the loss. "The idea of Babe dying was a terrible shock to me," he later remarked. "I had such faith in myself and believed that, somehow, I was going to beat the rap." But more—much more—was involved than the inability to surmount a personal challenge. Babe had filled a need that no one else could, and he felt very lost without her. He would call friends and say, I can't be alone, can you please come to dinner. On another occasion Paley complained to a friend, "My memory is so poor now. I can't even remember whom I sat next to at dinner last night." There were many people who cared about Bill Paley, and they were disheartened by what they saw. "After Babe died," said one friend, "he was very disoriented for about two years."

The impact was very evident at Black Rock. "He was a lost soul," said John Backe. "He would be invited to a meeting and wouldn't attend nine out of ten of them. And if he did walk into a room filled with CBS executives, his face would fill with panic until I got up and walked over to get him." Backe tried to comfort Paley by offering him frequent dinner invitations, and on other occasions when they attended social functions together, Paley would take Mrs. Backe's arm and stay with her the entire evening.

To help cope with the depression, Paley began to drink. He had never been more than a social drinker, sometimes having cocktails before dinner or wine with dinner. But now, as one friend commented, "He began to put down a lot of vodkas." The drinking soon became excessive. There were embarrassing moments for colleagues and friends, but no one had the courage to say anything to the chairman of CBS—until a female friend bluntly told him on one occasion that he was drinking too much. Paley was incredulous. He had always been in control, he had never had a drinking problem, and he refused to believe that he had one now. He began asking friends whether he was drinking too much, and they all gave him the answer he wanted to hear. But one of his long-time servants was beyond the point of fear in saying that the emperor had no clothes. When Paley casually asked his servant whether he thought he might be drinking too much, the servant replied, almost as casually, why, of course, don't you remember that I had to put you to bed last night? Paley did not remember and it scared him. And that was end of his excessive drinking.

As with the termination of his smoking habit, he had the discipline to do whatever he decided was in his own best interest.

Through all of this Paley could maintain only a sporadic interest in the affairs of his company. He still reviewed the pilots, and he continued to play a role in the selection of network programs. But by now the players had changed considerably. After being rebuffed by three earlier presidents, Paley was finally able to get Backe to fire Jack Schneider as president of the Broadcast Group. Prior presidents had agreed that Schneider could sometimes be irritating, but they all felt his value as a broadcaster far outweighed that cost. Backe was eager to put his own team in place. Paley had told him that he would be chief executive in name and in practice, and Backe was taking the chairman at his word.

Ironically, the new CBS president chose to replace Schneider with Gene Jankowski, an executive who had a background similar to Schneider's—a long tenure with CBS, primarily in sales and management, with virtually no experience in programming. On the surface, that appeared to be a considerable risk for both men. CBS had slipped to second place behind ABC and was losing affiliates to that network and third-place NBC. But Jankowski more than justified his appointment. He was open, optimistic, and willing to delegate authority to those with more experience than himself, and by the 1979–80 season, CBS was on its way to becoming number one again.

The changes at the News Division were equally profound. In 1978 Dick Salant, after sixteen years as the president, had reached the age of sixty-five—a company milestone for everyone but the chairman. But unlike other executives, Salant, highly respected within the industry, was able and willing to move on to another network. NBC had hired him as its new vice chairman with responsibility for news. At first Paley was shocked and hurt. Loyalty to CBS, to his company, played a large role in the chairman's assessment of people, and he expected Salant to retire to a professorship, a nonprofit corporation, perhaps even to write his memoirs, but *not* to a rival network. Paley had planned to give Salant the "S" from the facade of the old CBS headquarters on Madison Avenue, but that idea was shelved when Salant announced his plans.

Paley had always suspected that Salant's first loyalty was to Stanton. After all, despite Stanton's statements to the contrary, Salant had to know that he had been replaced as News president in 1964 to satisfy the chairman's wishes. And Salant probably recognized that he had been restored as News president when Fred Friendly unexpectedly resigned in 1966 only because Stanton still thought highly of him and there was no one else immediately available. Paley was convinced, in short, that Salant viewed

him as the villan, and the move to NBC, thought Paley, seemed to confirm
it. Still, he was not entirely sure, and he asked Jack Loftus to attend
Salant's farewell party to determine whether the departing News president
bore any ill will toward him. To Paley's surprise, Loftus reported back
that Salant had been very gracious in his references to the chairman,
speaking of him in glowing terms. That softened Paley immediately, and
he said to Loftus, "Maybe we should give him the 'S.' Ask Kidder what
he thinks." But Meade remained offended by Salant's willingness to work
for NBC, and Salant never got his letter.

By 1979, Bill Leonard had become the News president, and he used his
close relationship with the chairman to engineer what seemed to be the
News Division's most important victory of that period: retaining Dan
Rather to replace Walter Cronkite as anchor for the "Evening News." In
terms of stature and dollars, the issue was clearly a critical one. "The CBS
Evening News" had dominated the ratings since the late 1960s, and
Cronkite had become arguably the most trusted man in America. With
his retirement approaching in 1981, CBS needed an orderly transition to
someone who could command respect and maintain the ratings. There had
been many suitors for Cronkite's position over the years—Harry Reasoner, Charles Kuralt, John Hart, and others. But when Cronkite began
to plan his retirement, only two remained in the running: Rather and
Roger Mudd. Both were highly talented journalists with long, distinguished records at CBS News. Leonard and his colleagues found it difficult to choose between the two, and at first the News president tried to
sell both on the notion of a Rather–Mudd team that would score as well
as Huntley–Brinkley had. But neither Rather nor Mudd liked the idea,
and when ABC seemed to be on the verge of signing Rather, CBS realized
that the decision had been made. The premier news network could not
afford to take the chance—which seemed very real—that Rather would
succeed at the come-from-behind competitor.

Paley did not play any role in the initial negotiations. He of course
respected Mudd, but he no doubt remembered that Mudd had let him
down when the chairman chose him to anchor coverage of the 1964
Republican Convention. Rather had no similar blemishes on his record
and, in fact, seemed to improve with each passing year. Paley admired the
way Rather, as White House correspondent, had stood up to President
Nixon, and in one of their meetings, the CBS chairman had mentioned to
David Halberstam that Dan Rather was destined to be the next Ed Murrow. (Upon being told that, Rather said it was surely the kiss of death—
whenever they are about to fire you, they make the comparison to Murrow.) After leaving the White House beat, Rather had narrated some

special reports and had then assumed a position as a correspondent on "60 Minutes," which had become the number-one show in television and probably the network's biggest money-maker—points that could not be forgotten in assessing Rather's value to CBS.

As the negotiations with Rather reached their final stages, a decision was made to bring in the chairman. "He had to approve the contract," said Leonard, "and he was in complete shock when he saw the dollars involved." ABC had signed Barbara Walters years earlier for $1 million a year, and Rather was deemed to be even more valuable than that. Reports circulated that he had been offered $3 million a year by ABC, and CBS would have to make a comparable bid to stay in the running. Eventually Paley gave his assent to a long-term contract that would give the new anchorman $2 million a year for ten years plus other benefits.

The depth of the commitment only heightened Paley's anxiety about the future. He had no doubts that Rather could maintain the high quality of the "Evening News" and saw no need to watch the show with any more regularity than he had in the past. (The conventional wisdom around Black Rock was that there need be no concern about mistakes on the "Evening News" since the chairman would never see them.) But Paley did worry about the ratings, which he read at his leisure the following day. Would Rather be able to preserve the high ratings to justify the astronomical investment the network had made in him? "We told Paley that he could expect a drop in the ratings intially," said Leonard. "It would naturally follow any change. But that made him very, very nervous. And when the ratings *did* drop right after Rather took over in the spring of 1981, Paley wouldn't rest. He wanted something done about it right away." Little could be done to improve the situation, and so Paley pressed for a change. He was not about to fire his star performer, however. By March 1982 Van Gordon Sauter had replaced Leonard as News president.

By then other, more fundamental changes had occurred at CBS. Backe had taken a long, hard look at the company's structure, and he soon became convinced that CBS was now *too* diversified. It was no longer just a media company. Its products and services included medical textbooks, musical instruments, musical publishing, and a variety of other endeavors far removed from broadcasting. And while the company had never achieved the chairman's arbitrary goal of generating half its income from non-broadcast services, the investment of money and energy in those areas was still substantial. In Backe's mind, the diversion of resources helped to explain CBS's slide from the number-one position in the ratings. He subscribed to the principle that the company should focus on what it did well, and by early 1979 he had devised a business plan to sell all of the company's interests except those directly related to media and entertainment. It would reduce the company's overhead and allow it to invest more resources in broadcasting.

Although he was now chief executive, Backe could not move forward with the plan without the approval of Paley and the rest of the board. He made an attempt to explain his proposal to the chairman, but it proved to be a frustrating experience. "We briefed him and de-briefed him many times," Backe recalled, "but we couldn't get him to focus on it." But the CBS president was persistent. He believed in his plan, and he was determined to have it adopted. By late 1979 Paley finally gave his assent, and the rest of the board quickly followed. Backe felt confident that the company's future—and his own—were now more secure. It was only a matter of time, he thought, before he could replace Paley as chairman of the board.

But it was not to be. Paley had become disillusioned with Backe. True, he was a superb manager, but, in the chairman's eyes John Backe lacked the perspective and personality to manage a media company, especially Bill Paley's media company. Few people were closer to Paley's thinking at the time than Kidder Meade, and he vividly remembered the conclusions that had been reached. "Backe had the leadership capacity but lacked the intellectual capacity," said Meade. "He had been the head of the publishing division and rarely read a book. We talked once about doing a special on George Orwell, and he didn't know who Orwell was. He was contemptuous of poetry and did not seem to care for cultural matters." Beyond the issue of taste were the complaints that Backe had become too involved in the News Division, which was supposed to operate with a large degree of independence from management. "We had a terrible time keeping him out of the editing business," said Meade.

Paley also had doubts that Backe had the kind of commitment to the company that the chairman wanted. Paley recognized that even the most dedicated executive could have interests outside CBS, but there were limits. Backe surprised the chairman one day by saying that he was planning to take some time off during a critical period to take flying lessons. "And Paley decided," said Meade, "that he was more interested in planes than he was in CBS."

Beyond all these specific complaints was the personal side of it. Paley resented Backe's eagerness to exercise power outside the watchful eye of the chairman. Almost from the first day of his tenure, Backe was asking board members when the seventy-five-year-old Paley was going to retire. ("Well," said Marietta Tree, "his mother is in her nineties and just had her own art exhibition in Palm Beach.") Of course, Paley had told Backe that he would be retiring soon, but the chairman wanted to do it according to his schedule, not Backe's.

Taken together, the portrait that formed in Paley's mind was not a positive one. As he later observed, Backe lacked "vision" and "had not grown in the job." And in drawing these conclusions, Paley could not help making a comparison to Frank Stanton. He had come to CBS from the academic world without any background in business or in broadcasting. He had watched, he had listened, he had learned, and he had evolved into a widely respected leader in the industry. And more than that, he had demonstrated an extraordinary devotion to Bill Paley and CBS. To be sure, Paley had had doubts about making Stanton chief executive. But all of that was now forgotten. In retrospect, Stanton's many strengths assumed even larger proportions. "Frank was terrific," Paley commented at one point during this time period. "He was a very good man, and particularly in certain respects there was no one better than he. He was a top guy for that office of president while I was chairman of the board." The conflicts that had emerged in Stanton's last few years had been erased. "It was," said Paley, "a very healthy and very productive and very successful relationship."

Paley was not the only to to be making the comparison to Stanton. The former CBS president commanded considerable respect among the board and the senior staff, and there were repeated references to Stanton and how he had handled certain issues. Backe did not appreciate these reminiscences, and at one meeting he exploded, saying, "I'm tired of hearing about Stanton. He doesn't run the goddam company any more." The outburst may have silenced the comments, but it could not suppress the doubts that people felt. In late 1979 Paley suggested to the board that they intiate an "assessment" to determine whether the future required a new CBS president. And although there was no specific timetable for any action, one promising candidate appeared to be Thomas H. Wyman.

Like Taylor and Backe, Tom Wyman had no background in broadcasting. He was a fifty-year old corporate executive who had made his mark with Polaroid and various food companies. A tall, handsome man with graying hair, Wyman already knew some of the CBS board members and was highly recommended by other business executives. "He had some legendary friends who spoke very highly of him," said Kidder Meade. He was described as "polished" and "dynamic." And he was also accomplished. A graduate of Phillips Academy and Amherst, he had parlayed his intelligence and personality into executive positions with Nestle, Polaroid, Green Giant, and finally as vice chairman of Pillsbury Company.

In the winter of 1980 Wyman was asked by an executive search firm whether he had any interest in joining the CBS board. Wyman was intrigued by the possibility, and in due course he was invited to dinner at Paley's elegant Fifth Avenue apartment. As on earlier occasions, the interview consisted of general discussion, with Paley doing most of the talking. "We talked about life and happiness and broadcasting," said Wyman, although "he talked a little bit more about broadcasting than I did, and we had a very pleasant time." At the end of the evening, Paley asked Wyman to join the board. Wyman responded that he would be glad to accept if Paley could wait about six months. He had other commitments that would have to be met and his schedule could not be cleared before the summer. Paley was satisfied with with that response. "Great," he said. "Let's keep in touch."

In April 1980 Wyman was sitting in his Minneapolis office when his secretary told him that Mr. Paley was on the phone. Since the two men had had periodic conversations over the preceding months, there was nothing unusual in that. But Paley's inquiry was most unusual. "Are you going to be in New York this weekend?" he asked, as though everyone— even people a thousand miles away in Minnesota—went to New York for the weekend. No, said Wyman, I'm going to a Pillsbury meeting in California. Can you change your plans? Paley asked. No, I really can't, Wyman responded, and besides, what's so important about this weekend? Well, said the CBS chairman, Henry Kissinger is going to be in town and I'd like you to meet him. Wyman suspected that other reasons were on Paley's mind, especially when he asked Wyman when he *could* be in New York. The Pillsbury executive persisted—you'll have to tell me why I need to come to New York. Paley relented. It's hopeless with Backe, he replied. I've got to replace him. At first Wyman thought Paley wanted recommendations for replacements, and he immediately responded that he would be of little help in the search for a new president. I don't know any broadcast executives, he told Paley. I only know grocery people. No, no, Paley responded. I want you to take Backe's place. And so plans were made for Wyman to journey to New York in early May to meet with Paley and the board.

Long before Wyman reached New York, Backe heard the rumors that Paley was searching for a new president. He found that hard to believe, but he checked with some board members, who assured him that all was well. But then Backe heard that Paley had a dinner scheduled with Wyman. The CBS president was frustrated, hurt, and angry. He felt that he had served the company well, and he was not going to let Paley push him aside the way he had dismissed Arthur Taylor. Nor was he going to wait for the drama to unfold. On the afternoon of April 25, he went to Paley's office and demanded an explanation. The seventy-eight-year-old chairman initially denied the reports of his scheduled dinner with Wyman and his search for a new president. There's nothing to it, he said. Backe would not accept that. "Don't lie to me," he told Paley. "I know all about your meeting with Wyman. I know all the details." Paley's anger erupted immediately. "I'm the founder of this company," he replied. "It's my company, and I can do what I want." "Not with me, you can't," retorted the CBS president. And with that he started to walk out the door—which only infuriated Paley even more. "You can't walk out on me," he began to shout. But Backe kept walking and closed the door as the CBS chairman was still standing at his table, yelling at the departing executive.

Backe immediately telephoned the board members to advise them of the meeting. He could not, would not, continue as chief executive, he said, unless the board reined in Paley's power. In Backe's view, the chairman was no longer capable of playing a major role in the management of the company. Indeed, he felt Paley was disruptive. He would come to the office infrequently, would rarely stay for more than a few hours when he did show up, would sometimes fall asleep at meetings, and would—despite his sporadic involvement—constantly challenge decisions that had been made in his absence. Backe had reached the breaking point. "I can't run this company when he keeps changing his mind and second-guessing everything," said the beleaguered executive.

The board was sympathetic, and some members were anxious to develop a compromise. However much they wanted an "assessment" of future needs, and however deep their doubts about Backe's leadership, no one was waiting in the wings to replace him if he should leave. The board wanted time to determine an appropriate course, but Backe was not willing to give it to them. He wanted a specific agreement—right then— that Paley would step down as chairman, that he would no longer enjoy the prerogative to do as he chose. It could not be Bill Paley's candy store any longer.

The board was not prepared to go that far. All of the board members had been selected by Paley himself. Most had known him a long time, all cherished their relationships with him, and they would not allow Backe to succeed in an open confrontation with the chairman. So the board's executive committee—Roswell Gilpatric, Henry B. Schaat, and Franklin A. Thomas—went to Backe and told him that he would have to resign. There could be no compromise based on his terms.

An agreement was reached that Backe's resignation would be made public after the CBS affiliates meeting in Los Angeles. For the sake of the network, appearances had to be maintained until the right moment. Backe dutifully attended the meeting and received the congratulations of broadcast executives from around the country. CBS was number one again, the slide in financial fortunes was over, the future looked bright. At 7:30 in the morning of May 8, Backe left the Bel-Air Hotel, boarded a CBS plane, and flew back to New York. He arrived in New York around 3:30 P.M.,

went to his office at Black Rock, and handed in his letter of resignation
around six. CBS announced his departure at 9:30 that night.

The public reaction was one of shock and disbelief. CBS's abrupt dismissal of Taylor three and a half years earlier remained fresh in the press's
memory, and the headline in *Broadcasting* magazine, the premier trade
journal, captured it all: HISTORY REPEATS AT CBS; BACKE OUT AS PRESI-
DENT. The article described Backe's departure as "stunning and unexplained," suggesting that the root of the problem was Backe's deteriorating relationship with the CBS chairman. Paley tried to defuse that
speculation, saying, "I thought we were getting along pretty well." As for
reports of an angry confrontation with Backe, Paley acknowledged only
that there had been a meeting, that the company was undergoing an
"assessment" of its future needs, that it was a "prudent thing for the
company to do from time to time," and that he had tried to correct
Backe's erroneous impression that a decision had been made to replace the
CBS president. "It was an open question," Paley told *Broadcasting.*

In fact, however, the matter had already been decided. It was not a
question of whether Backe would be replaced, only a question of when.
To outsiders, it was unclear why any "assessment" for new leadership had
to be made after such a short time. The company was doing well on all
fronts, and financial analysts gave the management high marks. As John
Reidy of Drexel Burnham Lambert observed, "Backe's personal stock on
Wall Street was probably at its peak." Paley saw it differently. CBS's
resumption of the leadership in programming reflected the input of the
chairman and the network programming executives—not Backe; and the
company's strong financial posture reflected Kidder Meade's success in
promoting the company's virtues. ("We worked very hard to create that
image," said Meade, "to show that the company was coming back.")
There were many—including Backe—who would have provided a different perspective on the company's success, but none of that mattered. Bill
Paley was calling the shots.

Still, the public criticisms about Backe's dismissal were embarrassing
to the company and to Paley—especially since Wyman had not yet agreed
to become CBS president. (He had not even met the board members yet.)
Bill Leonard, who was CBS News president at the time, remembered
discussing Backe's departure as he and Paley flew to a meeting on the
company plane. "Why'd you do it?" he asked the chairman. "I had to,"
said Paley. "He wasn't the right guy." "Well, you knew you would get
a lot of flack for firing him, didn't you?" said Leonard. Paley said he knew
that, but it could not alter the decision. "I just had to do it," he repeated.

Tom Wyman's appointment as CBS president was announced on May
22, 1980. He would get a three-year contract at $800,000 a year, plus a

$1 million bonus for joining CBS. It was a lucrative deal, but reporters could not resist asking Wyman whether he had any reservations about his ability to succeed where Taylor and Backe had failed. "Clearly there was a huge awkwardness in the events of the last months," said Wyman. "But I really am persuaded that the CBS board was very much involved with Paley in the performance evaluation process." Wyman acknowledged that the board had not handled the situation well, but he had no fault with any assessment of an executive's performance. "Obviously, anybody in any job, this one included for certain," the new CBS president observed, "has got to be evaluated, and by stern standards. I'm not nervous about that," he added with a laugh. "I'm nervous about passing the test."

One key factor in Wyman's expectations remained unmentioned: Paley had agreed to step down as chairman. There was no specific timetable, only a general commitment that it would happen within a year or so. Paley and the board members told the new president that they merely wanted to satisfy themselves that he was in fact the right choice.

Wyman accepted the commitment as a reasonable approach. After all, however impressive his credentials, Wyman was not a broadcaster. For its part, the board was hopeful that there would be no need to change course again. Despite its failure to support Backe, the board was deeply concerned about his departure. Coming so soon on the heels of Taylor's dismissal, the change in leadership would create turmoil within the organization and undermine public confidence in the company's stability—critical factors in the management of a large, publicly-owned conglomerate. The board consisted of members who were loyal to Paley, but they were all, without exception, conscientious men and women. Their first priority had to be to the company, and they could not sit by idly and accept the risk that the chairman would want a new assessment and a new replacement at any time in the near future. They were now of one mind on the key issue. After years of resistance, Bill Paley would have to face what others at CBS had been forced to accept: retirement.

However much he dreaded the prospect, Paley was not one to retreat to a life of quiet solitude and wait for the inevitable. Whatever his title, he wanted to be active, he had to be active. Given that goal, he had to have a good relationship with Wyman, and the new president made it easy. "Tom Wyman is not unskilled in the art of getting along with people," said Kidder Meade, "and he and Paley had a big honeymoon." The two men spoke with each other frequently during the day in meetings, on the telephone, and at lunch. But it was not just a professional relationship. In contrast to previous presidents, Wyman spent considerable time with Paley after business hours. Wyman and his wife Betsy often dined with Paley at his Fifth Avenue apartment, accompanied him to restaurants, and even vacationed with him in Japan. Bill Paley was very happy, and for those who asked, he would tell them that the company had finally selected an appropriate successor.

Part of Paley's pleasure was the leeway Wyman afforded him in programming matters. Although he was not as intimately involved in the process as in earlier years, Paley still played a central role in shaping the network's television schedule. He was there to review the pilots, to ask questions, and to make suggestions. In most cases, Paley was simply reacting to the groundwork laid by Jankowski's staff. But on some occasions the chairman was prepared to take the initiative.

Norman Lear remembered the occasion when Paley asked to see him in New York. "All in the Family" had been terminated, with most of the principal actors moving on to different challenges. The major exception was Carroll O'Connor, Archie himself, who continued on in a new series called "Archie Bunker's Place," a spin-off which had Archie running a tavern and reacting to controversy without the presence of Edith, Gloria, or Michael. Although not nearly as successful as "All in the Family," the show was nonetheless a mainstay of the CBS schedule. Paley watched the entire schedule, and he wanted to tell Lear about his reaction to "Archie Bunker's Place." "He was very disturbed about the quality of the show," said Lear, "and he explained that one of the principal actors was 'over-performing'—engaging in exaggerated movements that undermined the character's credibility." To illustrate his point, Paley walked from behind his French gaming table to show Lear what he meant. The producer was taken aback by the performance of Paley himself. "He was very funny," said Lear, "but it was also clear to me that he had really studied the matter closely, and he was dead right in his criticism. So I went back to Alan Horn, who was running the show, and they made the change."

Paley had other proposals to improve programming, and not all of them were confined to broadcasting. He was captivated by the opportunities offered by cable. The FCC had recently eliminated regulations that had hampered cable's growth, a move that coincided with and even helped to advance the expanding interest in cable service. Almost one fourth of the nation's homes were now wired for cable, and communications analysts were forecasting an imminent future where virtually all major population centers would be wired and where subscribers would pay $20, $30 and even more each month to take advantage of specialized programming on systems with 36 channels or more.

Paley wanted to be a man of the future. Throughout the 1960s CBS, led by Peter Goldmark, had experimented with Electronic Video Recording, a device that would have enabled people to use their television sets to watch prerecorded programs. Paley liked the idea of being a pioneer for the new technology, but he was wary of the financial commitment and the competition that video cassette programs could pose to CBS network programs. He listened, he watched, and he vacillated. He was not sure that the public was prepared to accept EVR, and he was not about to repeat the same mistake he had made in pushing for color television and buying Hytron. So, after an expenditure of millions of dollars, he decided against the venture.

None of those doubts seemed to plague Paley when it came to cable. He believed it would soon be reaching most of America's homes, and he wanted CBS to be there. He did not want his network to miss this parade, and he pushed to have the company develop a cable component. In early 1980 he went with Wyman to meet with FCC chairman Charles Ferris to urge that the commission lift its ban on network ownership of cable systems. And when a reporter asked whether he was truly committed to new video technologies, Paley responded, "Nobody around here has been pushing harder than I have. I've been very sensitive to the whole field and the need to get going and the need to get manpower in place for us to do it properly."

The proposal eventually accepted by management was to develop a special cable channel that would offer high-quality cultural programming—ballet, opera, symphony, drama—a concept that held special appeal for Paley. He had always viewed himself as a man of culture and refined taste. For decades he had bridled at the suggestion that commercial television catered to the lowest common demoninator. Now his network could offer the best of entertainment, the kind of programming "elitists" said was far too rare on commercial television. And, more than that, the programming would be free to cable subscribers. CBS was convinced that demand for its channel would be sufficiently high to be supported entirely by advertisers, and the company announced it would spend $100 million over three years to bring its new channel to the nation's homes.

The expectations were wonderful, but the realities were less assuring. As the country entered a recession in the early 1980s, demand for cable services leveled off and in some cases decreased. Much of the hope for the new technology was soured by cable operators who could not deliver what they had promised and by a realization that many people were not yet prepared to pay $20 or $30 a month for programming. Although it would be free to subscribers, the CBS channel's survival depended on a sufficiently large subscriber base to attract advertisers. By 1982 reports circulated within the industry that CBS might abandon its proposed channel, and much of the indecision could be laid at the chairman's office. "CBS had invested millions, and faced the prospect of losing more," said one executive. "The future was very uncertain, and Paley couldn't make up his mind." There were some, like Norman Lear, who urged Paley to proceed with the project, but neither Paley nor Wyman could ignore the huge financial losses that the company had already incurred or the likelihood that they would continue. In the fall of 1982, after an expenditure of almost $30 million, CBS announced that it was cancelling plans for a cultural cable channel.

The decision did not come easily to Paley. He had invested so much hope in the enterprise, and he no doubt viewed it as an appropriate cap to a productive career. He almost never discussed business matters at social gatherings, but Arthur Schlesinger, Jr., a social companion for almost thirty years, remembered one exception at a dinner that was held at Paley's Fifth Avenue apartment the day CBS announced that there would be no cultural cable channel. "It's the greatest disappointment of my life," Paley told Schlesinger. "I had really hoped to make something of it."

Other disappointments continued to weigh on Paley's mind as well. He would never fully recover from Babe's death, and years afterward friends would comment that Paley still felt her loss and could not be entirely reconciled to a life without her. There were outward signs of Babe's absence. Kiluna was sold to developers. It could not be the same without Babe, and beyond that, the estate was now more than anything Paley wanted for himself. He bought a home in Southampton, but friends noticed that he did not seem to have the same enthusiasm for Long Island's eastern shore as he had had for its north shore.

Still, Bill Paley remained a man committed to overcoming despair and to maximizing the fun and laughter and good times. And to Paley, that required interaction with people. He rarely attended concerts, plays, or other public events and, despite the huge screens at his homes in Southampton and Nassau, he rarely watched movies. (In earlier days the children used to take bets on how long it would take Paley to walk out of a movie being shown in the projection room at Kiluna.) He preferred the wit and gaiety of good conversation, and most of his social life consisted of dinners with a highly select group of friends, who included Jacqueline Onassis, Oscar de la Renta, Henry Kissinger, Rex Harrison, and other luminaries from the worlds of theater, politics, and fashion. His interest in travel also remained undiminished. There would be long retreats in the Bahamas and trips to Paris, Marrakesh, London, and other distant cities. And always there would be female companionship. "He likes women," said Irene Selznick, who remained a close friend. "It doesn't have to be sexual. . . . It doesn't have to be artistic. It doesn't have to be professional, personal, social. He likes them." And friends noticed that he had no trouble finding attractive women to spend time with him. "Despite his age," said one friend, "he's still a handsome man."

None of this social activity included his sister Blanche, who was now in her seventies and living quietly in an ocean-front home in Palm Beach. Paley's relationship with his sister over the years had remained largely unchanged. Polite but distant. Much of Paley's contact with his sister had reflected his genuine affection for her husband, Leon Levy, who remained a CBS director until his last years. But Levy was now dead, and that had an obvious impact on Paley's desire to see his sister. "Leon was the salt of the earth, as far as Paley was concerned," said one colleague, "and he acted as a buffer with Blanche, who always seemed jealous of Bill's success with CBS. When Leon died, it changed everything."

Although Paley could enjoy a social life without his sister, he could not be content with a retirement that offered nothing but a social calendar. He knew that about himself, and, if he had any doubt about an appropriate course, he had his father as an example. Bill Paley would make his "retirement" a productive one, pursuing ventures that had been foreclosed to him because of his involvement with CBS. And even before he stepped down as chairman, he had set his sights on one opportunity that seemed well suited to his interests and lifestyle.

It concerned *The International Herald Tribune,* the presitgious daily newspaper published in Paris and read by foreign-based Americans and Europeans interested in current events in the United States. The *International Herald* stock was divided in equal thirds among three partners— *The New York Times, The Washington Post,* and Whitcom Investment Company, the firm founded by Paley's brother-in-law Jock Whitney. The years had finally caught up with Whitney. He had suffered a major heart attack in 1976. His convalescence was slow, and his activities remained severely restricted. There were further setbacks, and by February 1982 he was gone. In the meantime, Paley's friend Walter Thayer, who had been recruited by Whitney in the early 1960s, had taken over the management of Whitcom, and in the late spring he suggested that Paley become publisher of the *International Herald* after his retirement from CBS. Whitcom would sell Paley its one third interest in the paper, thus making him eligible for the position. Paley loved the idea, and he jumped on it.

Both Thayer and Paley were confident that the *Times* and the *Post* would be eager to have the CBS chairman as the *International Herald*'s publisher. *Post* publisher Katharine Graham and *Times* publisher Punch Sulzberger were Paley friends and people who would surely welcome his contribution. Thayer communicated the proposal to Graham and Sulzberger, and Paley, confident that the responses would be affirmative, rushed to Paris to lay the groundwork. He took up residence at the Ritz and went to the *Herald*'s offices to advise a surprised staff that he would soon be the publisher.

All these plans and expectations were soon dashed by Graham and Sulzberger. They decided that they did not want their friend Bill Paley as the publisher. A complex of personal and business factors shaped their perspectives. However zestful he might feel, the fact remained that Paley was eighty-one years old and could not possibly have the energy that would be required for the job. And more than that, as a friend with firm views about management, Paley would be more difficult to control than an employee with no personal relationship to the owners. And lastly, if *Herald* stock was to be offered for sale, there were sound financial reasons for the *Times* and the *Post* to increase their respective stakes. It was a difficult situation for both Graham and Sulzberger—neither wanted to hurt their friend of many years—but business realities could not be ignored.

A meeting was convened at a fashionable home on Long Island's eastern shore, and Graham and Sulzberger informed Paley of their decision. They also told him that they would not even let him buy Whitcom's interest in the *Herald.* Under the prevailing agreement, the *Post* and the *Times* had a right of first refusal, which entitled them to buy Whitcom's stock before it could be sold to a third party. Graham and Sulzberger informed Paley that they would exercise that right.

Paley was shocked by Graham and Sulzberger's revelations. He simply could not believe that these two people, friends of his, would shut him out. People did not say no to Bill Paley very often, and he had not expected a negative answer on a matter that had become very important to him. "Bill really wanted to do that," said Thayer. "He thought he could add something, and he was very upset when the *Times* and the *Post* turned him down. He was very disturbed about it."

Paley did eventually become a general partner in Whitcom (which held onto its *Herald* stock) as well as a member of the *Herald*'s board of directors. But the decision by Graham and Sulzberger precluded him from devoting the amount of time to the enterprise he had originally anticipated. Still, Paley would not dwell on what might have been. He had numerous interests, ample funds, and he would pursue other ventures. And to assist him in those activities, Paley hired Raymond K. Price in January 1983.

A man of with high intelligence, good political instincts, and substantial experience in large organizations, Price, fifty-two, was ideally suited to advise Paley. His first professional career had been as a journalist, working for *Life* and *Collier's* magazines and then joining the *New York Herald Tribune* in 1957 as an assistant to its new owner, Jock Whitney. Price was soon working closely with Whitney, as well as with Thayer, who was also involved with the paper's management. Eventually, Price became editor of the editorial page, a position that expanded both his influence and his contacts. It was during that period that Price had his first interaction with Bill Paley. In 1967 he arranged a dinner at Le Cirque, one of New York's finer restaurants, for himself, Whitney, Thayer, Paley, and Richard Nixon, who was then beginning his campaign for the presidency. The dinner at Le Cirque was later followed by another at Paley's apartment and then a meeting at the offices of one of Jock Whitney's other companies.

Although the dinners and meetings did not benefit Paley's relationship with Nixon to any great extent, they did mark a turning point for Price. He joined Nixon's campaign staff and followed him to the White House as his chief speechwriter. The Watergate scandals did not affect Price's reputation or his loyalty to Nixon, and when the former president departed for San Clemente in August 1974, Price followed him to assist in the writing of Nixon's memoirs and his subsequent books.

Paley contacted Price in the fall of 1982 to inquire whether he might be interested in working for him. Paley explained that he would be stepping down as CBS chairman at the annual stockholders meeting the following spring, that he would be engaged in a variety of activities, and that he needed someone to assist him on whatever might come up. Price was intrigued by the offer. Although he had known Paley only casually, the job would offer a new environment and a new boss—important considerations after having spent thirteen years working for Richard Nixon.

Price began his new job on January 1, 1983, and he was not disappointed. He liked Paley. He was dynamic, curious, entertaining, full of life. "I only wish I had known him twenty years earlier," said Price. Their working relationship was, from the start, a harmonious one. And few matters received as much attention or required more collaboration in those first days of 1983 than the speech Paley would give to the stockholders on the day he stepped down as chairman.

It would not be easy. To begin with, however much he may have believed his earlier statements to Backe and Wyman that he would be retiring soon, Bill Paley did not want to retire. The date for his "departure" was not something that he had chosen of his own free will. It had been pressed upon him by the board. After Wyman had been at CBS for a year or so, the directors went to him and said, business is great, you're great, and shouldn't we get on with this transition and make you chairman? At first Wyman deflected the suggestion, saying that his relationship with Paley was good and that there was no need to foster the bad feelings that would surely be generated when Paley was told of the board's decision. After all, the new CBS president told the directors, You spend most of your days in offices across town; I have to see him every day. But eventually Wyman agreed that the time was ripe and that there was no sense in delaying the decision.

The board had not relished the prospect of confronting Paley with the ultimatum. A delegation had been dispatched to see the chairman, and it was headed by the director who knew Paley best: Benno Schmidt, Sr. He was president of J.H. Whitney Company, Inc., one of Jock Whitney's many enterprises, and he had been a social and professional colleague of Paley's for many years. Still, Paley did not take the news well. "He went on a rampage," said one former CBS executive, "calling the board sons of bitches and threatening to throw them into the street. The atmosphere on the thirty-fifth floor was very bad. Paley couldn't imagine himself without CBS and vice versa."

Paley gave no hint to Price of any hostility toward the board or the retirement that they planned to impose on him. Instead, Paley focused on what he should say in his final remarks as chairman. The speech would, in some special way, have to capture the pride, satisfaction, and emotion that Paley felt. CBS was his company, it had been his life. But more than that, CBS represented, in his eyes at least, all that was good in broadcasting. The speech could reflect on that, but there could be no recriminations or regrets about his forced retirement. Bill Paley would go out like a champion.

At 2 P.M. on Wednesday, April 20, 1983, Paley, dressed in a dark blue suit, white shirt, and dark tie, called the stockholders' meeting to order in the large studio of the CBS television station in St. Louis. He then began to read the speech that Price had drafted. Paley had never been an eloquent speaker, and this speech was the most difficult he had ever had to make. He did not deviate from the text and showed none of the charm that came so easily to him. It was a moment he thought he would never have to face.

Paley began with a review of broadcasting history, saying that television and radio had revolutionized the communications industry, that he was proud of the role that CBS had played in that revolution, and that he was "certain" that, under Tom Wyman, CBS would "maintain and deserve that reputation for quality that has become as much a company trademark as the CBS eye." His voice then began to crack as he spoke of himself. "It's difficult to tell you what a jumble of emotions I feel at this time. The memories crowd in. The battles. The victories. The disappointments. The triumphs. And through it all," he observed, "the people. In those early days, Ed Klauber. Paul Kesten. Through so much of it, Frank Stanton. And the stars. Jack Benny, Bing Crosby, Lucille Ball, so many more.

Those who made CBS News the standard of excellence for an industry and a generation: Ed Murrow. Eric Sevareid. Walter Cronkite. And there were so many others. Scores, hundreds, thousands, who worked at all levels and in all departments at CBS, and who together gave CBS its heart and its mind and its muscle." It was, to be sure, something to be proud of, and for those remaining in power, something to look forward to. "And now," Paley concluded, "I'd like to salute Tom Wyman and all of his team, and to wish for them as much fun, as much zest, as much enthusiasm, and as much deep-down satisfaction, as I've had from these fifty-four wonderful years at CBS."

As Paley concluded, the hundreds in attendance rose to give him a loud, standing ovation, one that brought a broad smile to the face of the departing chairman. It was the only event marking his retirement. He did not want any celebrations to commemorate the occasion—perhaps because, for all his stature and accomplishment, there was still something about him that was shy, that recoiled from public displays of any kind of emotion. Or perhaps it was because, despite his willingness to yield the chairmanship of the board, Bill Paley did not believe, in his heart, that he would really be leaving CBS, never to exercise leadership over it again. As his friend Lew Wasserman told a reporter shortly afterward, "As long as Bill Paley has breath in his body, he will *be* CBS."

In the meantime, other activities began to crowd his calendar. He had become chairman of the Museum of Modern Art, and he continued to devote considerable energy to the Museum of Broadcasting, which he had founded in 1976 and which was located in a building next to the park on Fifty-third Street that had been dedicated to his father. He also branched out into new areas. He was, at bottom, a man filled with curiosity about any number of subjects, and now was an opportune time to pursue some of them. And to share many of these pursuits, he decided to join forces with Frank Stanton.

The two men had rarely seen each other in the years immediately after Stanton had retired. It had been an awkward period for both of them, and there was no one who could bring them together. But the years had washed away much of the bad feeling that had grown between them, and they began to have lunch together, to see each other at different board meetings, and then to invest in projects—like genetic engineering and the development of artificial intelligence (computers that simulate the reasoning process)—that seemed to capture the wonder of a new technological age. It was exciting activity, and when Norman Lear once asked Paley what kept him so youthful, the retired chairman had a quick answer: "All these new interests."

He also began to consider the prospect of writing a new autobiography.

"Paley was never satisfied with his 1979 book," said Ray Price. "He was still chairman of CBS when he wrote it, and he felt unable to be completely candid about events and people." Of course, there had been no lack of candor in the book when it came to describing his feelings about David Halberstam, Daniel Schorr, Peter Goldmark, and others who had publicly criticized him. But there had been a certain inhibition about other people. "He was friends with so many people," Kidder Meade observed, "and even if they were dead, their wives and children might still be around. Readers kept looking for something that wasn't there and felt cheated."

He did receive numerous inquiries from authors who were preparing biographies of him, and at least one of the inquiries received serious consideration. But Paley had a basic fear about entrusting to someone else the task of chronicling his life. They might get the facts right, but he worried that they might not convey the sense of fun and laughter that has been the mainstay of his life. "You must remember," said Price, who discussed the subject with Paley many times, "that the joy of living well is important to him. Joy is an essential word in understanding him. And it's one of the reasons why he isn't going to die any time soon. The zest for life keeps him going." And beyond the spirit of the book was the matter of control. Paley could never be sure that someone else would tell the story as he wanted it to be told. He had taken risks with other writers—David Halberstam the most prominent of them—and had never been satisfied with the results. He was taking no more chances.

By early 1986 he had recruited David Harris, a young writer, to assist him in preparing the new book. Harris was directed to interview colleagues, friends, and associates, but Paley took more than a passing interest in the project. He began dictating hours and hours of recollections into a tape recorder, boasting to Arthur Schlesinger at one point that he had more than forty hours of tapes already completed. He also met frequently with Harris, spending time with the writer in New York City, Southampton, and the Bahamas so that Harris could, as Paley had once told Martin Mayer, get a sense of his varied lifestyle.

In putting his new book together, Paley looked back upon the past with considerable satisfaction. He felt he had accomplished much, and there was no shortage of awards to confirm that view. For years he had been receiving honors from diverse sources, including induction as one of the charter members of the Television Hall of Fame in 1984 (with James Arness coming out of seclusion, at Paley's request, to make the introduction to a television audience of millions). Paley could also feel more secure about the relationships with his children. Differences of viewpoint remained, the past had not been forgotten. But as he advanced in years, the children had rallied around the patriarch, offering support and compan-

ionship. Bill, for example, now saw his father frequently. When Paley
came to Washington for business, Bill would invariably join him for lunch
(and Paley would invariably ask his son to return to New York for a short
visit). Kate had also reconciled with her father. She would see him in New
York, spend weekends with him at Southampton, and—having become
deeply involved in Christian theology—use these occasions to urge her
father to attend church (a suggestion which Paley appreciated but felt
unable to accept).

However satisfied he might feel with his past and present life, only one
thing really mattered to Bill Paley: CBS. It had been a part of his life
longer than any wife or offspring, and he viewed it through the prism of
the most caring parent. He might not be chairman any longer, but he kept
a close watch on its fate, hoping, perhaps believing, that he could somehow take over if Wyman should ever falter. On the day of his retirement,
a reporter asked Paley where he wanted to channel his energies. The
answer was quick and firm. "I would go right back into broadcasting,"
he said. "It's in my blood. I love broadcasting. It's important. There are
great ups and downs. That is the kind of life some people like, and I like
it very much." The reporter did not have to ask where Paley would like
to pursue those ups and downs.

In the first days of his retirement, the possibility of Paley's return to
power did not appear that unrealistic. To begin with, he remained CBS's
single largest stockholder, with 1,930,767 shares, or 6.51 percent of the
total issued, representing a market value of approximately $135 million.
Moreover, the board had not completely pushed him out the door. He still
had his two-thousand-square-foot office on the thirty-fifth floor, and although Arthur Judson was the one who had founded the company in
1927, the board had conferred upon him the title of Founder Chairman.
The title did not give him any additional prerogatives, but it was at least
a recognition of his special status. The board also gave him a long-term
consulting contract with an annual fee of $200,000 (half his base salary
as chairman) and named him chairman of its executive committee. While
that committee never met, Paley did remain active in board deliberations.
He attended the meetings and hosted a lunch in his private dining room
when the board gathered on the second Wednesday of every month. From
all appearances, then, it seemed that Bill Paley's voice would still command respect in the decision-making process.

Other developments, however, soon conveyed a different message.
Wyman did not consult Paley as frequently, and some of the new chairman's decisions were disturbing to his predecessor. The company's jets,
long a symbol of Paley's status, were sold; the company no longer distributed garment bags, cuff-links and other gifts to those who attended

affiliate meetings; and there was even talk that Wyman was prepared to eliminate some of the executive dining rooms and reduce the size of the kitchen staff—proposals that Paley found incomprehensible. But nothing was more crushing to the former chairman than Wyman's decision to exclude him from some of the programming meetings.

From any practical perspective, there was ample justification for the decision. However broad his experience, and however sure his touch, Paley did not have the energy to keep up with the process. He rarely took time to review the marketing and financial studies that were distributed prior to the programming meetings. After a while, the lack of preparation became evident. Those attending programming meetings began to notice that the former chairman would ask the same questions over and over again, making points about early radio or television that were irrelevant to the discussion at hand. People began to roll their eyes when Paley spoke, and many were embarrassed by the situation. "Choosing television programs is a complicated process," said one CBS executive who attended those meetings. "If you're a Rhodes Scholar and you come in to watch the pilots cold, you're tragically behind. If you're eighty-three and you're not a Rhodes Scholar, it's pitiful."

At first Wyman and the other executives were tolerant of Paley's disruptions. He was an integral part of CBS history, his accomplishments were considerable, and no one wanted to offend him. But patience has its limits. "The eye-rolling became pretty bad," said one executive, and Wyman decided that something had to be done. Too much time was being taken to accommodate Paley's repeated questions. So Wyman went to Paley's office and suggested, as diplomatically as he could, that Paley not attend the first few programming meetings and that he wait until the group was prepared to make its final decisions. Paley recognized the suggestion for what it was, and he bluntly told Wyman that if he couldn't attend all the meetings he wouldn't attend any of them.

Retirement had become a humiliating experience for Paley. He was watching the trappings of his empire discarded, his throne being dismantled, his position undermined. Tom Wyman was in control now. Bill Paley, however glorious his past, had become little more than an observer.

Paley could complain about these developments to friends and associates, but the CBS board was now loyal to the new chairman. Some of the board members were close to Paley—Roswell Gilpatric, Marietta Tree, and Walter Cronkite—but the other nine members of the board (aside from Wyman himself) were Wyman's friends and supporters. He had the votes and, after his first full year of leadership, the performance to justify them. In 1984 CBS earned a record $212 million on $4.6 billion in revenues—figures that undercut any hope Paley may have had of being restored to a position of power within the company. But fate was not kind to Tom Wyman in 1985, and it all began with Senator Jesse Helms.

In January the conservative legislator announced his support of a campaign by Fairness in Media, a conservative media watchdog, urging fellow conservatives to buy CBS stock so that they could take over the network and become "Dan Rather's boss." Despite studies showing otherwise, Helms and his associates maintained that "The CBS Evening News" had a liberal bias and that the only way to eliminate it was to change the ownership. Although Wall Street gave little credence to the group's likelihood of success, the campaign generated considerable media attention and did require CBS to file a lawsuit against the group to insure that its campaign was not successful.

The media attention increased when it was disclosed in February that arbitrageur Ivan Boesky and a group of investors had acquired 8.7 percent of CBS's stock, thus making the group the company's largest stockholders and raising the question whether they could succeed in a hostile takeover. The debate intensified in April when Ted Turner, sometime America's Cup skipper and owner of superstation WTBS, announced a $5.4 billion offer to purchase 67 percent of CBS stock—the quantity required under the corporation's by-laws to take over the company. While the price of CBS stock was hovering around $90 per share, Turner said his proposal would give each stockholder notes and bonds worth approximately $175 per share. Most Wall Street analysts scoffed at Turner's proposal, observing that his offer included no cash and relied instead on what had become known as "junk bonds," securities that were based more on hope than on assets.

At first, CBS management gave little credence to Turner's offer. As board member and former FCC chairman Newton Minow later commented, he considered Turner's offer "dead on arrival." But Turner's much-publicized pursuit raised questions whether CBS stock was grossly undervalued and whether some of the company's thousands of stockholders might be tempted to take a chance with Turner. Wyman and his senior staff could not risk that possibility. They convened a "war council" to explore the measures that should be taken in court, at the FCC, on Wall Street, and with the Securities and Exchange Commission to prevent Turner from even being allowed to tender his offer to stockholders.

Paley was extremely disturbed by the prospect of someone taking over CBS against its will. "He was very upset," said Price. "He didn't want to have his child kidnapped." He was particularly unsettled by the prospect that the kidnapper might be Ted Turner, a flamboyant figure who proposed to finance his public offer by selling off all of CBS's assets except its television operations (if and when he should ever gain control). To

Paley, the proposal was unthinkable. He had spent almost twenty years in pursuit of diversification, and Turner's plan would undo all he had accomplished.

As always, Paley was full of ideas and proposals. He even suggested that perhaps the company should be taken private so that the public would be unable to decide CBS's fate. In the meantime, he felt compelled to make a statement to the public. In his mind, he was the company's founder, the person who had groomed the corporate infant into a giant $5 billion conglomerate. The public, especially those people who were shareholders, would want to know what he thought. *The New York Times* was contacted and asked to send a reporter to Paley's office on the thirty-fifth floor so that he could communicate his views through the "paper of record."

On April 30, 1985, *Times* reporter Sally Bedell Smith was ushered into the chairman's office. Amid priceless art and memorabilia of CBS history, Paley read his statement. "CBS is strong; CBS is healthy," he stated. "But that strength and health are the products of more than a half a century of careful, concerned nurturing by a great many very dedicated people. To throw this away," he continued, "would be a tragedy. To risk its loss would be to trifle recklessly with the company's future and with the public interest." Paley expressed his support for Wyman's management and the need to maintain a diversified company. CBS is "soundly structured," he said, "not just for the present but for the long-term future." Paley did not mention Turner by name, and when Smith asked what he thought of the Atlanta-based broadcaster, Paley would say only, "If you read between the lines you can tell what I think."

Despite Paley's public opposition and management's low opinion of Turner, the offer moved forward at the SEC and the FCC (where prior commission approval was required). Wyman and his war council decided that dramatic action had to be taken to end the threat of a takeover. On July 3, 1985, CBS announced that it was borrowing $954 million to buy back one-fifth of the company's stock at $150 a share, or $32 more than the current stock price. Since it was based on cash and standard bonds, the CBS offer was immediately deemed to be better than Turner's. Stockholders flooded CBS with commitments, and by the end of July, CBS and its supporters held enough stock to prevent Turner from ever reaching the magic figure of 67 percent. Turner's threat, for all practical purposes, was eliminated.

Although the company's independence had been preserved, the cost was high. In fighting Turner and other takeover threats, CBS had been forced to increase its debt from $370 million to $1 billion, while the equity in the company dwindled from $1.5 billion to $519 million. To recover from this dramatic financial shift, Wyman was forced to announce cost reductions in operations and the sale of certain assets, including the network's St. Louis television station. The prosperity of the previous year had become a distant dream.

The dream became a nightmare as other transactions turned sour. And they marked the beginning of Paley's assault to recapture control of CBS—the company that, in his mind, had always been his. In the spring of 1985 CBS had paid $362.5 million to buy twelve consumer magazines owned by Ziff-Davis Publishing Company. Within weeks it was learned that the CBS offer was many millions more than the bid of the nearest competitor, and then CBS claimed that Ziff-Davis had made misrepresentations concerning the magazines' profits, a claim that was followed by CBS's lawsuit against the seller. However justified, CBS's complaints did little to enhance Tom Wyman's image on Wall Street. "To make an acquisition of that magnitude without doing your homework enough to know the proper price is inexcusable," one financial analyst told *The New York Times,* "and then to lay the blame on Ziff is very sloppy."

Criticism in a newspaper, even a national newspaper like the *Times,* was the least of Wyman's problems. Paley was resurfacing. He had had a lunch with media baron Rupert Murdoch, who had purchased some of Ziff-Davis's other magazines. Murdoch bluntly told Paley that Wyman had handled the Ziff-Davis deal badly, that he had overpaid by millions, and that he had poorly served CBS interests. "Murdoch kept rubbing it in," said one of Paley's close associates, "and it gave Paley something to talk about. He desperately wanted back into the company, and now he had an angle."

Unfortunately for Wyman, the Ziff-Davis transaction appeared to be only the tip of the iceberg. Contrary to Paley's statement to *The New York Times*, the company's structure did not appear sound. CBS's non-broadcast ventures had turned sour—the Theatrical Film Division had lost $40 million, the company's $57 million purchase of the Ideal Toy Company had turned into a losing proposition, and TriStar Pictures, the joint movie venture with Home Box Office and Columbia Pictures, had to be sold because of conflicting commitments among the participants. Although many of these activities had been initiated under Paley's regime, and although the retired chairman had enthusiastically endorsed some of them when they had been initiated, the failures were now Wyman's. By the end of October 1985 *The New York Times* reported that Wyman was receiving mixed reviews on Wall Street, that "the company seems in disarray," and that "a number of Wall Street analysts are skeptical that Mr. Wyman's demonstrated skills can solve those problems."

Paley had similar concerns. He had read the reports which Wall Street analysts had issued on CBS, and their critical comments filled him with anger and frustration. ("How do those guys get in the building?" he demanded of one CBS executive after reviewing a particularly scathing report.) But for Paley it was not simply a question of money and finances and corporate structure. In his eyes, programming remained the key, and on that score he was especially troubled by the plight of the News Division. The need to reduce costs had led to the firing or forced retirement of approximately one hundred staff members, almost ten percent of the entire division workforce. And of those who remained, many complained that Executive Vice President Van Gordon Sauter, who had supervisory responsibility over the News Division, did not appreciate the CBS tradition which, it was said, placed public responsibility above corporate profits. To rectify the situation, "60 Minutes" producer Don Hewitt devised a scheme to have the corporation sell CBS News to a group composed of himself, Dan Rather, Mike Wallace, Morley Safer and Diane Sawyer. Paley later told his friend that the proposal was a fool's errand, and, to no one's surprise, Broadcast Group President Gene Jankowski rejected the offer when Hewitt made it over lunch one day.

Still, morale within the News Division remained extremely low. "The CBS Morning News" was consistently scoring behind ABC's "Good Morning America" and NBC's "Today" show, Rather's ratings started to dip, and the number of documentaries had been drastically reduced. CBS had, with Paley's support, always emphasized hard news. Now the focus started to change. "The line between entertainment and news was steadily blurred," CBS correspondent Bill Moyers later observed. "Our center of gravity shifted from the standards and practices of the news business to show business. In meeting after meeting, [ABC's] 'Entertainment Tonight' was touted as the model—breezy, entertaining, undemanding. . . . Pretty soon, tax policy had to compete with stories about three-legged sheep," said Moyers, "and the three-legged sheep won."

It was all very distressing to Paley, who started to complain more frequently to friends and associates and even to board members that Wyman did not understand the CBS news tradition, that his financial management had proven to be unwise, and that he did not have the personality or skills to be the chairman of a business that ultimately depended on creativity. Paley's complaints gained credibility when CBS lost its number one position in entertainment programming to NBC—a development which also, in Paley's eyes at least, cast doubt on the wisdom of his exclusion from the program selection process.

The overwhelming majority of the board nonetheless remained committed to Wyman. Unlike Paley, they did not see better programming as the cure to the company's complicated problems. ("Paley thought better programming was the answer to everything," said one CBS executive who was close to the board. "It's like a baseball pitcher with a good fastball who always wants to throw his fastball, regardless of the situation.") And unlike Paley, most board members believed that Wyman had performed admirably under trying circumstances. "He had to keep the troops' spirits up, he had to keep the wolves at bay, he had a board to deal with, he had a founder to keep happy, [and] he had to deal with wild swings in the stock market," said board member and Ford Foundation President Franklin A. Thomas. "I think," Thomas added, "Tom has done an extraordinarily good job." Thomas's sentiments were echoed by the full board when it voted in April 1986 to give Wyman the biggest bonus ($293,859) he had ever received in his six years with the company.

Paley found the board's position incomprehensible. He kept telling board members that Wyman was ruining the company, that something had to be done, but the board seemed deaf to his pleas. Even one member who was sympathetic to Paley was not prepared to take his complaints at face value. "I thought it was only natural," said this board member. "After all, I knew that he wanted to be where Wyman was." Paley was plagued by frustration. He repeatedly asked his personal attorney, Arthur L. Liman, why won't they believe me? And Liman repeatedly replied, because you fired all those other presidents. Roswell Gilpatric, who had been on the board since 1970, supported Liman's explanation. "There have been five presidents of CBS since I've been on the board," said Gilpatric. "It keeps you on the alert because it's always Paley versus the president."

Despite his many complaints, Paley remained on cordial terms with Wyman. The two men still spoke with each other frequently and still had lunch at least once every few weeks. Indeed, in an ironic twist of fate, Wyman saved Paley's life at one of their lunches and thus preserved the octogenarian's ability to carry on his fight for control. The two men were dining on pork chops in Paley's dining room one May afternoon when Wyman suddenly noticed that Paley's face was redder than usual. In an instant Wyman knew that a piece of food had lodged in Paley's throat and that emergency measures would have to be taken immediately. Paley remained calm, however. He stood up and waved Wyman over to a corner of the dining room. Wyman then stood behind Paley and put his arms around the former chairman's considerable girth in an attempt to apply the Heimlich Maneuver. He gave Paley two considerable blows to the chest, and on the second effort a huge piece of pork chop came sailing out of Paley's mouth in a perfect arch. The two men then resumed their lunch as though nothing had happened.

However grateful he might be to Wyman, Paley was not about to abandon his pursuit of a change in leadership. And by then there was one new board member who was growing increasingly sympathetic to that pursuit: Laurence A. Tisch. A balding man who stood five feet eight inches, with the slight paunch of middle age, Tisch was, at sixty-three, twenty-one years younger than Paley. His rise to fame and fortune was truly spectacular. After graduation from New York University and one semester at Harvard Law School, Tisch made an investment that would, in time, make him one of the wealthiest men in the country. He saw an ad announcing the sale of a resort hotel on the New Jersey shore and persuaded his family to sell the summer camp it owned and take the $20,000 to buy the hotel. Thus began the development of a hotel chain that would give Tisch and his brother Bob the resources to buy a string of rundown movie theatres owned by the Loews Corporation (the company name they retained for their operation), the Lorillard tobacco company, and the CNA insurance company. By 1985 the Tisch brothers' Loews Corporation had $16.1 billion in assets and $589 million in profits, and the brothers themselves could claim a personal worth reported to be $1.7 billion.

A fortune of that size required investment, and Tisch was known as one of the country's smartest investors. He himself managed the company's $13.5 billion portfolio, aided by one of his four sons who is an investment banker (the other three being employees of Loews). He prided himself on being a cautious investor who is always prepared for the worst and unwilling to take risks that could mean exorbitant losses. As one son told reporter Ken Auletta in the spring of 1986, "We're bargain hunters and bottom pickers." At times this strategy had backfired. In 1982, for instance, Tisch decided to stay away from the stock market because of inherent volatility, thus missing the bull market that brought the Dow Jones average to the brink of the 2000 mark. But those were the exceptions. Larry Tisch rarely missed a good investment opportunity.

Investment was not the only consideration, however, when Tisch responded to CBS's offer in July 1985 to buy back its stock at $150 a share. To be sure, Tisch believed that a purchase of CBS stock at that price could mean greater profits for Loews. But Tisch also had a sense of public responsibility, and he was disturbed by CBS's constant battles to preserve its independence against extremists like Jesse Helms and corporate raiders like Ted Turner. CBS was not just any company. It was one of three major television networks, institutions that informed the nation and shaped the political landscape. Such power was not to be treated lightly. Tisch had used his money and influence to benefit other causes—especially New York University and Israel—and he was prepared to do likewise for one of the country's premier news organizations. As NYU President John Brademas explained, the Tisches "have a deep sense—certainly a moral one and maybe a religious one as well—that, if one has wealth, one has an obligation to give." If Tisch used his wealth to buy enough CBS stock, he could prevent Jesse Helms or anyone else from taking over the company.

As he walked off the tennis court at the exclusive Century Club in Westchester County in early 1985, Tisch raised the issue with his friend Jim Wolfensohn, an investment banker who also happened to be a CBS director. "Larry passed on to me," said Wolfensohn, "that if we ever needed help on this public policy issue, he would offer it." Tisch repeated the offer of help after Turner's takeover bid escalated the tension and the costs for CBS. "What I said," Tisch recalled saying, "was, 'Look, fellas, if you're looking for a white knight, consider us a potential.' "

The invitation remained unanswered for months. Wyman's first meeting with Tisch occurred in spring 1985 and involved a short discussion concerning Jewish groups who could be asked to oppose Turner's bid at the FCC. There was no further conversation until Tisch telephoned in July to say that he had just purchased 5 percent of CBS's stock and to reiterate that he had no intention of making a bid for the company. Paley was advised of the purchase and had to wonder what it signified. He did not know Larry Tisch. Indeed, when he first learned of the Loews' stock purchase, Paley confused Tisch with real estate developer Robert Tishman. But after learning Tisch's true identity, Paley did not extend any overtures to the new CBS stockholder—at least not initially. But Tisch kept buying CBS stock, until by the fall he had acquired almost 12 percent of the company, a level that enabled him to surpass Paley (who had raised his percentage to about 8) as the largest single stockholder. At that point the CBS board invited Tisch to become a member, and Paley decided to invite the Loews executive to his Fifth Avenue apartment one afternoon for tea and sponge cake.

The retired CBS chairman was obviously interested in probing Tisch's views on corporate management in general and Tom Wyman in particular. But he would be discreet about it. He would not even ask good friends for assistance. One who could have been helpful was Walter Thayer, who already knew Tisch. But Paley was not one to involve social friends in business situations. "He never discussed it with me," said Thayer, "even though he knows that I know Tisch very well."

From that first meeting Tisch and Paley no doubt recognized that, in some respects, their goals and personalities were very compatible. Like Paley, Tisch does not like open confrontations. "He doesn't get passionate," said one former Loews board member. "He does things gently." Tisch also seemed to share Paley's interest in preserving CBS as an independent company that would not be beholden to any political faction or a larger corporation. And like Paley, Tisch had begun to believe that CBS could benefit from changes. One obvious example was the CBS organization chart. Tisch was startled to see that the company had forty-two presidents and vice presidents, and he pointedly asked at a board meeting whether all those executives didn't bump into each other and create bottlenecks. Tisch operated Loews with a very lean staff and plainly saw the elaborate CBS structure as inefficient.

Of course, most of the CBS organization had been established while Paley was still chairman and could not be a basis for criticizing Wyman. But other aspects of CBS operations were tying the noose around Wyman's corporate neck. Walter Cronkite was becoming more and more vigorous at board meetings in attacking Wyman's leadership of the News Division, and the company's financial performance continued to move in the wrong direction. In 1985 CBS earned only $27 million, which represented almost a 90 percent decline from the previous year. Much of the problem was beyond the control of Wyman or any other corporate officer. The growth of competition in the video marketplace—primarily through cable television—had reduced the television networks' share of the audience from 87 percent in the 1980–81 season to 76 percent in the 1985–86 season. The economy had also proved soft, and, instead of the expected annual increase in revenues, advertising on network television decreased from $8.5 billion in 1984 to $8.3 billion in 1985.

Still, many complained that CBS could weather the economic doldrums better through more efficient management. "It is still fat everywhere," said one Wall Street media analyst. Tisch was certainly becoming more and more inclined to that view, and his opinions were becoming more and more important. He had continued to buy CBS stock, and by the summer of 1986 he represented almost 25 percent of the company's ownership. The board was concerned. Tisch had said that he had no intention of taking control, but could he be trusted? Wyman raised the issue with Tisch and inquired whether the Loews executive would sign a "standstill agreement" committing himself to that position. Tisch refused, saying that he was a man of his word. The response left Wyman's future in doubt. Although Tisch had not openly challenged his leadership, Wyman knew that Tisch's stock ownership, as well as his stature, would make his voice a powerful one at any board meeting to decide the company's fate.

Unfortunately for Wyman, Tisch was becoming more and more disenchanted with the performance of CBS in general and its chairman in particular. Like Paley, he was appalled at the way Wyman had handled the Ziff-Davis negotiations. He was even more concerned about the deterioration in CBS's financial health, and, like Paley, had become convinced that Wyman was ruining the company. New York financier Felix Rohatyn, a good friend of Tisch's, told one board member in the late summer that "Larry is very, very angry." Trouble was in the air.

For those who were skeptical of Tisch's motives, there was evidence that he was laying the groundwork for a change in leadership. He was readily available to the press and to financial analysts to talk about CBS's problems. And in August he candidly told Wyman that he did not think the former food executive was the man for the job. Tisch's refusal to sign the standstill agreement was acquiring more and more significance, and many board members were plainly worried that Tisch would take control and make CBS a subsidiary of Loews.

These concerns made Francis Vincent's overture all the more attractive. He was president of Coca-Cola's entertainment division, and he had a proposal for Tom Wyman. As the two men were having lunch in August, Vincent said that Coke was prepared to buy CBS. Although the details would have to be negotiated, Vincent made it clear that Coke would probably offer about $170 a share for CBS stock—a substantial improvement over the then-current market price of about $130 a share. Wyman left the lunch without giving Vincent a response, saying only that he would discuss it with the board.

For those who supported Tom Wyman and feared Larry Tisch, the timing and substance of the offer could not have been better. With its ownership of Columbia Pictures and its aggressive strategy, Coke had become a major player in the video marketplace. And more than that, Coke had the vast resources and the wholesome image that most board members would seek in any acquiring company. So Wyman made individual appointments to speak with various board members to determine whether the proposal warranted further consideration. Wyman's selection of directors was not happenstance. He made appointments with directors who would probably be sympathetic to Vincent's proposal; and he excluded two directors who were bound to be vigorous in their opposition: Bill Paley and Larry Tisch.

In August and early September, Wyman spoke with eight directors, and all of them were interested in Coke's offer. Although Wyman and those directors represented more than two-thirds of the board membership, they knew that nothing could be decided without formal board action and the concurrence of Paley and Tisch. So the board members urged Wyman to raise the Coke proposal at the board meeting that was planned for September 10. Acceptance of the offer would protect CBS from a hostile takeover and insure CBS's independence. Paley might be persuaded to support the proposal on that basis; and if Tisch had no interest in controlling the company, as he had repeatedly said, he might go along as well.

However reasonable, these hopes were illusory. Paley had no interest in making CBS a subsidiary of any company, no matter what its attributes. For his part, Tisch was not willing to relinquish the influence which he now wielded over CBS's fate. "Tisch was concerned about Wyman," said one CBS director, "and he wanted to take a more active interest in the company." So, while Wyman was gathering support for the Coke proposal, Tisch and Paley began to formulate a strategy to terminate Wyman's employment with CBS.

Shortly before the board's September meeting, Tisch went to see Paley. The former chairman was not entirely comfortable with Tisch's dominant stock ownership in CBS. However strong their mutual interests, Tisch was still a remote figure and certainly beyond Paley's control. But Tisch knew how to push those concerns to the background. Through their own stock positions and the support of friends, he and Paley controlled more than a third of CBS's stock—more than enough to control the company. Together, he and the former chairman could force Tom Wyman's resignation. Together they could restore Paley's influence in the selection of television programs. And together they could fight any takeover attempts and thus insure that CBS remained an independent company. For Paley it was an irresistible offer, and he readily gave his assent to an alliance with the Loews executive. While Wyman had not informed either man of the Coke offer, their alliance foreclosed any chance that the offer would be accepted.

On the afternoon of Sunday, September 7, Marietta Tree went to see her old friend Bill Paley at his Fifth Avenue apartment. Tree had been in Italy in August. She did not know about the Coke offer, but she had heard rumors that Wyman might be replaced and that the issue might even be raised at the board's meeting the following Wednesday. Paley responded to Tree's inquiries with a recitation of rapidly changing developments. "Bill spoke with great emotion," said Tree. The company, he told her, was being torn apart by Wyman, and to prove his point he gave Tree an advance copy of the next day's *Newsweek.* The cover featured a broken CBS "eye" with the headline, "Civil War at CBS: The Struggle for the Soul of a Legendary Network." Paley's voice broke as he described the humiliation to "his company." His company. Others might have the titles, they might even own more stock, but it was always his company.

Paley explained to Tree that the situation would come to a head at the board meeting on Wednesday, that Wyman would be told to resign, that Paley would be named board chairman, and that someone else would be appointed chief executive. The new CEO might be Stanton, Tisch, or perhaps even Broadcast President Gene Jankowski. There was also a possibility that a committee would handle the responsibilities temporarily. But one thing was for sure: Wyman would not be there on the following Thursday.

Later that evening Paley went to a birthday party for a friend. Although he had hopes for a new beginning later that week, he was not his usual upbeat self. "Bill was in a great depression," said Tree, who also attended the party. "He was very morose the entire evening, and Don and Marilyn Hewitt attended to him all night, trying to console him."

The next day Paley was in his office when Wyman came to see him. Wyman obviously wanted to solicit Paley's support for an expected show-down at the board meeting, but the retired chairman made it clear immediately that there was no hope of a change of heart. Wyman explained his view that Larry Tisch was on the verge of taking control of CBS, that Paley could not stop any such takeover by himself, and that the board could take preventive action if Paley was agreeable. Paley was not interested in those kind of preventive measures. Gently but bluntly he told Wyman that other issues had priority in his mind and foremost among them was the need for a change in management. The meeting was cordial, but Wyman left with the knowledge that he would face a powerful adversary when the board convened on Wednesday.

Rumors of an organizational upheaval circulated as the board prepared to gather for its meeting on September 10, 1986. "High anxiety," said *Broadcasting* magazine. "It is clearly not atmosphere as usual," commented one senior CBS executive. "It is clear the atmosphere is a circus." Although both Paley and Tisch refused to talk to the press, many people speculated that they might join forces to demand Wyman's resignation.

The following Tuesday, September 9, the directors convened for dinner at the Ritz Carlton. Everyone attended except for Tisch and Wyman. The absence of the Loews executive was not coincidental. He and Paley had decided that the conversation would be less inhibited without Tisch there; and more than that, it would avoid any suggestion that he was trying to take over the company. Later news stories reported that Wyman had planned the dinner, that he had cancelled it at the last moment (presumably to avoid a showdown before the next day's board meeting), and that the dinner had been resurrected over his objection; in fact, Wyman had not planned the dinner, had not cancelled it, and, contrary to contemporaneous news accounts, probably welcomed the informal discussion—without Tisch present—in the hope that it would lead to unanimous support for the Coke proposal.

It was a buffet dinner—a format that avoided the need for waiters who might overhear conversations that were meant to be private. The atmosphere was somber, the conversation was animated, and the debate lasted far into the night. The ultimate issue was simple: Should Tom Wyman be replaced. Paley spoke first. "The company is going to pot," said the retired chairman. He then recited the particulars of what he saw as Wyman's failures: "a record of unsuccessful acquisitions, inattention to the talent and creative aspects of the business, particularly in the flagship News Division, inability to control overhead costs, [and] failure to anticipate declines in operating earnings. . . ." Paley continued that he had met with Wyman the day before and had told him that he should resign for the good of the company. Paley also made it clear that the advice to Wyman was a command and not a suggestion. As he told the assembled directors, "Larry and I have the votes."

Paley's reference to Tisch was no surprise to anyone. The board had previously designated Roswell Gilpatric, Frank Thomas, and Jim Wolfensohn as a committee to ask Tisch for his views about Wyman, and Tisch had told them candidly that the CBS chairman should be replaced. Not surprisingly, he cited the same reasons now being offered by Paley at the dinner.

The board members asked questions of Paley and each other, and several times Paley left the room with Liman, who was also attending the dinner, to review specific issues that had been raised. The members would break up into small groups, usually leaving Tree and Cronkite to themselves (on the assumption that they were already Paley loyalists). Then, upon Paley's return, the board would reassemble and the discussion would resume.

Some of the board members were now prepared to agree with Paley's assessment. "There were poor executive decisions," said one director, "and after looking at all the figures and the situation, I came to believe that Bill was predominately correct." Of equal significance, many board members—even some of those who had talked with Wyman earlier—were beginning to have doubts about the wisdom of the Coke deal. If it indicated a willingness to consider Coke's offer, the board would be legally obligated to consider offers from other companies as well, and the highest bidder might not be a company as desirable as Coke. As one board member later explained, "It was no simple matter. The issue was whether you wanted to open it up to auction or keep the company independent."

Despite the power block aligned against him, and despite these growing doubts about his performance and his proposals, most of the directors at the dinner wanted to keep Wyman as chairman. They continued to believe that he had been the victim of unfortunate circumstances and that he might yet be able to turn the company around. They were anxious to hear what Wyman would say in his report at the board meeting on the following day. Perhaps he would offer a plan for recovery that would mollify

Paley and Tisch. And perhaps, somehow, some way, discussion of the Coke proposal would inspire new thoughts on how to deal with the problem of hostile takeovers. The dinner broke up shortly before midnight without a vote, and Paley left the Ritz Carlton without knowing whether his open challenge to Wyman's leadership would be the last act of a fading emperor or the first step in his restoration to power.

Wyman began the board meeting on Wednesday morning with a status report on key issues and some proposals to resolve them. Board members sympathetic to Paley were not impressed with the chairman's perform-ance. "He was rambling and vague and unwilling to deal head on with the problems that existed and the decisions that had to be made," said one director. His response to the problems at the News Division were espe-cially disturbing. The board members had already recognized that Wyman was not a "hands on" chairman. Still, some were disappointed that he did not have a specific plan to halt the deterioration in service and morale at the News Division, and one director asked Wyman why he did not make more frequent visits to the News Division (even though the News Division was supposed to operate largely independent of manage-ment and even though Paley had spent virtually no time at the News Division in his last years as chairman). "Tom is an absolutely wonderful guy," said one director sympathetic to Paley, "but he simply didn't under-stand the business. He might be a textbook CEO for a company that makes things, but he didn't understand the news and entertainment business where everyone is a star and everyone has to be paid attention to."

Three hours into his report, Wyman described the inquiry he had received from Coca-Cola. Wyman did not realize that support for the proposal had diminished, literally almost overnight, and he now recom-mended that CBS pursue the inquiry. He explained that the sale of CBS to the multibillion dollar soda company would forever protect CBS from a hostile takeover. And more than that, the marriage of the two companies would give CBS a compatible partner in the expansion of its business in the video marketplace.

Later it would be reported in the press that Wyman had solicited the offer from Coke on his own initiative, that the board was "shocked" by the disclosure of his talks with Coke, and that the disclosure played a significant role in the board's decision to oust Wyman. Citing "well-informed sources," for example, *The Washington Post* said that Wyman had had "secret discussions" with Coke without the board's knowledge, that his willingness to bring the Coke proposal to the board was "a gamble that was to cost him his job," and that, according to one source, " 'Wyman shot himself in the foot.' " Citing "sources close to CBS," *The New York Times* similarly reported that Wyman had "tried to sell CBS to Coca-

Cola" without the board's knowledge, that the proposal left the directors " 'flabbergasted,' " and that the disclosure " 'convinced everyone that Wyman was not the man for the job.' "

Although they helped to make the board's decision to fire Wyman more palatable to Wall Street and the public at large, these reports bore little resemblance to the truth. The only directors who could have been shocked and flabbergasted by the Coke offer were Paley, Tisch, and their known supporters on the board. Almost everyone else—a clear majority—were well aware of the offer, had expressed an interest in it, and had even urged Wyman to bring the proposal to the board meeting for discussion. As one director later observed, "Tom was not nailed by the Coke deal."

None of that mattered, however. Tisch was the first to speak after Wyman had finished his presentation to the board. "I won't sell my shares," he said in a voice that left no room for debate. Paley quickly echoed that sentiment, and the Coke deal was dead. Wyman then left the room so that the board could discuss the future of the company without the inhibition of his presence.

Frank Thomas and Harold Brown began the discussion by asking for assurances from Paley and Tisch that CBS would remain an independent company—one that would not become a subsidiary of Loews or be subject to the direction of Larry Tisch. Not surprisingly, Paley immediately gave his commitment to the principle of CBS remaining independent. Tisch endorsed that principle also, saying that Loews had never intended to assume control, that he had never initiated any effort to replace Wyman, and that he had expressed his views on Wyman's performance only when asked to do so by a committee of the board.

At that point, Paley joined in, repeating the arguments he had made the previous night. "I expressed the view," he later explained, "that Mr. Wyman should resign because he no longer enjoyed the confidence of employees, shareholders, and the public, and could not lead the company in the difficult period ahead." Tisch now openly agreed with the retired chairman, saying that CBS needed new leadership. Marietta Tree and Walter Cronkite added their voices to the chorus of criticism, observing that, after long deliberation, they too had reached the conclusion that Wyman should resign "for the good of the corporation." Paley then made the proposal that reflected the culmination of months of thinking and planning and waiting: Wyman's responsibilities as chief executive officer should be temporarily turned over to a committee of the board that would include Tisch as chairman as well as Paley and several outside directors. Paley added that he should be named as acting board chairman and that a committee should be established to search for Wyman's successor.

The board asked Paley and Tisch to withdraw from the meeting so that they could discuss Paley's proposal freely. Left to themselves, the remaining directors again reiterated their commitment to keeping CBS an independently-owned company. If they could not pursue attractive deals with companies like Coca-Cola, they certainly did not want to become a stepchild of Loews. The board also agreed that Wyman would have to resign. It was no longer a question of whether his performance had been adequate in the past. He could not be effective in the future with the company's two largest shareholders openly opposed to his retention. And besides, if Wyman were asked to resign now, the board could probably give him a better deal than if he were forced to leave after months of turmoil (an observation that proved to be prophetic—Wyman received a settlement package valued at $4.3 million).

The next issue was Wyman's replacement. The board members were opposed to Paley's proposal to vest the chief executive's powers and responsibilities in a committee. That route would create risks of confusion and delay at a time when the company needed a sure hand at the tiller. Much better, they believed, to have a single chief executive officer who could be accountable for CBS's management. And while there was no one who had been screened and accepted as a successor to Tom Wyman, the board knew one person who could ably fill that role on a temporary basis: Larry Tisch. And to help revive CBS's image as a quality company that could regain the glories of the past, the board decided to accept Paley's offer to become acting chairman of the board.

The board's deliberations by now had occupied many hours. Dinner had been brought in, and the directors were emotionally drained. But they were satisfied that they had now settled on a course that would be good for the company, well received by most of the staff, and endorsed by Wall Street. They asked Tisch to rejoin the meeting, and he quickly agreed to accept the temporary assignment as acting chief executive. It was the kind of challenge that he loved.

Henry Schacht and Frank Thomas were soon dispatched by the board to ask Wyman for his resignation and to discuss the settlement of his contract. Tisch and two other board members walked down to Paley's office to advise the retired chairman of the board's conclusions. He could not have been more pleased. His gamble had succeeded. True, the board did not accept his proposal to create a committee (with him on it) to exercise the powers of chief executive. But the basic goals had been achieved. Tom Wyman was out. And Paley himself had been resurrected to a position of power that he had never wanted to leave. He returned to the boardroom and, with great emotion, acknowledged the decision that had brought him back into the company.

Late in the evening, Paley and Tisch, both wearing broad smiles, walked out to meet the assembled press and talk to them about the change in leadership. In his statement, Paley said that he was "delighted" by the board's selection of Tisch as acting chief executive. "Larry has not only proven his extraordinary ability as a businessman and leader in the success of his own company, Loews," said Paley. "But most important he shares the values and principles that have guided the company throughout the period of its growth." Paley did not have to add that he also subscribed to those principles and values.

The news of the dramatic shakeup was well received at CBS and Wall Street. Tisch had made his reputation as an executive who could transform financially-troubled companies into money-making machines. Despite his lack of experience with media companies, most seemed to assume that those talents could be applied to CBS as well. And while Paley would not be exercising the kind of power that he had in earlier years, his presence generated the reactions that the board could have anticipated, especially in the News Division. "To have the man who built the thing in the first place back in charge," said CBS correspondent Mike Wallace, "everyone will welcome that." Morley Safer, another correspondent on "60 Minutes," agreed. "Even if it's only symbolic," he said, "it's a very important symbol."

There was one potential problem in all this euphoria: the FCC. Fairness in Media, the conservative group aligned with Senator Helms, immediately filed a complaint with the commission, saying that there had been a change in control at CBS that, under the Communications Act, required the approval of the FCC. CBS lawyers were prepared to fight the complaint. They did not want the FCC reviewing the board's decision and determining whether it was acceptable. But the issue was a controversial one, and a reporter raised the question with Tisch and Paley at a press conference a few days after Wyman's ouster. What did the two men think of the complaint by Fairness in Media—and how could they dispute the fact that there had been a change in control?

Tisch and Paley were in very relaxed moods, sitting on the edge of the desk in Tisch's new office, their feet dangling over the top. Tisch responded first, saying that CBS shortly would be filing an appropriate application with the FCC to cover the change in control. At that point, the eighty-four-year-old Paley, obviously better versed in these regulatory matters, interrupted to say, No Larry, we won't be filing any applications with the FCC. There had been no change in the board (except for Wyman's departure) and no change in the stockholders; there has been a change only in the officers who manage the company and who serve at the board's pleasure.

Paley reiterated these points in a letter he sent to the FCC a few days later. Although drafted by CBS attorneys, the letter reflected Paley's true sentiments. "For my whole career," the letter said, "I have fought to maintain CBS's independence, and the events of the last few weeks have reaffirmed, rather than undermined, this principle."

In theory, it sounded entirely accurate and reasonable. As a practical matter, however, the board was not about to disregard the firm decision of two stockholders owning one-third of the company. The board members could express their views, they could review the record, but the alternatives were shaped by the knowledge of what Tisch and Paley would accept. "It was simple arithmetic," said one board member. "We were not going to go against Paley and Tisch."

Nonetheless, the FCC issued a decision on October 20, 1986, concluding that there had been no change in control that warranted its review. The agency explained that it had placed particular reliance on the company's "active and independent Board of Directors that has been and remains openly antagonistic to CBS coming under the domination of an outside party."

Whatever the legalities, there was no doubt who was now controlling the day-to-day decisions. For Tisch, the appointment as CBS's chief executive meant more than the protection of a $750 million investment. "This is no longer a financial investment for him," said one friend. "He believes that this is an investment for history, for his children, for financial reasons, and out of a desire to become a corporate statesman." And, as Bill Paley had discovered decades earlier, it was fun as well. "It's been a fascinating experience," Tisch told *Broadcasting* magazine, "in a very interesting business." And like Paley, Tisch said he was committed to spending whatever was necessary to secure the kind of programming that would return CBS to the number one position. "We will stop at nothing to put on better programming," he explained. "We will spend any amount of money for programming, for news, anything that reaches the American public. That is our obligation." Paley would not have said it any differently.

The appointments for Tisch and Paley were supposed to have been only temporary, and a search committee was established to recruit successors to both men. But the committee remained inactive, no candidates were interviewed, and it was only a matter of time before the appointments became permanent. On the evening of January 13, 1987, all the board members (except for Cronkite, who was in Australia covering the America's Cup) gathered in the board room at Black Rock to consider the issue. The board wanted assurances that Tisch would not dismantle the entire empire, that however great the need to cut costs, certain components of the company—including Columbia Records—would be retained. One participant said the meeting became "boisterous" at times, but the result was unaffected. The board's decisions were ratified at its formal meeting on the following morning, and on January 14, 1987, it was announced that Tisch would be chief executive and that the eighty-five-year-old Paley would be the board chairman. "We've taken a good hold of things," the new chairman told the press, but he added that there was still a need to recruit successors for him and Tisch. "I don't think," he explained, "that either of us is prepared to last in these jobs for too long."

In the meantime, he would do what he could to restore CBS to its position of preeminence in network programming. He spent much of the fall and winter analyzing program proposals, talking with producers, and even taking trips to California to review pilots for new programs. Time had changed many things, but not for Bill Paley. He was back where he had always wanted to be, where he felt he always belonged. "He's very happy," said his good friend Walter Thayer. "Very happy indeed."

Having It All

The weather was anything but pleasant as I walked up Fifty-third Street in Manhattan toward Black Rock—a blanket of low-lying gray clouds covering the skyline, a nagging drizzle, and a temperature hovering around fifty degrees. But the weather was the least of my concerns on this mid-April day. Every thought was focused on the one o'clock luncheon appointment with Bill Paley. After more than three years of research and writing, he had finally agreed to see me.

There had been a time when I thought this meeting would never take place. I had written him in the spring of 1984 to ask whether he would be willing to cooperate with me in the preparation of a biography. His executive assistant, Frank Mewshaw, had written to say that Paley was out of town and would respond in due course. After weeks of silence, I telephoned Mewshaw, only to be told that Paley was thinking about it. Later calls generated the same answer, until, finally, Mewshaw confided that Paley was troubled that his cooperation might require an inordinate amount of time—an understandable concern for a man of eighty-two with wide-ranging interests. I had tried to defuse that problem, saying that Paley could give me as much or as little time as he chose—but any time would be better than none. Mewshaw suggested that I convey those sentiments in another letter. I was happy to comply, but it was all for naught. After a couple of months, Paley finally replied by letter that he was flattered by my interest but that he could not agree to my request for an interview. No explanation was offered.

I made additional calls to Mewshaw asking whether there was any hope of Paley changing his mind. Although sympathetic to my inquiry, Mewshaw could offer nothing but good wishes. Eventually he told me that Paley was planning to do another book on his life. At first I was incredulous. Paley's autobiogrpahy had already been published in 1979, and it was inconceivable to me that a person could write two autobiographies within the space of five years. But then it was announced that Bantam would publish a "tell-all" autobiography by the former CBS chairman, and Paley was quoted as saying that the commitment would preclude cooperation with anyone else preparing a book about him or CBS.

I soon learned that Paley's refusal to make himself available did not mean active opposition to my project. Mewshaw was very helpful in providing me with access to some CBS records; John Minary, Paley's confidential assistant for more than forty years, was receptive to my inquiries to check facts; and personal friends and close colleagues of Paley's were willing to talk with me about the man, his record, his family, and his social life.

By January 1987 the manuscript was virtually completed, and I decided to make one last effort. There were a number of sensitive subjects on which I had some questions. And beyond that, I wanted to afford Paley one last opportunity to give me the benefit of his recollections and opinions. I had no expectation that he would give me any time, but that was a decision for him to make.

For weeks there was no response. That was hardly surprising. The telephone call finally came at ten o'clock on a Sunday morning in late March. When the voice at the other end of the line said, "Hi, this is Bill Paley," my first reaction was to wonder which of my friends would play this kind of practical joke. But then the voice added, "I'm sitting here with John Minary, going over my mail. I have your letter, and I'd like to take advantage of your offer. Can we meet?" I knew then that the voice was genuine, and I was quick to honor the request. Mewshaw later called to say that Mr. Paley would like to have lunch with me in his private dining room on April 13.

As I walked down the steps to the entrance on Fifty-second Street, I could appreciate the appeal that Black Rock held for Paley and Stanton. The lines of the tall building were straight and clean. There were no signs to mar the simplicity of the design—only a relatively low placement of letters indicating that it was the CBS headquarters. The security guard took note of my name as I signed in, smiled, and then picked up the phone to advise Mr. Paley that his scheduled visitor had arrived. By the time I stepped out into the spacious foyer on the thirty-fifth floor, a well-dressed, middle-aged woman was standing by the desk and addressed me by name.

I was directed to the anteroom in Paley's office by a young, attractive secretary. While I admired the art on display—several Ben Shahn sketches, a Matisse, and a still-life by Goldie Paley herself—Frank Mewshaw stopped by to say hello, a waiter in a white coat asked what I would like to drink, and then, finally, another attractive woman came by to say that Mr. Paley was ready to see me.

He was seated behind the French gaming table in the corner of his office and stood up immediately as I walked in. Although he had just recovered from a two-month bout with pneumonia, the eighty-five-year-old CBS chairman looked quite healthy. He still carried the slight paunch he had acquired years earlier, but it was camouflaged well by the dark blue suit, white shirt, and wide blue tie with green markings.

From the beginning the conversation was relaxed and animated. In a gravelly voice, Paley expressed what seemed to be genuine surprise at my appearance, saying that, from all accounts, he had expected a person more advanced in years. He then spoke of his own youth, repeating the story of how he had made a serious commitment at the age of eighteen to retire by thirty-five—only to discover that he enjoyed broadcasting too much to walk away from it. After a short time he rose and invited me to follow him across the anteroom and into his private dining room. The small table was already set, with his apple juice (a perennial favorite), awaiting his arrival.

As I surveyed the trappings of Paley's environment, I could not help but recall Mike Dann's comment months earlier. "When I come back in my next life," said Dann, "I want to come back as Bill Paley. Because he's had it all." And so it seemed. But it was not a rags-to-riches story. Bill Paley had the good fortune to have a father who was driven, who was a shrewd businessman, and, perhaps most importantly, was willing to devote considerable time to his young son. This close contact left an indelible imprint on young Willie. "My father was my best friend," Paley remarked at lunch. And there was nothing Willie would not do for his best friend. "At fourteen or fifteen years old," Paley remembered, "I used to dream about being a salesman, going to cigar stores and making them buy *his* cigar. I wanted everybody to own his cigar . . ."

For his part, Sam Paley wanted nothing more than to see his only son enjoy life to the fullest. "Never has a father brought so much pleasure to bear on his son as he did to me," said Paley over his clam chowder. "Everything I did was right. He got vicarious pleasure out of my success. And he got vicarious pleasure because I spent my money." At an early stage, Paley decided to live extravagantly—with his father's blessing. Paley recalled the vast sums he spent to decorate his triplex on Park Avenue when he first came to New York. "Now, an ordinary man would have said, 'Now, son, it's going to your head. How dare you spend that much money. You don't have to live that way.' Which I didn't," Paley quickly added. "But I wanted to. And he wanted me to, too. And everything I did of that kind, he would sort of lean back and smile at me."

However close the ties between them, Sam could not give his son the one thing he longed for most in the 1920s—a job with glamour. And so it was only natural that Bill Paley would turn to the opportunity to manage a small radio network in New York. "This thing called broadcasting excited me terrifically," Paley recalled at lunch. He had experienced unbridled joy in buying a small crystal set in Philadelphia and staying up to all hours of the night to listen to distant signals that would come and go without warning. "Pittsburgh was easy," he said. "Chicago was pretty difficult. Kansas City . . . oh, my God . . ." And I could see his facial expression change as he reached back for that long-ago memory. "I got so excited," he remembered. "This was about two o'clock in the morning. I ran upstairs and got my father up. He came downstairs. I said I wanted him to hear something. But by the time we got there we had lost the signal. My father was sore as hell."

None of that prevented Sam from approving his son's request to join United Independent Broadcasters. In retrospect, it was an incredibly farsighted decision. Radio was starting to revolutionize mass communications in the 1920s, and Bill Paley had the good fortune to be there in the beginning. But as a young broadcaster, Paley was not there to engage in social experiments. He was there for the fun of it. And for him, much of the fun was in making money. So he did not want to take chances. He only wanted to know what would work. He searched for performers who would bring listeners—and with them, advertisers—to his fledgling network.

As CBS began to reach millions and make millions, Paley began to sense the power of his creation. People, important people, wanted to hear him speak, listen to his views, and, incredible as it once seemed, gain access to his radio network. It might have been an entertainer, a member of Congress, or sometimes even the president of the United States. It was all very heady stuff for a young man whose only credential was a college degree. "Radio was going so fast," he commented at lunch, "you just couldn't keep up with it." And Paley could not help but recall the many friends in Philadelphia who had counseled him against going to New York because radio was, in their views, just a passing fad. "All those people," said Paley with a smile, " . . . they couldn't believe it when they heard what was happening."

Ironically, Paley's sense of his own power mushroomed in the late 1930s and early 1940s because CBS was not quite as successful as he wanted it to be. There was time, large blocks of time, that remained unsold and was, therefore, available for Ed Murrow's reports and other broadcasts that offered information and opinion about current events. When war erupted, the public's need for news almost completely eclipsed the desire to be entertained. Now listeners wanted to know about their husbands, their sons, and other loved ones caught in a war an ocean away. Listeners started to shift to CBS, knowing that the junior network would have the latest developments and the most informed opinions. It enhanced CBS's ratings and inflated Bill Paley's stature.

The postwar years and especially the advent of television marked a further and almost unbelievable expansion in Paley's power. For so many years he had gone to so many people, hat in hand, to ask for financial assistance, to ask them to perform, or to ask them to buy advertising time. Now they came to him. Broadcasting was big money for all concerned, and Paley alone had the discretion to choose who would get what. With a nod of the head he could make or break a program producer, decide whether a nationally known senator could have access to millions of viewers, and determine whether a performer would remain a household name or become a half-forgotten legend. Sitting in the confines of his office at Madison Avenue and then Black Rock, he could choose the programs that millions of people would see every night and control the political information that millions of voters would have before any election. It was power almost unimaginable, and in other hands the consequences could have been disastrous for the country.

Bill Paley did not want the power abused. He wanted fairness and balance in news programs. The principle was instilled in him by Ed Klauber, but Paley was the one who made it the mainstay of CBS's approach in covering current events. "To me, the policy is so strict," he remarked, as the waiter served the roast chicken, "everybody I hired had to come in and I had to give them a lecture about giving the people all they needed on every issue that was of importance." Over the decades, many would debate whether the principle had been followed in specific instances, but few would challenge the principle itself. There were, to be sure, other voices at the FCC and elsewhere that supported the principle, but Paley gave it a legitimacy that made its acceptance that much easier.

His only regret, he told me, was that the FCC had—at his own urging—made the "fairness doctrine" a formal policy and had required every broadcaster to honor it. In retrospect, Paley felt that it was inconsistent with the press's First Amendment rights for the government to be telling a broadcaster how to be fair. "Nothing has really hurt us," he commented, "but I do not like the idea of that being a rule of law on the books saying you have to do it. It's a different thing altogether." Still, he agreed with me that his support for the principle of fairness was one of his most significant contributions to the development of broadcasting.

His contribution to entertainment programming was equally profound. Although many of the stars and program formats found their beginnings on NBC, CBS was the network that pushed the notion of entertainment to new heights. Bill Paley was prepared to delegate the authority and spend the money to create programs that would make people laugh and listen and even learn. If he achieved that goal, he would not only bring more listeners and viewers to his network, he could also feel satisfied that he had brought something worthwhile into people's lives.

In all of this, however, he had no intention of catering to the educated elite. Broadcasting, after all, was a mass medium, not a class medium, and he constantly told people that *The New York Times* would be a very different paper if it had a circulation of forty million. Still, he wanted a certain quality in all that his network offered, and that sense of taste, of high-mindedness, affected most of those who occupied senior positions at CBS. Mike Burke had explained it to me a few months before he died in the winter of 1987. "One took enormous pride in the fact that you worked for an outfit that was top-class in its field," said Burke. "The world championship team. And he made that possible. Of course, he had Stanton and all those others who made it work. But he established the climate. He had a passion for excellence. And it wasn't just his concern for quality," Burke added. "It was the sweep of his interests. From the Picassos he hung in his office to the kind of building that would house CBS to news to programming. The passion for quality is the one phrase that captures the essence of the man." Jack Schneider, whose relationship with Paley was far from tranquil, agreed. "Working for CBS was a mission," he remarked. "A holy calling." And it was a mission, a dream, that Paley never relinquished. Even as a retired chairman with little to do, he would have lunches with young correspondents, reminding them of the CBS tradition and urging them to retain that standard of excellence that had been nurtured by Murrow, Cronkite, and so many others.

None of this was done casually. Paley had understood from the beginning that he could not do it alone. The standards might be his, but the network's performance would have to depend on the dozens, hundreds, and then thousands of employees who applied those standards in the network's daily operations. He was more interested in success than in flattery, and so he wanted to surround himself with men (there being few women executives of high rank at CBS) who were talented, aggressive, and even smarter than himself. At first, it was an impossible prescription to fill. "I had all kinds of trouble hiring people," he remembered. In the 1920s, most people saw radio as a business with no future. "Imagine," Paley remarked, his eyes wide. "Very bright people, listening to it, knowing about it, saying it was a gimmick. A passing fad."

The situation changed as radio matured. Soon CBS had the executive talent it needed, and Paley afforded them broad discretion to do their jobs, supporting them even when he had doubts (as long as the executive remained confident of his course). But as Lou Cowan, Jim Aubrey, and many others discovered, everyone—the chairman excepted—was expendable and replaceable. The issue was raised at our lunch, and Paley displayed an almost disarming sensitivity toward the prospect of having to fire someone. "My first fear," he said, "is what's he going to tell his wife when he gets home at night? That's where I start. It must be awful. That's the thing that gets me. Other things are important, but your own intimate life is the thing that's affected more than anything else."

None of this concern prevented him from doing whatever would best serve the company's interests. "Paley was ruthless about getting rid of people who were in the way," said former News president Bill Leonard. "He might care about the person, but he wouldn't let it interfere with the decision." Leonard drew an analogy to an army general in a war. "If you're worried about the sight of men getting killed in battle," he observed, "you shouldn't be a general. You might care deeply about the human loss, but you can't let that affect your decision if you have to send men into battle." Another former CBS executive had the benefit of a close relationship with Paley over many years and was more pointed in his characterization of the chairman's approach to personnel matters. "You must remember," said this executive, "that Bill Paley has no morals. No ethics. He doesn't care about anyone or anything. He's autocratic. But—" And now the man smiles. "I could see him on the street again, he'd give me that bear hug, and he could win me over."

Charm. It was one of the most dominant features, perhaps the most dominant feature, of Paley's personality. It was plainly in evidence for the two hours we spent together: the smile, the firm handshake, the warm inquiry about the family, the humorous anecdote. But it was not something that was extended to everyone. Many executives at CBS—especially those not involved in programming—knew that. And even for those who *were* involved in programming, there were limits, particularly after 1959.

That was a watershed year for Bill Paley and for CBS. His lung operation may have spared him the immediate fear of cancer, but it demonstrated, in some perverse way, his own mortality. He might escape death now, but who knew about tomorrow? "It was a funny kind of let-down," he said, between mouthfuls of chicken and salad, "because I was almost sure I had cancer. . . . I had a nurse who was a faithful little girl . . . and I remember her yelling in my ear as I was coming out of the operation, 'Nothing there, nothing there. You're okay. You're okay.' I heard it through a haze or something. But as I started to recuperate, I just couldn't control these awful feelings I had. That's when I invented it. That's why I was two different people."

He began to think about what he should do to make life more fun, more challenging, more worthwhile. His tenure as chairman of the Materials

Policy Commission had been an enjoyable and productive venture, and he became even more proud of the experience as time went on. After his operation he wanted something that would be an even greater public honor—ambassador in Europe. It was a fitting position for someone of his stature, for a life that could end at any moment.

While he struggled with his own mortality, Bill Paley's company went through its own transition. The quiz-show scandals graphically demonstrated that television was no longer just another form of entertainment. It was now an integral part of the nation's social structure, a phenomenon that would be watched closely by the nation's decision-makers. CBS, like NBC and to a lesser extent ABC, would have to be more careful in supervising the programs sent over the nation's airwaves.

For the most part, Paley was not there to exercise that supervision. But the company prospered beyond belief in his absence. Broadcasting had always been a profitable business, especially after World War II, but now the profits were simply incredible. Jim Aubrey's stewardship generated millions and millions of dollars in earnings that surpassed even Paley's greatest hopes. "He had great ability," Paley said of Aubrey. "He was on his way to any place he wanted to get to." Bill Paley wanted a quality company and he had a sense of pride about his network, but he could not disregard the kind of money being generated by Aubrey's regime. The ratings and the profits became even more important. The perspective was captured best by the story that Mike Dann likes to tell about the time when he was chief of programming in the 1960s—he enters the chairman's office to tell him the good news, that CBS has nine of the top ten programs in daytime television, the "soaps," and Paley's response tells it all: "That damn NBC always hangs in there for one."

Some executives, like Lou Cowan, tried to warn Paley about the dangers of seeking larger and larger profits every year, that that kind of pursuit could not be maintained without cost to the nature and quality of the network's programs. But Paley could not be turned aside. It was all a question of how he defined leadership. At lunch he spoke of the only three "great" leaders he had known—Franklin D. Roosevelt, Winston Churchill, and Chaim Weizmann. These men, he said, had "vision and power and substance. The sort of greatness I like." And as someone who aspired to greatness as the chairman of a publicly traded media empire, Paley decided that his first priority had to be to the thousands of people who held CBS's stock. After all, how would they feel if dividends did not increase or, worse yet, were reduced? And beyond the stockholders was the New York financial community—it too would assess his leadership on the basis of the company's monetary success.

There were many people who would have gladly challenged these priorities, but by the time Paley adopted this view, there was no one who could confront him. Ed Murrow was gone, his independence so emasculated that, by 1960, he didn't even know if he had a job with CBS. Paley's camaraderie with the other correspondents was all but over. The lone exception was Charles Collingwood, but he was in Europe most of the time and could not be there to comment on the decisions being made on a daily basis. Paley became more and more distant, hermetically sealed away from anyone who would tell him he was wrong about anything.

The only occasional exception was programming, and even then there were limitations. Jack Schneider remembered the time when he was reviewing program issues with the chairman and other executives, and, in an effort to make a point about his own viewing habits, Paley said in a matter-of-fact way, "I think we can all agree that I have a typical American home." At that, Schneider rolled his eyes and threw his pencil in the air, knowing that it was a debate that could never be won. The insulation from reality was too great.

The insulation spared Paley from many uncomfortable moments. He never had to worry about firing someone, or telling a fading performer that the contract would not be renewed, or advising a president that he could not have access to the network for a speech. He was shielded from confrontation with almost every adverse influence, every troubling message. Everything was done for him—even the most personal tasks. One CBS executive recalled the occasion when Paley, now in his eighties, explained the need for his valet, saying, "I can't remember the last time I tied my own tie."

Despite this protective atmosphere, Paley never forgot that he was ultimately in charge. The firing of Lou Cowan in December 1959 was a case in point. Stanton was the one asking, pushing, almost demanding that Cowan sign a letter of resignation. Paley was unavailable, but he did not pretend to be uninvolved when I put the question to him. "I certainly take full responsibility," he replied. "Nothing like that could have happened without my assent."

Unfortunately for Paley, by the early 1970s much of the public began to feel that Paley was chairman in name only, that Stanton was the one who really ran the company. After all, he was the one defending the company against charges of distorted broadcasts in "The Selling of the Pentagon." Paley reasserted his control when Nixon special counsel Chuck Colson called to complain about Walter Cronkite's special on Watergate. Paley concurred. Everyone inside CBS would know that Bill Paley was the one calling the shots, that he was the one charting the company's course. All he had to do was call a meeting and voice his concerns.

Those outside the CBS family could not be controlled that easily. And the older and more insulated he got, the more quickly Paley would focus on those outside critics, inflating the significance of their positions and the impact of their comments. Some CBS executives tried to counsel caution, to place the matter in perspective, saying that no criticism could undo the incredible achievements of a lifetime. But Paley was now beyond reasonable discussion when it came to these outside critics. And for those who might have believed otherwise, there was David Halberstam.

He was, to be sure, an important political writer, and many important people read his books. But his articles about Paley and CBS appeared in a magazine with a circulation of only 300,000—a universe small by television standards, where a program had to have a weekly audience of thirty million to escape the axe. Halberstam coveted coverage by the media, and he knew that powerful people are particularly sensitive to confrontation. But the CBS chairman's reaction surprised even him. "What is it about a man who's had so much richness in his life and comes apart because one person writes a book?" Halberstam later mused. "It's very sad," he said, almost answering his own question, "that a man could have a life of that much accomplishment and be so fragile, so vulnerable."

The subject of Halberstam occupied a good part of our lunch. "I don't even remember now what upset me so much," said Paley, ". . . but I have to admit that at the time it hurt me very much that he was . . . saying things about me that were absolutely untrue." He did feel, however, that Halberstam "was trying to find some weakness in me about my religious association." He recalled, for example, an inference in Halberstam's work that his family had changed its name after arriving in America to avoid any suspicion that they were Jewish. And he resented the implication in Halberstam's work that he had married Babe Cushing, in part at least, to enhance his position with the exclusive WASP society in New York. Paley insisted that was preposterous. "I had enough confidence at that time, I promise you," he said with unusual vigor. "I wasn't looking for someone to help me jump up the ladder. I just fell in love with her madly. And she fell in love with me madly."

Paley acknowledged that he had indeed ordered someone to tape Halberstam's speeches in Tulsa and elsewhere. But he could not see anything sinister about that. "The request had nothing to do with his behavior," he remarked. "Just with the content of the speech and nothing else." Even so, the ultimate objective was not obtained. Halberstam remained beyond comprehension and certainly beyond control. "I couldn't understand the guy," said Paley. "He was a great mystery. And we didn't get along."

There was some merit to Paley's complaint, because there was some material in Halberstam's articles that was in error. But the errors were relatively minor and disguised the real source of Paley's concern. He had, in a very real sense, become an emperor who was supposed to be beyond reproach, royalty whose subjects were to be loyal and unquestioning. "He is a very powerful man," said one former CBS president, "and, in his world, the truth is what he says it is." It was certainly a position with benefits—he could enjoy the company of the most glittering and engaging people in the worlds of politics and entertainment and society; he could travel from New York to Nassau to Paris and back again without the need to make arrangements for himself; and he could be whisked away in his maroon limousine to any restaurant of his choosing (or anywhere else) at a moment's notice. He could control so much—and yet he could not command the respect and affection of all who knew him.

He had equal difficulty in deciding when—and to whom—he would give up his positions as chairman and chief executive officer of CBS. Although he skirted the question at first, he soon agreed at lunch that he had a compelling need to stay as long as he could—no matter what. "That feeling within me was strong enough to prevail . . . against Stanton," he said, "which was hard for me to do, but I admit that I did it, knowing how much he wanted it. One of those compulsions you just can't get rid of. . . . Whether I was protecting myself or protecting the company, I don't know," he confessed. "But I convinced myself that it wasn't only for me; it was also because I thought I was so effective and important [to CBS] to maintain what I was doing for a while longer."

Although the added years began to sap his energy, the desire to hang on remained. And so no anointed successor could ever be satisfactory. He gave different reasons to explain why different successors were inadequate, but no one could pass his test. The standard of comparison was himself and there was only one Bill Paley. That was clear when the conversation turned to Tom Wyman.

Paley told me that he had always felt that "the head of this company ought to have a creative sense, and, if he can't be creative himself, at least understand creative people and be able to assess things." While Wyman had had an extraordinary career in the corporate world, and while Paley himself said that the former CBS chairman was "brilliant," there was nothing in his record to indicate that he had the slightest notion about running a business that revolved around news and entertainment. In retrospect, it seems obvious that Paley had allowed Wyman to enter the CBS arena knowing, if only subsconsciously, that he had a handicap that Paley could exploit if Wyman should falter. And not surprisingly, Paley did lay all of CBS's later problems at Wyman's feet. "He was dragging the company down," Paley told me. "I never saw it go so bad in my life. . . . So when Larry [Tisch] arrived on the scene . . . and was as dissatisfied, pretty quickly as I was . . . it was natural for the two of us to get together and get him out."

However victorious his collaboration with Paley, Tisch faced the same high standard of acceptance that Wyman had. Although he remarked that Tisch is a "shrewd businessman," Paley refused to comment on the controversy that had erupted weeks earlier concerning the budget cuts and deteriorating morale at the news division—the same problems that had been part of the basis for forcing Wyman's resignation. But a close associate of Paley's later agreed that Paley was very frustrated by the controversy and the illness which had prevented him from playing a more active role in dealing with it. "The people here now," said this associate, with obvious reference to Tisch, "are making the same mistakes that Wyman made. They're not studying the problems. They think you can resolve everything through numbers alone without regard to the functions involved." It was clear that, in this associate's view, there was really only one person who knew who to handle the situation. "Paley is a showman and a businessman," he said, "and it's not easy to find people who combine both talents."

Although he would not talk about Tisch's stewardship of CBS, Paley did want to discuss other material in my manuscript. He had obviously been briefed about some sensitive matters in the manuscript—even though I had not given it to him and even though the manuscript was supposed to be within the protective custody of the publisher. His ability to gain access to the manuscript was, in some small way, a reflection of the power Paley could wield. Still, the issues uppermost in his mind did not concern his involvement with CBS or his place in history. Instead, they centered around his family and his personal life. The emphasis graphically demonstrated that, for all his stature, Bill Paley had to grapple with the same problems that could strike any man in the street.

By three o'clock a young woman brought in notes to remind Paley about another visitor who was waiting for a scheduled appointment. We got up from the dining table, leaving behind most of the dessert of fresh raspberries and bananas, walked into the anteroom, shook hands, and agreed to talk on the phone at a later time about a few lingering questions.

As I left Black Rock, I could easily understand the appeal Bill Paley had held for so many people. And in some strange way, the lunch had left me with a better sense of how far he had come from those first days at United Independent Broadcasters. But Paley had paid a price, in some respcts a heavy price, for all that he had achieved. His single-minded devotion to CBS limited the time and energy and emotion he could give to other people. That was true of colleagues, friends, and sometimes even family. But there were obviously no regrets. He had grown up with CBS, it was his, and he was very proud of what he had done. He may not have had it all, but he had had more than enough to satisfy his seemingly unquenchable thirst for life. The time was long past when he could effectively rule the CBS empire, but none of that really mattered. Bill Paley had become a sovereign, and, when all was said and done, he would exit a sovereign. From his perspective, no one could ask for more.

Author's Note

I first conceived the idea of doing this biography when Bill Paley was inducted as one of the first members of the Television Hall of Fame in March 1984. Having been involved in broadcasting for more than ten years as a lawyer, I was certainly aware of his stature but only generally aware of his impact on broadcasting. While some books, most notably David Halberstam's *The Powers That Be,* had provided some insight into Paley's background, it seemed to me that there was much more to know.

Of course, any biography of Bill Paley would have to involve much about the history of CBS. Although he was not really its founder, Paley has been with the company since its infancy. He is the one who has nurtured it, molded it, and developed it into a major force in the worlds of journalism, politics, and entertainment. Still, however close the ties, Paley is not CBS, and there is much about CBS and its history that had to be overlooked in the preparation of this biography. This book is, first and foremost, the story of Bill Paley and only secondarily the story of CBS. I was principally interested in recounting the evolution of a person, not a company.

In tracing a person's evolution, there is an understandable tendency to become an amateur psychologist, and biographers are no exception. Current biographies often focus on the psychological underpinnings of the subject, offering opinions on the influence of people and events on a person's psyche. The practice has become so common that many reviewers, and perhaps many readers, have come to expect some kind of psychological analysis in every biography.

I have resisted the temptation to offer psychological conclusions about Bill Paley. While I think they would be invaluable to any understanding of the man and his impact, I am not equipped to make well-informed psychological judgments. Although I have some limited background in the field, I am not a psychologist. My background is in broadcasting, history, politics, and law. Those looking for something more in this book will be disappointed. Still, I would like to think that this work will provide much raw material for those with a psychological bent. And for those only interested in fascinating history, the story of Bill Paley's life has much to recommend it.

In my effort to tell that story, I have relied primarily on unpublished documentary sources and hundreds of interviews of Paley himself, his family, his colleagues, his friends, and his adversaries. Some of the interviews were found in libraries, others were located in private papers to which I had access, and the remainder I conducted myself. At the risk of omitting some who deserve credit for helping me, I would like to acknowledge my considerable debt to the many people across the country who contributed to this project.

David Halberstam generously gave me access to his private papers at Boston University, which included thousands of pages of correspondence and interview notes with Paley, family members, colleagues, friends, and others who had contact with him over a long life; and while some of that material had already been used in the preparation of *The Powers That Be,* much of it had never been utilized in any published source. Don West, managing editor of *Broadcasting,* the industry's principal trade journal for more than fifty years, gave me access to the magazine's "morgue" on Paley, which included, among other items, a seventy-seven-page transcript of an interview with Paley in 1976. Former CBS correspondent Dan Schorr was equally generous in providing me with copies of transcripts of his many hours of interviews with Paley (and Frank Stanton) in 1977. And Martin Mayer made available documents reflecting his 1976 effort to prepare, with Paley's assistance, a history of CBS News.

Another invaluable source was the unpublished autobiography of Louis G. Cowan, who first met Paley during the war years and later became president of the CBS Television Network. The material was given to me by Cowan's daughter, Holly Cowan Shulman, and provided much insight into the slow transformation of Paley as CBS matured from a relatively small communications company into a media empire.

Other interviews and documentary materials were located in libraries throughout the country. Those of particular importance were the Oral History Research Collection at Columbia University (which contains interviews with many people prominent in CBS history, including Louis G. Cowan, Arthur Judson, H.V. Kaltenborn, and Goddard Lieberson); the Broadcast Pioneers Library in Washington, D.C. (which houses, among other items, interviews with Ike and Leon Levy); the Library of Congress in Washington, D.C. (which has, among other items, Eric Sevareid's papers as well as copies of Edward R. Murrow's papers); the Dwight D. Eisenhower Library in Abilene, Kansas (which includes a voluminous amount of correspondence with and about Paley between 1943 and 1964); the John F. Kennedy Library in Dorchester, Massachusetts (which has correspondence with and about Paley as well as interviews with people such as Benno Schmidt, Sr., who are close friends and colleagues); the Lyndon Baines Johnson Library in Austin, Texas (which has thousands of pages of correspondence with and about Paley and Frank Stanton, who was particularly close to President Johnson); and the Harry S. Truman Library in Independence, Missouri (which has voluminous files concerning Paley's participation in the Materials Policy Commission).

I want to thank Joan Simpson Burns for granting permission to inspect and quote from the interview of Goddard Lieberson at Columbia University. I also appreciated the research assistance of Randy Mock, who reviewed materials at the Eisenhower Library.

I was equally fortunate to have had assistance from people and records at Paley's alma mater, the University of Pennsylvania. The people to be thanked are Lee Zimmerman of Zeta Beta Tau Fraternity and Margaret Gilbert, director of the Alumni Records Office.

The Freedom of Information Act proved to be only marginally beneficial. The records available from the Central Intelligence Agency and the Federal Bureau of Investigation did confirm the existence of a relationship between the respective agencies and CBS. In the case of the FBI, the records indicate that there was close cooperation between the network and the agency during the 1940s and the 1950s. But the records did not shed any significant light on Paley's personal relationship with the agencies or their personnel.

I also had the benefit of talking with former CBS executives and others who had had an opportunity to observe Paley in his professional and personal lives. Some of these individuals requested anonymity because of their present or former associations; I have honored those requests. Indeed, I decided early on in the project that it was impractical to use footnotes because there were too many occasions on which the source would have to remain unidentified.

Still, there are scores of people who can and should be thanked publicly for talking and corresponding with me. In a few cases the exchange was brief (although almost always helpful); and in many other instances individuals were kind enough to give me many hours over the course of one, two, and sometimes many conversations. Sometimes an individual would protest that he or she really had nothing to offer, that they knew Paley only casually—and would then spend the next hour or so providing telling recollections and insightful observations.

As might be imagined, there were numerous instances in which people's recollections collided with each other—and sometimes with published comments that the interviewee had reportedly given other authors. In almost every case I tried to present individuals with the contrasting recol-

372 Author's Note

lectionslections in the hope of eliminating the conflict. Sometimes that approach worked; and in those instances where it didn't, I ultimately had to make choices based on a variety of factors, including other known facts and recollections.

In any event, I would like to thank the following people for giving me the benefit of their memories of events and people that in some cases date back more than sixty years: Harry Ackerman, James Arness, James T. Aubrey, Jr., John Backe, Edward Barrett, Joan Benny, Edward Bernays, Simon Michael Bessie, Les Brown, the late Michael Burke, George Burns, Philip Coombs, Geoffrey Cowan, Kenneth Cox, Mike Dann, Norman Dorsen, Lou Dorfsman, Irving Fein, Myer Feldman, Henry Gerstley, Jackie Gleason, Jack Gould, Katharine Graham, Jap Gude, David Halberstam, H.R. Haldeman, Nathan Hamburger, Don Hewitt, Dorothy Paley Hirshon, Ann Honeycutt, Richard W. Jencks, Norman Lear, Robert E. Lee, Lionel Leffret, Bill Leonard, Jack Loftus, Ernie Martin, Martin Mayer, Kidder Meade, Sig Mickelson, Donald Mills, John Minary, Janet Murrow, Shirley McClure, Tac Nail, William O'Shaugnessy, William S. Paley, Raymond K. Price, Jr., Joseph L. Rauh, Jr., Joe Ream, David Riesman, Dean Rusk, Richard Salant, James Sax, Arthur M. Schlesinger, Jr., John A. Schneider, David Schoenbrun, Daniel Schorr, Holly Cowan Shulman, Helen J. Sioussat, Howard K. Smith, David Sonenberg, Frank Stanton, Arthur R. Taylor, Walter Thayer, Jonathan Tourtellot, Kip Tourtellot, Marietta Tree, Gloria Vanderbilt, Al Warren, Doris Klauber Wechsler, Don West, Robert Wussler, Len Zeidenberg.

I would especially like to thank Kip Tourtellot for providing me with a copy of a privately published pamphlet that included a eulogy which Paley gave at Arthur Tourtellot's funeral.

Douglas Katz, David Sonenberg, and Don West took time from their own hectic schedules to read the book in manuscript form. Their comments and suggestions were invaluable—but I alone remain responsible for any errors of fact or mistakes in judgment.

My agent, Ted Chichak, deserves special thanks for his early encouragement and his many efforts on my behalf. Tom Dunne and Laura Jack, my editors at St. Martin's Press, were always available to offer enthusiasm and sound advice, and for that I am very grateful.

Words are always inadequate to thank my wife, Jan. She reviewed every word of the draft (sometimes several times) and was always available, no matter what her other commitments, to discuss every aspect of the project.

And finally, Lindsay and Brett—two very special children.

L J P
Potomac, Maryland

Selected Bibliography

Of all the secondary sources, the most important proved to be contemporaneous periodicals, especially *Broadcasting* magazine, *Newsweek, The New York Times, Television Digest, Time,* and *The Washington Post.* Beyond these publications were many books and articles which shed considerable light on Paley and the people and events important to his life. The following list represents the most helpful additional publications:

"And All Because They're Smart," *Fortune* (June 1935), p.80

Desi Arnaz, *Book* (1976)

Ken Auletta, "Gambling on CBS," *New York Times Sunday Magazine* (June 8, 1986), p.35

Erik Barnouw, *History of Broadcasting (Vol.I): Tower of Babel* (1966)

Erik Barnouw, *History of Broadcasting (Vol. II): The Golden Web* (1968)

Erik Barnouw, *History of Broadcasting (Vol. III): The Image Empire* (1970)

Sally Bedell, *Up the Tube: Prime-Time in the Silverman Years* (1981)

Edward Bernays, *Biography of an Idea* (1962)

Peter W. Bernstein, "CBS Fights to Regain the Title," *Fortune* (Jan. 29, 1979), p. 58

Kenneth Bilby, *The General: David Sarnoff and the Rise of the Communications Industry* (1986)

Stephen Birmingham, *The Rest of Us: The Rise of America's Eastern European Jews* (1984)

Les Brown, *Television: The Business Behind the Box* (1971)

Michael Burke, *Outrageous Good Fortune* (1984)

Geoffrey Cowan, *See No Evil: The Backstage Battle over Sex and Violence on Television* (1979)

Carl Dreher, *Sarnoff: An American Success* (1977)

John Henry Faulk, *Fear on Trial* (1964)

Fred Friendly, *Due to Circumstances Beyond Our Control* (1968)

Gary Paul Gates, *Air Time: The Inside Story of CBS News* (1978)

Peter Goldmark, *Maverick Inventor* (1973)

David Halberstam, *The Powers That Be* (1979)
Irving Howe, *World of Our Fathers: The Journey of the East European Jews to America and the Life They Found and Made* (1976)
E.J. Kahn, Jr., *Jock: The Life and Times of John Hay Whitney* (1981)
Murray Kempton, "The Fall of a Television Czar," *The New Republic* (April 3, 1965), p. 9
Alexander Kendrick, *Prime Time: The Life of Edward R. Murrow* (1969)
Eugene Lyons, *David Sarnoff* (1966)
Barbara Matusow, *The Evening Stars* (1983)
Martin Mayer, *About Television* (1972)
———, *Making News* (1987)
Robert Metz, *CBS: Reflections in a Bloodshot Eye* (1975)
Sig Mickelson, *The Electric Mirror: Politics in an Age of Television* (1972)
David McClintick, "What Hath William Paley Wrought?" *Esquire* (Dec. 1983), p. 286
Jack Newfield, *Robert Kennedy: A Memoir* (1969)
Richard Oulahan and William Lambert, "The Tyrant's Fall That Shocked the TV World," *Life* (Sept. 10, 1965)
William S. Paley, *As It Happened* (1979)
———,"Radio Turns South," *Fortune* (April 1941), p. 77
Kenneth T. Reed, *Truman Capote* (1981)
Daniel Schorr, *Clearing the Air* (1978)
Irene Selznick, *A Private View* (1983)
William L. Shirer, *The Nightmare Years: 1930–1940* (1984)
Helen J. Sioussat, *Mikes Don't Bite* (1943)
A.M. Sperber, *Murrow: His Life and Times* (1986)
Elizabeth Thomson, *Harvey Cushing: Surgeon, Author, Artist* (1950)
Paul W. White, *News on the Air* (1947)

Index